The Economics of Gender Equality in the Labour Market

This book evaluates the global labour market in the context of gender equality, and the associated policies and regulations, particularly in developing markets, to recommend measures for encouraging gender equality. It exposes the barriers that women employees encounter as well as some of the societal and workplace policies they, specifically, are subject to. Important themes within this topic include participation rates, the looming gap in hourly pay, availability of part-time and full-time positions, value and social status associated with jobs held by men and women.

The book examines how global gender policy objectives, such as gender equality in careers, gender balance in decision making and gender dimensions in research, can be incorporated into policy frameworks. The book analyzes the gendered nature of assumptions, processes and theories. The juxtaposition between family and work, tradition and modernity, and dependency and autonomy clearly still seems to be misunderstood. Therefore, the book asks whether work improves women's positions in society and/or changes their roles in their families. The authors explore and uncover the connections among employment, entrepreneurship, migration economies and gender global labour markets and provide helpful solutions to the perceptions surrounding women's status, risks and inequality that limit their economic participation.

This insightful read provides comprehensive details on a variety of themes and encourages further research on policies that are key to promoting gender equality. The book will appeal to postgraduate students and researchers of labour and feminist economics, the economics of gender, women's studies and sociology.

Meltem İnce Yenilmez is an associate professor in the Department of Economics at Yaşar University, Turkey; a research associate at Five College Women's Studies Research Center at the University of Massachusetts Amherst, USA; and a visiting researcher in the Department of Sociology at Lund University, Sweden. In addition to her academic positions, Meltem's career includes work in the impact of various forces of economics and social change on the constitution of gender relations and women's empowerment. Her expertise encompasses cyclical patterns of female employment and wage differentials to discrimination, care work and employment patterns in developing countries as well as issues related to gender and development. Aside from the two books she has published, her work also includes women in sports, occupational segregation and gender wage gap.

Gül Ş. Huyugüzel Kişla is an assistant professor in the Department of Economics at Ege University, Turkey. She completed her undergraduate study, MA and PhD in economics at Ege University. She worked at Yaşar University from 2007 to 2009. Afterwards, she joined Ege University as academic staff, where she has been working since 2009. Currently, her primary research interest is macro finance, labour productivity and currency crises.

Routledge Studies in Gender and Economics

Using Fiscal Policy and Public Financial Management to Promote Gender Equality
International Perspectives
Janet G. Stotsky

The Economics of Gender Equality in the Labour Market
Policies in Turkey and other Emerging Economies
Edited by Meltem İnce Yenilmez and Gül Ş. Huyugüzel Kişla

For more information about this series, please visit www.routledge.com/Routledge-Studies-in-Gender-and-Economics/book-series/RSGENECON

The Economics of Gender Equality in the Labour Market

Policies in Turkey and other Emerging Economies

Edited by Meltem İnce Yenilmez and Gül Ş. Huyugüzel Kişla

Routledge
Taylor & Francis Group
LONDON AND NEW YORK

First published 2021
by Routledge
2 Park Square, Milton Park, Abingdon, Oxon OX14 4RN

and by Routledge
52 Vanderbilt Avenue, New York, NY 10017

Routledge is an imprint of the Taylor & Francis Group, an informa business

British Library Cataloguing-in-Publication Data
A catalogue record for this book is available from the British Library

Library of Congress Cataloging-in-Publication Data
A catalog record for this book has been requested

ISBN:978-0-367-69401-2 (hbk)
ISBN: 978-1-003-14165-5 (ebk)

Typeset in Times New Roman
by Apex CoVantage, LLC

Words cannot express how grateful I am to my mother, father, mother-in-law and father-in-law for all of the sacrifices they have made on my behalf and whose love and guidance are with me in whatever I pursue. They are the ultimate role models. I wish to thank my sisters for whom I have no words to describe the meaning of their love and support. Most importantly, I owe my deepest gratitude to my loving and supportive husband, Özgür, and my wonderful beloved son, Bryan Poyraz, who provides unending inspiration, and being such a good boy always cheering me up. You are the best thing that is still happening to me.

Meltem İNCE YENİLMEZ

I dedicate this book to my lovely parents who raised me as a strong daughter, to my warm-hearted husband who made me a loving wife, and to my beautiful son who made me a caring mother.

Gül Ş. HUYUGÜZEL KIŞLA

Contents

List of figures ix
List of tables xi
List of contributors xiii
Preface xv

1 **Bridging the gender gap in emerging economies for a better future of work for all** 1
MELTEM İNCE YENILMEZ

2 **Women's labor force participation and gender discrimination in the labor market** 17
MEHMET ŞENGÜR

3 **The gender-responsive budgeting: a way of coping with gender inequalities** 44
UMUT HALAÇ

4 **Gender equality in the finance sector: closing gaps or another "old boys' club"?** 57
BEGÜM YURTERI KÖSEDAĞLI

5 **Is there gender equality in employment indicators? A comparative study for emerging markets** 73
MELIH ÖZÇALIK

6 **The relationship between minimum wages and youth employment in OECD countries** 106
M. AKIF ARVAS

7 **Gender gap in the labour market: a comparative view for youth and adults** 127
FATMA DIDIN SÖNMEZ AND YASEMIN ÖZERKEK

8 **An assessment of the gender (in)equality in education** 152
GÜL S. HUYUGÜZEL KIŞLA AND TARIK KIŞLA

9 **Intersectional challenges in the labor market: the case of Roma women** 172
MERAL UZUNÖZ AND ASLIHAN YURDAKUL

10 **What makes labor markets inaccessible for women migrants? From "triple disadvantage" to multiple challenges** 187
MEHMET GÖKAY ÖZERIM AND ELIF ÇETIN

11 **Femvertising: a new concept for female empowerment in advertising** 204
EMEL YARIMOĞLU

12 **Evaluation of labor market issues in sport and exercise environment in Turkey** 223
GÖZDE ERSÖZ

13 **How patriarchal power structures undermine women's empowerment and gender equality: the case of Nigeria** 239
ÖZGÜR TÜFEKÇI AND MOHAMMED HASHIRU

Index 255

Figures

4.1	The Gender Gap in Employment in Financial Activities (%)	61
4.2	Women Representation in Financial Services Firms in North America, 2017 (% share)	61
4.3	Women Representation in Different Subsectors of Financial Services Firms in North America, 2017 (% share)	62
4.4	Average Share of Women on Bank Boards, 2013 (%)	63
4.5	Double Glass Ceiling in Banking Industry	64
4.6	Gender Balance Index (GBI) Scores (%)	65
4.7	Gender Balance Index, Central Banks, 2018–2019 (%)	66
4.8	The Unadjusted Gender Pay Gap in Financial and Insurance Activities in European Countries, 2017 (%)	67
4.9	The Share of Employees Aspiring for a Senior Position in Financial Firms (%)	68
5.1	Labor Force Participation Rate (F)	83
5.2	Labor Force Participation Rate (M)	84
5.3	Wage and Salaried Workers (F)	84
5.4	Wage and Salaried Workers (M)	84
5.5	Contributing Family Workers (F)	85
5.6	Contributing Family Workers (M)	85
5.7	Unemployment Rate (F)	86
5.8	Unemployment Rate (M)	86
6.1	Minimum Wage and Employment Relationship	109
6.2	The Population Projections of Youth Cohort in OECD (2018–2030) (%)	111
6.3	OECD Youth Employment Rate (2000–2018)	112
6.4	Minimum Wage Relative to Average Wages of Full-Time Workers (Average of 2000–2018)	114
6.5	The View of Dependant Variable for Countries	119
6.6	Histogram of Minimum-to-Mean Wage Ratios (2000–2018)	120
7.1	Youth and Adult Unemployment Rates by Country	132
7.2	Variations in Unemployment Across Countries (1995–2018)	133
7.3	Unemployment Gap Versus Real GDP Per Capita (1995–2018)	136
7.4	Unemployment Gap Versus Relative Cohort Size (1995–2018)	137

7.5 Adult and Youth LFP Rates (%) by Country (2014–2018) 138
7.6 Gender Unemployment Gap and Gender LFP Gap (%) by Country (2014–2018) 138
7.7 Gender Gap Employment Rate by Country (2014–2018) 139
7.8 Gender Employment Distribution Across Sectors by Country (2014–2018) 140
7.9 Roots of the Companion Matrix 145
7.10 Impulse-Response Functions 147
8.1 Youth Literacy Rates (Female, Male, Total) 155
8.2 Adult Literacy Rates (Female, Male, Total) 155
8.3 Enrollment Rates for Preprimary Education (Total, Female, Male) 156
8.4 Enrollment Rates for Primary Education (Total, Female, Male) 157
8.5 Enrollment Rates for Secondary Education (Total, Female, Male) 157
8.6 Enrollment Rates for Tertiary Education (Total, Female, Male) 158
8.7 Female Teachers in Primary Education (%) 159
8.8 Female Teachers in Secondary Education (%) 159
8.9 Female Academic Staff in Tertiary Education (%) 159
8.10 The General Structure of the Formal Education System 161
8.11 Literacy Rates in Turkey 166
8.12 School Enrollment Rates in Turkey 166
8.13 Female Teachers in Turkey 166
8.14 Enrollment Rates in Tertiary Education by Field of Study 167
13.1 Trends in Seats by Women in Nigeria's National Parliament (%) 243
13.2 Proportion of Seats Held by Women in National Parliaments (%) – Nigeria 244

Tables

1.1	Ordinary Least Squares Estimates of the Determinants of Gender Equality	11
2.1	Labor force participation rate for female, 2000–2018, (15+)	22
2.2	Labor force participation rate for female, 2000–2018, (15+)	23
2.3	Labor force participation rate for female, 2000–2018, (15+)	24
2.4	Labor force participation rate for female, 2000–2018, (15+)	24
2.5	Labor force participation rate for female, 2000–2018, (15+)	25
2.6	Employment in agriculture, female percentage (2000–2009)	27
2.7	Employment in agriculture, female percentage (2010–2018)	27
2.8	Employment in industry, female percentage (2000–2009)	29
2.9	Employment in industry, female percentage (2010–2018)	29
2.10	Employment in services, female percentage (2000–2009)	30
2.11	Employment in services, female percentage (2010–2018)	31
2.12	Own-account workers, female percentage (2000–2009)	31
2.13	Own-account workers, female percentage (2010–2018)	32
2.14	Gender parity index of the gross enrolment ratio in primary and secondary education (2009–2017)	33
2.15	Wage and salaried workers, female percentage (2010–2019)	34
2.16	Variables and data descriptions	36
2.17	Wald chi2 and Hausman Test	36
2.18	Durbin-Watson and Baltagi-WuTest	37
2.19	Pesaran CD, Friedman and Frees Tests	37
2.20	Model Estimations	38
4.1	Financial Sector's Employment Share in Total Employment, by Gender and by Region (%)	60
5.1	Employment Indicators of Brazil (%)	78
5.2	Employment Indicators of Russia (%)	79
5.3	Employment Indicators of India (%)	79
5.4	Employment Indicators of China (%)	80
5.5	Employment Indicators of South Africa (%)	81
5.6	Employment Indicators of Turkey (%)	82
5.7	Cross-Section Dependency Test	88
5.8	CADF Test	88

5.9 CIPS Test 89
5.10 Lag Order Selection from VAR Model (Female) 90
5.11 Granger Causality Test from VAR Model (Female) 91
5.12 Variance Decomposition Model (Female) 92
5.13 Lag Order Selection from VAR Model (Male) 96
5.14 Granger Causality Test from VAR Model (Male) 96
5.15 Variance Decomposition Model (Male) 98
6.1 Descriptive Statistics of the Variables 118
6.2 Panel Estimation Results for Total Youth Employment (Model 1) 121
6.3 Panel Estimation Results for Male Youth Employment (Model 2) 122
6.4 Panel Estimation Results for Female Youth Employment (Model 3) 123
7.1 Global Gender Gap Index Performance of Countries 130
7.2 Unemployment Rates for the Young and Adults by Gender (%) 134
7.3 The Elasticity of Gender Unemployment Gap with Respect to Unemployment 143
7.4 MBIC, MAIC and MQIC Information Criteria 145
7.5 Estimation Results 146

Contributors

Mehmet Akif ARVAS is an associate professor in the Department of Economics at Van Yüzüncü Yıl University, Van.

Elif ÇETİN is an assistant professor in the Department of International Relations at Yasar University, Izmir.

Fatma DİDİN SÖNMEZ is an assistant professor in the Department of Economics at Bilgi University, Istanbul.

Gözde ERSÖZ is an associate professor in the Department of Physical Education and Sports Teaching at Fenerbahce University, Istanbul.

Umut HALAÇ is an associate professor in the Department of Economics at Yasar University, Izmir.

Mohammed HASHİRU is a doctoral student in the Department of International Relations, Karadeniz Technical University, Trabzon.

Gül S. HUYUGÜZEL KIŞLA is an assistant professor in the Department of Economics at Ege University, Izmir.

Meltem İNCE YENİLMEZ is an associate professor in the Department of Economics at Yasar University, Izmir.

Tarık KIŞLA is an associate professor in the Department of Computer Education and Instructional Technology at Ege University, Izmir.

Melih ÖZÇALIK is an associate professor in the Department of Economics at Celal Bayar University, Manisa.

Mehmet Gökay ÖZERİM is an associate professor in the Department of International Relations at Yasar University, Izmir.

Yasemin ÖZERKEK is an associate professor in the Department of Economics at Marmara University, Istanbul.

Mehmet ŞENGÜR is an assistant professor in the Department of Economics at Osmangazi University, Eskisehir.

Özgür TÜFEKÇİ is an associate professor in the Department of International Relations, Karadeniz Technical University, Trabzon.

Meral UZUNÖZ is a professor in the Department of Economics at Yıldız Technical University, Istanbul.

Emel YARİMOĞLU is an associate professor in the Department of Business Administration at Yasar University, Izmir.

Aslıhan YURDAKUL is a doctoral student in the research group Demography and Sociology at University of Pompeu Fabra, Barcelona.

Begüm YURTERİ KÖSEDAĞLI is a research assistant in the Department of Economics at Ege University, Izmir.

Preface

The traditional approach to gender can no longer help accomplish growth and economic resilience as the knowledge economy has become greatly competitive and global. Policymakers may have talked about accomplishing the UN Millennium Development Goals, through inclusive development, but have failed to develop models that can transform their hot air into actions. Employment still excludes a great number of people. Opportunities to transform policy and developmental decisions are still not open to a great number of people because of their disability, sexual orientation, age, ethnicity, gender or financial condition. Even so, when gender comes into the picture, alongside any of these attributes, many people within such categories cannot access the opportunities that can improve their lives and help them gain control over their destinies. This book provides insights through holistic and multidisciplinary gender analysis of diverse metrics, models and frameworks to uncover business, economic and organizational development practices that can prove effective to eradicate the gender gap. It challenges readers to rethink conversational perceptions of women in the labour market, and to consider how vital women are to eradicating adverse economic issues.

Gender equality not only focuses on empowering people, but it equally has a moral angle. It is about upholding fairness and equity across cultural, social and political areas. It is also a critical factor that can drive happiness and well-being across the globe. Nations are already making progress towards gender equality. In education, for example, girls are reaching higher academic achievements compared to boys and are less likely to drop out of school.

However, there are still lingering issues as men typically earn more than women, have greater opportunities to grow in their careers, and are less likely to spend their final years in poverty. Gender inequality stops nations from harnessing the vital contributions that females add to the economy and can waste years of investments that could be used by educating the young female population. It must be said that for a nation to maximize its talent pool, equal changes be given to males and females to foster equal contributions at home and in the workplace. This further improves not only their well-being but also the well-being of society.

Gender is an enormous issue as new economies, consulting firms and businesses are developing reforms that particularly target society. Estimates currently show that women have a huge part to play in the consumer sectors of the economy, and gender-based violence is hampering significantly the values of employees and the performance of many typical businesses. Nevertheless, notions of diversity, flexibility and gender, although for everyone, have become interlinked with females. Hence, executives and diversity programs concurrently use these notions when discussing women, especially female participation in leadership positions. Therefore, when diversity programs occur, they undervalue the importance of diversity, flexibility and gender as they only reinforce the ideas that women should only work within the household or in caregiving positions. Therefore, the conversation must stop aligning wage gap, childcare, flexibility, diversity and gender as though they are women's issues. Businesses today understand that competitiveness can only be gained through diversity and flexibility. Therefore, for these businesses to navigate the complexities of the global environment, they must drive a change in gendered language and stop it from aligning parenting with women only. For instance, the advantages of diversity thinking should be enforced in decision making, which Friedman (1993) aligns with moral and friendship grounds: "The greater the diversity of perspectives one can adopt for assessing rules, values, principles and character, the greater the degree of one's autonomy in making moral choices".

Instances like this highlight the benefits of improved gender balance and cultural diversity and can help organizations make better decisions. *The Economics of Gender Equality in the Labour Market* provides insights on why gender diversity must become a priority. It further offers insights on the advantages of gender diversity and economic empowerment, particularly how they can reform organizations and economies. The chapters across the book further discuss a vast range of issues in an attempt to revolutionize perceptions of values and structures alongside existing practices. However, this is only a starting point. To further redefine this field of study and increase its attractiveness, there is a need to focus results on research, and on the benefits that businesses can gain. Therefore, frameworks, practical tools and methodologies should be created in that direction to analyze current laws, policies, academic fields and structures from a gender perspective. This will help businesses understand the impacts of gender equality on economics and profitability through the overlay of sociological perception, and further offer necessary foundational insights on the emerging contemporary society. Through this approach, the reader can easily make his or her own decisions about what must be done in contemporary society to embrace gender diversity. Overall, this book provides deep insights on society and the perspectives of gender and economics.

Meltem İNCE YENİLMEZ
Gül Ş. HUYUGÜZEL KIŞLA

1 Bridging the gender gap in emerging economies for a better future of work for all

Meltem İnce Yenilmez

"The world of the future is in our making. Tomorrow is now."

Eleanor Roosevelt

Introduction

Ongoing debates discuss gender disparity in labor market participation and economic opportunities. There are perceived gaps in economic opportunities for men and women, and this has significant impacts on labor productivity and earnings. Owing to these incidents, the types of jobs have brought about significant differences in human capital.

In truth, when one assesses the number of women against the number of men across industries, fields, professions, firms and sectors, it is impossible to overlook the gaping hole between men's and women's jobs. This gap shows that evolving economic development and restructuring of avenues of employment is not enough to disrupt the gender segregation witnessed. By evaluating global data, it is easy to see that women dominate lower-impact jobs and work in or manage small establishments. In Turkey, the ratio of employed women is far less than that of men. Statistics released in 2014 show that out of every four women in Turkey, only one is employed. And women are segregated in the labor force. Most women are employed in low-paying and low-skilled jobs, for example, in the textile industry and in agriculture. Gender inequality in Turkey's employment is responsible for the underutilization of women in the labor force. Although there has been a considerable rise in women's employment, there is still a serious need for a policy that will ensure an equal opportunity role for both males and females in the work environment. There are many contributing factors to the skewed involvement of women in the labor force. The gender difference in employment roles and the social roles of women contribute to the imbalance in the labor force. There's also an unfair job requirement set by employers and the lack of required qualifications of unemployed women plays a significant role in the low population of women in labor force. The gender difference in labor force has social, economic, political and cultural contributing factors. Addressing these issues should involve a constant effort and creation of policies that will eliminate the gender bias in workplaces.

In the informal sector, the situation is even worse as women in this sector are primarily overrepresented among unpaid family workers. On a general note, women rarely rise to powerful positions in the labor market. Over the years, there have been several misconceptions about women in leadership. Most of these women are seen as arrogant, disrespectful, pushy and stubborn, whereas men who occupy the same capacity are regarded as being ambitious with excellent leadership skills. Other assumptions view women as subordinates to men who would not do well when asked to lead. The social belief of a woman's role being in the bedroom has done little to help them in developing the leadership qualities necessary to succeed. Another assumption is that women often follow others' opinions at the expense of what they feel is right, thus making them unfit to lead. Once people feel a leader is not in control, they mostly ignore the leader's decisions. Also, women are known to prefer an inclusive and collaborative style of leadership, further contributing to the view that they are not confident of ruling on their own.

Another contributing factor to the low involvement of women in leadership is the social role of women being the primary caregivers in families and the other household responsibilities that are expected of them. In Turkish society, women are required to put the needs of their families above their careers and other ambitions. According to research, women who make it to the top of their careers are usually unmarried, without children, or focused on their careers before starting a family. As a result, companies believe that women will most times place their families over their careers and in return limit the responsibilities given to women. To be at the top of one's career, there are moments when one needs to do overtime at work – this, however, conflicts with women's social roles at home – thereby making it difficult for women to create a healthy work/life balance. Networking plays a crucial role in a professional's journey to the top. Networking is the backbone of any business, but women's roles limit them from participating in these networking activities. Also, most networking activities, such as clubbing and golf, are male-oriented.

Due to inadequate access to better opportunities, the perceived gender gap reinforces institutional and labor market failures. For instance, women prefer to work in jobs with flexible working arrangements, to be able to combine work and their domestic responsibilities. These working arrangements, which are primarily informal or part time, carry significantly lower earnings than formal and full-time jobs. With the higher number of women working in such positions, there is decreased motivation to become active participants in the labor market.

Therefore, women mainly specialize in nonmarket work more than market work, which deepens the segregations in time use, access to inputs, market, and institutional failures that traps women in lower-paying positions. To break out of this trap, there must be interventions to lift time constraints, improve women's access to productive jobs, and correct market and institutional failures.

Feminist economic theory focuses on the marginalization of women in traditional institutions and other positions in society. Women are marginalized and are excluded from many activities and situations because of the norms, traditions and discriminatory laws that are still abundant. Therefore, women face severe difficulties attaining positions associated with elevated status, power and money. This challenge is linked with the philosophy concerning laws and norms that the differences between roles played by women and those represented by men determine the kinds of opportunities they can encounter (England, 1993). Therefore, these gender roles significantly affect the chances women have of pursuing individual achievements such as education or career growth. When these women enter the labor market, they encounter restrictions, and the economic opportunities available for them are limited.

Traditional values also limit the number of opportunities women can access to the economy, especially in male-dominated employment positions. Nevertheless, gender roles can be used in evaluating and assessing the connections between gender roles and inadequate economic opportunities for women.

In Turkey, family units are perceived to have men as breadwinners and representatives of their own family. The perceived role is also seen as a prestigious position and held high socially. On the other hand, women are perceived as managers, caretakers or organizers of all household functions. This position may be valued if the household runs smoothly. Therefore, many women face intense pressure to eliminate their search for formal employment or higher education.

Nevertheless, limited opportunities for women in the labor market are a significant concern not only for Turkey but for the world at large because they lead to substantial adverse effects and can hinder any country from reducing poverty and attaining sustainable growth. It is therefore not surprising that the United Nations Millennium Development Goals (MDGs) place women's empowerment and gender equality as one of its primary goals. These obstacles to growth are also the reason why many nations around the world are changing, structuring and aligning policies to tackle the issues of gender inequality. This chapter examines the extent, structure, nature and characteristics of the prevalence of the looming gap between the number of women against men in Turkey's labor force, and the reasons for its existence.

The goal is to develop strategies toward bridging the gender gap in the Turkish labor market. Bridging this gender gap is vital for many reasons. As stated earlier, it can help tackle poverty due to the direct and interrelated contributions to the welfare of the household. It also improves the position held by women as they can now take part in family decisions and making sure that primary income is used for necessities such as health care and children's education. Secondly, gender equality, in terms of employment, has to be enhanced based on the internationally recognized standpoint that every individual is deserving of the same opportunities. This comes from the perspective of fundamental rights.

The World Bank (2012) observed that gender equality in all forms of employment is not only about empowering women but ensuring equity, decreased efficiency loss, fairness, increased productivity, increased social protection contributions, opening tax bases, improved decision making concerning development, business and economic freedom, increased innovation and competition, improved business expansion opportunities for stronger, inclusive development and growth.

Therefore, gender equality sits as the most significant development challenge across Turkey. Over 78.3 percent of women around the globe are killed (ILO, 2019), whereas the women's employment ratio was just 51.9 percent. In Turkey, 65.7 percent of men are employed, while over 28.9 percent of women employed in the population. Therefore, the women working actively as part of Turkey's economy are just 33.5 percent, which is lower than the worldwide average of 48.7 percent. Nevertheless, during the year, women in Turkey have witnessed social exclusion due to employment choices and jobless rates, which also triggered the currency crisis that began in August 2018. Additionally, analysts predict that the employment to dependency ratio will be abnormally high by the end of the year 2018. Therefore, this chapter looks in particular at the main drivers of the gender gap in employment in Turkey and toward finding the best policies that can transform the Turkish labor market into a more inclusive setup while promoting gender equality.

Barriers to women's employment opportunities

Diverse works of literature outline demographic factors, globalization, political systems, economic development, cultural and social norms, education, availability of infrastructure, macroeconomic factors, perceptions and expectations as primary factors influencing gender equality in employment. Current evidence points to the fact that development is positively affected by an increase in female labor participation.

Studies, lectures and discourses have tried to assess the reasons why female labor participation usually takes a plunge before rising as economic development improves. Boserup (1970) provides insights that during the early stages of development in any country, men tend to displace women in the labor force because they already have the knowledge and skills to take on better positions. Nevertheless, this phenomenon may also take a different shape (bringing about the establishment of another focus on the effects of income and substitution). Therefore, when development occurs, the unearned income in the household rises, which reduces the motivation for women to work outside the home. This negatively affects the growing revenues grossed by women and leads to a condition called "income effect," which means that households with higher income provide more avenues for leisure for women.

On the other hand, the substitution effect works in the opposite direction such that when female wages rise, more women are motivated to enter the labor market (Goldin, 1995; Mammen and Paxson, 2000; Bloom et al., 2009; Chaudhuri, 2009; Tam, 2011). Niemi and Lloyd (1981) also provide a different insight into the independent and positive impacts on female labor force participation brought on by inflation. Therefore, the effects of increasing inflation will not significantly negatively affect the lower earnings of women as opposed to their counterparts (Cardoso, 1992).

Nevertheless, Sakellariou (2011) also presents additional insights on the fractures in female-male participation in the labor force within rural societies, citing that deviations in profile (demographic data) and educational fulfillment of the population influence the inequality between men and women participating in the economic. Therefore, increments in education and literacy levels witnessed contribute to the growth and expansion of the female labor force participation. Patacchini et al. (2012) who observed, systematically, that an increase in the level of education also supports these views and diminishing effects of fertility choices can positively affect women's participation in the labor market, with significant differences witnessed in different institutional and welfare settings across EU countries. Concerning Turkey, there have been some policies and changes over the last decade that have reduced gender inequality and provided opportunities for women to participate in the Turkish labor market. Nevertheless, the growth within this period is still low in comparison with other developed EU countries.

In other literature related to women employment in Turkey, education has become an essential factor that influences the female labor participation in Turkey (Er, 2013; Önder, 2013; Kılıç and Öztürk, 2014; Inan and Aşık, 2015). Therefore, it is crucial to analyze women's employment with respect to the perceived gender inequality in education and how it influences the growth of female labor participation. Tansel (2002) has previously evaluated the rate of female involvement in Turkey through time-series evidence of cross-provincial determinants. He discovered that female education strongly and positively affects female labor participation. He equally found there were regional disparities in female labor force participation. According to his results, Central Anatolia, Southeast Anatolia, East Anatolia and the Mediterranean had lower rates of female participation than Marmara, while the Black Sea had higher rates of female participation. Nevertheless, Aegean and Marmara had almost the same (in the participating female labor force). In a different study by Rankin and Aytac (2006), it was observed that the gender differences in schooling depend primarily on the level of urbanization across provinces on a macro-structural level.

Beyond education, Turkey's reluctant growth in female labor participation may also be influenced by the patriarchal family beliefs that remain dominant in Turkey. According to Caner et al. (2015), reforms fail to increase the participation of females in schools, even with the perceived reduction in school dropout rates across the country. The study used data from 1998 to 2003 from the Turkish demographic and healthy surveys to observe the effects of the 1997 education reform. They equally noted that even in cases where the mother's views on gender roles were expressed, the reductions in school dropout rates were almost the same for girls and boys.

A different study by Filiztekin and Karahasan (2015) also provides insights into the spatial dimensions of gender inequality in education in Turkey. This study used district-level data from 1990 to 2020, and findings indicated that different societal segments had varying levels of improvement. They also confirmed the theory, and the rural populations negatively affected female education. Therefore, the female population and rural population were observed as the most disadvantageous individuals, leading to the highest spatial spillovers as observed among these significantly unequal groups of the society. At some point in the past decade, the government in Turkey embraced secularism and began enacting policies and changing curriculums to boost gender equality in educational systems across the country (Çimen and Bayhan, 2018).

More recently, the government has significantly diminished Turkey's improvements in educational sectors through an overarching curriculum reform that barely touches on women's rights and gender roles and equally states almost nothing on equality (The Educational Reform Initiative, 2016–2017).

In 2012, Turkey ranked among countries with the most profound gender gaps, according to the World Economic Forum Gender Gap Report. This report ranks countries using four key factors: health and life expectancy, political participation, educational attainment and economic participation and opportunities (Hausmann et al., 2012). In 2018, these figures remained alarming as Turkey ranked 130th out of 149 countries, making the country one of the worst states for wage inequality. The gender inequality problem in emerging countries is disturbing. Between 2013 and 2015, these figures improved, but owing to the changes made by the present government, this figure has plunged, leading to the status quo of the 2018 Gender Gap Index (World Economic Forum, 2018).

Nevertheless, further research observed that when women seek educational accomplishments, their fertility rates decreased, which also positively influenced infant mortality rates, improved quality of childcare and augmented educational opportunities for girls. Unfortunately, the number of Turkish women attaining higher educational achievements is low when compared to their counterparts.

The TÜİK Research in 2018 provides data on literacy levels in Turkey: 3.5 percent of men over the age of 15 are illiterate, whereas 6.8 percent of women in the same age group are illiterate. Therefore, one in every ten women in Turkey is illiterate, with educational attainments for women diminishing after elementary school, which further confirms the gender gap in educational accomplishments and opportunities (TÜİK, 2018). Other research in 2017 further highlights that for every 100 Turkish women holding a college degree, there are over 158 Turkish men with similar degrees. Nevertheless, the TÜİK research equally highlights that the majority of women in urban areas have at least a high school degree, whereas only 18 percent in the rural areas have comparable degrees.

Women's participation in labor markets is widely acknowledged as a necessity for development. Unfortunately, for Turkey, there have been regular fluctuations in the years past. In 1990, 34 percent of women participated in the labor market, but these rates decreased to 30.6 percent in 2000 and to 25.4 percent in 2004. In 2009, the rates increased to 26.1 percent and had so far expanded to 34.9 percent – a figure attained in 2019. Nevertheless, it is also important to note that over 91.2 percent of women who participated in the labor market have access to social protection.

It is equally important to note that Turkey in 2003 passed an employment law forbidding the differentiation of pay scales by gender. However, these laws were not enforced, and so the gender-based discrimination continues, leading to culturally segregated employment opportunities and gender-based layoffs whenever there is an economic crisis in Turkey.

Naturally, Turkey has also undergone several structural and legal changes over the years, especially concerning its commitment to achieving economic development. These ongoing developments have also helped increase awareness in women about their rights to participate in all aspects of modern society. Nevertheless, many of the reforms in Turkey have failed to provide full cooperation, and some of the reforms in the most recent years have led to further restrictions in traditional gender roles (Köroğlu, 2006).

According to Dökmen (2006), gender inequality is an impediment to achieving a truly democratic and modern society. This means that societies with unequal opportunities for men and women to access all aspects of society limit the growth of real democracy. Therefore, Turkey falls within this unfortunate class of societies because family responsibilities, access to education, participation in labor markets and politics are not fully granted to women. Thus, the Turkish women's labor market has significantly declined over the years and therefore demonstrates an urgent situation that must be addressed. In that regard, the first step to overcoming all impediments is gender equality in education. With education, women will be less eager to procreate unscrupulously and will push for quality health care and education for their children. All of this will, in turn, transform the labor force into a more productive outlay and strongly impact the growth of the economy.

There have been many notable reforms and movements toward eradicating gender inequality in Brazil for the past ten years. However, the impacts are still insignificant, and gender inequality is still considerably high. Nevertheless, the country has successfully enacted policies to reduce the rate of women's illiteracy and created programs that would help improve the lives of women within lower-income positions. However, even as the government has been striving to improve labor force participation within the last ten years, the number of women entering the labor market remains low, and so the effects of these programs and policies are hardly felt. 2014's estimates of women representation were about 43.8 percent of the overall labor force, while the numbers for 2000 and 2005, respectively, were about 41.2 percent and 43 percent (World Economic Forum, 2014). Nevertheless, statistics also show that 24.7 percent of the total female population had part-time jobs, while 59.4 percent participated fully. Furthermore, studies also showed that the effects of "Bolsa Familia" on participation within the official labor market were insignificant, and it also had small but significant negative effects within the informal labor market. Therefore, even as the gender gap decreased across informal and formal sections of the Brazilian labor market, there have been higher gaps within unexplained dimensions of the market. For instance, in 2001, the unexplained areas within the formal sector were 33 percent of the overall 34.9 percent (11.6 percentage points), and, in 2010, the numbers are at about 45 percent (9.86 percentage points). Within the informal sector, unexplained proportions were about 75 percent in 2001 (35.1 percentage), but those numbers rose to about 84 percent (30.5 percentage points) in 2011 (Almeida and Packard, 2018). According to Cameron and Suarez (2018), educational attainment is one of the driving forces of these differences and further explains the enormous wage disparities within the informal and formal sectors. Additionally, Cameron and Suarez

(2018) sheds insights on the prevalence of "sticky floors" as one of the pressing issues affecting the kind of wages most women earn. The lowest deciles of the wage distribution had the largest gender wage disparities, which decreased over the other sides of the dispersion, within the formal and informal sectors.

South Africa also had receding numbers in gender wage disparities, which was 16 percent in 2014 as compared to 40 percent in 1993. However, this decline only happened between 1993 and 2007, but has been in the same position of 16 percent for a long time now. On further analysis, the rate of expanded unemployment (without adding the number of job searches) even increased to 37.2 percent in 2018, whereas it was about 30.9 percent in 2008. Within these periods, rates for women are greater than those for men. Rates for female unemployment in 2018 was about 29.5 percent as against 25.3 percent for the male population, going by formal unemployment definitions. However, concerning expanded definitions, women had over 7.5 percentage points higher unemployment rates when compared to men (Stats, 2018). Therefore, the present study aims to critically assess the principal drivers of the gender gap in employment within South Africa, Turkey, Indonesia and Brazil. The study is necessary for discovering the right policies that can revolutionize the emerging global market to promote gender equality.

Method

This section provides insights on analytical measurements carried out on the determining factor of gender equality driving emerging employment systems. The present study uses data from 1990 to 2019 to analyze the fundamental features of gender equality in employment in Brazil, Indonesia, South Africa and Turkey.

The dependent variable is the ratio of female to male employees for the age group 15–64 over the period (in percentage) and stands for gender equality in employment. Therefore, ratio specifies the gender gap. Thus, value increments would mean improvements in gender equality. The economic development, as well as other control variables, serves as independent variables.

Dependent variable

Gender equality is the dependent variable in this study and is calculated using the methodological observations put in place by the United Nations for evaluating the GDI (Gender Development Index). Nevertheless, the UN equally designed the GDI to include the HDI (Human Development Index). On this account, the UN's HDI measures standard of living, longevity, education and health. Therefore, the GDI is a useful tool as it also evaluates life expectancy, income access and education.

Independent variables

Economic development: The nation's real gross domestic product (GDP) per capita and the squared version of real GDP per capita are jointly used for the representation of economic development. Therefore, the study will uncover the relationship between gender equality and economic development and the extent of this relationship. The real GDP growth rate will also be used on separate terms to determine the possibilities of an economic decline or slowdown and how it affects gender equality.

Infrastructure: Recent innovations have shown that infrastructural developments are the way of the future. However, women (especially those in a rural setting) have to spend an enormous amount of time carrying out household chores. Due to the massive amount of time spent on household chores, which significantly reduces the time spent in the labor market, infrastructure is key to a significant turnaround. Providing infrastructures such as access to energy, transport, childcare centers and ICT infrastructure can diminish the amount of time spent away from the labor force. It has equally been confirmed that when innovations help women streamline processes, it empowers these women, in turn, opening opportunities for growth in the economy and breaking down information barricades. It can also help women come together to take collective actions and bring about more development to society.

Democracy: Democracy is also an essential variable in the present study because true democracy demands equal political opportunities for men and women. This is because it is assumed that when societies practice real democracy, they have a higher respect for the rights of humanity and, by extension, women's rights as opposed to authoritarian systems. In the present study, the Polity IV index ranges from –10 to +10 and is used as a proxy. In the same vein, the "consolidated democracy" is given the code +10, while hereditary monarchy is coded as –10. The study tests the relationship between gender equality and democracy from 1990 to 2019 in Brazil, Indonesia, South Africa and Turkey. It is potentially possible that because democratic countries encourage female employment, more profound levels of freedom should augment and dynamically push equality.

Gender empowerment: The present study uses the UN's gender empowerment measure (GEM) in revised form to analyze the relative significance between political and professional arenas in explaining the differences between GI and GDI. The GEM has three main components: the share of women in parliamentary seats, the share of women in earned income and the relative weight of women in administrative and professional positions. According to the United Nations, the values range from 0.120 as low for Niger to a high of 0.810 for Norway. These data is available for over 102 countries since 1999. In this study, only two components are used in measuring GEM as an indicator of women's empowerment. These two components include the share of women of parliamentary seats and the relative weight of women in administrative and professional positions. This adjustment is made because the GDI measure for this study already contains the third component (share of women in earned income).

Macroeconomic stabilization: The domestic investment rate and the inflation rate are used to evaluate macroeconomic stabilization. According to some experts, inflation may not harm women in lower-earning positions; further, still, inflation may encourage women to take part actively. Therefore, it is expected that macroeconomic stabilization positively influences gender equality in employment. The other indicator, the nation's domestic investment rate, is evaluated (a percentage of gross domestic product (GDP). Higher investment rates mean the government has more resources at its disposal to establish social and economic problems, including problems for employment creations.

Education: Education is also an independent variable in this study. It is based on the premise that education can shape one's perceptions and reduce incidents of patriarchy, thereby eliminating rigid norms and customs. The level of education can also help the general population accept and understand gender equality dynamics. Therefore, women with a higher level of training will have more top motivations to become active participants in the economy's development and aim for higher earnings and opportunities.

Model

Macroeconomic data sets come from TÜİK, WHO, WDI, UNDP, GEM, ILO for selected countries. The Gender Equality Index is taken from World Bank's Online database, except democracy from the Polity IV Project Online (2016) and democracy that is from the Eurostat.

The equation for gender equality in employment evaluation is written as follows:

$$\log GE_{it} = \alpha_i + \beta_1 \log\left(RGDP_{it}\right) + \beta_2 \log\left(RGDP_{it}^2\right) + \beta_3 \log\left(INFRUST_{it}\right) + \beta_4 \left(DEMOC_{it}\right) + \beta_5 \left(DEMOC^2_{it}\right) + \beta_6 \left(X_{it}\right) + \beta_7 \left(Z_{it}\right) + \varepsilon_{it}$$

$$(i = 1, \ldots, N;\ 1, \ldots, T)$$

Where

- GE is the measure of gender equality in the selected countries at time t.
- β_1 is the elasticity of gender equality concerning real per capita income α_i is the fixed effect representing differences between countries.
- β_2 is the gender equality elasticity with respect to RGDP (quadratic real per capita GDP).
- β_3 refers to the flexibility of gender equality concerning INFRUST (infrastructure).
- β_4 represents the coefficient of DOMEC (democracy).
- β_5 represents the coefficient of democracy's quadratic.
- β_6 is the coefficient of gender empowerment measure.
- β_7 is the coefficient of independent variables.

- X is the control variables, including the share of women in parliamentary seats, the share of women in earned income and the relative weight of women in administrative and professional positions.
- Z represents the independent variable and includes inf (inflation), (% of GDP) (inv) (domestic investment), popg (growth rate of the population), urban (urban population share) and educ (secondary school enrolment ratio).
- ε is an error term that includes errors in the gender equality measure.

Results and analysis

Table 1.1 shows the outcomes of using the equations of employment to estimate gender equality (1) in the model; real GDP per capita's coefficient is observed as statistically significant and negative. The squared real GFP is utilized as an explanatory variable to test the hypothesis of this study that real GDP is significantly improving gender equality in employment. The quadratic term was observed as affirmative and substantial at the 5 percent level. This was the same for the coefficient of infrastructure variable. It means that gender equality in employment can improve strategically with improvements in infrastructural levels. These results provide a relationship between gender equality in employment and real

Table 1.1 Ordinary Least Squares Estimates of the Determinants of Gender Equality

Variable	*Countries' Values*
Log of Real GDP per capita	−4.817 (−2.54***)
Log of Real GDP per capita2	1.614 (1.98**)
Democracy	0.931 (3.59**)
Democracy2	0.136 (2.21**)
Inflation (%)	−1.491 (−4.18**)
Domestic investment (%GDP)	0.691 (2.21**)
Urban population share (%)	0.547(5.38***)
Population growth (%)	0.343 (2.06**)
Infrastructure	0.419 (2.41***)
Gender equality in education	0.169 (4.83***)
Women in parliamentary seats share (%)	2.387 (1.94**)
Women in earned income share (%)	0.441 (2.68***)
Weight of women in administrative and professional positions share (%)	0.214 (1.84*)
Adjusted R-squared	0.8703
F-statistic	69.12
Prob>F	0.0000
N	21

Source: Author's estimations

Note: t-values are in parentheses; *** = 1% significant level; ** = 5% significant level; * = 10% significant level.

GDP per capita. Nevertheless, greater levels of real GDP per capita also negatively related to gender equality in work, but that effect is not constant.

Democracy is also statistically significant and positive. The quadratic variable for democracy is equally positive and statistically significant, which indicates that GE (gender equality) and true democratic practices work together. In addition, gender empowerment can also positively affect or lead to higher levels of gender equality. Rising inflation can also bring about profound levels of GE, as observed in the results of this study. These findings may be explained with the following scenarios. More women can be motivated to enter the labor market to seek supplemental earnings when real wages are reduced.

Increasing urbanization rates are found to be positively associated with increasing gender equality in employment in Brazil, Indonesia, South Africa and Turkey. As seen in Table 1.1, this effect is statistically significant at the 1 percent level. The results show that a 1 percentage point increase in urbanization rate is associated with a 0.55 percentage point increase in gender equality in employment in Brazil, Indonesia, South Africa and Turkey. Furthermore, our results suggest that rising population growth rates have a statistically significant effect on gender equality in employment in Brazil, Indonesia, South Africa and Turkey. These results support the positive results of Eastin and Prakash (2013) for gender gaps in labor force participation.

Gender equality in education has positive and statistically significant (at 1 percent level) association with gender equality in employment. A 1 percentage point increase in gender equality in education enrollment is associated with a 0.17 percentage point increase in gender equality in employment in Brazil, Indonesia, South Africa and Turkey as a whole. This supports the hypothesis that education increases people's awareness of cultures and social norms that exist in industrial countries where women are, in most circumstances, entitled to the same freedoms and opportunities as those extended to men (Chen, 2004).

Nevertheless, the rate of domestic investment is also found to be positive and significant in relation to gender equality. To explain these findings, it is vital to assess the impacts of efficient and effective policies as well as well-selected target requirements and audience associated with primary investment projects. The effect of education on gender equality is also substantial and is observed to drive gender equality positively. Therefore, education can provide platforms to transform existing cultural and social norms to see the importance of granting equal opportunities to men and women.

Conclusion and policy recommendations

Gender inequality is a multidimensional problem and can only be solved by implementing strategies that cut across all macro and micro factors influencing the prevalence of this issue; therefore, suggestions for development require lengthy periods for complete implementation. As developing countries, Brazil, Indonesia, South Africa and Turkey must deal with their gender inequality issues to attain significant growth.

Because gender inequality in Brazil, Indonesia, South Africa and Turkey has social, cultural and economic dimensions, reforms and policies must cut across these dimensions. Panel evidence over the period 1990 to 2019 suggests that quadratic real per capital GDP increments, increased democracy, higher ICT infrastructure availability, higher prices and education increase significantly increases gender equality in employment, whereas profound levels of real GDP per capita and higher gross domestic investment lowers it.

Owing to these findings, domestic investments such as good governance, transparency and strengthening accountability are essential areas for improvement to significantly augment and fill the gap between genders in Brazil, Indonesia, South Africa and Turkey's economies. Awareness programs should be enacted to enlarge the civil society landscape. Besides, good governance can help implement, monitor and evaluate the success of all programs instituted for bridging that gender gap. At the design stage for each program, the governments should focus all efforts on meeting legitimate targets that leverage all-stakeholder ownership through collaborations with the civil society, private sector and other development agencies. All stakeholders must become active participants to ensure the establishment and implementation of the programs and projects. This is especially important because efficient decisions depend on the development of objective, transparent and coordinated processes to fully achieve the milestones for each program.

Beyond the importance of good governance, women should be trained in entrepreneurship and encouraged to take risks to build businesses and become employers as well. Concerning good governance, the government should also implement policies that can boost investments in human capital and open up better opportunities for women in the workforce. These policies should promote upskilling, practical training and education for workforces with lower skill sets. By implementing educational reforms and upskilling that augments the needs of the industry, Turkish women will be motivated to build skills to match working environments and improve their positions tremendously. Governments should also help foster working environments and societies that promote the views of women by enforcing anti-discrimination laws, empowering women and supporting equal opportunities. Therefore, the governments of Brazil, Indonesia, South Africa and Turkey should institute programs that dialogue with conglomerates to create employment opportunities for women through skills development, planning and matching. Skill mismatches will also be addressed by improving training programs and closing the gap between vocational and tertiary educational institutions as well as the private sector. Concerning training programs, emphasis should be on initiatives carried out in real-world scenarios to give all existing participants and graduates the chance to be a part of the revolution. The governments should also partner with private sectors and other relevant stakeholders to correct institutional policies pertaining to gender equality. This would strengthen the economic positions of the countries and lead to stronger university–industry connections.

This can be achieved by getting the academic boards and private sector representatives to work together toward developing curriculums that foster gender equality. These steps will no doubt bring about private sector funding for scholarships, research and internships. Therefore, the government's efforts will not only increase opportunities for women but also utilize the human capital effectively in Brazil, Indonesia, South Africa and Turkey and reform the education curriculum. Other measures should target government expenditure on introducing laws that would establish better investment climates toward formalizing the informal sector.

Through the present study, a number of possible instruments can be established to handle inequality in all forms and includes labor market training, employment schemes, access to educational opportunities, nutritional awareness and increased health care awareness and opportunities. Land and property rights reforms can also be established toward growth and acceptance of equality between gender in the country. On the path of education, providing access will reduce inequality, as more women will be motivated to seek educational accomplishments and move up the corporate ladder to better-paying positions. When it improves educational institutions, it provides a double dividend that not only reduces gender inequality in employment in the short term but increases the avenues to break through the poverty trap. Therefore improving the quality and providing access to education should also be accompanied by investments in workplaces to accommodate the newly educated men and women adequately. The policies enacted should also be transferred to cultural/social norms and practices. Therefore, the educational system can be used to change the perception of the upcoming generation. Indeed, integrating the principles of gender equality into the school curriculum will transform society from the early years and help combat discriminatory social norms. In addition, the government should implement policies that promote women's participation in public settings and increase access to information that enlightens on the role of women in society. There is no doubt that inclusive growth and development fostered by inclusive governance is critical to eliminating the different treatments meted to male and female participants in the emerging labor markets.

Besides the aforementioned strategies, the governments can also enact awareness programs that can be aired on the media to help others become aware of the direct impacts of discriminatory practices on the economy. These programs will help individuals gain better insights on the importance of individual support to help boost the emerging economies by eliminating gender-based unfair practices in their workplaces. Without implementing all of the reforms and strategies outlined in this chapter, the current unemployment rate of women is a time bomb that may disrupt Brazil, Indonesia, South Africa and Turkey's seamless economic growth and development in the future.

References

Almeida, R. K. and Packard, T. G. (2018). *Skills and Jobs in Brazil: An Agenda for Youth*, International Bank for Reconstruction and Development/The World Bank: Washington DC.

Bloom, D., Canning, D., Fink, G. and Finley, J. (2009). Fertility, female labor force participation and the demographic dividend. *Journal of Economic Growth*, 14, 79–101.

Boserup, E. (1970). *Women's Role in Economic Development*, St. Martin's: New York.

Cameron, L. and Suarez, D. C. (2018). *Sticky Floors in Developing Countries – A Distributional Analysis of the Formal and Informal Sector*, Australian Gender Economics Workshop, 26 March 2018.

Caner, A., Guven, C., Okten, C. and Sakalli, S. O. (2015). Gender roles and the education gender gap in Turkey. *Social Indicators Research*, 129(3), 1231–1254.

Cardoso, E. (1992). *Inflation and Poverty*, Working Paper No. 4006, National Bureau of Economic Research, Cambridge, MA.

Chaudhuri, S. (2009). *Economic Development and Women's Empowerment*, Working Paper, University of Wisconsin, Eau Claire.

Chen, D. H. C. (2004). *Gender Equality and Economic Development: The Role for Information and Communication Technologies*, World Bank Policy Research Working Paper 3285, The Knowledge for Development Program, Washington, DC.

Çimen, C. A. and Bayhan, S. (2018). *Ders Kitaplarında Sekülerizm ve Toplumsal Cinsiyet Eşitliği Araştırması Sonuç Raporu* [Secularism in Class Books and Findings of the Gender Equality Report], Karşılaştırmalı Eğitim Derneği, Elf Publication.

Dökmen, Z. Y. (2006). *Toplumsal cinsiyet*, Sistem Yayıncılık: İstanbul.

Eastin, J. and Prakash, A. (2013). Economic development and gender equality: Is there a gender kuznets curve? *World Politics*, 65(1), 156–186.

Er, Ş. (2013). Türkiye'de Kadınların İşgücüne Katılım Oranını Etkileyen Faktörlerin Bölgesel Analizi. *Öneri Dergisi*, 10(40), 35–44.

ERI (2017). *Education Observatory Report, 2016–2017*. Education Reform Initiative, Istanbul. Retrieved from: http://en.egitimreformugirisimi.org/education-monitoring-report-2016–17/

Filiztekin, A. and Karahasan, B. (2015). *Mapping the Educational Attainment in Turkey: In EY International Congress on Economics II* (EYC2015), Ekonomik Yaklasim Association: Ankara, Turkey (No. 285).

Goldin, C. (1995). The U-shaped female labor force function in economic development and economic history. In *Investment in Women's Human Capital* (Ed. T. P. Schultz), The University of Chicago Press: Chicago, IL.

Hausmann, R., Tyson, L. D. and Zahidi, S. (2012). *Küresel cinsiyet uçurumu raporu 2012*, Dünya Ekonomik Forumu.

ILO (2019). *World Employment Social Outlook: Trends 2019*, Geneva: International Labour Office.

Inan, F. and Aşık, G. (2015). *Making Economies Work for Women: Female Labour Force Participation in Turkey*, OXFAM and TEPAV Report.

Kılıç, D. and Öztürk, S. (2014). Türkiye'de Kadınların İşgücüne Katılımı Önündeki Engeller ve Çözüm Yolları: Bir Ampirik Uygulama. *Amme Idaresi Dergisi*, 47(1), 107–130.

Köroğlu, F. (2006). *Okul yönetiminde cinsiyet etkeni ve kadın öğretmenlerin okul yöneticiliği talepleri Bingöl ili örneği*, Yayımlanmamış Yüksek Lisans Tezi: Elazığ.

Mammen, K. and Paxson, C. (2000). Women's work and economic development. *Journal of Economic Perspectives*, 14(4), 141–164.

Niemi, B. T. and Lloyd, C. B. (1981). Female labor supply in the context of inflation. *The American Economic Review*, 71(2), 70–75.

Önder, N. (2013). Türkiye'de Kadın İşgücünün Görünümü. *Çalışma Dünyası Dergisi*, 1(1).

Patacchini, E., Cipollone, A. and Vallanti, G. (2012). *Women Labor Market Performance in Europe: Trends and Shaping Factors*, Centre for European Policy Studies: Brussels.

Sakellariou, C. (2011). *Determinants of the Gender Wage Gap and Female Labor Force Participation in EAP*, Paper commissioned for the EAP Gender Report.

Stats sa. (2018). *How Do Women Fare in the South African Labour Market?* Statistics South Africa. Retrieved from: http://www.statssa.gov.za/?p=11375

Tam, Henry (2011). U-shaped female labor force participation with economic development: Some panel data evidence. *Economic Letters*, 110(2).

Tansel, A. (2002). *Economic Development and Female Labor Force Participation in Turkey: Time-Series Evidence and Cross-Province Estimates*, METU/ERC Working Paper No. 02/3 Middle East Technical University, Ankara, Turkey.

Türkiye İstatistik Kurumu (TÜİK). (2018). *Cinsiyet ve eğitim durumuna göre aylık ortalama brüt ücret ve yıllık ortalama brüt kazanç tablosu.*

World Bank (2012). *World Development Report 2012: Gender Equality and Development*, World Bank. Retrieved from: https://openknowledge.worldbank.org/handle/10986/4391

World Economic Forum (2014). *The Global Gender Gap Report*. Retrieved from: http://www3.weforum.org/docs/GGGR14/GGGR_CompleteReport_2014.pdf

World Economic Forum (2018). *The Global Gender Gap Report*. Retrieved from: www3.weforum.org/docs/WEF_GGGR_2018.pdf

2 Women's labor force participation and gender discrimination in the labor market

Mehmet Şengür

1 Introduction

Every individual needs income to take part in economic and social life. The fact that the type and amount of income is different does not change the obligation of individuals, who are a social entity, to earn income. The most familiar/traditional way of making individual income is to be involved in the production process in any way. Simply, whatever production factor a person has, he or she will get that type of income. At the end of this sharing process, which is also called the functional distribution of income, everyone will have a certain amount of income. Although the working class is at a lower level in terms of getting a share from income, it constitutes an important group within the income group. Therefore, the income earned by individuals has an important role in terms of economic activities. When we consider that income earners constitute a large part of the population, it is seen that they have a determining feature both in terms of individual expenditure and consumption and national total demand.

Wage is a compensation for the work done and it will also be the resource for the expenses to be made and the expenses one wants to make. It is clear that obtaining high wages will also mean more spending or consumption. The amount and type of spending will also vary from person to person. All we have said so far is based on the assumption that individuals have a job and are earning income. But what if individuals do not have a job to work at? Or if there is no income? In this case, it will be very difficult for them to exist in social and economic terms.

Being involved in the labor market is a desirable or must-have situation for people, as it means earning income. Particularly participation of the women in the labor force is extremely important for them and, more importantly, for the society. On average, the population is equal in terms of the number of women and men in most countries worldwide. In this case, the absence of women in the labor force means that half of the population remains idle. In addition, when women are not involved in the labor force, there is a lack of income and subsequent poverty. If a woman is poor, her children will also be a poor as a result. Another problem for women in the labor market is that they do not have equal positions and wages with men even if they enter the market in sufficient numbers.

In this chapter, initially, information is given about the concepts such as labor market, wage, social exclusion and gender inequality. Afterwards, the ratio of participation of women in the labor market and whether the wages earned in the labor market differ by gender are examined for different countries. Finally, factors such as wage and education, which have an impact on the participation of women in the labor force, were analyzed within the framework of the established model and suggestions were offered.

2 Labor market and wage

Wage is a compensation for the work done and it will also be the resource for the expenses to be made and the expenses one wants to make (Case and Fair, 2006). Factor markets are markets where production factors are bought and sold. The labor market is also a marketplace where supply and demand of labor, which is one of the factors of production, exists. Wage can simply be defined as the share that the labor which participates in the labor force takes from production.

Labor markets are also regulated by supply and demand forces like all other markets in the economy (Mankiw, 2012, p. 376). The individual labor supply curve shows that the amount of labor provided by anyone depends on the ratio of wage which that person has earned. As the wages of the workers increase, the amount of labor they offer will increase. Therefore, the relationship between wages and the amount of labor will be positive and upward (Krugman and Wells, 2010).

The labor market labor supply curve is determined based on the decisions of household individuals on labor supply (Parkin, 2012, pp. 422–424). The labor supply curve has a positive slope and will vary depending on how individuals respond to wage changes. If there is an increase in wages, individuals are expected to increase the amount of labor supply. Because people will try to buy more goods and services with higher wages. Individuals may prefer to increase their labor supply, i.e. to work or not to work. However, the point that should not be forgotten is that with increasing wages, leisure time becomes a more expensive commodity (Case and Fair, 2006).

It is especially important how an individual member of the labor market will make a choice regarding how many hours a week s/he will work. When we think about this preference, we need to know these three factors very well: the first of these is the selection objects, the second is the elements that restrict the selections and finally the pleasures that affect or direct the selections. You may think of working or leisure time as a choice or selection object. However, individuals will actually have chosen only one at a moment in time and will be faced with one. If a preference has been made for working, the hours to work will have been selected. In fact, the hours left for leisure will also have been determined. If individuals waive their leisure time, they get paid a wage in return as a reward. Income is gaining the ability to purchase consumer goods, but it is the result of a situation where leisure time is also waived (Estrin et al., 2008). Although the labor supply curve is an increasing function of wages and it has a positive slope, it is normal to observe changes in labor supply from time to time. According to Mankiw, the reasons for this change in the amount of labor supply are changes in trends or preferences, changes in alternative opportunities and migration (Mankiw, 2012). If the preference of individuals is to work, labor supply will increase due to the amount of labor. Similarly, increases in the amount of labor in the areas receiving migration and in the sectors the labor force is directed towards as well will be observed.

The labor demand curve shows the firm's effort to minimize the cost of the amount of labor against changing wages (Besanko and Braeutigam, 2010, p. 266). The labor demand amount of any firm is determined at the point where the marginal product value of labor equals the wage ratio. Therefore, the labor demand curve of a firm is obtained from the marginal product value curve (Parkin, 2012, p. 420). The labor market has a different structure from other markets. Labor force demand is derived or derivative demand. In other words, labor is not an end product offered directly to consumers, but it is used for the production of goods and services. In order to make the demand for labor more understandable, we should focus on companies that want to hire labor in order to produce goods and services and to offer more sales (Mankiw, 2012, p. 376). It is understood here that labor demand is a decreasing function of wages and it also has a negative slope.

The marginal product value of any factor is equal to the value of the additional output obtained from this factor using an additional unit. Therefore, the marginal product value of labor will also be equal to the output value obtained by the use of an additional unit of labor. In this case, the marginal product value (VMPL) of labor will be equal to the multiplication of the unit output price (P) and the marginal product (MPL) of labor (Krugman and Wells, 2010, p. 514).

If the marginal product value of labor is greater than the cost of a worker, that is the wage, firms will be demanding for labor. Otherwise, if the cost of labor demand is higher than its contribution to additional output, labor will not be demanded.

A number of factors affect the demand for labor. The main factors can be listed as changes in technology, changes in output prices, changes in the supply of other factors. If technological change is oriented towards increasing labor productivity, demand for labor will increase. However, if the technology changes mostly in the direction of robotic production, it will lead to a decrease in labor demand. As the price of the goods produced by the firms increases, the firm will want to produce more and the demand for labor will shift to the right. Similarly, if the price of the produced goods decreases, the demand for labor decreases and shifts to the left. As the supply or price of other factors involved in production changes, it will also change the demand for labor, depending on the amount of labor and the degree of substitution (Mankiw, 2012; Parkin, 2012; Krugman and Wells, 2010).

The market labor demand is derived by considering the labor demands of the companies. Market labor demand consists of the sum of all the amount of labor demanded by all firms in the market at each wage level (Parkin, 2012). Wages in a competitive labor market are equal to the marginal product value of labor. It is also adjusted to balance labor supply and demand. In this case, the balance wage level in the labor market is determined at the point where labor supply and demand are equal (Mankiw, 2012, p. 384).

At the point where the market labor supply and labor demand are equal, the balance wage level has been determined. If there is an increase in the level of equilibrium wage, labor supply, that is, the number of those who want to work, will increase. However, firms will not assume a positive attitude towards demanding additional labor at high wages, and even a decrease in labor demand will occur. In this case, unemployment will occur because the labor supply will be more than the demand for labor. On the contrary, if the market balance wage decreases, the number of people who want to work at low wages will decrease and the labor supply will shift to the left. Labor demand will increase at low wage level, but there will not be enough labor to meet this demand. In such a situation, there will be a lack of labor supply or extra labor demand in the market.

3 Participation of women in the labor market, social exclusion, gender inequality and poverty

Poverty is a situation where individuals cannot meet minimum consumption when viewed from a monetary perspective. Poverty can be defined as the deprivation of welfare in the society or it can have different definitions, such as poverty of home, food, health and education (Haughton and Khandker, 2009). In such a situation, measurement of it is commonly made on the basis of comparing the resources required for the consumption bundle. In this comparison, if the individual or household does not have enough resources to meet their basic needs, they will be defined as poor (Foster, 1998, p. 335). Poverty is basically associated with the inability to have enough income to sustain life, which in absolute terms defines poverty. Besides absolute poverty, the concept of relative poverty, which provides information about the proximity to the average welfare level in society, is also important.

Relative poverty provides information about the distribution of income for people in different income groups. On the other hand, relative poverty only shows whether an individual is poor and the numerical size of the poor (Khusro, 1999, p. 51). For us, the point here is whether women are in poverty rather than whether the society is in poverty as a whole.

The concept of women's poverty was used for the first time in America in 1978. Pearce introduced the phenomenon of women's impoverishment between 1950 and 1970 based on the fact that women living in America constitute 75% of the total poor (Pearce, 1978). Now, "feminization of poverty" has been added to the concepts of poverty and it has been revealed that women suffer most from poverty in the society.

It would not be correct to address women's poverty in a single dimension. In addition to the inequality and discrimination they face in the labor markets, women are pushed to the secondary position in comparison to men in many social fields due to structural inequality in society (Bradshaw and Linneker, 2003, p. 9).

The most determining reason why women fall into poverty is inequality in the labor markets. In addition to the unequal wage in the labor markets, shouldering responsibilities such as marriage, maternity, divorce and financial weakness also impoverish women (Goldberg and Kremen, 1990, pp. 4–7).

According to Buvinić (1997), women attribute poverty to two main reasons: discrimination in the labor market and inability to access adequate educational opportunities. Another concept that needs to be addressed along with women's poverty is social exclusion. Because it would be wrong to think that women are only unequal or devoid in terms of income. Feminization of poverty covers many economic and social fields, materially and morally.

The concept of social exclusion was used to explain the social transformation in France in the 1980s. The concept of "social exclusion," first used by sociologists, has become widespread over time and has attracted the attention of all social sciences. Social exclusion generally refers to the weakness of a person or group in society in terms of economic and social participation (Silver, 1994). With the advent of the concept of social exclusion, it was also observed that women were the most affected by this situation. It is clear that women will feel the negative effects of social exclusion in an environment where poverty is feminized. As the concept of social exclusion has become widespread, the situation has started to be expressed as mass deprivation and poverty instead of on an individual level.

As a result of the new forms of poverty and exclusion, it is seen that deep distinctions occur between the lowest groups, which experience mass weakness, and the highest groups. The most important negative aspect of this situation is the polarization between the living groups in the society. With technology and new types of production, the current unemployment ratio will also increase rapidly. When this situation is considered, the most important problem will be whether integration with the large excluded and weak population in the society will be ensured (Bhalla and Lapeyre, 2004, pp. 4–5). Countries tend to support the weakest segments in society to avoid social and economic crises. This support will be in terms of social and economic empowerment.

Empowerment can basically be defined as having personal power, being able to make and implement individual choices, having a dignified life and campaigning for fundamental rights (Narayan et al., 2002, p. 13). Empowering women will also be an important political topic, as they experience the most inequality in the social and economic spheres in society. Therefore, our study is based on the participation of women in the labor force, which is among the main reasons for women to fall into poverty and social exclusion.

3.1 Indicators of participation of women in the labor force, wages and gender inequality

In this section, the labor force participation ratio of women, wages and the status of various gender-based parameters for development in the largest developing countries are examined. Tables and graphs are created in line with the data obtained from World Bank (WB). These countries are Argentina, Australia, Bangladesh, Brazil, Canada, China, Egypt, France, Germany, India, Indonesia, Italy, Japan, South Korea, Mexico, Pakistan, Philippines, Russian Federation, South Africa, Turkey, United States and Vietnam. For these countries, whose data are available, the participation ratio of women; whether they are self-employed or not; employment status in different sectors such as agriculture, industry and services; and

Table 2.1 Labor force participation rate for female, 2000–2018, (15+)

	Argentina	*Australia*	*Bangladesh*	*Brazil*	*Canada*
2000	50.38	54.62	26.52	50.27	58.65
2001	50.00	55.19	26.77	51.28	58.95
2002	48.82	55.40	27.03	52.63	60.13
2003	49.43	56.05	27.28	52.95	61.14
2004	50.06	55.80	27.54	53.99	61.26
2005	49.42	57.05	27.80	55.12	60.93
2006	49.94	57.61	27.92	54.83	61.20
2007	49.02	58.20	28.40	54.59	61.89
2008	48.12	58.66	28.89	54.49	61.99
2009	48.82	58.82	29.38	54.97	61.87
2010	47.83	58.71	29.88	53.58	61.86
2011	48.10	58.95	30.37	52.17	61.60
2012	48.19	58.83	30.86	53.08	61.61
2013	47.79	58.71	31.36	52.98	61.68
2014	47.16	58.65	31.87	52.86	61.09
2015	47.83	59.07	32.38	53.38	60.77
2016	48.48	59.25	32.89	53.32	60.81
2017	49.12	59.69	35.85	54.17	61.02
2018	48.97	59.65	36.00	54.03	60.85

Source: Data from database: Gender Statistics (World Bank-modeled ILO estimate)

schooling ratio according to gender equality index are presented by creating tables with data obtained from the World Bank (World Bank, 2019a, 2019b).

When we look at Table 2.1, we see the labor force participation ratio of women in Argentina, Australia, Bangladesh, Brazil and Canada for the period 2000–2018. While the labor force participation ratio of women in Argentina was around 50.3% in 2000, this ratio dropped to 48.9% in 2018. In Australia, participation of women in the labor force was 54% and above in this 19-year period. While the participation ratio of women in the labor force in Brazil was 50.2% in 2000, it increased to 60.8% in 2018. In Canada, participation ratio of women is, from the year of 2000 to 2018, increased from 58.6% to 60.8%. Among these five countries, the labor force participation ratio of women in Argentina decreased by approximately 1.5% in 19 years. Unlike Argentina, there has been an increase in the labor force participation ratio of women in four other countries. For the 2010–2018 period, Bangladesh was the country that increased its participation of labor force ratio the most among the five countries – by approximately 10%. However, despite this 10% increase, the labor force participation ratio of women in Bangladesh is as low as 36% by the year of 2018 (Table 2.1).

The labor force participation ratio of women in China is extremely high. Women were involved in the labor force at 71% in 2000; however, with a decrease of almost 10%, it went down to 61% in 2018. Although labor force participation of women decreased in China in 2018, it is almost three times that of India and Egypt. Even though labor force participation of women in Egypt increased by 3% in the 19-year period, it was only 22.8% in 2018. Similarly, for India, the labor force participation ratio of women are quite low, even less than in Egypt. On the contrary, the labor force participation ratio of women in India decreased by around 7% from 2000 to 2018. In France and Germany, between 2000 and 2018, the labor force participation ratios of women were on average 50% and above. In Germany, the labor force participation ratio of women was 55.2%, with an increase of approximately 6% in 19 years by 2018 and 50.3% in France (Table 2.2).

Table 2.3 shows the participation ratio of women in the labor force in Indonesia, Italy, Japan and South Korea in the period 2000–2018. The labor force participation ratio of women in Indonesia is quite high compared to some countries in Europe, such as Italy. Despite the occasional decreases, the labor force participation ratio of women in Indonesia in 2018 increased to 52.2% from 51.6% in 2000 (Table 2.3).

When we look at the participation of women in the labor force in Mexico, it is observed that it increased from 38.8% in 2000 to 43.7% in 2018. This ratio, which was 47.7% in the Philippines in 2000, decreased to 45.7% at the end of 19 years. The labor force participation ratio of women in Pakistan is very low (Table 2.4).

Table 2.2 Labor force participation rate for female, 2000–2018, (15+)

	China	*Egypt*	*France*	*Germany*	*India*
2000	71.01	19.91	48.60	49.06	30.38
2001	70.20	20.08	48.35	49.36	30.72
2002	69.33	18.84	48.57	49.63	31.07
2003	68.42	19.25	49.81	49.99	31.43
2004	67.55	19.72	49.69	49.81	31.80
2005	66.77	20.23	50.12	50.70	32.17
2006	66.07	20.79	50.16	51.49	30.81
2007	65.46	22.75	50.51	52.01	29.50
2008	64.92	21.50	50.69	52.13	28.23
2009	64.38	22.69	50.97	52.53	27.01
2010	63.78	22.63	50.92	52.79	25.83
2011	63.57	22.04	50.77	53.66	24.39
2012	63.40	22.50	50.93	53.70	23.02
2013	63.18	23.39	51.08	54.31	23.19
2014	62.93	23.69	50.83	54.51	23.35
2015	62.61	22.55	50.73	54.61	23.50
2016	62.23	22.85	50.68	54.96	23.66
2017	61.84	22.73	50.44	55.21	23.80
2018	61.26	22.83	50.34	55.25	23.60

Source: Data from database: Gender Statistics (World Bank-modeled ILO estimate)

Table 2.3 Labor force participation rate for female, 2000–2018, (15+)

	Indonesia	*Italy*	*Japan*	*South Korea*
2000	51.06	35.44	49.26	48.82
2001	49.24	36.02	49.21	49.29
2002	47.16	36.56	48.61	49.79
2003	47.09	37.02	48.50	49.07
2004	46.56	38.26	48.30	50.10
2005	45.51	37.86	48.37	50.39
2006	45.49	37.97	48.44	50.60
2007	49.48	37.75	48.55	50.51
2008	50.23	38.39	48.60	50.19
2009	50.36	37.90	48.81	49.24
2010	51.12	37.78	48.72	49.49
2011	51.05	37.94	48.35	49.71
2012	51.60	39.16	48.29	50.02
2013	50.88	39.03	49.03	50.29
2014	50.77	39.40	49.47	51.45
2015	50.76	39.00	49.85	51.90
2016	50.92	39.64	50.59	52.24
2017	52.17	40.10	51.41	52.74
2018	52.24	40.00	51.39	52.75

Source: Data from database: Gender Statistics (World Bank-modeled ILO estimate)

Table 2.4 Labor force participation rate for female, 2000–2018, (15+)

	Mexico	*Philippines*	*Pakistan*	*Russian*
2000	38.88	47.74	16.06	54.69
2001	38.18	47.71	15.95	53.54
2002	38.92	47.57	16.08	54.54
2003	38.45	47.04	16.95	54.29
2004	40.65	46.72	17.87	54.75
2005	41.32	47.55	18.37	55.22
2006	42.51	47.97	18.92	55.58
2007	42.91	48.04	19.21	56.17
2008	42.78	47.53	19.67	56.09
2009	43.32	48.30	20.74	56.25
2010	43.16	48.49	21.74	55.92
2011	43.49	49.26	22.09	56.15
2012	44.55	48.84	22.35	56.08
2013	44.55	48.78	22.62	55.78
2014	43.55	49.56	22.96	55.73

	Mexico	*Philippines*	*Pakistan*	*Russian*
2015	43.89	49.07	23.92	55.58
2016	43.95	48.62	23.81	55.72
2017	43.66	45.51	23.70	55.30
2018	43.78	45.71	23.90	54.91

Source: Data from database: Gender Statistics (World Bank-modeled ILO estimate)

Table 2.5 Labor force participation rate for female, 2000–2018, (15+)

	South Africa	*Turkey*	*United States*	*Vietnam*
2000	49.02	26.29	59.03	72.05
2001	49.42	26.83	58.81	72.00
2002	49.11	27.55	58.59	71.95
2003	47.20	26.21	58.46	71.88
2004	45.08	23.38	58.15	71.78
2005	46.97	23.30	58.24	71.67
2006	48.35	23.05	58.34	71.58
2007	47.38	23.11	58.26	71.48
2008	47.92	23.99	58.46	71.43
2009	46.29	25.48	58.14	71.40
2010	44.73	27.03	57.50	71.31
2011	45.20	28.32	56.93	71.46
2012	45.42	28.88	56.70	71.97
2013	46.39	30.10	56.29	72.90
2014	46.61	30.24	56.11	73.19
2015	47.80	31.48	55.83	72.95
2016	47.80	32.51	55.99	72.64
2017	48.92	33.57	56.31	72.70
2018	48.85	33.52	56.05	72.65

Source: Data from database: Gender Statistics (World Bank-modeled ILO estimate)

Table 2.5 shows the participation ratio of women in labor force in South Africa, Turkey, the USA and Vietnam between the years 2000 and 2018. Vietnam is the country with the highest labor force participation ratio of women among these four countries. Almost three-quarters of women are involved in the labor force in Vietnam. Turkey, among these four countries, has the lowest ratio of labor force participation of women. In Turkey, the labor force participation ratio of women was 33.5%, with the increase of 7% in this period. The 7% increase is a relatively positive development, but it is quite a low labor force participation ratio compared to other countries (Table 2.5). For the period of 2000–2018, the labor force participation data of women from 22 countries are listed alphabetically. Country data in alphabetical order is presented in Table 2.1 to Table 2.5.

Participation of women in the labor force is very crucial both individually and socially. There are many factors that affect labor force participation. These factors can affect the entire labor force. However, some factors especially affect labor force participation of women. Among the factors affecting labor force participation, dozens of factors such as development level of countries, industrialization, capital accumulation of countries, marginal productivity of labor, technology-based production, education, traditions, age, gender, taxes, subsidies, price of manufactured products can be listed. When the level of economic and social development is low in a country, women's labor force participation rates are also decreasing. Women cannot take part in the labor market, as job opportunities will be very limited in countries where industrialization lags behind. The stronger the capital structure of the country's economies, the easier it will be to finance investments. As a result of easier investment, job opportunities for individuals will also increase. Similarly, government subsidies and tax cuts to investors accelerate women's participation in the labor market, because investors will either increase their existing investments or make new investments with these supports. The increase in the education level of women also increases the productivity of labor, and women can get jobs easier. Apart from these, the sexist viewpoint and traditions in some societies prevent women's participation in the labor market. Women's labor force participation rates are decreasing as a result of the thought that put men at the first position and employs women only in household responsibilities.

However, factors such as gender, traditions, mindset in the country, the sector which is worked in and the level of education affect women more and negatively compared to men. Some of the variables that affect the labor force participation of women are presented in the following tables, with data obtained from WB.

Employment numbers of women in the agricultural sector in the period 2000–2009 are shown in Table 2.6. In Argentina and the USA, the share of women employed in agriculture remained below 1% in the ten-year period. While the employment ratio of women in the agricultural sector in the USA was 0.86% in 2000, it decreased to 0.68% in 2009. In Argentina, the employment ratio of women in the agricultural sector was 0.24% and 0.39% in the same years (Table 2.6).

We can see the course of women employment in the agricultural sector in Table 2.7 for the period after 2009. According to 2010 data, Pakistan is the country with the highest women employment ratio in the agricultural sector.

When we look at the women employment ratio in industry, which is another important sector in the economy, we see that it is extremely low compared to the agricultural sector. The country with the highest share of women employment in the industry sector was China, with a ratio of 26.5% in 2000. After China are countries such as Russia, Mexico, Japan and Italy, with the approximate ratios of 21–22%. The countries with the lowest share of women employed in industry were Egypt and Bangladesh in 2000. At the end of the next nine years after 2000, the women employment ratio in the industrial sector decreased in countries other than Vietnam, Turkey, India, China and Bangladesh. One of the reasons for these

Table 2.6 Employment in agriculture, female percentage (2000–2009)

	2000	*2001*	*2002*	*2003*	*2004*	*2005*	*2006*	*2007*	*2008*	*2009*
Argentina	0.24	0.30	0.47	0.97	0.97	0.72	0.49	0.42	0.35	0.39
Australia	3.43	3.45	3.03	2.62	2.68	2.45	2.37	2.29	2.22	2.22
Bangladesh	78.78	77.44	75.96	74.28	72.48	70.49	68.19	67.52	66.86	66.25
Brazil	14.41	15.48	15.94	15.58	15.66	15.66	14.75	13.79	13.03	12.15
Canada	1.65	1.34	1.36	1.32	1.29	1.35	1.38	1.31	1.21	1.19
China	46.94	46.94	46.94	46.02	43.82	41.73	39.54	37.77	36.59	35.13
Egypt	39.41	31.92	27.57	39.07	46.78	46.66	43.33	46.56	45.62	46.06
France	2.84	2.82	2.78	2.68	2.64	2.28	2.22	2.14	1.83	1.88
Germany	2.11	2.07	1.96	1.83	1.70	1.73	1.61	1.61	1.32	1.25
India	74.38	73.90	73.43	72.82	72.11	71.43	70.40	69.23	68.21	66.98
Indonesia	46.74	44.52	45.40	47.54	44.62	44.38	41.13	41.40	41.36	39.94
Italy	4.35	4.37	3.93	3.69	3.16	3.26	3.32	3.06	2.83	2.66
Japan	5.55	5.28	4.96	4.90	4.71	4.57	4.44	4.30	4.25	4.11
South Korea	12.25	11.31	10.67	10.14	9.25	8.93	8.64	8.27	7.93	7.51
Mexico	6.56	5.80	5.93	5.00	5.31	4.82	4.54	4.49	4.32	3.83
Philippines	24.05	24.31	24.63	24.24	23.75	23.49	23.15	22.74	22.37	22.12
Pakistan	65.04	64.91	64.71	64.41	65.92	67.25	69.11	72.75	75.34	72.88
Russian Federation	11.72	9.32	8.94	8.16	7.71	7.91	7.64	6.82	6.60	6.40
South Africa	8.46	7.14	8.43	7.22	7.08	5.38	5.41	5.11	4.19	3.63
Turkey	64.72	62.00	59.14	55.73	50.74	47.36	43.54	42.60	40.11	37.79
United States	0.86	0.84	0.83	0.81	0.78	0.75	0.74	0.66	0.68	0.68
Vietnam	66.28	64.97	63.13	61.71	59.99	56.96	53.78	51.48	50.82	50.02

Source: Data from database: Gender Statistics (World Bank-(World Bank-modeled ILO estimate)

Table 2.7 Employment in agriculture, female percentage (2010–2018)

	2010	*2011*	*2012*	*2013*	*2014*	*2015*	*2016*	*2017*	*2018*
Argentina	0.38	0.28	0.28	0.22	0.15	0.07	0.03	0.01	0.01
Australia	2.28	1.89	1.92	1.67	1.83	1.85	1.69	1.65	1.63
Bangladesh	65.53	65.32	65.02	64.73	64.36	63.86	63.38	59.84	59.43
Brazil	11.57	11.01	5.90	5.67	5.21	5.05	4.76	4.29	4.23
Canada	1.11	1.10	1.11	1.09	1.05	1.01	1.14	0.96	0.95
China	33.75	31.91	30.75	28.64	26.83	25.97	25.12	24.44	24.24
Egypt	42.87	43.37	37.59	42.87	43.22	40.21	38.40	36.88	36.66
France	1.76	1.87	1.83	1.84	1.64	1.64	1.62	1.58	1.56
Germany	1.20	1.18	1.10	1.01	1.01	0.96	0.89	0.88	0.87
India	65.61	62.80	59.97	59.58	59.09	58.60	58.16	57.63	57.06
Indonesia	38.40	36.79	35.26	33.91	33.37	32.61	30.07	28.82	28.53

(*Continued*)

Table 2.7 (Continued)

	2010	*2011*	*2012*	*2013*	*2014*	*2015*	*2016*	*2017*	*2018*
Italy	2.71	2.63	2.57	2.43	2.40	2.43	2.51	2.35	2.31
Japan	3.93	3.72	3.54	3.38	3.30	3.22	3.05	2.99	2.96
South Korea	6.88	6.75	6.32	6.11	5.63	5.10	4.72	4.47	4.41
Mexico	3.86	3.90	4.10	3.86	3.69	3.66	3.57	3.74	3.69
Philippines	21.75	21.40	20.93	20.11	20.19	18.69	17.30	15.32	15.15
Pakistan	74.08	74.45	74.82	75.15	73.19	72.06	73.14	72.96	72.72
Russian Federation	5.56	5.68	5.41	5.40	5.15	5.11	5.01	4.03	3.99
South Africa	3.78	3.45	3.60	3.49	3.20	4.24	3.89	3.72	3.66
Turkey	39.20	39.27	37.10	35.56	32.77	31.00	28.59	28.20	27.89
United States	0.74	0.77	0.76	0.67	0.70	0.74	0.77	0.77	0.75
Vietnam	51.19	50.95	49.51	48.78	48.13	45.45	43.49	41.47	41.11

Source: Data from database: Gender Statistics (World Bank-(World Bank-modeled ILO estimate)

decreases in the employment ratio of women in the industrial sector is the global financial crisis in 2008 (Table 2.8).

China, Vietnam, Russia, India and Mexico are the countries with the highest women employment share in the industry sector. The country with the lowest share of women employment in the industry sector is Egypt with 5.9%. Egypt's women employment share in the industry sector is at a low level of 6.8%, even by 2018. As in the previous decade, China has the highest women employment ratio for this nine-year period (Table 2.9).

The share of women employed in the services sector is quite high compared to other sectors. With a ratio of 12.5%, Bangladesh is the country with the lowest women employment ratio in the service industry in 2000. It is seen that India is in second place and Pakistan is in third place after Bangladesh (Table 2.10).

The countries with the highest share of women employed in the service industry in 2010 are USA, Canada, Argentina, Australia and France. On the contrary, the countries with the lowest women employment ratio in the service industry are Pakistan, India and Bangladesh (Table 2.11).

There are many factors that affect women taking part in labor market or economic activities. Although some of these factors are about the market and its components, others are about social structure and institutions. Women working for someone else or being self-employed are possible determinant circumstances. The ratios of self-employed women in 2000 and 2018 are presented in Table 2.12 and Table 2.13.

The countries with the highest ratio of self-employed women are India, Indonesia and Vietnam in 2000. The ratio of self-employed women is around 56.5% in India, 31.5% in Indonesia and 30% in Vietnam. Countries with the lowest ratio of self-employed women are Germany, France and the USA, with an approximate ratio of 4% in 2000. In 2009, although there is a decrease in the ratio of self-employed women, India is in first place with a ratio of 53%, as it was ten years ago (Table 2.12).

Table 2.8 Employment in industry, female percentage (2000–2009)

	2000	*2001*	*2002*	*2003*	*2004*	*2005*	*2006*	*2007*	*2008*	*2009*
Argentina	10.32	10.42	9.40	11.17	10.79	10.60	10.60	10.37	10.17	9.62
Australia	10.23	9.51	9.53	9.54	9.36	9.31	9.50	9.32	9.31	8.90
Bangladesh	8.65	9.01	9.51	10.11	10.83	11.65	12.50	12.62	12.75	12.89
Brazil	13.11	12.68	12.49	12.58	12.71	13.06	12.81	12.98	13.36	12.99
Canada	11.45	11.30	11.50	11.33	11.32	10.80	10.46	10.21	9.71	8.94
China	26.56	26.17	25.78	25.85	26.53	27.15	27.77	28.09	28.22	28.37
Egypt	6.86	10.13	10.36	6.16	5.78	4.91	6.01	6.15	5.54	5.12
France	13.96	13.85	13.25	12.30	12.41	11.97	11.61	11.43	10.85	10.20
Germany	18.28	17.88	17.62	16.92	17.01	16.02	16.01	15.95	15.01	14.56
India	11.66	12.07	12.52	13.01	13.61	14.13	14.68	15.34	15.99	16.72
Indonesia	14.97	16.12	15.78	15.16	14.21	15.91	15.36	15.03	14.58	14.42
Italy	20.53	20.44	20.11	19.88	17.74	17.38	16.71	16.48	15.86	14.83
Japan	21.56	20.77	19.74	19.37	18.43	17.41	17.38	17.35	16.55	15.36
South Korea	19.09	18.50	17.99	17.89	17.76	16.58	15.97	15.57	15.18	13.75
Mexico	22.08	21.83	20.51	19.52	19.25	18.85	18.78	18.08	17.44	16.24
Philippines	13.28	12.51	11.78	11.60	11.40	11.23	11.05	10.86	10.74	10.61
Pakistan	15.71	15.69	15.66	15.65	15.37	15.06	14.87	12.47	12.02	12.58
Russian Federation	22.30	23.26	23.01	22.19	21.60	21.05	20.54	20.13	19.14	17.90
South Africa	15.29	16.38	17.52	16.88	17.23	16.85	16.90	16.13	13.13	13.13
Turkey	11.60	12.27	13.86	14.63	16.00	16.12	16.43	16.16	15.84	15.33
United States	12.71	11.86	10.98	10.78	10.46	10.24	10.06	10.05	9.60	8.68
Vietnam	10.12	11.15	11.70	12.97	13.73	14.79	15.91	16.09	16.52	16.98

Source: Data from database: Gender Statistics (World Bank-(World Bank-modeled ILO estimate)

Table 2.9 Employment in industry, female percentage (2010–2018)

	2010	*2011*	*2012*	*2013*	*2014*	*2015*	*2016*	*2017*	*2018*
Argentina	9.38	9.95	9.46	8.92	8.33	8.59	8.86	9.11	8.98
Australia	8.61	8.53	8.36	8.30	8.32	7.83	8.09	7.62	7.58
Bangladesh	13.05	13.49	13.94	14.42	14.90	15.41	15.94	16.78	16.74
Brazil	12.27	11.58	12.62	12.22	11.94	11.66	10.77	10.68	10.58
Canada	8.54	8.97	9.00	8.73	8.60	8.55	8.53	8.49	8.40
China	28.59	29.04	29.06	29.41	29.72	29.32	29.14	28.79	28.27
Egypt	5.93	5.09	5.51	5.06	5.02	5.62	6.21	6.85	6.81
France	10.06	10.44	10.16	10.03	9.57	9.30	9.17	9.79	9.65
Germany	14.27	14.19	14.16	14.01	14.17	13.87	13.81	13.87	13.63
India	17.57	18.25	18.77	18.75	18.72	18.67	18.62	18.69	18.75
Indonesia	14.94	15.06	15.77	15.73	15.42	15.76	15.99	16.66	16.49

(*Continued*)

Table 2.9 (Continued)

	2010	*2011*	*2012*	*2013*	*2014*	*2015*	*2016*	*2017*	*2018*
Italy	14.10	14.23	13.80	13.69	13.34	13.23	12.90	12.76	12.60
Japan	14.94	14.68	14.71	14.68	14.71	14.77	14.55	14.15	14.01
South Korea	14.35	14.39	13.97	13.60	13.73	13.77	13.34	13.71	13.54
Mexico	16.18	16.02	15.94	16.26	16.59	16.74	17.09	17.52	17.36
Philippines	10.43	10.27	10.07	10.13	10.09	10.01	9.94	9.89	9.78
Pakistan	11.52	11.43	11.29	11.14	12.96	14.52	14.11	14.07	14.05
Russian Federation	17.80	17.20	17.18	16.96	16.59	16.13	16.06	15.77	15.69
South Africa	13.04	12.97	12.28	12.43	12.06	11.76	11.94	12.24	12.14
Turkey	15.95	15.24	14.95	15.39	17.18	16.25	15.98	15.67	15.49
United States	8.46	8.73	8.78	8.83	8.85	8.84	8.70	8.71	8.49
Vietnam	17.26	16.56	16.84	16.96	17.50	19.32	20.77	21.81	21.66

Source: Data from database: Gender Statistics (World Bank-(World Bank-modeled ILO estimate)

Table 2.10 Employment in services, female percentage (2000–2009)

	2000	*2001*	*2002*	*2003*	*2004*	*2005*	*2006*	*2007*	*2008*	*2009*
Argentina	89.44	89.28	90.13	87.85	88.25	88.68	88.91	89.21	89.49	89.99
Australia	86.34	87.04	87.44	87.84	87.96	88.24	88.14	88.39	88.47	88.89
Bangladesh	12.57	13.55	14.53	15.61	16.69	17.86	19.31	19.87	20.39	20.86
Brazil	72.48	71.84	71.57	71.84	71.63	71.27	72.44	73.23	73.61	74.87
Canada	86.90	87.35	87.14	87.35	87.40	87.85	88.15	88.49	89.08	89.87
China	26.49	26.89	27.28	28.13	29.65	31.12	32.68	34.14	35.19	36.50
Egypt	53.73	57.95	62.08	54.77	47.44	48.43	50.66	47.29	48.84	48.81
France	83.20	83.33	83.98	85.02	84.95	85.75	86.16	86.43	87.32	87.92
Germany	79.61	80.05	80.42	81.25	81.29	82.25	82.38	82.43	83.67	84.19
India	13.96	14.02	14.05	14.17	14.28	14.44	14.92	15.42	15.80	16.30
Indonesia	38.30	39.36	38.82	37.30	41.17	39.71	43.52	43.57	44.06	45.65
Italy	75.12	75.19	75.96	76.43	79.10	79.36	79.97	80.46	81.31	82.51
Japan	72.89	73.95	75.30	75.73	76.86	78.01	78.18	78.34	79.20	80.53
South Korea	68.66	70.19	71.34	71.96	72.99	74.49	75.39	76.16	76.89	78.74
Mexico	71.36	72.37	73.56	75.47	75.44	76.33	76.67	77.42	78.24	79.93
Philippines	62.67	63.17	63.59	64.16	64.84	65.28	65.80	66.40	66.89	67.27
Pakistan	19.25	19.40	19.64	19.94	18.70	17.70	16.02	14.78	12.64	14.54
Russian Federation	65.98	67.42	68.05	69.64	70.69	71.05	71.82	73.05	74.26	75.71
South Africa	76.25	76.49	74.06	75.90	75.69	77.76	77.69	78.76	82.68	83.24
Turkey	23.68	25.73	27.00	29.64	33.26	36.52	40.03	41.24	44.05	46.88
United States	86.43	87.30	88.19	88.41	88.76	89.00	89.21	89.29	89.72	90.65
Vietnam	23.60	23.88	25.16	25.32	26.28	28.25	30.31	32.43	32.66	33.00

Source: Data from database: Gender Statistics (World Bank-(World Bank-modeled ILO estimate)

Table 2.11 Employment in services, female percentage (2010–2018)

	2010	*2011*	*2012*	*2013*	*2014*	*2015*	*2016*	*2017*	*2018*
Argentina	90.24	89.76	90.25	90.86	91.52	91.33	91.11	90.87	91.01
Australia	89.10	89.58	89.73	90.04	89.86	90.32	90.23	90.72	90.79
Bangladesh	21.42	21.20	21.04	20.85	20.74	20.73	20.68	23.38	23.83
Brazil	76.17	77.41	81.48	82.12	82.85	83.29	84.48	85.03	85.19
Canada	90.35	89.93	89.89	90.19	90.34	90.44	90.33	90.55	90.65
China	37.66	39.05	40.19	41.95	43.46	44.71	45.74	46.77	47.50
Egypt	51.21	51.54	56.90	52.07	51.76	54.17	55.39	56.26	56.53
France	88.18	87.69	88.00	88.13	88.78	89.07	89.21	88.63	88.79
Germany	84.54	84.63	84.74	84.98	84.82	85.18	85.30	85.25	85.50
India	16.82	18.95	21.26	21.68	22.19	22.74	23.22	23.69	24.19
Indonesia	46.65	48.15	48.96	50.36	51.21	51.63	53.94	54.52	54.98
Italy	83.19	83.14	83.63	83.88	84.26	84.34	84.59	84.89	85.08
Japan	81.14	81.60	81.76	81.94	81.99	82.00	82.40	82.86	83.04
South Korea	78.77	78.86	79.70	80.30	80.64	81.13	81.94	81.82	82.04
Mexico	79.96	80.08	79.97	79.88	79.72	79.61	79.34	78.74	78.94
Philippines	67.82	68.33	69.00	69.76	69.72	71.31	72.76	74.78	75.07
Pakistan	14.41	14.12	13.89	13.72	13.85	13.42	12.75	12.97	13.22
Russian Federation	76.64	77.11	77.42	77.64	78.25	78.76	78.92	80.19	80.32
South Africa	83.18	83.58	84.12	84.08	84.74	84.00	84.18	84.04	84.20
Turkey	44.85	45.50	47.95	49.05	50.05	52.75	55.43	56.13	56.62
United States	90.81	90.50	90.46	90.50	90.45	90.42	90.52	90.53	90.75
Vietnam	31.55	32.49	33.65	34.25	34.37	35.24	35.74	36.71	37.24

Source: Data from database: Gender Statistics (World Bank-(World Bank-modeled ILO estimate)

Table 2.12 Own-account workers, female percentage (2000–2009)

	2000	*2001*	*2002*	*2003*	*2004*	*2005*	*2006*	*2007*	*2008*	*2009*
Argentina	18.79	19.65	18.39	16.57	16.61	16.58	15.80	15.06	15.12	15.70
Australia	8.08	8.23	8.60	8.37	8.23	8.51	8.09	7.92	8.11	8.15
Bangladesh	15.47	15.52	15.63	15.74	15.74	15.73	15.94	17.48	19.11	20.79
Brazil	21.00	22.94	23.38	23.45	23.17	23.81	23.43	22.99	22.49	22.01
Canada	8.65	7.93	8.25	8.24	8.06	8.22	8.11	8.36	8.38	8.95
China	28.67	28.70	28.69	28.56	28.48	28.32	28.18	28.10	28.00	27.97
Egypt	12.25	11.79	6.80	13.37	13.76	13.85	10.86	14.76	10.58	12.73
France	3.87	3.87	3.77	3.95	3.68	3.76	4.18	4.01	3.78	4.09
Germany	3.83	3.73	3.76	4.01	4.23	4.86	4.90	4.94	4.83	4.89
India	56.63	55.36	53.96	52.75	51.38	50.17	51.05	52.02	52.75	53.81
Indonesia	31.49	29.83	32.12	28.34	30.37	27.84	30.53	32.33	33.10	32.41
Italy	14.11	14.17	14.19	14.24	14.31	13.80	13.70	13.47	12.95	12.59

(Continued)

Table 2.12 (Continued)

	2000	*2001*	*2002*	*2003*	*2004*	*2005*	*2006*	*2007*	*2008*	*2009*
Japan	6.75	6.24	5.99	5.86	5.77	5.63	5.41	5.25	5.05	5.07
South Korea	18.16	18.52	18.32	16.76	17.72	17.78	17.59	17.23	16.94	16.07
Mexico	20.76	21.81	22.93	23.89	23.93	22.41	22.30	22.33	22.31	23.43
Philippines	29.90	30.86	30.98	30.74	30.25	30.08	29.79	29.09	28.76	28.38
Pakistan	16.97	16.97	15.89	16.03	15.89	16.03	15.75	14.03	13.61	13.61
Russian Federation	7.97	6.14	5.95	5.47	5.62	5.95	5.72	5.41	5.35	5.35
South Africa	13.77	20.60	14.15	14.61	13.95	16.30	15.33	13.90	11.44	10.55
Turkey	12.81	13.10	12.68	12.39	10.04	13.59	12.59	11.56	11.09	12.84
United States	3.91	3.86	3.77	3.82	3.80	3.71	3.72	3.63	3.46	3.53
Vietnam	30.29	28.21	29.29	30.76	31.20	34.71	38.15	41.44	44.46	46.94

Source: Data from database: Gender Statistics (World Bank-(World Bank-modeled ILO estimate)

Table 2.13 Own-account workers, female percentage (2010–2018)

	2010	*2011*	*2012*	*2013*	*2014*	*2015*	*2016*	*2017*	*2018*
Argentina	15.18	14.88	15.22	15.86	16.24	16.83	17.45	18.00	18.00
Australia	8.20	8.08	8.01	7.63	8.00	7.95	8.12	8.11	8.10
Bangladesh	22.77	24.01	25.25	26.47	28.63	30.65	32.49	38.41	38.58
Brazil	21.40	20.90	17.32	17.25	17.18	17.97	18.88	19.58	19.56
Canada	8.70	8.56	8.72	9.02	8.93	9.07	8.97	9.11	9.09
China	27.82	27.72	27.70	27.69	27.66	27.71	27.69	27.59	27.50
Egypt	15.56	13.93	13.43	11.17	9.95	6.30	8.33	8.61	8.68
France	4.61	4.65	4.71	4.82	5.39	5.32	5.46	5.72	5.70
Germany	4.96	5.11	5.08	4.90	4.81	4.66	4.67	4.63	4.63
India	54.89	52.94	50.89	51.38	51.92	52.50	53.04	53.52	53.97
Indonesia	30.63	29.11	27.50	27.73	28.44	28.42	30.23	31.31	31.54
Italy	12.61	12.36	12.49	12.13	12.73	12.35	12.27	11.63	11.63
Japan	4.94	4.76	4.36	4.23	4.34	4.08	3.92	3.88	3.94
South Korea	15.33	14.83	14.55	14.18	13.78	13.49	13.26	13.53	13.70
Mexico	22.73	22.97	23.13	23.21	22.50	22.90	23.05	22.23	22.20
Philippines	28.17	27.80	27.23	27.25	27.25	27.51	27.72	28.58	28.57
Pakistan	14.06	16.08	15.79	15.55	19.23	21.06	19.84	19.96	20.17
Russian Federation	4.63	5.04	4.80	5.13	4.96	5.03	5.12	4.23	4.22
South Africa	10.57	10.16	9.62	9.40	8.49	8.99	8.97	9.47	9.46
Turkey	12.90	11.79	10.89	10.83	9.20	8.93	8.91	9.50	9.55
United States	3.48	3.42	3.48	3.47	3.34	3.28	3.22	3.30	3.27
Vietnam	43.47	44.53	46.01	46.43	41.61	40.58	40.28	39.73	39.83

Source: Data from database: Gender Statistics (World Bank-(World Bank-modeled ILO estimate)

When we consider the self-employed women ratio in 2010, India, Vietnam and Indonesia are the top countries. Countries with the lowest ratio of self-employed women are the USA, Russia, Japan, France and Germany. The results here are largely similar to those between 2000 and 2009. Bangladesh reached a rate of 38.5% in 2018 and became the country with the highest increase, with a change of about 16% between 2009 and 2018. After Bangladesh, Pakistan became the second country, with a 6% increase in the proportion of self-employed women (Table 2.13).

The high number of self-employed women does not indicate that women have more say in the national economy by itself. There can be many reasons behind this. In countries such as the USA, France and Germany where the self-employed women ratio is low, it is difficult to say that they are less visible. In fact, it is likely to see self-employed women more in countries such as Pakistan and India due to reasons such as security, traditional roles and some other reasons.

The gender equality index value is obtained as a result of comparing the schooling rates of female students with those of male students at any educational level in the academic year and proportioning them. When the calculated index value is "1," it is understood that there is no gender difference in schooling rates, which means equality is provided. If the index value is less than 1, there is inequality in favor of male students; if it is greater than 1, the inequality is in favor of female students (www.tuik.gov.tr). When we look at Table 2.14, Pakistan is the country

Table 2.14 Gender parity index of the gross enrolment ratio in primary and secondary education (2009–2017)

	2009	*2010*	*2011*	*2012*	*2013*	*2014*	*2015*	*2016*	*2017*
Argentina	1.05	1.04	1.04	1.03	1.03	1.03	1.03	1.02	1.02
Brazil	1.04	..	1.03	1.03	1.03	1.03	1.02	1.02	1.00
Canada	0.99	0.99	0.99	1.00	1.01	1.01	1.01	1.01	1.01
China	1.00	0.99	0.99	1.00	1.01	1.01	1.01	1.01	1.01
Egypt	0.98	0.97	0.97	0.99	0.99	1.00	..	0.99	0.99
France	1.00	1.00	1.00	1.00	1.01	1.01	1.00	1.00	1.00
Germany	0.96	0.96	0.96	0.96	0.96	0.97	0.97	0.96	0.96
India	0.99	0.99	1.00	1.00	1.07	1.07	1.07	1.10	1.08
Indonesia	0.98	1.02	1.02	1.01	0.98	0.98	0.99	1.00	0.99
Italy	0.99	0.99	0.99	0.99	0.99	0.99	1.00	1.00	0.98
South Korea	1.00	1.00	1.00	1.00	1.00	1.00	1.00	0.99	1.00
Mexico	1.02	1.03	1.02	1.02	1.02	1.02	1.03	1.04	1.04
Philippines	1.02	..	..	..	..	1.02	1.01	1.01	1.02
Pakistan	0.83	0.82	0.82	0.82	0.81	0.83	0.83	0.84	0.85
Russian Federation	0.99	..	0.99	0.99	0.99	0.99	0.99	0.99	0.98
South Africa	1.00	1.00	1.00	1.00	..	1.02	0.96	1.02	1.01
Turkey	0.94	0.95	0.95	0.96	0.98	0.98	0.98	0.98	0.96
United States	1.01	1.00	1.00	0.99	1.00	1.00	1.01	1.00	0.99

Source: Data from database: Gender Statistics (World Bank)

with the highest inequality in favor of any gender and after Pakistan, Turkey and Germany follow.

When we look at the ratio of women employment among workers with salaries and wages, the top countries are Russia, the USA, France and Germany. In these countries, the proportion of women with salaries and wages between 2010 and 2018 is 90% or more. In South Africa, Japan, Australia and Canada, it is seen that the ratio of women with salaries and wages is over 85% in the period of 2010 to 2018.

When the data are analyzed in the 2010–2018 period, the countries that had the lowest ratio of women with salaries and wages are India, Bangladesh and Pakistan. Bangladesh, which had a 16.5% ratio of women with salaries and wages in 2000, was the country that showed the highest increase by 2018, with an increase of approximately 15%. Although Bangladesh is the country with the highest rate of increase in nine years, it is still very low compared to many other countries, with a rate of 31.8% in 2018. Turkey, showing an increase of around 13% from 2000 to 2018, is the second country with the highest increase after Bangladesh. In terms of women with salaries and wages, Vietnam is the third country, with the highest increase, a 10% increase. However, Vietnam's situation is far behind, as in 2018 compared to other country examples, just like Bangladesh (Table 2.15).

Table 2.15 Wage and salaried workers, female percentage (2010–2019)

	2010	*2011*	*2012*	*2013*	*2014*	*2015*	*2016*	*2017*	*2018*
Argentina	80.66	81.32	81.29	80.90	80.54	79.89	79.18	78.57	78.58
Australia	86.72	87.05	87.34	87.78	87.44	87.44	87.41	87.56	87.56
Bangladesh	16.56	17.98	19.47	21.03	23.39	25.74	28.09	31.17	31.89
Brazil	71.23	72.61	75.49	75.36	75.78	74.90	74.58	73.57	73.62
Canada	88.46	88.52	88.53	88.22	88.32	88.07	88.26	88.14	88.15
China	45.29	46.20	47.01	47.78	48.54	49.20	49.90	50.63	51.32
Egypt	52.04	52.82	56.25	52.01	51.11	51.47	65.76	62.96	63.42
France	92.45	92.28	92.39	92.32	91.88	91.83	91.61	91.46	91.48
Germany	91.58	91.51	91.66	91.90	92.02	92.25	92.35	92.45	92.47
India	12.46	14.49	16.75	17.10	17.51	17.94	18.35	18.77	19.22
Indonesia	34.44	36.33	38.56	39.61	39.64	41.55	41.90	41.64	42.39
Italy	81.49	81.75	81.70	81.78	81.57	81.71	81.95	83.02	83.05
Japan	88.17	88.67	89.28	89.61	89.81	90.28	90.85	91.11	91.14
South Korea	72.98	73.71	74.23	75.01	75.77	76.74	77.35	77.35	77.47
Mexico	65.60	65.25	65.50	66.26	67.23	67.05	67.37	68.34	68.42
Philippines	52.84	53.02	54.33	55.58	55.08	56.48	57.85	59.32	59.62
Pakistan	20.72	21.38	23.00	24.67	26.55	24.86	24.13	24.57	25.11
Russian Federation	94.07	93.79	94.00	93.64	93.78	93.74	93.64	94.53	94.54
South Africa	85.35	85.86	86.92	87.04	88.18	87.93	87.66	87.15	87.14
Turkey	50.98	51.93	54.60	56.87	60.52	62.08	63.71	63.67	64.02
United States	94.42	94.50	94.41	94.43	94.64	94.74	94.84	94.72	94.78
Vietnam	28.03	28.74	29.16	29.43	30.59	34.23	35.79	37.73	38.31

Source: Wage and salaried workers, female ((World Bank- modeled ILO estimate)

4 Application for the determination of factors affecting participation of women in the labor force

4.1 Method and model

Panel data analysis is mostly the result of examining cross-sectional variables consisting of individuals, households, regions, countries or another group in a certain time dimension (Baltagi, 2005). In the time series analysis, which reflects a single country example, problems have started to occur in obtaining data in terms of time dimension. Researchers have had a tendency to work with extremely large data within a short time range. If the behavior between units is different, panel data analysis provides researchers with considerable ease in modelling. However, providing such flexibility is not available in the time series analysis. In such a case, the analyzes have now shifted to panel data analysis on the basis of cross-sectional diversification and heterogeneity (Greene, 2012). If the cross-sections of the data sets used in the analysis are of the same length, balanced panel data analysis will be applied. If the data sets have different cross-sectional lengths, unbalanced panel data analysis will be preferred (Wooldridge, 2003). The factors that affect the ratio of participation of women in the labor force were analyzed through the following model. In the model, FLFP stands for female labor force participation, WSWP for ratio of wage- and salary-earning women, UNFP for the ratio of unemployed women in the female labor force, OWFP for the ratio of self-employed women, GCEP for the ratio of government consumption expenditures to Gross Domestic Product, GNI for per capita purchasing power, GSP for the ratio of total savings to GDP, SGPI for the gender equality index in primary and secondary education, and GHEP represents the ratio of the state's domestic health expenditures to GDP.

$$\begin{aligned}\mathbf{FLFP} = \beta 0 + \beta 1\left(\mathbf{WSWP}\right)\mathbf{it} + \beta 2\left(\mathbf{UNFP}\right)\mathbf{it} + \beta 3\left(\mathbf{OWFP}\right)\mathbf{it} \\ + \beta 4\left(\mathbf{GCEP}\right)\mathbf{it} + \beta 5\left(\mathbf{GNI}\right)\mathbf{it} + \beta 6\left(\mathbf{GSP}\right)\mathbf{it} + \beta 7\left(\mathbf{SGPI}\right)\mathbf{it} \\ + \beta 8\left(\mathbf{GHEP}\right)\mathbf{it} + \mathbf{uit}\end{aligned}$$

$$\mathrm{i} = 1, \ldots .19(\text{Country}) \qquad \mathrm{t} = 1, \ldots 19(2000 - 2018)$$

The data of 19 countries included in the study between 2000 and 2018 were obtained from the World Bank database. Since the type of data used is available for the specified years, a period limitation has been made. Period limitation has been made until the date, which can be reached for the developing countries, and the largest countries in terms of national income in the world economy.[1]

Using the Hausman test, it is decided which model to use in panel data analysis. The researcher will examine the differences between the coefficients of fixed effect and random effect models with the help of the Hausman test and decide which one to choose (Ahn and Moon, 2001; Hsiao, 2014).

When we look at the results of the Hausman test, for the model that is formed, it is seen that there is no statistical and systematic difference between the results of fixed effect estimation method and random effect estimation

Table 2.16 Variables and data descriptions

Type	*Code*	*Explanation*
Dependent Variable	**FLFP**	Labor force participation rate, female (% of female population ages 15+)
Independent Variables	**WSWP**	Wage and salaried workers, female (% of female employment)
	UNFP	Unemployment, female (% of female labor force)
	OWFP	Own-account workers, female (% of female employment)
	GCEP	government final consumption expenditure (% of GDP)
	GNI	GNI per capita, PPP (current international $)
	GSP	Gross savings (% of GDP)
	SGPI	School enrollment, primary and secondary (gross), gender parity index (GPI)
	GHEP	General government health expenditure (% of GDP)

Table 2.17 Wald chi2 and Hausman Test

Wald chi2		*Hausman*
chi2	Prob>chi2	chi2(8) = (b-B)'[(V_b-V_B)^(-1)](b-B) = 3 321,8
76541.45	0.000	Prob>chi2 = 0.000 (V_b-V_B is not positive definite)
Ho: sigma(i)^2 = sigma^2 for all i		Test: Ho: difference in coefficients not systematic

method. After obtaining such a result, in the estimation of the model, the fixed effect model was preferred with the assumption that the fixed effect models are consistent.

Changing variance problems in the models that are formed in panel data analysis should also be tested. The presence of variance problems in models is investigated by using the Wald test (Hayes and Cai, 2007; Stock and Watson, 2008).

The results of the Wald test for our model are given in Table 2.17. When we look at the results of the Wald test in the table, it is seen that there is a changing variance problem in our model. In order to see the effect of the changing variance problem and to eliminate this problem, our model was also analyzed by a robust regression method that makes predictions by using resistant errors.

In models formed in panel data analysis, whether there is a problem of autocorrelation is tested by GDW (Durbin-Watson Test; Bhargava et al., 1992) test and LBI-test (Baltagi and Wu, 1999). If the model has autocorrelation and also a changing variance problem is found in the test result, estimation is made by using a clustered method for consistent results (Wooldridge, 2003; Williams, 2000; Rogers, 1993). According to the results of the Durbin-Watson and Baltagi-Wu tests in the table, there is a problem of autocorrelation in our model. Therefore, our model will be re-estimated by a clustered standard errors method.

Table 2.18 Durbin-Watson and Baltagi-WuTest

Durbin-Watson	Baltagi-Wu(LBI)
0.393	0.706
Basic threshold value "2"	

Table 2.19 Pesaran CD, Friedman and Frees Tests

Pesaran CD Test	*Friedman Test*	*Frees Test*
0.639, Pr = 0.14	2.448 Pr = 0.0014	3321
Critical values from Frees' Q distribution		
alpha = 0.10 : 0.1360		
alpha = 0.05 : 0.1782		
alpha = 0.01 : 0.2601		

Pesaran, Friedman and Frees tests can be used to determine the inter-unit correlation problem in the cross-section data. If problems such as correlation between the units, changing variance and autocorrelation are detected as a result of the tests, it is necessary to re-estimate with a different method. In such a case, the method developed by Driscoll and Kraay (1998) is used to obtain deviation-free results (Hoyos and Sarafidis, 2006; Driscoll and Kraay, 1998).

In our model, tests for determining the correlation between units are included in Table 2.19. As a result of Pesaran CD and Frees tests performed to determine the correlation between units, a correlation was detected between the error terms in our model. Although this problem was not detected in the Friedman test, we preferred to re-estimate with the Driscoll-Kraay method to obtain more consistent results from our model.

4.2 Findings

Table 2.20 includes the results of four models: linear regression model prediction, robust regression model prediction using resistant errors, cluster method prediction with clustered standard errors and prediction by using the Driscoll-Kraay method.

The estimation results of the basic model with four different methods are given in Table 2.20. It was determined that some of the independent variables were statistically significant for all models and some variables were statistically significant only in some models.

The effect of women working for a salary or wage on the labor force participation of women ratio was statistically significant at 1% in all four models. However, despite the statistically significant results, the direction of the effect was negative. A one-unit increase in employment of women with a salary or wage had a 0.20 unit reduction effect on labor force participation rates.

Table 2.20 Model Estimations

FLFP *Variables*	*(1)* *Mode l*	*(2)* *Robust*	*(3)* *Cluster*	*(4)* *DK*
WSWP	-0.208***	-0.208**	-0.208**	-0.208***
	[0.033]	[0.074]	[0.074]	[0.051]
UNFP	0.045***	0.045***	0.045***	0.045***
	[0.006]	[0.012]	[0.012]	[0.006]
OWFP	-0.044**	-0.044	-0.044	-0.044*
	[0.018]	[0.031]	[0.031]	[0.026]
OWFP	0.131***	0.131*	0.131*	0.131***
	[0.029]	[0.074]	[0.074]	[0.024]
GNI	0.104***	0.104***	0.104***	0.104***
	[0.013]	[0.033]	[0.033]	[0.011]
GSP	0.032*	0.032	0.032	0.032
	[0.018]	[0.035]	[0.035]	[0.019]
SGPI	-0.179*	-0.179	-0.179	-0.179*
	[0.092]	[0.221]	[0.221]	[0.117]
GHEP	-0.064***	-0.064	-0.064	-0.064***
	[0.016]	[0.040]	[0.040]	[0.009]
Constant	3.124***	3.124***	3.124***	3.124***
	[0.175]	[0.315]	[0.315]	[0.169]
Observations	273	273	273	273
F	18.41	4.670	4.670	46.96
Prob > F	0.000	0.00318	0.00318	
R-squared	0.375	0.375	0.375	
Number of countrycode	19	19	19	
rho	0.992	0.992	0.992	
sigma	0.313	0.313	0.313	
sigma_e	0.0279	0.0279	0.0279	
sigma_u	0.312	0.312	0.312	
r2_w	0.375	0.375	0.375	0.375
r2_b	0.367	0.367	0.367	
r2_o	0.122	0.122	0.122	
r2_a	0.308	0.356	0.356	
corr	-0.540	-0.540	-0.540	
N_clust		19	19	
Number of groups				19
lag				2

Standard errors in brackets *** p<0.01, ** p<0.05, * p<0.1

The unemployment rate of women variable is also statistically significant, at 1% in all models. The effect of the ratio of women without jobs on labor force participation of women is positive. A one-unit increase in unemployed women ratio increases labor force participation of women rates by 0.04 units.

The fact that women are self-employed is statistically significant at the level of 5% for the first model and 10% for the fourth model. The fact that women are self-employed has a negative impact on labor force participation rates. This negative effect and severity appear to be the same in almost all models. A one-unit increase in self-employment reduces labor force participation of women ratio by 0.04 units.

The effect of the increase in the total consumption expenditures of the state on the labor force participation ratio of women is statistically significant in all models. The effect of the consumption by state expenditures was found to be significant at the level of 1% in the first and fourth models and 10% in the second and third models. The direction of the effect of this variable, which is significant in all models, is also positive. A one-unit increase in the consumption expenditures of the state increases the labor force participation rates of women by 0.13 units.

Expressing the purchasing power per capita, GNI variable is also statistically significant at 1% in all models. It is observed that the increase in purchasing power per capita supports the participation of women in the labor force. A one-unit increase in purchasing power per capita increases the labor force participation rate of women by 0.1 units.

The effect of total savings on labor force participation ratio of women was statistically significant only in the first model. Although it is not statistically significant in all models, the total savings increase in the country positively affects labor force participation ratio of women.

The gender equality index in primary and secondary education is statistically significant in the first and fourth models. The effect of gender equality index on education is negative. In other words, a one-unit change in favor of male students has a decreasing effect on the labor force participation rates of women by 0.17 units.

The impact of public health spending on labor force participation of women is significant at 1% in the first and fourth models. The direction of the impact of public health spending on labor force participation ratio of women is negative in all models. A one-unit increase in public health spending reduces labor force participation ratio of women by 0.06 units.

5 Conclusion and evaluation

It is out of the question that women, who make up half a country's population, are not involved in economic and social life. The absence of women in the labor market means a material and spiritual loss, both individually and nationally. The negative experiences of women about their social, economic and legal status in the past centuries have no place in this age. With the historical process, women have gained their economic and social rights and become more visible in the society. However, despite all these developments, women are sometimes pushed to the background compared to men in the economic field. There are many reasons why women remain in the background compared to men. Many factors, such as the country or region people live in, social structures and institutions, the responsibilities and roles women undertake, the economic and social development levels of the countries and the education level, can be listed among these reasons.

Women, who participate in economic activities as men, should be in equal conditions in the labor market. They should not be more disadvantaged than men in matters such as the nature of the jobs they work, the positions they hold, the amount of income they earn and the amount time spent working.

In our study, the place of women in the labor force market is presented by tabulating the numerical data of selected countries. Then, the factor that has an impact on the labor force participation rate of women for the same country group, other than a few, is analyzed through the established model. After estimating the model with four different methods, four different analysis results are obtained. It was found that most of the results of the analysis had similar results for all models. When we look at the details of the analysis results, per capita purchasing power, public consumption expenditures, unemployed women rates and savings have been found to affect labor force participation of women positively. On the other hand, it was determined that working for a salary or wage, self-employment, public health expenditures and gender index in education negatively affect the labor force participation ratio of women.

The increase in the consumption expenditures of the state encourages production by increasing demand in the economy. As a result of firms or producers turning towards more labor force and women employment for increase in production, the labor force participation ratio of women also increases.

Women being self-employed decreases the labor force participation ratio. This is the result of women not being able to be workers anywhere when they choose to work for themselves. Besides, security or social structure may have an effect on women preferring to be self-employed.

The increase in purchasing power per capita increases the participation of women in the labor force. This situation can be interpreted as an increase in per capita income. This will be more reasonable when we think that women are involved in the labor force to earn individual income. The labor force participation ratio will increase again, as more work or more working time will be required for more income.

According to the results of the analysis, the effect of women employment with salary or wages has a negative effect on their involvement in the labor force. This situation increases the chance that women are mostly employed in informal and low wage jobs. The income of the women working in regular and legal jobs will also be continuous. However, the income earned by women working in informal and temporary jobs will also be periodic.

If the gender equality index in education is in favor of male students, labor force participation rates of women are negatively affected. In other words, women with low or lack of education are also unable to participate in the labor market. The relationship between education level and income has been empirically established in many studies. In general, an increase in education level and income increase act in unison. Therefore, with an increase in the education level of women, the ratio of participation in the labor force and their incomes will increase.

Of course, it is not possible to limit the factors that affect women's participation in the labor force with the variables in our model. It is also likely that there are numerous factors that affect participation of women in economic life and the labor force. The selected country examples and the size of the data obtained are the limitations of our study. This study has revealed a number of factors that affect the labor force participation ratio of women within the frame of selected countries and established models. However, it is evident that this is not enough, and that there are many factors and variables to be discussed.

The role of women in society and the responsibilities of women are always heavier than those of men. Women should no longer experience problems such as gender inequality, physical and sexual violence, social exclusion, lack of security, and social and economic weakness. For this to happen, it is important for girls to access educational opportunities as easily as boys. Women must receive equal pay with men when they do the same job. Women should always be able to choose whatever role they want, not only a secondary role compared to men. Childcare and housework should not be seen as the single and basic duty of women, and it should be accepted that women exist in economic and social fields. In short, women should not be exposed to any economic or social inequality only because they are women. It should also be remembered that individuals in societies and states should increase their positive efforts even more rapidly.

Note

1 Argentina, Bangladesh, Brazil, Canada, China, Egypt, France, Germany, India, Indonesia, Italy, South Korea, Mexico, Pakistan, Philippines, Russian Federation, South Africa, Turkey, USA.

References

Ahn, S. C. & Moon, H. R. (2001). Large-N and Large-T Properties of Panel Data Estimators and the Hausman Test. *USC Center for Law, Economics & Organization*, Research Paper No: C01-20.

Baltagi, B. H. (2005). *Econometric Analysis of Panel Data*. 3rd ed. England: JW &Sons.

Baltagi, B. H. & Wu, P. X. (1999). Unequally Spaced Panel Data Regressions with AR (1) Disturbances. *Econometric Theory*, 15(6), 814–823.

Besanko, D. A. & Braeutigam, R. R. (2010). *Microeconomics*. 4th ed. Hoboken, NJ: John Wiley & Sons.

Bhalla, A. S. & Lapeyre, F. (2004). *Poverty and Exclusion in a Global World.* 2nd ed. New York: Palgrave Macmillan.

Bhargava, A., Franzini, L. & Narendranathan, W. (1992). Serial Correlation and the Fixed Effects Model. *The Review of Economic Studies*, 49(9), 533–549.

Bradshaw, S. & Linneker, B. (2003). *Challenging Women's Poverty: Perspectives on Gender and Poverty Reduction Strategies from Nicaragua and Honduras*. London: Catholic Institute for International Relations.

Buvinić, M. (1997). Women in Poverty: A New Global Underclass. *Foreign Policy*, 108, 38–53.

Case, K. E. & Fair, R. C. (2006). *Principles of Microeconomics*. Harlow, UK: Pearson Education Company.

Driscoll, J. & Kraay, A. (1998). Consistent Covariance Matrix Estimation with Spatially Dependent Data. *Review of Economics and Statistics*, 80, 549–560.

Estrin, S., Laidler, D. & Dietrich, M. (2008). *Microeconomics*. 5th ed. Edinburgh: Pearson Education and Prentice Hall.

Foster, J. (1998). *Absolute Versus Relative Poverty*. Working Paper 98-WOI, Department of Economics and Business Administration, Vanderbilt University, Nashville, Tennessee.

Goldberg, G. S. & Kremen, E. (1990). *The Feminization of Poverty: Only in America?* No. 117. Westport, CT: Praeger Publishers.

Greene, W. H. (2012). *Econometric Analysis*. Boston: Pearson Education.

Haughton, J. & Khandker, S. R. (2009). *Handbook on Poverty & Inequality*. Washington: World Bank Publications.

Hayes, A. F. & Cai, L. (2007). Using Heteroskedasticity Consistent Standard Error Estimators in OLS Regression: An Introduction and Sofware Implementation. *Behavior Research Methods*, 39(4), 709–722.

Hoyos, R. E. & Sarafidis, V. (2006). Testing for Cross Sectional Dependence in Panel Data Models. *The Stata Journal*, 6(4), 482–496.

Hsiao, C. (2014). *Analysis of Panel Data*, No. 54. Cambridge: Cambridge University Press.

Khusro, A. (1999). *The Poverty of Nations*. New York: Springer.

Krugman, P. & Wells, R. (2010). *Microeconomics*. New York: Worth Publishers.

Mankiw, G. (2012). *Principles of Microeconomics*. 6th ed. Mason, OH: South Western Cengage Learning.

Narayan, D., Stern, N., Nankani, G., Page, J. & Jorgensen, S. (2002). *Empowerment and Poverty Reduction: A Source Book*, PREM. Washington, DC: The World Bank.

Parkin, M. (2012). *Microeconomics*. United States of America: Pearson Education, 10th edt Inc. Addison Wesley Longman.

Pearce, D. (1978). The Feminization of Poverty: Women, Work, and Welfare. *Urban and Social Change Review*, 11(1), 28–36.

Rogers, W. H. (1993). Regression Standard Errors in Clustered Samples. *Stata Technical Bulletin*, 13(3), 19–23.

Silver, H. (1994). Social Exclusion and Social Solidarity: Three Paradigms. *International Labour Review*, 133, 531.

Stock, J. H. & Watson, M. W. (2008). Heteroskedasticity-Robust Standard Errors for Fixed Effects Panel Data Regression. *Econometrica*, 76(1), 155–174.

Williams, R. L. (2000). A Note on Robust Variance Estimation for Cluster-correlated Data. *Biometrics*, 56(2), 645–646.

Wooldridge, J. M. (2003). Cluster-Sample Methods in Applied Econometrics. *American Economic Review*, 93(2), 133–138.
World Bank (2019a). Retrieved from https://databank.worldbank.org/source/world-development-indicators
World Bank (2019b). Retrieved from https://datacatalog.worldbank.org/dataset/gender-statistics.

3 The gender-responsive budgeting

A way of coping with gender inequalities

Umut Halaç

1 Introduction

For the past 25 years, the international community has recognized that gender inequality must be eliminated for sustainable economic growth and full social development (Klasen, 1999; Hewitt and Mukhopadhyay, 2002; Rubin and Bartle, 2005). Such sustainability and equality issues at the forefront, countries are invited to be aware of and pay attention to the concepts of equal resource distribution and income generation, which support and emphasize gender equality while creating their budgets. More than 60 countries responded to this call by stating that they will organize their national and/or local government budgets as gender-responsive budgets.

Gender-responsive budgeting is not a well-known concept among academics, public managers and practitioners. Gender-responsive budgeting is a topic that has started to attract relatively more attention in the last 25 years (Elson, 2002a). It has been encountered more frequently since the early 2000s and has started to gather related stakeholders around this issue. Initially, gender-responsive budgeting was thought to raise the issue of gender inequality higher and make gender inequality issues a mainstream component of macroeconomic policies (Holvoet, 2006). However, the subject, which started to lose its former popularity throughout time, eventually fell to a position that may only contributed to the objectives of economic efficiency and effectiveness (Sharp, 2003).

As we underline before gender-responsive budgeting is a relatively new subject that is dependent on a relatively small number of researchers and needs additional work, especially regarding its successes and failures. In this study, gender-responsive budgeting will be defined, the lessons learned in this process will be evaluated and possible contributions of the subject on the gender equality will be discussed. We hope that this study will contribute to the gender-responsive budgeting issue to reach the value it deserves, to increase the number of academicians, public officers and practitioners interested in the subject and to become a concept that is considered at every stages of budgeting process.

2 Defining the gender-responsive budget

In 1979, the UN General Assembly adopted the "Convention on the Elimination of All Forms of Discrimination against Women (CEDAW)" as known as the "international bill of rights for women". CEDAW set out what constitutes gender discrimination and suggest a pathway for the countries to eliminate the gender discrimination on national level (UNDAW, 2004). At the fourth World Conference on Women held in Beijing in 1995, representatives of 171 governments reiterated CEDAW's commitment to end discrimination against women. By October 2004, 179 of the 191 UN member nations were party to CEDAW, had bound themselves to do "nothing in contravention of its terms" (UNDAW, 2004).

Both CEDAW signatories and Beijing conference attendees defined "the equal treatment of women and men in government budgets as central to ensuring gender equality". The platform for action adopted in Beijing specifically called on governments to "incorporate a gender perspective into the design, development, adoption and execution of all budgetary processes as appropriate in order to promote equitable, effective and appropriate resource allocation and establish adequate budgetary allocations to support gender equality" (United Nations, 1995).

Various terms, including "gender budgets", "women's budgets", "gender-sensitive budgets" and "gender-responsive budgets" have been used to describe public budgets that incorporate the gender perspective into their budgeting processes. In this study, we use the *gender-responsive budget* term to indicate, "a government budget that explicitly integrates gender into any or all parts of the decision-making processes regarding resource allocation and revenue generation" (Rubin & Bartle, 2005). Similarly, a "gender-responsive budgeting" has been defined as "a gender-based assessment of budgets, incorporating a gender perspective at all levels of the budgetary process and restructuring revenues and expenditures in order to promote gender equality" (Council of Europe, 2009). In general, gender-responsive budgeting "involves using the tools, techniques and procedures of the budget cycle in a systematic way to promote gender equality" (OECD, 2017).

3 The need for a gender-responsive budget

A public budget determines the government's priorities by showing what it plans to spend over a period of time and how it will allocate and finance these expenditures. Government budgets are presented in a financial aggregation, without reference to men or women. Therefore, the budget appears to be gender neutral. However, budgeting decisions (revenues and expenditure) have different effects on men and women in a society. Therefore, the budget, contrary to what it is supposed to be, is not gender neutral and ignoring such differences is called "gender blindness" (Elson, 1999). It is obvious that government policy that deliberately treats men and women differently in budgeting terms should not be gender blind. Gender blindness refers in particular to the unintended consequences of fiscal policy because of economic and social differences between men and women.

Despite commitments to promote gender equality, in practice, most countries do not ignore gender equal public policies or not prioritize them (Daly, 2011). As a result, many disparities and inequalities between genders have been placed at the core of public policies and the allocation of public resources (OECD, 2016f).

Some countries are dealing with gender budgeting as a way to resolve these disparities and inequalities. Gender budgeting helps apply gender equality to normal budgeting routines, thereby filling the gap between policy making and budgeting.

In recent years, studies have been pioneered by international organizations considering its leading role in "promoting gender equality", that is ensuring gender equality in the design of all public policies and the use of policy instruments. Recommendation on Gender Equality in Public Life (OECD, 2015) provides "a multidimensional approach in promoting gender equality as a fundamental principle of modern public governance, including the development of gender-responsive policies, the role of gender budgeting, and the closing of the gender gap in leadership and public employment". From this point of view, gender budgeting is seen as the practice of promoting gender equality in the budgeting process.

Gender inequalities persist in education, employment, entrepreneurship and public life opportunities and outcomes. Gender budgeting involves the systematic use of the tools, techniques and procedures of the budget cycle to promote equality in several areas. Gender Budgeting Practices Survey (OECD, 2016b) shows that almost half of OECD countries promote, plan, or actively think about gender budgeting. OECD analysis shows that wide varieties of gender budgeting approaches are applied. Only half of the OECD countries can currently point to specific examples of impact, but in many countries the introduction of gender budgeting is relatively new, so a wider range of effects may become more apparent in the future.

It has been advocated maintaining a better gender balance in policies, organizations and society as being beneficial, not only to reduce inequalities and to ensure fairer communities, but also to strengthen productivity (OECD, 2016a; IMF, 2017). There is a broad agreement on the potential of gender budgeting to play an important role in making public policies more gender responsive (Rubin & Bartle, 2005; OECD, 2016a; IMF, 2017).

Reviews of gender budgeting vary between two complementary views. On the one hand, they point out to a technical tool or a set of tools and techniques to support gender budgeting, allocations and decisions. On the other hand, they focus on gender-responsive logic to make gender issues more visible, to ensure change and to eventually promote gender equality. In fact, it is often claimed that the implementation of gender-specific instruments requires gender- sensitive logic, perception and cultural change. At the same time, the lack of such a cultural change can easily be an excuse for not introducing new systems or justifying failure in the gender-responsive budget implementations. However, tools can often be the driving force of change

> the means through which new ideas, values, and beliefs are introduced, become accepted and then embodied in routines, habits and thus become part of a renewed culture. Likewise, gender budgeting does not only require an existing culture, but can become an important driver of cultural changes, with the two "sides" of gender budgeting feeding each other in a virtuous circle.
>
> (Rubin & Bartle, 2005)

4 Gender-responsive budget initiatives

The term "gender-responsive budget initiative" will be defined as "an organized movement to influence government to incorporate a gender perspective into its budget decisions". Thus included, more than 60 countries have undertaken gender-responsive budgeting initiatives at the national and/or local levels of government (Budlender & Hewitt, 2003). The first gender-responsive budget initiative was undertaken in Australia in 1984 and executed in 1985.

As Sawer (2002) mentioned, in order to eliminate gender inequality, the gender analysis should have embedded into the central policy processes, including the public budget process called as "mainstreaming". What is known as the "Women's Budget Statement" required that all departments in the government provide detailed reports showing the impact of their programs on women. They were also investigated to identify methods to improve program outcomes in meeting women's needs (Budlender & Hewitt, 2002). Over time, all the states and regions of Australia followed the lead of the central government and implemented their own gender budgeting initiatives. Although the Australian initiative proves that it has no lasting effect at the federal level, there is evidence that it continues to inform budget decisions at state and regional levels (Sawer, 2002).

The Australian experience has brought international interest in gender-responsive budgeting as a path to gender inequality, but it took ten years for the next initiatives to take place in South Africa and the Philippines. The initiative in South Africa was managed in 1995 by the partnership of two policy-based research civil society organizations and newly elected Parliament members, as well as the Women's Budget Initiative, a partnership of the Gender and Economic Policy Group of the Committee of Finance (Budlender, 1998, 2003; Budlender & Hewitt, 2002). Despite its slow start, the Women's Budget Initiative analyzed budgets for all 27 ministries covered by the national government and published its results annually. The Initiative also inscribed guides and papers (the famous one is "Money Matters" which was translated into many languages) to inform the other gender budgeting initiatives.

The gender-responsive budgeting initiative in the Philippines started in 1995 as part of a gender and development movement. The General Grants Act, which approves the country's national budget, required all national institutions to set aside 5 percent of their gender and development budgets. In 1998, local governments had to do the same. This 5 percent allocation means, "to provide national agencies and local governments . . . with a budget for programs that would enhance the . . . capability for gender-responsive planning and budgeting" (Flor & Lizares-Si, 2002).

Australian, South African and Philippine experiences were followed by gender-responsive budgeting initiatives worldwide. Some have originated from the government, but mostly civil society groups are usually undertaken by non-governmental organizations working to promote gender equality. As Rubin and Bartle (2005) indicated,

> in some countries, gender-responsive budgeting is actually integrated into one or more stages of the budget cycle at the national or subnational government

levels. In other countries, initiatives are still at the formative stage in which one or more government programs are gender-analyzed or workshops for groups such as government employees, non-governmental organizations and other representatives of civil society.

According to the Survey of Gender Budgeting Practices (OECD, 2016b) the majority of OECD countries (59 percent of respondents) do not explicitly undertake gender-responsive budgeting. Actually, there appears that there is no consensus on what the gender-responsive budgeting is. Most of the OECD countries (90 percent) indicate the use of tools to promote gender equality. Several countries have reported that "mainstreaming" responsibility of gender equality is with the line ministries' responsibility to advance this agenda in the relevant policy areas, and consequently no special role for the budget process is envisaged. Nearly half of OECD countries (15 out of 34 members) report that they have introduced (Austria, Belgium, Finland, Iceland, Israel, Japan, Korea, Mexico, Netherlands, Norway, Spain, Sweden), plan to introduce (Italy) or are actively considering the introduction (Turkey, Czech Republic) of gender-responsive budgeting.

5 Lessons learned

We cannot fully evaluate the implementation stages and results of gender-responsive budgeting initiatives, since the vast majority relies on outdated open to public sources. However, these initiatives were found to have some common aspects during their implementation. Thus, we can draw out some preliminary lessons from these initiatives. We believe that the preliminary lessons reached in the context of the conclusions drawn from the attempts so far will support the efforts to integrate the gender issue into the budget preparation stages in the future, despite the need for more empirical evidence of gender-responsive budgeting. The preliminary lessons drawn from the experiences can be categorize as (i) commitment from both government and civil society stakeholders, (ii) level of government, (iii) political environment and (iv) availability of technical expertise and data disaggregated by gender (Rubin & Bartle, 2005).

5.1 Commitment of government and civil society stakeholders

The first step to be taken for the integration of the gender perspective into the budget is government decision makers have to recognize the existence of gender inequality in the society and accept the budget policy as a way to promote equal treatment of men and women. In the elections held in Australia in the early 1970s, a government that was more sensitive to women's needs came to power. Feminists, as known as "femocrats" have been hired to fulfill the new government's commitment to gender equality. "In line with their commitment to mainstreaming, Australian femocrats became increasingly concerned with the need for an effective way to mainstream gender perspectives and gender accountability into budgetary processes" (Sawer, 2002). In the Philippines initiative, the government began by accepting gender inequalities amongst the steps to be taken to democratize and promised to eliminate gender inequality from national to subnational regulations (Flor & Lizares-Si, 2002). In Rwanda, the president and other leaders who have struggled to bring their country together after years of civil war and genocide use gender-responsive budgeting as a way to overcome gender inequalities and poverty. As a strong indicator of these reforms, the Ministry of Gender and Women in Development was established in 1999, so the government has demonstrated how eager it is (Diop-Tine, 2002).

Even though governments' commitment to gender equality is crucial for implementing gender-responsive budgeting, stakeholders outside the government also need to recognize and advocate the importance of gender-responsive budgeting.

Supporting gender-responsive budgeting initiatives by stakeholders outside the government is a very encouraging situation, at least in its early stages. Such supports are thought to force governments to make decisions on related issues. However, when gender-responsive budgeting initiatives are supported only by the government, budgetary practices generally continued as long as the respective governments are in power. For example, although gender-responsive budgeting initiatives in Australia were initially supported by feminist nongovernmental organizations and women in civil society, support from non-government stakeholders declined over time, as links to the desired intensity could not be established. Therefore, it has been observed that despite the efforts of the central government, federal governments have abandoned gender-responsive budgeting initiatives (Sawer, 2002).

In this context, for gender-responsive budgeting initiatives to be sustainable, government and non-governmental stakeholders should be included in the process and regularly informed about the process. By doing so, they will be able to embrace such initiatives and, if necessary, force governments to continue the process.

5.2 Level of government

The majority of gender-responsive budgeting initiatives have been implemented by national governments. But in Australia, South Africa and the Philippines, the subnational level governments as well as the national government have launched their own gender-responsive budgeting initiatives. With the guidance of the national government in Australia, states and territories have started their own initiatives, and even when the national government's initiatives have slowed down, it has been observed that local governments have continued their own initiatives strongly (Sawer, 2002). Although Budlender (2002) emphasized, "at this stage there is very little activity inside government", the South Africa experience is often referred to as the most successful gender-responsive budgeting initiative. In addition to the initiatives of the national government, Gauteng Province, which is one of the richest regions of the South Africa, has adopted the gender-responsive budgeting approach since 2000 and started to prepare its budget accordingly (Budlender & Hewitt, 2002). In 2001, the Berlin city parliament of Germany launched gender budgeting for selected expenditures, starting with selected city districts (German Agency for Technical Cooperation, 2004).

It can be said that the implementation of gender-responsive budgeting initiatives at the subnational level has developed in line with the decentralization of budget functions that have become widespread in the world. In such decentralization trends, residents are more likely to engage with decision-making process (Bellemy, 2002). In many countries where decentralization involves devolution, national government priorities for gender-responsive budgeting will clearly influence what will happen at the subnational level.

5.3 Political environment

Political environment and social values in the country can be counted among the most important factors affecting the acceptance of gender-responsive budgeting initiatives. Gender-responsive budgeting initiatives in South Africa started with the increase in the number of women in Parliament and a government that accepted that one of the country's biggest social and political changes was to make gender-responsive budgeting. It is also clearly accepted that such initiatives are one of ways to end the racial discrimination. In Rwanda, which is one of the most difficult places to implement gender-responsive budgeting initiatives, the new president who came to power tried to use gender-responsive budgeting as a way putting together the country after the years of civil war and genocide. He thinks that these initiatives are one of the ways to achieve and maintain peace (Diop-Tine, 2002). In the United States, San Francisco is the only government implementing the gender-responsive budget. As a matter of fact, San Francisco recognized as the most progressive and pioneering state in policies aimed at improving the situation of women and minorities within the country. In addition, it is the only government in the United States to adopt a CEDAW ordinance (protect human rights and to act to eliminate discrimination against women and girls) which was adopted in 1998 by the Board of Supervisors. With a decision taken by the Board of Supervisors in 2003, they asked all departments in the city to determine the possible effects of the budget cuts planned for the 2004 budget on selected groups, including women. In fact, this is the one of the first steps of gender-responsive budgeting and the first initiatives have been started for the integration of gender into the budget (City and County of San Francisco, 2003a). While many departments reported that budget cuts would not have a specific impact on selected groups, the Department of Human Services predicted that two out of three people who would be affected by budget cuts would be women (City and County of San Francisco, 2003b). In fact, these results can be seen as an indication that such initiatives, at first, are underestimated even in San Francisco. Besides, it can be perceived as a proof that the technical expertise is insufficient to make the necessary calculations.

5.4 Technical expertise and data availability

One of the main requirements of gender-responsive budgeting is the need to collect the gender-based data or gender-disaggregated data to be used in the budget process. Many countries do not collect gender-based data. Without gender-disaggregated data, the budget cannot be analyzed in terms of gender and its unintended gender effects cannot be measured. The lack of disaggregated gender data has been identified as a serious impediment to implementing gender-responsive budgeting (Balmori, 2003).

The lack of disaggregated data is not just a technical challenge. However, it is a factor that makes it difficult and prevents budget experts in government and civil society from preparing gender-responsive budgets. As seen in many examples, outside experts are brought in gender-responsive budgeting initiatives and the budgets are planned to be prepared under the leadership of these experts. The problem here is not about how eligible these outside experts are in their subjects. The problem arises from the fact that outside experts are not enough familiar to the culture and political structure of the country or region in which they prepare a gender-responsive budget.

6 Challenges

Although gender-responsive budgeting initiatives vary between countries, the difficulties encountered during the implementation of these initiatives can be evaluated in three main categories.

- "*gender-informed resource allocation* whereby individual policy decisions and/or funding allocations take into account the impact of the decision on gender equality";
- "*gender-assessed budgets* where the impact of the budget as a whole is subject to some degree of gender analysis"; and
- "*needs-based gender budgeting* where the budget decisions are underpinned by a prior assessment of gender needs".

(Rubin & Bartle, 2005)

As mentioned before, the first step to resolve any inequality is to acknowledge the existence of inequality and a problem. The categories just mentioned should be considered as obstacles encountered during the solution of the inequalities. Actually, these problems also include steps to be taken to find solutions to inequalities. Thus, detailed information can be obtained about the existence of inequality and the policies that should be developed to eliminate inequality. In fact, these categories are intertwined with each other and complement each other, in that those which have gender-assessed budgets generally undertake gender-informed resource allocation and countries that do needs-based gender budgeting also generally have gender-assessed budgets.

Apart from this categorization, other problems faced by gender-responsive budget initiatives are briefly listed in the OECD report (OECD, 2016f).

- "*Wide variety of gender budgeting approaches*: There is no standard model of gender budgeting in countries".
- "*Gender budgeting is legally underpinned*: Most countries with gender budgeting have a legal foundation for their gender budgeting practice, although the nature and intention of the legal provisions vary".

- "*Evidence of systematic gender-proofing through the budget cycle*: Two of the most frequently used gender budgeting tools are *ex ante* and *ex post* gender impact assessments, suggesting a systematic continuum of gender-focused policy assessment across the budget cycle. However, the rigour and impact of these approaches appear variable".
- "*Evidence of broad application of gender perspectives*: Half of the countries which undertake gender budgeting apply a gender perspective in resource allocation and performance setting. However, there is relatively limited application of gender perspective in spending review".
- "*Limited use of comprehensive* ex ante *needs assessment*: Few countries currently undertake a comprehensive gender equality needs assessment to gain insights into the priority gender issues arising from the current disposition of public policies and of public resources".
- "*Limited evidence of positive impact*: Out of 12 OECD countries with some form of gender budgeting, half of them could point to specific examples where the gender-budgeting tool had brought about significant changes in policy design and/or outcomes. As the introduction of gender budgeting is still relatively new in a number of countries, greater evidence of impact may appear in future".
- "*Reliance on a co-ordinated approach*: The practice of gender budgeting typically involves co-ordination between a number of government departments, such as the Ministry of Finance and the Ministry of Equality".

(OECD, 2016f)

7 Future endeavors

In order to make gender-responsive budgeting more understandable and more widespread, the number of academicians interested in the subject should be increased. In this context, working areas related to gender-responsive budgeting can be listed as follows. Of course, researches to make gender-responsive budgeting more visible are not limited to the areas listed here. In fact, interdisciplinary studies that extend beyond these areas should be encouraged more.

- The availability of gender-specific data sets and statistics play an important role in determining gender inequalities. Moreover, with the help of these data, political interventions can be designed more easily and their effects can be easily measured.
- Especially in countries that implement the performance-budgeting approach, a clear link needs to be established between measurable outputs and budget allocation. For this, budget distribution and gender-responsive feature should be clearly defined in this type of budgeting approach. This will reveal the effect of the budget on reducing gender inequality.
- It is not possible to maintain the gender-responsive budgeting approach externally as patched to the budget. If the gender-responsive budgeting approach is to be a permanent feature of modern budgeting, it should be included in the normal annual budget preparation routine.

- Gender-responsive budgeting approach should be subject to audit like any budget approaches. Such budgets containing gender-disaggregated budget information should be subjected to two types of audits: "gender audit" and "civic audit". Or there should be a hybrid method that consists of a mixture of these two types of control.
- Most fundamentally, gender budgeting should not be viewed as a bureaucratic adjustment exercise. Policies developed in all areas of public policy should be intrinsically linked to gender-responsive budgeting. The allocation of resources should be compatible with the gender-responsive budgeting approach in terms of re-prioritization and re-allocation decisions.
- Beyond its traditional economic dimensions, the effects of gender-responsive budgeting on growth and productivity should be evaluated from different perspectives.

8 Final remarks

Even if all kinds of inequality have started to form a central place in the context of academic research, it is obvious that much progress should be made regarding the solution of inequalities. Although gender inequality is becoming more and more visible, it is not among the priority issues of many governments and political parties. Today, political agendas, especially shaped by populist approaches and social media trends, are often influenced by issues that can quickly attract the attention of voters. From this point of view, gender issues are located at the bottom of the "urgent to-do" list and even cannot be included in the list.

However, even in the European Union, which previously acknowledged the existence of gender inequality and working to reduce inequality, concerns are growing about the weakening of social agenda, including its gender equality policy. Recent changes to the European Employment Strategy have left gender equality in the forefront and apparently focused on men's employment, ignoring gains in increasing women's employment during the Lisbon process (Crouch, 2015; Villa & Smith, cited in Barry, 2014).

One of the tools proposed to reduce and eliminate gender inequalities is the gender-responsive budgeting approach. A gender-responsive budget is a government budget that explicitly integrates gender into any or all parts of the decision-making process regarding resource allocation and revenue generation. More generally, gender budgeting can become an important tool to raise awareness not only among academics and experts, but also among citizens. In order to raise awareness, it should be ensured that the benefits and effects of gender-responsive budgeting approach on policies and political choices are easier to see to the public. To ensure this, data and information regarding gender-responsive budgeting should be easily accessible and understandable by its own stakeholders.

A further step will be to explore the potential of gender budgeting with the participation of stakeholders. Gender budgeting should be established as a participatory structure and as a joint production form in supporters and advocates. This type of structure is very important for the sustainability of the budget

(Anessi-Pessina, Barbera, Sicilia & Steccolini, 2016; Barbera, Sicilia & Steccolini, 2016).

The UK Women's Budget Group underlines that gender-responsive budgeting can be done by bringing together two sets of knowledge that have been separated from each other, "knowledge on gender equality and knowledge on public policy and finance". The first challenge to those responsible for preparing the budget is determining the relevance of gender to the respective policy sectors. Beyond that, analysis from a gender perspective depends on the correct setting of gender equality goals and redirecting the gains of the budget towards these goals. From this perspective, gender expertise has very important duties. Understanding – what are the effects of gender in society and policy, which data should be collected, how this data be used, which analysis method can be applied – is vital for determining meaningful gender equality targets in the budget process.

In the era of Big Data, it may seem like a paradox to say that gender-disaggregated data could not be collected in a sufficiently reliable and healthy way that would facilitate gender-responsive budgeting. However, our failures in collecting gender-disaggregated data are in an undeniable situation. Lack of necessary data or difficulty in working with limited data is one of the biggest obstacles to gender-responsive budgeting initiatives. Similarly, the lack of technical specialists and lack of resources can also prevent successful implementation of the gender budget. Given the lack of data, resources or capacity, and the lack of commitment of leaders and relevant decision makers, it is not possible to implement gender-responsive budgeting. Gender-responsive budgeting can be adapted and integrated into any budget format. Gender-responsive budgeting does not require a new budget format. As a basic logic, gender needs to be included in the decision-making process in budgeting, regardless of format.

Gender budgeting is no longer just a concept advocated by feminist or radical movements. It is now a phenomenon promoted by most international and supranational institutions as a good practice. This can provide strong support for international and "top-down" adoption. However, it may also cause gender-responsive budgeting to be perceived as another "élite" technical tool imposed by high "technocracies". Increasing the involvement of national governments, civil society and potential stakeholders should be encouraged to overcome this dangerous trend.

As mentioned earlier, the first step in gender-responsive budgeting is taken by stakeholders inside and outside the government accepting the existence of gender inequality. They should then show that this inequality must be closed and that they are willing to change their thoughts and behavior to close the gap. And if they are willing to provide the necessary funds and time to support gender-disaggregated data collection and analysis, gender-responsive budgeting has the potential to change the budget decision making process and become a budget reform.

We believe that gender-responsive budgeting has the potential to reduce gender inequalities around the world. We hope this research will lead to an in-depth discussion of gender-responsive budgeting among academics, practitioners, and decision makers, and to make the issue stand out.

As Elson writes,

> The focus on gender inequality can be structured so as to take account of other forms of inequality, such as class, race. . . . The key question might be reformulated, for example, as: does this fiscal measure improve, worsen, or leave unchanged, the position of the most disadvantaged women?
>
> (Elson, 2002b)

References

Anessi-Pessina, E., Barbera, C., Sicilia, M., & Steccolini, I. (2016). Public Sector Budgeting: A European Review of Accounting and Public Management Journals. *Accounting, Auditing & Accountability Journal*, 29(3), 491–519.

Balmori, H. H. (2003). *Gender and Budgets: Overview Report*. Brighton, UK: BRIDGE.

Barbera, C., Sicilia, M., & Steccolini, I. (2016). What Mr. Rossi Wants in Participatory Budgeting: Two R's (Responsiveness and Representation) and Two I's (Inclusiveness and Interaction). *International Journal of Public Administration, 39*(13), 1088–1100.

Barry, U. (2014). Gender Perspective on the Economic Crisis: Ireland in an EU Context. *Gender, Sexuality & Feminism, 1*, 82–103.

Bellemy, K. (2002). Gender Budgeting. Background Paper, Council of Europe's Informal Network of Experts on Gender Budgeting.

Budlender, D. (1998). The South African Women's Budget Initiative. Background Paper No. 2, Community Agency for Social Enquiry.

Budlender, D. (2002). A Profile of Country Activities. In *Gender Budgets Make Cents: Understanding Gender Responsive Budgets*, edited by Debbie Budlender, Diane Elson, Guy Hewitt, and Tanni Mukhopadhyay, 131–164. London: The Commonwealth Secretariat.

Budlender, D. (2003). *Engendering Budgets: A Practitioner's Guide to Understanding and Implementing Gender-Responsive Budgets*. London: The Commonwealth Secretariat.

Budlender, D., & Hewitt, G. (2002). *Gender Budgets Make More Cents: Country Studies and Good Practices*. London: The Commonwealth Secretariat.

Budlender, D., & Hewitt, G. (2003). *Engendering Budgets a Practitioners' Guide to Understanding and Implementing Gender-Responsive Budgets*. London: The Commonwealth Secretariat.

City and County of San Francisco, Board of Supervisors. (2003a). Resolution Urging City Departments to Consider a CEDAW Gender Analysis and Impact on the City's Equal Access to City Services for Limited English Speakers Ordinance Prior to Proposing Departmental Budget Cuts and/or Staff Cuts.

City and County of San Francisco, Board of Supervisors. (2003b). Summary of CEDAW Gender Analyses of Budget Cuts.

Council of Europe (2009). Gender Budgeting: Practical Implementation, Handbook. Council of Europe, Directorate General of Human Rights and Legal Affairs.

Crouch, C. (2015). Can the European Union Abandon Social Policy? Paper presented at UCD Society of Politics and International Relations 'Understanding the Eurozone Crisis' Seminar Series, November.

Daly, M. (2011). What Adult Worker Model? A Critical Look at Recent Social Policy Reform in Europe from a Gender and Family Perspective. *Social Politics, 19*, 1–23.

Diop-Tine, N. (2002). Rwanda: Translating Government Commitments into Action. In *Gender Budgets Make More Cents: Country Studies and Good Practices*, edited by Debbie Budlender and Guy Hewitt, 117–131. London: The Commonwealth Secretariat.

Elson, D. (1999). *Gender-Neutral, Gender-Blind, or Gender-Responsive Budgets? Changing the Conceptual Framework to Include Women's Empowerment and the Economy of Care*. Gender Budget Initiative Background Papers. London: The Commonwealth Secretariat.

Elson, D. (2002a). Integrating Gender into Government Budgets within a Context of Economic Reform. In *Gender Budgets Make Cents: Understanding Gender Responsive Budgets*. London: The Commonwealth Secretariat.

Elson, D. (2002b). Gender Responsive Budget Initiatives: Some Key Dimensions and Practical Examples. Paper presented at the Conference on Gender Budgets, Financial Markets, Financing for Development, February 19–20, Berlin, Germany.

Flor, C., & Lizares-Si, A. (2002). The Philippines: Getting Smart with Local Budgets. In *Gender Budgets Make More Cents: Country Studies and Good Practices*, edited by Debbie Budlender and Guy Hewitt, 98–116. London: The Commonwealth Secretariat.

German Agency for Technical Cooperation (2004). *Gender Advisory Project: The Berlin* Initiative. Ober-Ramstadt: League for Pastoral Peoples Publishing.

Hewitt, G., & Mukhopadhyay, T. (2002). Promoting Gender Equality through Public Expenditure. In *Gender Budgets Make Cents: Understanding Gender Responsive Budgets*. London: The Commonwealth Secretariat.

Holvoet, N. (2006). The Differential Impact on Gender Relations of 'Transformatory' and 'Instrumentalist' Women's Group Intermediation in Microfinance Schemes: A Case Study for Rural South India. *Journal of International Women's Studies*, *7*(4), 36–50.

IMF (2017). *Gender Budgeting in G7 Countries*. Washington, DC: IMF.

Klasen, S. (1999). Does Gender Inequality Reduce Growth and Development: Evidence from Cross-Country Regressions. Policy Research Report on Gender and Development Working Paper Series, 7. The World Bank, Washington, DC.

OECD (2015). *Recommendation of the Council on Budgetary Governance*. Paris: OECD Pulishing.

OECD (2016a). Promoting Inclusive Growth through Better Regulation: The Role of Regulatory Impact Assessment. OECD Regulatory Policy Working Papers, No. 3, OECD Publishing, Paris.

OECD (2016b). *2016 OECD Survey of Gender Budgeting*. Paris: OECD Publishing.

OECD (2016f). *Gender Budgeting in OECD Countries*. Paris: OECD Publishing.

OECD (2017). *OECD Performance Budgeting Survey 2016*. Paris: OECD Publishing.

Rubin, M. M., & Bartle, J. R. (2005). Integrating Gender into Government Budgets: A New Perspective. *Public Administration Review*, *65*(3), 259–272.

Sawer, M. (2002). Australia: The Mandarin Approach to Gender Budgets. In *Gender Budgets Make More Cents: Country Studies and Good Practices*, edited by Debbie Budlender and Guy Hewitt, 43–64. London: The Commonwealth Secretariat.

Sharp, R. (2003). *Budget for Equity: Gender Budget Initiative Within a Framework of Performance Oriented Budgeting*. New York: UNIFEM UN.

United Nations. (1995). *Beijing Declaration and Platform for Action*. www.un.org/womenwatch/daw/beijing/platform/plat2.htm

United Nations Division for the Advancement of Women (UNDAW). (2004). *Convention on the Elimination of All Forms of Discrimination against Women*. www.un.org/women watch/daw/cedaw/

4 Gender equality in the finance sector

Closing gaps or another "old boys' club"?

Begüm Yurteri Kösedağli

1 Introduction

Gender inequality may emerge in various forms and disguises all over the world. Although the progress achieved towards gender equality under the Millennium Development Goals[1] cannot be underestimated, the ongoing discrimination and violation towards girls and women all around the world shows that there is still room for improvement. For this reason, the "gender equality and women's empowerment" is now included in the UN's Sustainable Development Agenda as one of the 17 goals to be achieved by the year 2030.

Unfortunately, the labor market is no exception to the discrimination against women as the gender gap is affirmed to be one of the most insistent problems in the labor market. The slight increase of the ratio of female to male labor force participation rate (from 66.5% in 1990 to 66.9% in 2018)[2] shows the phenomenon that women are less likely than men to participate in the workforce persists for a long time. Although the social norms and socio-economic constraints preventing women to participate in the labor market vary across countries; gender role conformity, religion, work-life balance, marital status, lack of affordable care for children and limited access to transportation are among the most common reasons of the gender gap in the labor market (International Labour Office [ILO], 2017).

It's no secret that women made important gains in recent decades in terms of human capital (schooling and labor market experience) mostly in developed countries (Blau and Kahn, 2017). Considering that women constitute 30% of economic graduates and 50% of business and social science graduates in United States and United Kingdom, the fact that their share of employment in financial activities is higher than men's in most of the regions as well as across the world may point to gender diversity in the financial sector (Sahay et al., 2018; ILO, 2017). According to Equileap's's[3] Global Top 200 list in 2018, the financial sector is the second-best performing sector (following the communications sector) as 27% of companies reaching the Top 200 operate in the financial sector (Equileap, 2018).

Nevertheless, Equileap (2019) reports that the women representation in highest levels of management remains low although 36 of the top 100 companies globally are from the financial sector. Similarly, women account for only 19% of top senior executives in financial firms in the USA which is lower than the average

USA women overall (Chin et al., 2018). This situation brings the gender balance in financial sector into question, especially for the leadership positions, banking, and executive boards as well as financial governance.

In the light of this information, this chapter aims to analyze the role of women in financial sector's labor market in developed and developing countries and to assess if the financial sector is a case for closing gaps or is another old boys' club like many other sectors. For this aim, the first section briefly discusses the importance of gender diversity and women representation in finance sector, the second section provides evidence on the different aspects of gender inequality in the finance sector's labor market and the last section is dedicated to discuss the reasons of gender gap and necessary policies to ensure that financial sector is (more) gender balanced.

2 The importance of gender diversity and women representation in finance sector

In a world where only 17.95% of firms have female top managers (the highest ranking manager or the chief executive officer, CEO) in 2018,[4] there is a vast literature on the effects of gender diversity on firm's performance, usually focusing on how women presence in boardrooms or CEO gender affect the performance in terms of returns or decision-making process. Despite some mixed results, it's found that companies with more women board members have higher profitability and better stock performance (Christiansen et al., 2016) and that female CEOs are more cautious than men in corporate decision making (Faccio et al., 2016).

There is also a remarkable and growing literature on the role of gender diversity in financial sector generally based on the relationship between gender diversity in bank boards and the bank's performance. Cabo et al. (2012) reveals that European banks with higher proportion of women on boards, have lower risk and less leverage while Garcia-Meca et al. (2015) finds that the women presence in bank boards have a positive impact on governance and profitability in developed economies. Similarly Gulamhussen and Santa (2015) finds that female presence in bank boardrooms (boards, supervisory boards and audit committees) has a positive influence on bank's performance and a negative impact on risk taking in OECD countries. Likewise, Sahay et al. (2017) finds that banks with greater share of women on bank boards have higher capital buffers and lower nonperforming loans ratio and that higher share of women on banking supervision boards can be associated with higher overall banking stability worldwide. Owen and Temesvary (2018), finds a non-linear relationship between female participation and bank performance in 90 bank holding companies in the USA. This non-linear relationship states that once the female share on bank boards reaches a critical level (which is around 13–17%), more gender diversity is associated with better bank performance (measured by revenue to expense ratio, return on assets, Sharpe ratio and stock price growth).

As the literature shows, there are various positive impacts of women presence in top-decision making positions on increasing a bank's performance (both in terms of increasing profitability and decreasing risk) and hence maintaining banking sector stability which is an important element of the financial soundness of the economy. For this reason, the current situation in financial sector's labor market regarding gender balance needs to be examined in detailed.

3 Gender gap in financial sector's labor market

As of 2020, one may argue that a lot has been achieved towards gender diversity in economics and financial sector since some of the most important institutions are headed by women. To be honest, the examples are really appealing. The number of female CEOs in the *Fortune 500* list has increased to 33 in 2019 up from 24 a year ago, means that 6.6% of the highest grossing firms in USA are led by women,[5] while Christine Lagarde, the first woman managing director of IMF between 2011 and 2019, is appointed as the first woman president of the European Central Bank. Looking back, Janet Yellen served as the first and only chairwoman of the United States Federal Reserve between 2014 and 2018. Inga Beal, the former CEO in Lloyd's of London who served between 2013 and 2018, was the first woman appointed to this title in more than 330 years' history of the insurance market (Gould, 2014).[6]

All these appointments may seem a progress towards gender equality and we can think that it is better late than never to give more responsibilities to women. But the question is whether this is the common practice in today's finance world or not? To answer this question, the employment gap and wage gap in financial sector needs to be analyzed in detail.

3.1 Gender employment gap

A quick look in Table 4.1 reveals that both men's and women's employment share in financial activities worldwide has increased in the past 20+ years, reaching 1.5% and 2.1% of total employment, respectively. This increase has been valid in all geographical regions except Northern America (women's share), Northern Africa (men's share) and Europe (share of both) where the share of employment in financial activities has decreased since 1997. Yet, Northern America is the region with the highest share of financial employment in total employment for both men and women as of 2017, whereas sub-Saharan Africa has the lowest share.

Examining the difference between men and women's employment shares, it is seen that women's share has been always higher than men's in the financial sector across the world and in every region except Southern Asia. Besides, Northern America, Europe (except Eastern Europe) and Eastern Asia are the regions with higher share of women in financial activities than global average (2.1%) as of 2017, with respectively 5.6%, 3.3% and 2.7%.

For financial activities, the difference between men and women's employment share in total employment has increased in favor of women in Northern Africa, sub-Saharan Africa, America and the Caribbean, Eastern Asia, Eastern Europe and Central and Western Asia in the past 20 years. Despite a fall, Northern America is still the region with the highest positive bias in favor of woman. A difference

Table 4.1 Financial Sector's Employment Share in Total Employment, by Gender and by Region (%)

Year	*Gender*	*World*	*Northern Africa*	*Sub-Saharan Africa*	*Latin America and the Caribbean*	*Northern America*	*Arab States*	*Eastern Asia*	*South-Eastern Asia and the Pacific*	*Southern Asia*	*Northern, Southern and Western Europe*	*Eastern Europe*	*Central and Western Asia*
1997	♀	1.6	1.2	0.5	1.5	6.1	0.8	1.4	0.9	0.2	3.8	2	1.3
	♂	1.1	1	0.4	1.1	3.4	0.7	1	0.8	0.7	3.1	0.7	0.8
2007	♀	1.9	1.4	0.5	1.5	6.2	1.2	2	1.2	0.4	3.6	2.5	1.5
	♂	1.3	0.9	0.4	1.1	3.7	1	1.4	1.2	0.9	2.9	1.1	0.9
2017	♀	2.1	1.4	0.7	1.6	5.6	1.2	2.7	1.5	0.5	3.3	3	1.9
	♂	1.5	0.8	0.5	1.1	3.6	1.2	1.8	1.5	1.2	3	1.3	1

The table shows the financial sector's employment share in total employment by gender and by region for ten-year intervals since 1997.

Source: ILO, World Employment and Social Outlook: Trends for Women 2017

of 0.7% between men and women's employment points to a gender gap in financial sector employment in Southern Asia (Figure 4.1).

However, Figure 4.2 shows that the positive bias towards women's employment in financial sector differs in upper levels of financial services firms in North America. That is to say, while there's parity between men and women in entry-level staff,

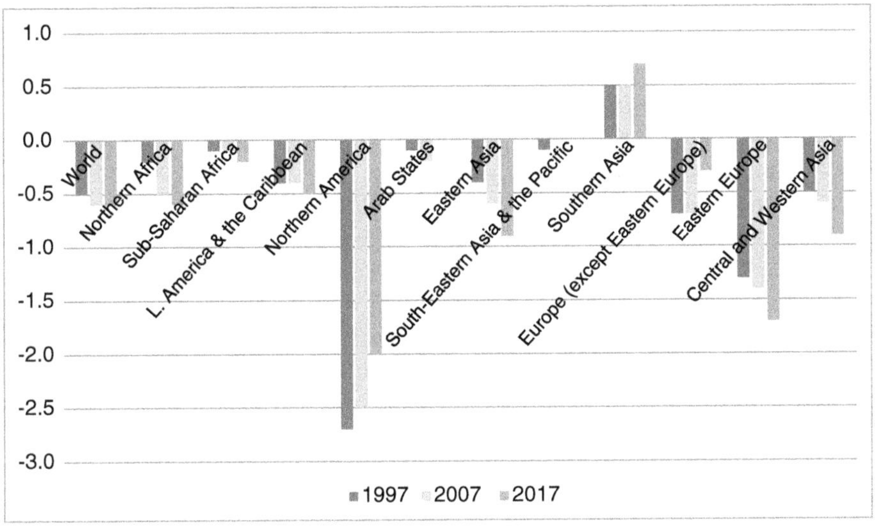

Figure 4.1 The Gender Gap in Employment in Financial Activities (%)

Source: ILO, World Employment and Social Outlook: Trends for Women 2017

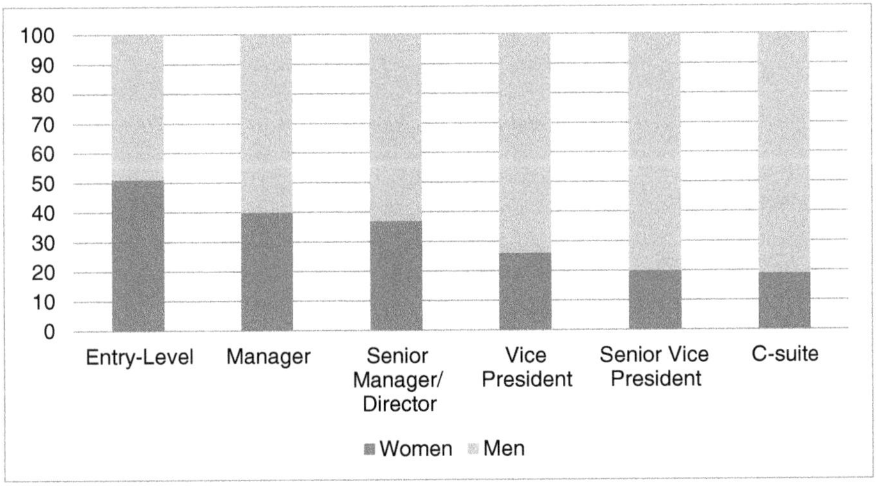

Figure 4.2 Women Representation in Financial Services Firms in North America, 2017 (% share)

Source: Chin et al. (2018)

this parity diminishes starting with the manager level where women represent 40% of total employees. Women are underrepresented in every step up the career ladder but especially in executive management team with accounting only 19% of top senior executives, known as the C-suite positions (CEO; Chief Financial Officer, CFO; Chief Operating Officer, COO; Chief Information Officer, CIO). Similarly, in a survey consisting 135,000 members in 151 countries, Adams et al. (2016) found that only about 18% of Chartered Financial Analyst (CFA)[7] are women, underlining the underrepresentation of women in top jobs of finance industry.

The gender gap in the senior management levels of financial firms vary across different subsectors. While women's representation is relatively higher in insurance, there is an acute lack of women roughly in all top positions in asset management and wholesale banking (Figure 4.3).

A detailed look in the banking subsector shows that globally, women occupied less than 20% of board seats of banks while less than 2% of bank CEO's were women in 2013. Contrary to popular belief, the representation of women on the bank boards isn't always higher in advanced economies (Figure 4.4). With an average share of 47.6%, Norway has the highest women representation on bank boards while there is no woman presence in a vast number of countries in the sample (Chile, Colombia, Hungary, Luxembourg, Malta, Pakistan, Peru, Qatar, Saudi Arabia, Sri Lanka and United Arab Emirates). Sahay et al. (2017) reports that the share of women's board participation in saving banks (45%) is higher compared to securities firms and banks (15%). Despite a progress after the Global Financial Crisis, women only hold less than 17% of board seats of banking supervisory agencies in 2015 and no relationship between the country/region's income

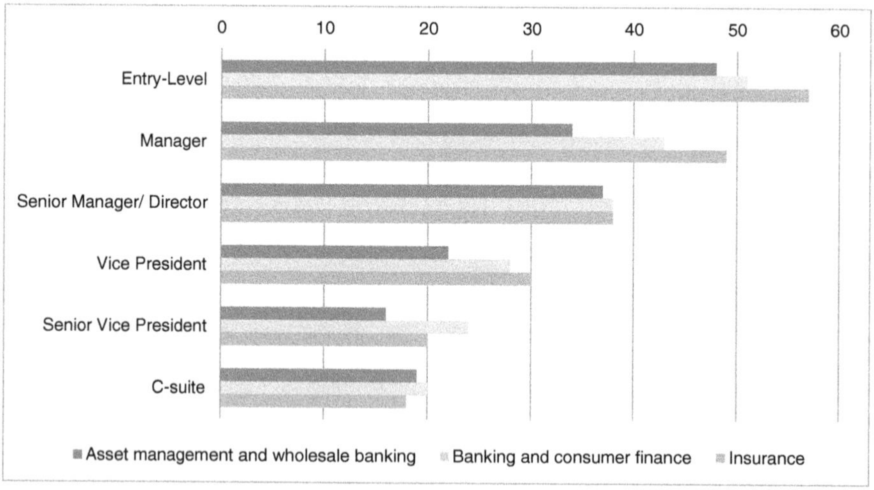

Figure 4.3 Women Representation in Different Subsectors of Financial Services Firms in North America, 2017 (% share)

Source: Chin et al. (2018)

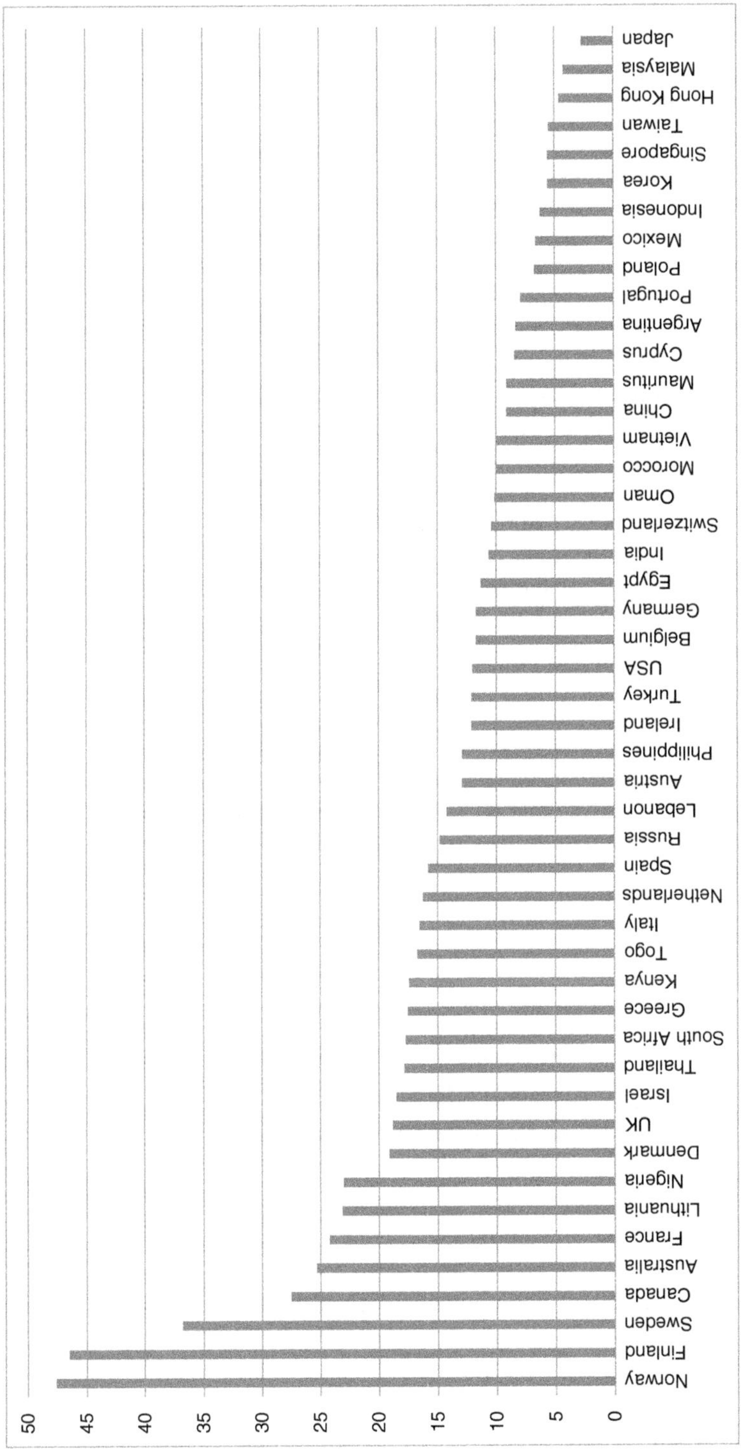

Figure 4.4 Average Share of Women on Bank Boards, 2013 (%)

Source: Sahay et al. (2017)

Note: The countries with no women representation on bank boards (Chile, Colombia, Hungary, Luxembourg, Malta, Pakistan, Peru, Qatar, Saudi Arabia, Sri Lanka and United Arab Emirates) are excluded from the figure.

level and women representation can be deduced as Eswatini's and Israel's shares are above 60% while the share of USA is below 13% (Sahay et al., 2017).

Based on an international comparison based on 71 banks in 20 countries; Ferrary (2017) shows that the representation of women in banking industry decreases in the higher levels of hierarchy with women representing only 37.58% of middle management and only 16.45% of the executive committee. These findings are in line with Sahay et al. (2017) and indicate that although banking industry achieved gender balance in terms of general workforce, a different picture emerges in the executive team, revealing a double "glass ceiling" in the industry (Figure 4.5).

On the other hand, the picture differs remarkably in the management of microfinance institutions. Hartarska et al. (2014) finds that the average proportion of women CEO's is 27% in 250 microfinance institutions[8] from 50 countries for the 1998–2009 period. Similarly, Dawson et al. (2016) reports that 25–30% of microfinance institutions' CEOs and 50% of lending officers are women. It is also reported that the female-led institutions have more females in boards (44% versus 23% in male-led institutions) and also are more likely to have a female as a chair of the board (43% versus 16% in male-led institutions).

Regarding the gender diversity in decision making positions, the Gender Balance Index[9] (GBI) represents the performance of individual institutions (central banks, pension funds, sovereign funds) on gender equality. As seen in Figure 4.6, the overall index score in 2019 increased to 24.8% from 19.4% in 2018 but is still lower than the score in 2017.

In the meantime, a different aspect of the gender gap in financial sector labor market is associated with financial decision-making positions in public institutions. With some achievements on becoming more gender diverse, 138 out of 173 (80%) central banks have at least one woman in top positions, while 35 central banks have no women at senior positions. The fact that 63 out of 173 central

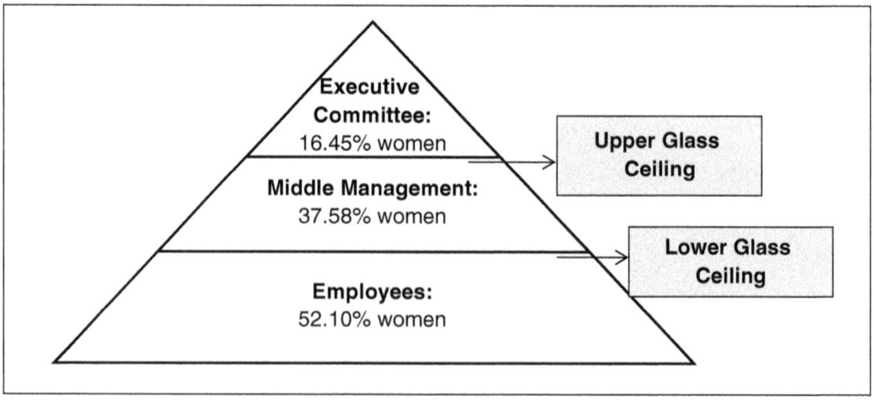

Figure 4.5 Double Glass Ceiling in Banking Industry

Source: Ferrary (2017)

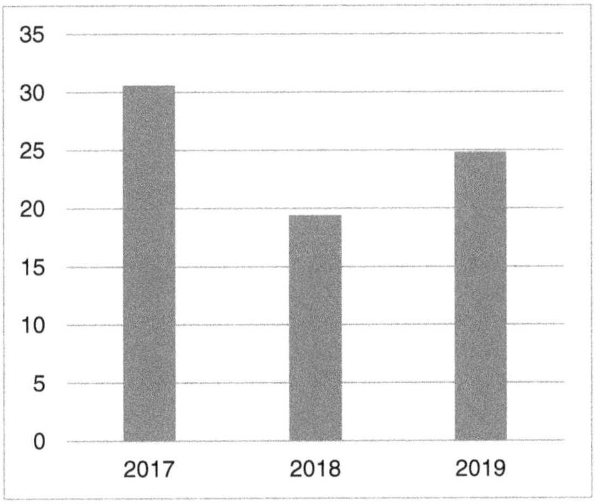

Figure 4.6 Gender Balance Index (GBI) Scores (%)
Source: Official Monetary and Financial Institutions Forum – OMFIF (2019)

banks have a woman governor or deputy governor and that only 14 central banks (8%) are governed by women shows that central bank governance is still highly masculine (OMFIF, 2019).

Encouragingly, the GBI for central banks shows that the women representation in senior positions has increased in all regions but one (the Middle East) in 2019 compared to 2018. However, there are large variations in women's representation in central bank governance across geographical regions. Despite no women representation in governance of its nine central banks (including Austria, the Czech Republic and Turkey), Europe leads the other regions while Asia Pacific has the worst performance (Figure 4.7).

However, a deeper look at the national central bank governors in European Union reveals the truth that the top positions and decision making in finance sector in EU is still highly dominated by men since there are no women governors in all 28 member states' national central banks as of 2019 and that only 21% of board members are women. The picture doesn't change for the finance ministers in EU member states as European Institute for Gender Equality (EIGE, 2017)[10] states that there are only two countries (Romania and Sweden) with a female finance minister.

The higher women representation in private banks in low and middle-income economies mentioned earlier also emerges in the case of central banks. The best performing countries regarding GBI of central banks include Iceland, Rwanda, Albania, Bulgaria, Timor-Leste, Bosnia and Herzegovina and Seychelles. The fact that only four central banks of G20 countries (Spain, Australia, Russia and France) are listed in the top 20 shows that the lack of women is more apparent in advanced economies' central bank governance (OMFIF, 2019, 12).

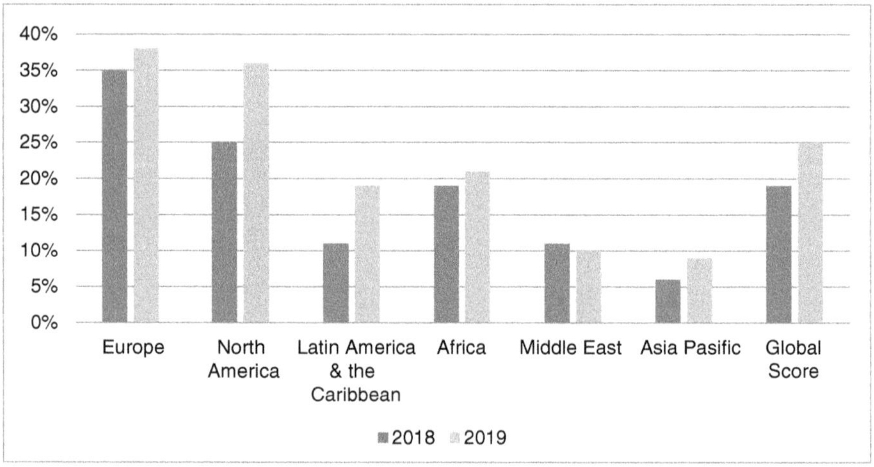

Figure 4.7 Gender Balance Index, Central Banks, 2018–2019 (%)
Source: OMFIF (2019)

3.2 Gender wage gap

As the relatively higher earnings in business and finance sectors attract young professionals and the increasing human capital of women (Bertrand et al., 2010), a positive bias emerges in favor of women in total employment share in finance industry and remarkable achievements on gender equality in terms of employment. However, the gender gap in top executive management and financial governance (detailed in the previous section) is not only limited to women's representation but also includes women's remuneration. The gender pay gap in the industry is alarming, especially in the developed economies.

In a survey among the graduating class for the period 1990–2006 of the University of Chicago MBAs, Bertrand et al. (2010) states that despite having identical income in the beginning of their career, a difference of 30 log points of annual earnings emerges in favor of male professionals five years after MBA completion. Not surprisingly, this difference doubles (60 log points) 10–16 years after MBA completion.

A survey on British firms reveals that, finance and insurance is one of the worst performing sectors in terms of gender pay gap with an average gap of approximately 23%, meaning that for every 1£ paid to a man, a woman earned 77£ in 2017. The situation is even worse for large retail and investment banks (Barr et al., 2019).[11]

A quick look at Eurostat's gender pay statistics reveals that, the gender pay gap in financial and insurance activities is remarkably evident in all European countries. Italy is the best performing country in terms of gender pay equality with a pay gap of 18% whereas Estonia is the worst performing with a gender pay gap of 40% (Figure 4.8).

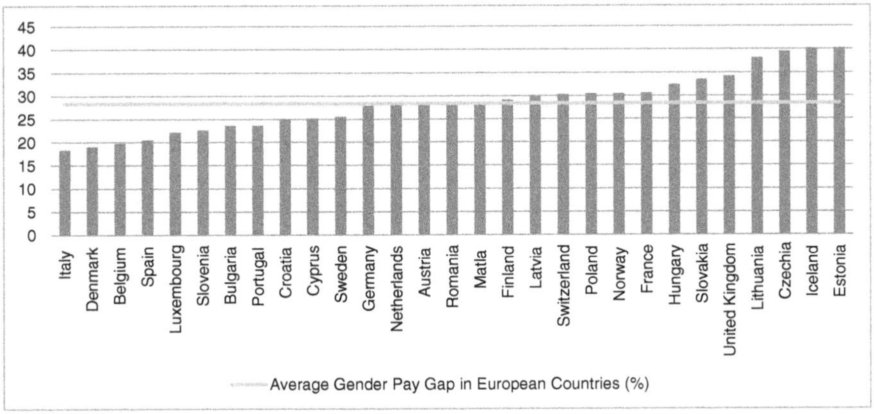

Figure 4.8 The Unadjusted Gender Pay Gap in Financial and Insurance Activities in European Countries, 2017 (%)

Source: Eurostat (https://ec.europa.eu/eurostat/statistics-explained/index.php/Gender_pay_gap_statistics#Highest_ gender_pay_gap_in_financial_and_insurance_activities)

On the other hand, New York State Department of Labor (2018)[12] reveals that the highest wage gap in New York State emerges in "finance and insurance and real estate and rental and leasing" industry where female median earnings are only 68.6% of male median earnings. This shows that the gender gap is persistent since the late 1990s as Roth (2006, 64) shows that women earned 40% less in average than their male co-workers in 1997 in Wall Street, the heart of financial businesses in New York City.

Given that the gender wage gap is clearly visible in developed countries, one can expect that the situation is not different at all in developing economies. In a survey among the female professionals in finance and banking industry in Turkey, Deloitte (2017) reveals that 69% of women feel at a disadvantage because of their gender whereas every one of two female professionals think that they're remunerated less than their male co-workers.

However, the most remarkable difference between developed and developing countries is the fact that while the gender wage gap is intensively discussed in developed countries, there's still room for detailed data and discussion regarding wage gaps in developing economies.

4 The reasons of the gender gap in financial sector and how to fight with?

The first step to ensure gender diversity in all sectors of the labor market is to understand the reasons behind. The remarkable human capital gains of women during the last decades points out that the gender gap in financial sector is related to socio-cultural and economical aspects rather than the lack of education.

First of all, the career interruption (a period of six months or more out of work) due to several reasons (the presence of children or caring for others) which results in future earning differences between male and female professionals are reported to be longer for women than men. Bertrand et al. (2010) states that only 4% of men, compared to 9% of women, have at least one career interruption one year after MBA graduation. While 10% of men have at least one career interruption ten years after graduation, this number is remarkably higher for women; 32% in the following nine years and 41% have at least one career interruption in the following 10–16 years after graduation.

Moreover, the highly competitive environment, male dominated nature, long working hours, travel commitments and inflexible schedules of the financial sector especially avoid women to aspire for a top position (Bertrand et al., 2010). Chin et al. (2018) states that the entry-level women in North American financial firms aren't enthusiastic on top positions as they cite a lack of interest, concerns about family–work balance, too much politics and pressure associated with the top positions and only 26% see themselves in a top position in the future while this ratio is 40% for men in entry level roles and 31% for entry-level women across all industries (Figure 4.9).

On the other hand, the lack of women in top positions does not help to encourage other young women about their future positions causing a vicious circle on the gender gap in senior management positions. Given the fact that, responsibility increases in the top-positions concerns on family–work balance also persists among women at the most senior levels complicating their pursuit of C-suite positions.

Hence, policies should be designed to first enhance the ambition of women to fix the leaky pipeline. Especially flexible work arrangements, remote working

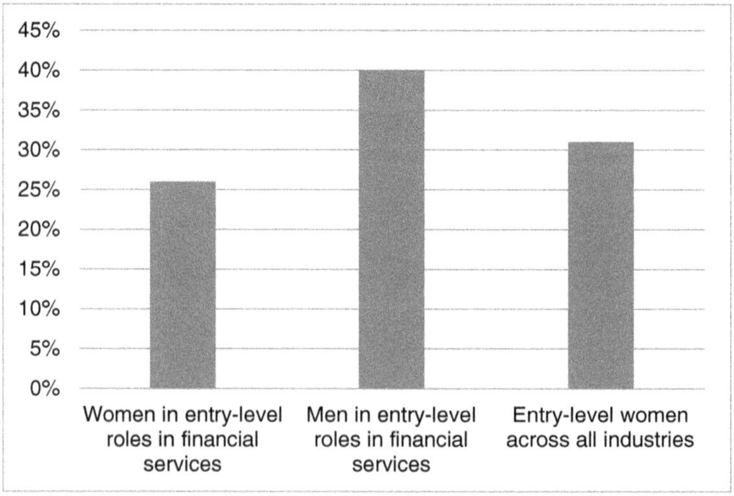

Figure 4.9 The Share of Employees Aspiring for a Senior Position in Financial Firms (%)
Source: Chin et al. (2018)

facilities, job-sharing, supporting part-time roles, facilities for nursing mothers and longer maternity leave policies may help women to maintain family–work balance and attract more females on these roles.

Another aspect is the importance of support provided by senior managers as entry-level women who received support, advice or mentoring from their managers or senior leaders have a higher chance of getting a promotion. Unfortunately the share of women who received support from their managers or senior leaders at the early stages of their career is lower than men (Chin et al., 2018). Thus, enriching leadership training and mentoring as well as coaching and sponsorship programs will help women in their pave to top senior management roles both in terms of enhancing the educational quality and networking.

At this point, changing corporate culture and introducing quotas will help to improve the presentation of women in business and financial sector. Therefore, commitment on gender equality at different levels and setting certain targets may help to reduce the male domination in the upper levels in financial governance.

Conclusion

The financial sector appears to be one of the best performing sectors in terms of gender diversity with women having a higher share of employment than men's in financial activities in most of the regions as well as across the world. However, a qualitative analysis shows that the situation in the sector differs for male and female professionals starting from the early career stages. This means that gender inequality emerges in every step up the career ladder as the women representation in top decision-making positions in private and public financial institutions remains to be low. However the literature shows that higher women presence in boardrooms have a positive impact on profits and stock performance in financial institutions while women representation is also associated with lower risk, less leverage, less risk taking and higher stability for banking industry; the gender diversity is remarkably important in finance sector.

In a world where women are educated better than ever before, the reasons of the gender employment gap in the financial sector is mostly based on socio-cultural and economical aspects rather than lack of education. Like other sectors, the most important reason appears to be the concerns on the family–work balance. The highly competitive environment, male dominated nature, long working hours, travel commitments and inflexible schedules of the sector discourages women to aspire for top positions where the pressure and responsibility is remarkable high, as the concerns on the family–work balance prevails. Causing a vicious circle, the underrepresentation of women in decision making positions of private financial institutions as well as central banks does not help to encourage other young women about their future positions.

On the other hand, the gender gap in the financial sector is also apparent regarding the remunerations of the male and female professionals. Despite being among the highest paying sectors, there is an acute gender wage gap especially in developed countries like United Kingdom and USA. The main reason of this gap arises due to the longer career interruptions of women which results in the difference of future remunerations. As the first step of the solution is to realize the problem, developed economies are in a better situation than developing economies as there is not much discussion on gender wage gap in the latter group.

Under these circumstances, it's no secret that there's still room for remarkable improvement for gender equality in the financial sector's labor market. Lagarde (2018)[13] expresses her thoughts on the necessity of a reform to include more female leaders in finance with the following sentence: "As I have said many times, if it had been Lehman Sisters rather than Lehman Brothers, the world might well look a lot different today" and underlines the importance of women representation to promote diversity not only to ensure prudence in decision making but also to sharpen thinking. It's believed that the higher representation of women in decision making will reduce the risk of *groupthink*,[14] which is believed to be the reason behind the 2008 Global Financial Crisis where most banks, regulators, central banks and academics failed to foresee the crisis coming.

To ensure gender diversity both in terms of employment and remuneration in the finance sector, the policies should be designated in a comprehensive aspect with a certain commitment on gender diversity. On one hand, enriching leadership training and mentoring programs may help to reduce the concern on work-life balance and to encourage women to aspire for a top career both in private and public institutions; on the other hand changing corporate culture and designing a new environment to diminish the male-domination in the industry by introducing some quotas for certain top positions as well as reassuring equal pay for equal job may lead to a more gender balanced finance sector. It should be kept in mind that, promoting gender equality in all sectors will be rewarding not only for women but also for men, and the financial sector has a huge potential to establish gender diversity in different levels considering the wide talent pool and the progress achieved so far.

Notes

1 Millennium Development Goals (MDGs) consist of eight development goals which all 191 member states of United States (UN) committed to help achieve in 2000 by the year 2015. For more information, please visit www.un.org/millenniumgoals/.
2 Worldbank, International Labor Organization (ILO) estimate.
3 Equileap, launched in 2016, is a nonprofit Netherlands-based organization providing data on gender equality in the corporate sector. Equileap's Global Top 200 list is a ranking to assess the gender equality between 3206 companies in 23 developed countries; for more information please visit https://equileap.org/about/.
4 Worldbank, Enterprise Surveys, https://data.worldbank.org/.
5 https://fortune.com/2019/05/16/fortune-500-female-ceos/.
6 www.theguardian.com/sustainable-business/gender-equality-finance-industry-progress-battles.
7 Chartered Financial Analyst is a credential granted by CFA Institute. It is a self-study program requiring one to have a bachelor's degree and professional work experience in investment decision-making process, in addition to passing a three-level sequential exam series. For more information, please visit www.cfainstitute.org/en.
8 A microfinance institution is a local organization that provides financial services to the communities who do not have access to traditional banking systems and also provides

access to credit and financial services to small businesses and entrepreneurs. It takes its origins from the microcredit concept, which is designed to help poor communities and low-income individuals.

9 The GBI is constructed to evaluate the presence of women and men in decision-making positions and represents the aggregate performance of individual institutions by a designated weighting scheme. For more information, please visit www.omfif.org/gender-balance-index-2019/.

10 https://eige.europa.eu/publications/gender-equality-financial-decision-making.

11 www.theguardian.com/world/ng-interactive/2019/apr/05/gender-pay-gap-what-did-we-learn-this-year.

12 https://labor.ny.gov/NYSDOL%20Pay%20Gap%20Study.pdf.

13 https://blogs.imf.org/2018/09/05/ten-years-after-lehman-lessons-learned-and-challenges-ahead/.

14 "Groupthink" is a term developed by Irvin L. Janis (1972) in his study entitled "Victims of Groupthink: A Psychological Study of Foreign-Policy Decisions and Fiascoes", where he examines the reasons behind the bad decisions (related to foreign policy) of groups consisting of highly intelligent individuals. Since then, the concept has been widely used in various fields such as organizational theory and management.

References

Adams, R., Barber, B., & Odean, T. (2016). *Gender Diversity in Investment Management: New Research for Practitioners on How to Close the Gender Gap*. Virginia: CFA Institute Research Foundation.

Barr, C., Kommenda, N., & Davies, C. (2019, April 5th). Gender Pay Gap: What Did We Learn This Year? *The Guardian*. Retrieved February 20th, 2020, from www.theguardian.com/world/ng-interactive/2019/apr/05/gender-pay-gap-what-did-we-learn-this-year

Bertrand, M., Goldin, C., & Katz, L. F. (2010). Dynamics of the Gender Gap for Young Professionals in the Financial and Corporate Sectors. *American Economic Journal: Applied Economics* 2, 228–255.

Blau, F. D., & Kahn, L. M. (2017). The Gender Wage Gap: Extent, Trends and Explanations. *Journal of Economic Literature*, 789–865.

Cabo, R., Gimeno, R., & Nieto, M. (2012). Gender Diversity on European Banks' Boards of Directors. *Journal of Business Ethics*, 145–162.

Chin, S., Nadeau, M.-C., & Krivkovich, A. (2018). *Closing the Gap: Leadership Perspectives on Promoting Women in Financial Services*. New York: McKinsey & Company.

Christiansen, L., Lin, H., Pereira, J., Topalove, P., & Turk, R. (2016). *Unlocking Female Employment Potential in Europe Drivers and Benefits*. Washington, DC: International Monetary Fund.

Dawson, J., Kersley, R., & Natella, S. (2016). *The CS Gender 3000: The Reward for Change*. Switzerland: Credit Suisse.

Deloitte. (2017). *Türkiyede finans dünyasında kadın*. Retrieved February 20th, 2020, from www2.deloitte.com/content/dam/Deloitte/tr/Documents/financial-services/turkiyede-finans-dunyasinda-kadin.pdf

EIGE. (2017, September 15th). *Gender Equality in Financial Decision-Making*. Retrieved February 20th, 2020, from European Institute for Gender Equality: https://eige.europa.eu/publications/gender-equality-financial-decision-making

EQUILEAP. (2018). *Gender Equality Global Report & Ranking*. Retrieved February 20th, 2020.

EQUILEAP. (2019). *Gender Equality Global Report & Ranking*. Retrieved February 20th, 2020.

EUROSTAT. https://ec.europa.eu/eurostat/statistics-explained/index.php/Gender_pay_gap_statistics#Highest_gender_pay_gap_in_financial_and_insurance_activities

Faccio, M., Marchica, M.-T., & Mura, R. (2016). CEO Gender, Corporate Risk-Taking, and the Efficiency of Capital Allocation. *Journal of Corporate Finance*, 193–209.

Ferrary, M. (2017). *Gender Diversity in the Banking Industry: An International Comparison*. Retrieved February 20th, 2020, from SKEMA Observatory on the Feminization of Companies: www.skema.edu/research/Documents/chairs/women-and-business/gender-diversity-banking-industry-2017-english.pdf

Fortune. (2019). *The Fortune 500 Has More Female CEOs Than Ever Before*. Retrieved from https://fortune.com/2019/05/16/fortune-500-female-ceos/

Garcia-Meca, E., Martinez-Ferrero, I., & Sanchez, I. (2015). Board Diversity and Its Effects on Bank Performance: An International Analysis. *Journal of Banking and Finance*, 202–214.

Gould, H. (2014, March 8th). *Gender Equality in Finance Industry: Progress Made and Battles Ahead. The Guardian*. Retrieved February 20th, 2020, from www.theguardian.com/sustainable-business/gender-equality-finance-industry-progress-battles

Gulamhussen, M., & Santa, S. (2015). Female Directors in Bank Boardrooms and Their Influence on Performance and Risk-Taking. *Global Finance Journal*, 10–23.

Hartarska, V., Nadolnyak, D., & Mersland, R. (2014). Are Women Better Bankers to the Poor? Evidence from Rural Microfinance Institutions. *American Journal of Agricultural Economics*, 96 (5), 1291–1306.

ILO. (2017). *World Employment Social Outlook: Trend for Women 2017*. Geneva: International Labour Office.

Janis, I. L. (1972). *Victims of Groupthink: A Psychological Study of Foreign-Policy Decisions and Fiascoes*. Boston, MA: Houghton Mifflin Company.

Lagarde, C. (2018). *Ten Years after Lehman: Lessons Learned and Challenges Ahead*. Retrieved February 20th, 2020, from IMF Blog: https://blogs.imf.org/2018/09/05/ten-years-after-lehman-lessons-learned-and-challenges-ahead/

New York State Department of Labor. (2018). *Closing the Gender Wage Gap in New York State: Pay Equity and Advancement*. New York: Department of Labor.

OMFIF. (2019). *Banking on Balance: Diversity in Central Banks and Public Investment*. Retrieved from www.omfif.org/gender-balance-index-2019/

Owen, A. L., & Temesvary, J. (2018). The Performance Effects of Gender Diversity on Bank Boards. *Journal of Banking and Finance*, 50–63.

Roth, L. M. (2006). *Selling Women Short: Gender and Money on Wall Street*. Princeton, NJ: Princeton University Press.

Sahay, R., Čihák, M., N'Diaye, P., Barajas, A., Mitra, S. K., Mooi, Y. N., & Yousefi, S. R. (2017). *Banking on Women Leaders: A Case for More?* IMF Working Paper.

Sahay, R., Cihak, M., & other IMF Staff. (2018). *Women in Finance: A Case for Closing Gaps*. IMF Staff Discussion Note 18/05, Washington, DC.

5 Is there gender equality in employment indicators?

A comparative study for emerging markets

Melih Özçalik

1 Introduction

In mainstream economics, the term of employment is described in two ways. The first is in the macroeconomic field and refers to the usage of all factors of production in full efficiency. Another meaning is in microeconomics and relates to household supply of labor in the market. We discuss the microeconomic aspect of employment in this chapter. Employment differs according to two economics schools: Classical economics and Keynesian economics. To this economic thoughts, the term of employment is all about whether wages are flexible or rigid. According to the flexible and rigid wage structure, short- or long-term unemployment varies.

According to the classical school of economics, there are two types of unemployment. However, this is not the case in Keynesian economics. There is an underemployment balance in Keynesian economics. This reveals that many types of unemployment are possible with the rigid wage model (Ahiakpor, 1997: 13–15; Stirati, 2012: 4; Chaudhry et al., 2011: 5–6).

The term of employment is an important macroeconomic indicator, whether for an underdeveloped, developing or developed country. A high employment rate means high production levels and high production levels means high GDP (gross domestic product). Additionally, the quality of labor factor is also important. The term "qualified labor factor" is related to the educated population, also known as human capital.

Countries where women are almost equal to men in economic and social life are called developed countries, whereas other countries are called developing or underdeveloped according to their social and educational levels (Kapucugil İkiz, 2015: 151).

In developed countries, a major part of employment is in the industrial sector. However, in underdeveloped and developing countries, employment is mostly in the service sector, and the agriculture sector occupies less work and less income in GDP.

Labor force and unemployment terms, just like employment, are also components of the labor market. However, unemployment is more significant in terms of its socioeconomic and psychological effects. Also, unemployment reveals the misery index along with inflation rate. This index is at especially high levels in underdeveloped and developing countries.

Another important aspect of employment is its diversity by gender. Until the middle of the last century, women mostly worked at housework and men worked in various jobs outside the home. The labor force participation rate of women increased gradually in developed countries, especially after World War II. However, female employment in developed countries is still not at equal levels to male employment. Moreover, equal employment rates are not currently available in underdeveloped and developing countries. In some underdeveloped countries, even the presence of women in working life is considered negatively. Gender identity in a country can also affect sectoral employment. The male employment rate is higher than the female rate in many sectors of employment (Cifre et al., 2018: 3). Employment rate is one of the major labor market topics. With the exception of some professions that require physical strength, it doesn't make sense to compare female labor with male labor. However, in the past, male labor was dominant in these countries, so this comparison is encountered in almost every sector.

There are many answers to why gender inequality is particularly apparent in employment. Parsons's view suggests that gender inequality is an effective way to create a division of labor to maximize resources and ensure efficiency. Engels's view sees society as a platform where social groups struggle for sovereignty. On the other hand, the feminist view is a structure that opposes all other views, gender inequality and male domination (Ewubare and Ogbuagu, 2017: 18). Since the liberal or market economy (market without interference) began to rise, an increase in production has made employment growth a necessity. This situation also made it necessary to increase female employment rates in underdeveloped and developing countries, and especially in developed countries. However, various cultural and social value judgments still prevent gender equality in employment.

2 Labor markets and female employment in emerging markets

The economy generally consists of two primary sectors: goods and services. Sectors that produce goods give physical products and use factors. Sectors that produce services give non-physical goods to the economy (Moyser, 2017: 21). Developing countries are generally known as the economies that have the service sector first and then the industrial sector. Also, female employment has been mostly concentrated in the service sector, especially in underdeveloped and developing countries.

Today, many scientists mention that artificial intelligence will increase and replace unqualified labor, especially in the industrial sector. However, qualified labor will remain as important in the future as it has been in the past.

Employment levels in all countries are affected by highly complex macroeconomic indicators, directly and indirectly. However, people living in underdeveloped countries in the Middle East and North Africa regions migrated due to wars and poverty. Therefore employment structures have changed (Otobe, 2017: 1). Today, discrimination of men and women in labor markets is one of the main problems. However, the worst problem is unemployment between labor market indicators.

Another important indicator of female employment is the labor force participation rate. There are many factors that affect women's participation in the labor market. The main factors used to determine permanent gender differences in the European labor markets are as follows (Eurofound, 2016: 21):

- Individual differences (such as age, education, nationality, work experience),
- Family and household situations (number of children, elderly relatives, marital status, unemployed spouse, etc.),
- Institutional and political regimes.

Apart from the fact that female labor force participation rate in the labor market has significant effects on the economy, it also affects women's welfare and society as a whole. Employment not only relates to income or financial earnings but also to enable households to engage with society and protect it as a social mechanism. This link between individuals and society also provides a sense of belonging, identity and participation.

In the second half of the last century there was an increase in the female labor force in Europe because of the war. Before that the view of the female labor force was negative, not only in underdeveloped and developing countries but also in developed and industrialized European countries. On the other hand, female employment increased in the industrial sector with a decrease in the male labor force after the war. Today, male and female employment is close to each other in developed countries.

The term "gender inequality" has mostly declined in social life since the 1970s. Workplaces are less reserved, women have moved to positions of power and responsibility, and men are more involved in childcare. Another important development is access to data regarding labor force participation rates and contributing family workers (Perron, 2009: 11). The increase in female employment rate stands out with its economic results and its social effects. Women in the labor market evaluate their lives more positively than women outside of the labor market. They have higher levels of economic security and improved social lives (Eurofound, 2016: 1). If female employers realize that there is a big gap between the minimum wage and wages that offered to them compared to male employers, female employment rate will be less than male (Humpert and Pfeifer, 2012: 2).

The challenge faced by almost all developing countries is the need for economic diversification and transformation in an environment that slows down global economic growth, as seen after the 2008 global economic crisis. Especially for women in developing countries, the future of work depends on how countries manage to diversify their economies and how women can benefit from new job opportunities created in non-agricultural sectors (Otobe, 2017: 11). In addition, "gender" in developing countries is the primary indicator of exclusion in the socioeconomic structure. Regardless of a person's socioeconomic level, there are also gender differences for welfare in similar countries. As a result, gender inequality is a feature of most societies. Men are generally better off in social, economic and political hierarchy (UNDP, 2013: 162).

According to İnce Yenilmez (2017: 486), in most underdeveloped and developing countries, social impact scales of men are higher than women. This shows that women are more disadvantaged than men. Moreover, this situation causes women to be in the background in politics, public institutions, family and in the private sector. In European countries, gender inequality was previously viewed as a matter of equality and justice. Discussions on a high pay gap between genders, differences in employment rates, poor representation in top management and boards of companies and inequalities in political representation are often addressed as gender inequality issues (Klasen and Minasyan, 2017: 17).

Many employment indicators are major problems that women face in the labor market with men. These problems include especially: women have lower activity rates and higher ratio of part-time workers, women work less than men, women are typically paid less than men in low-wage professions, women have less self-employment than men, and the gender gap in higher education is relatively small (Löfström, 2009: 25). If female employment was equal to men, countries would expect to be more resistant to internal and external shocks and have higher economic growth rates (Lagarde, 2019: 5). Male and female employment differences are also excused by managers, thereby paving the way for female employment to be lower than male employment. However, the fact that female employment is lower than male employment makes a difficult position for macroeconomic indicators in a country.

The difficulty of increasing economic growth is largely linked to the position of women in a country. Discrimination against women in education and employment not only harms women but also creates a cost for the whole society (Klasen and Lamanna, 2009: 117). Female employment and women's empowerment have an impact on economic growth. In addition, it has been revealed in many studies in the opposite situation. Accordingly, economic growth is indispensable for women's empowerment and gender equality (Duflo, 2012: 1054).

3 Employment indicators in BRICS and Turkey

This section indentifies some labor market indicators for BRICS countries and Turkey. Statistics are obtained from World Bank for the period 1991–2018. BRICS countries (Brazil, Russia, India, China and South Africa), which make up approximately 40% of the world's population and 20% of the world's GDP, will increase these values even more in the 21st century. It can be considered that BRICS countries will maintain their economic and strategic importance with their surface area, populations and GDP. This can be explained by the fact that they have a large population and obtain cheap production power, as well as having large consumer markets. However, the large areas that they cover reveal their potential to have underground resources likely to be used today and in the future. Some of them believe the term "BRICS", which has been in use since 2001, is a structure established by global financiers on increasing capital circulation.

In Turkey's case, foreign trade volume, especially after 1980, increased quickly in the Turkish economy. However, the employment rate did not increase rapidly. Today Turkey has upper ranks with its high unemployment rate and low employment rate among the world. Especially low female employment rates and high unemployment rates are some of the most important problems in Turkey (İnce Yenilmez, 2019: 71). Some of the employment indicators meanings are given here (https://ilostat.ilo.org/topics):

- Contributing family worker (percentage of employment): the workers who hold self-employment jobs as own-account workers in a market-oriented establishment operated by a related person living in the same household.
- Wage and salaried worker (percentage of employment): the workers who hold the type of jobs defined as paid employment jobs, where the incumbents hold explicit or implicit employment contracts that give them a basic remuneration that is not directly dependent upon the revenue of the unit for which they work.
- Labor force participation rate (percentage of population ages 15+): the proportion of the population ages 15 and older that is economically active; all people who supply labor for the production of goods and services during a specified period.
- Unemployment (percentage of labor force): the share of the labor force that is without work but available for and seeking employment.
- Youth unemployment (percentage of labor force between 15–24): the share of the labor force ages between 15–24 without work but available for and seeking employment.

Brazil's female employment indicators between 1991–2018 are shown in Table 5.1. Accordingly, the ratio of contributing family workers has declined from 13.2% to 3.6% over the years. The labor force participation rate has increased to around 11%; unemployment rate and youth unemployment rate have almost doubled. The wage and salaried workers variable is also increasing steadily.

In the early 1990s, the Russia differentiated its macroeconomic indicators with the change of its system and economy. The most important point that is seen in Table 5.2 is the deterioration in employment indicators in 1997–1998, which affected Asian countries and Russia economically. Apart from that, all the indicators kept their stable appearance for a 28-year period.

According to the Indian case (Table 5.3), almost all of the female employment indicators have been deteriorating for years. Particularly, while labor force participation rate decreases, unemployment rate and youth unemployment rate increases. However, the rate of wage and salaried workers is increasing. Contributing family workers rate decreases in employment.

In China's case (Table 5.4), the most important point in the table is that youth unemployment gradually increases while unemployment remains at almost the same rates. Besides, contributing family workers are gradually decreasing. The rate of wage and salaried workers is gradually increasing. This situation is in a certain trend.

Although South Africa is a new member of the BRICS group, it is similar to Russia in female employment data, particularly in contributing family workers and wage and salaried workers (Table 5.5). However, the unemployment rate and the youth unemployment rate are quite high.

Turkey's economy is similar to developing countries and especially BRICS countries concerning macroeconomic indicators (Table 5.6). Accordingly, while contributing family workers rate is decreasing, share of the wage and salaried workers rate in employment rate are increasing in Turkey.

Table 5.1 Employment Indicators of Brazil (%)

Years	*Contributing Family Workers*	*Labor Force Participation*	*Unemployment*	*Wage and Salaried Workers*	*Youth Unemployment*
1991	13.2	43.0	7.9	65.2	14.2
1992	12.9	44.1	8.1	65.2	14.8
1993	12.6	45.1	7.4	65.5	14.0
1994	12.4	46.2	7.7	66.0	14.3
1995	12.0	47.3	8.1	65.8	14.9
1996	10.3	46.3	9.6	68.2	16.8
1997	10.8	47.1	10.9	67.6	19.2
1998	10.2	48.0	12.6	67.6	23.2
1999	11.1	49.3	13.3	67.2	24.0
2000	9.8	50.3	12.8	66.8	23.3
2001	8.6	51.3	12.2	65.9	22.6
2002	8.6	52.6	11.9	65.3	22.9
2003	8.4	52.9	12.7	65.6	24.6
2004	8.2	54.0	12.0	66.1	23.4
2005	8.2	55.1	12.5	65.3	24.9
2006	7.2	54.8	11.4	66.5	23.1
2007	6.9	54.6	11.1	67.7	21.8
2008	5.9	54.5	9.9	68.6	20.3
2009	5.6	55.0	11.4	69.7	23.1
2010	4.9	53.6	10.4	71.2	21.3
2011	4.2	52.2	9.4	72.6	19.8
2012	4.6	53.1	9.1	75.5	19.8
2013	4.6	53.0	8.8	75.4	19.3
2014	4.3	52.9	8.1	75.8	18.8
2015	4.2	53.4	10.1	74.9	23.6
2016	3.5	53.3	13.5	74.6	31.1
2017	3.6	54.2	14.7	73.6	33.2
2018	3.6	54.0	14.4	73.6	32.5

Table 5.2 Employment Indicators of Russia (%)

Years	*Contributing Family Workers*	*Labor Force Participation*	*Unemployment*	*Wage and Salaried Workers*	*Youth Unemployment*
1991	0.1	58.5	5.1	99.4	13.1
1992	0.1	58.0	5.2	99.4	12.9
1993	0.1	56.2	5.8	99.2	13.9
1994	0.1	54.3	7.9	98.8	17.5
1995	0.2	53.7	9.2	98.3	20.0
1996	0.1	52.9	9.3	98.1	20.5
1997	0.1	51.9	11.5	96.6	24.1
1998	0.1	51.2	13.0	96.6	27.7
1999	0.1	54.6	12.9	90.8	25.8
2000	0.1	54.7	10.4	91.4	22.2
2001	0.1	53.5	8.6	92.8	19.2
2002	0.1	54.5	7.6	92.9	16.9
2003	0.1	54.3	8.0	93.6	18.8
2004	0.1	54.8	7.5	93.4	18.6
2005	0.1	55.2	6.9	92.9	16.8
2006	0.1	55.6	6.7	93.3	17.1
2007	0.1	56.2	5.6	93.4	14.4
2008	0.1	56.1	5.9	93.4	15.1
2009	0.3	56.3	7.7	93.4	18.8
2010	0.4	55.9	6.8	94.1	17.4
2011	0.3	56.2	6.1	93.8	15.8
2012	0.4	56.1	5.1	94.0	15.3
2013	0.4	55.8	5.1	93.6	15.0
2014	0.4	55.7	4.8	93.8	14.5
2015	0.4	55.6	5.3	93.7	17.3
2016	0.4	55.7	5.3	93.6	17.6
2017	0.4	55.3	5.1	94.5	17.2
2018	0.4	54.9	4.6	94.5	16.0

Table 5.3 Employment Indicators of India (%)

Years	*Contributing Family Workers*	*Labor Force Participation*	*Unemployment*	*Wage and Salaried Workers*	*Youth Unemployment*
1991	34.7	30.4	2.2	8.0	5.9
1992	34.4	30.5	2.3	8.1	6.0
1993	34.2	30.6	2.5	8.2	6.5
1994	33.9	30.8	2.5	8.4	6.7
1995	34.0	30.8	2.6	8.5	6.8

(*Continued*)

Table 5.3 (Continued)

Years	*Contributing Family Workers*	*Labor Force Participation*	*Unemployment*	*Wage and Salaried Workers*	*Youth Unemployment*
1996	34.0	30.7	2.6	8.6	6.9
1997	34.0	30.6	2.4	8.7	6.7
1998	33.9	30.5	2.4	8.9	6.6
1999	33.8	30.4	2.5	9.0	6.9
2000	33.8	30.4	2.4	9.1	6.8
2001	34.8	30.7	2.7	9.4	7.3
2002	35.9	31.1	3.1	9.7	8.2
2003	36.8	31.4	3.6	10.0	9.1
2004	37.8	31.8	3.9	10.3	9.7
2005	38.6	32.2	4.2	10.7	10.4
2006	37.4	30.8	3.7	11.0	9.8
2007	36.0	29.5	3.3	11.4	9.2
2008	35.1	28.2	3.0	11.7	8.9
2009	33.6	27.0	3.2	12.0	9.5
2010	32.1	25.8	3.3	12.5	10.1
2011	32.1	24.4	3.5	14.5	10.9
2012	31.9	23.0	3.7	16.8	11.8
2013	31.0	23.2	3.9	17.1	12.3
2014	30.1	23.4	3.8	17.5	12.4
2015	29.0	23.5	3.9	17.9	12.8
2016	28.1	23.7	3.8	18.3	12.9
2017	27.2	23.8	3.6	18.8	12.6
2018	26.3	23.6	3.6	19.2	12.9

Table 5.4 Employment Indicators of China (%)

Years	*Contributing Family Workers*	*Labor Force Participation*	*Unemployment*	*Wage and Salaried Workers*	*Youth Unemployment*
1991	43.5	73.1	2.1	26.6	3.8
1992	42.6	73.0	2.1	27.6	3.9
1993	41.7	72.9	2.3	28.7	4.5
1994	40.7	72.7	2.5	29.7	4.9
1995	39.8	72.5	2.6	30.6	5.2
1996	38.8	72.3	2.7	31.5	5.4
1997	37.9	72.0	2.8	32.5	5.7
1998	36.9	71.7	2.8	33.3	5.8
1999	36.0	71.4	2.9	34.2	6.0
2000	35.1	71.0	2.9	35.1	6.1

Years	*Contributing Family Workers*	*Labor Force Participation*	*Unemployment*	*Wage and Salaried Workers*	*Youth Unemployment*
2001	34.1	70.2	3.3	36.0	7.1
2002	33.0	69.3	3.6	37.1	7.8
2003	32.0	68.4	4.0	38.2	8.6
2004	31.0	67.6	3.9	39.2	8.4
2005	30.0	66.8	3.9	40.3	8.4
2006	29.1	66.1	3.8	41.4	8.2
2007	28.1	65.5	3.7	42.4	8.1
2008	27.1	64.9	4.0	43.4	8.7
2009	26.2	64.4	4.1	44.3	8.9
2010	25.4	63.8	3.9	45.3	8.6
2011	24.5	63.6	3.9	46.2	8.7
2012	23.7	63.4	4.0	47.0	9.1
2013	22.9	63.2	4.0	47.8	9.3
2014	22.1	62.9	4.0	48.5	9.4
2015	21.4	62.6	4.0	49.2	9.6
2016	20.7	62.2	3.9	49.9	9.5
2017	20.0	61.8	3.8	50.6	9.3
2018	19.4	61.3	3.8	51.3	9.4

Table 5.5 Employment Indicators of South Africa (%)

Years	*Contributing Family Workers*	*Labor Force Participation*	*Unemployment*	*Wage and Salaried Workers*	*Youth Unemployment*
1991	2.3	43.2	33.7	78.5	53.6
1992	2.3	43.9	33.9	78.5	54.4
1993	2.2	44.6	34.9	78.5	56.0
1994	2.2	45.3	35.3	78.5	57.0
1995	2.2	46.1	35.4	78.5	57.5
1996	2.1	46.6	35.7	78.5	58.1
1997	2.1	47.2	35.6	78.6	58.5
1998	2.0	47.8	35.2	78.6	58.3
1999	2.0	48.4	35.7	78.6	59.2
2000	2.0	49.0	35.9	78.7	59.6
2001	2.3	49.4	36.4	71.1	61.9
2002	1.8	49.1	41.1	78.1	67.2
2003	1.4	47.2	39.2	78.2	67.9
2004	1.3	45.1	36.2	79.0	65.6
2005	1.0	47.0	36.4	77.0	65.2

(*Continued*)

Years	*Contributing Family Workers*	*Labor Force Participation*	*Unemployment*	*Wage and Salaried Workers*	*Youth Unemployment*
2006	1.1	48.3	35.8	77.4	62.9
2007	0.7	47.4	33.1	79.5	60.8
2008	1.5	47.9	25.8	84.0	49.9
2009	1.5	46.3	25.6	85.4	51.9
2010	1.2	44.7	27.0	85.4	54.5
2011	1.1	45.2	27.2	85.9	54.6
2012	1.0	45.4	27.1	86.9	56.4
2013	1.0	46.4	26.5	87.0	55.4
2014	0.8	46.6	27.0	88.2	55.3
2015	0.8	47.8	27.5	87.9	54.9
2016	0.7	47.8	29.0	87.7	59.4
2017	0.7	48.9	29.5	87.1	58.7
2018	0.7	48.8	29.3	87.1	58.6

Table 5.6 Employment Indicators of Turkey (%)

Years	*Contributing Family Workers*	*Labor Force Participation*	*Unemployment*	*Wage and Salaried Workers*	*Youth Unemployment*
1991	53.3	33.9	7.1	33.7	11.9
1992	53.4	32.5	7.8	33.7	13.7
1993	55.7	26.6	9.4	32.1	16.2
1994	53.0	31.1	8.1	34.1	13.6
1995	52.4	30.8	7.3	34.5	13.3
1996	51.8	30.4	6.0	34.9	11.3
1997	52.4	28.6	7.8	34.6	15.2
1998	51.4	29.0	6.8	35.2	12.9
1999	50.3	29.8	7.6	35.8	14.0
2000	51.1	26.3	6.3	35.3	11.9
2001	52.5	26.8	7.5	33.7	14.4
2002	48.8	27.6	9.5	37.5	17.0
2003	48.2	26.2	10.1	38.7	18.7
2004	50.0	23.4	11.0	39.1	20.6
2005	41.7	23.3	11.2	43.8	20.4
2006	35.1	23.1	9.1	51.0	17.3
2007	34.3	23.1	9.1	52.7	17.3
2008	34.2	24.0	10.0	53.4	18.6
2009	34.5	25.5	12.6	51.3	22.2
2010	34.8	27.0	11.4	51.0	20.5
2011	35.0	28.3	10.1	51.9	18.8

Years	*Contributing Family Workers*	*Labor Force Participation*	*Unemployment*	*Wage and Salaried Workers*	*Youth Unemployment*
2012	33.2	28.9	9.4	54.6	17.6
2013	31.1	30.1	10.5	56.9	19.4
2014	29.0	30.2	11.8	60.5	20.0
2015	27.8	31.5	12.6	62.1	21.9
2016	26.0	32.5	13.6	63.7	23.3
2017	25.5	33.6	13.9	63.7	25.2
2018	25.1	33.5	13.6	64.0	24.4

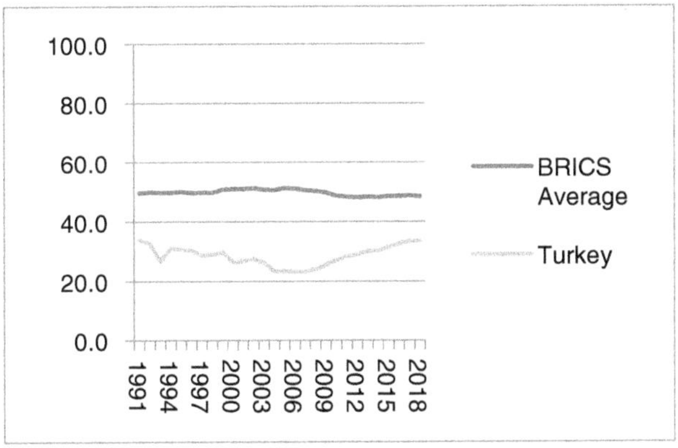

Figure 5.1 Labor Force Participation Rate (F)

Source: World Bank Statistics, 31.12.2020

Figures 5.1 and 5.2 show labor force participation rates for females and males between 1991 and 2018 (World Bank Statistics, 31.12.2020). Data is averaged for five BRICS countries. According to Figure 5.1, for females, BRICS countries have almost the same rate for labor force participation over years. However, there has been a slight increase in Turkey, especially since 2008. Male labor force participation rate averages in the BRICS countries and in Turkey have fallen since 1991. Turkey has experienced the most significant decline in this rate after the 2001 crisis. However, there has been a gradual increase since 2006. BRICS country average continues to decrease.

Data on female and male wage and salaried workers is shown in Figures 5.3 and 5.4 (World Bank Statistics, 31.12.2020). Data are average ratio for BRICS and ratio for Turkey. According to these figures, both of the indicators have an increasing trend. However, in Figure 5.4, it is seen that Turkey's BRICS exceeded the BRICS average from 2006.

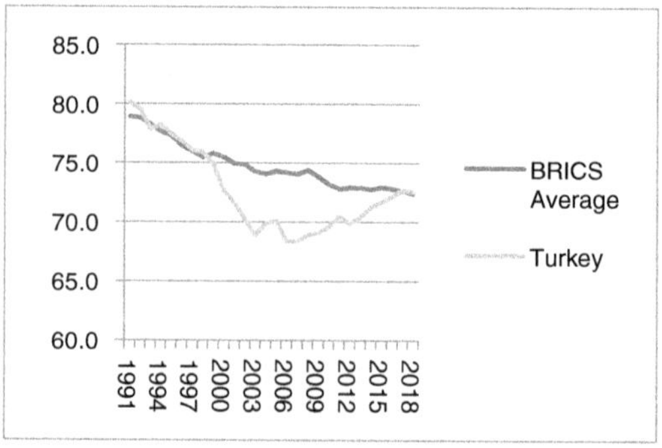

Figure 5.2 Labor Force Participation Rate (M)

Source: World Bank Statistics, 31.12.2020

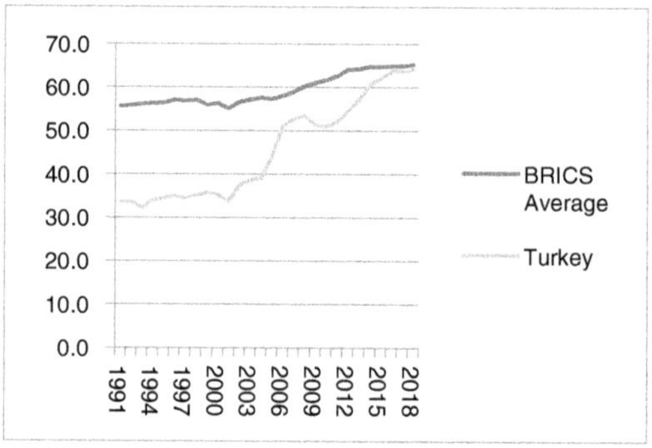

Figure 5.3 Wage and Salaried Workers (F)

Source: World Bank Statistics, 31.12.2020

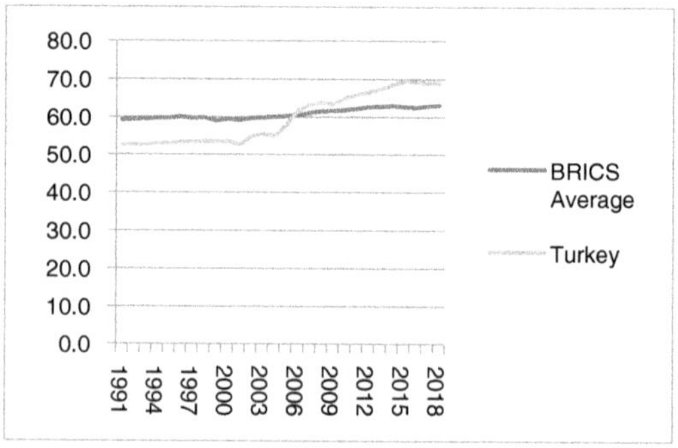

Figure 5.4 Wage and Salaried Workers (M)

Source: World Bank Statistics, 31.12.2020

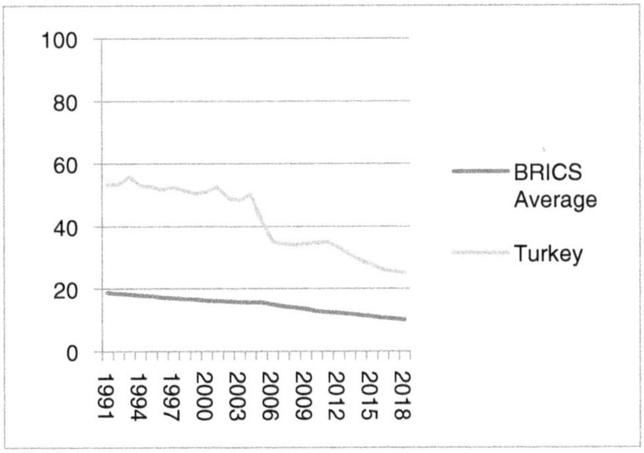

Figure 5.5 Contributing Family Workers (F)
Source: World Bank Statistics, 31.12.2020

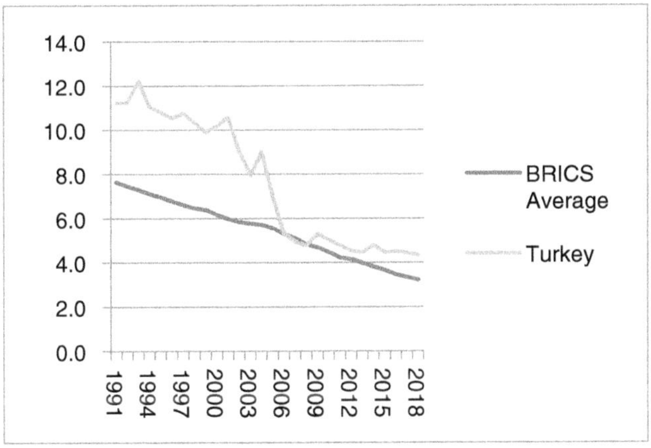

Figure 5.6 Contributing Family Workers (M)
Source: World Bank Statistics, 31.12.2020

Figures 5.5 and 5.6 display data on contributing family workers (World Bank Statistics, 31.12.2020). According to the figures, a definite decrease in average of the BRICS countries and Turkey is observed. This trend is much greater in the male figure.

Female and male unemployment rates are shown in Figures 5.7 and 5.8 (World Bank Statistics, 31.12.2020). Both figures show a non-linear trend over years. However, the male unemployment rate has the same pattern between countries.

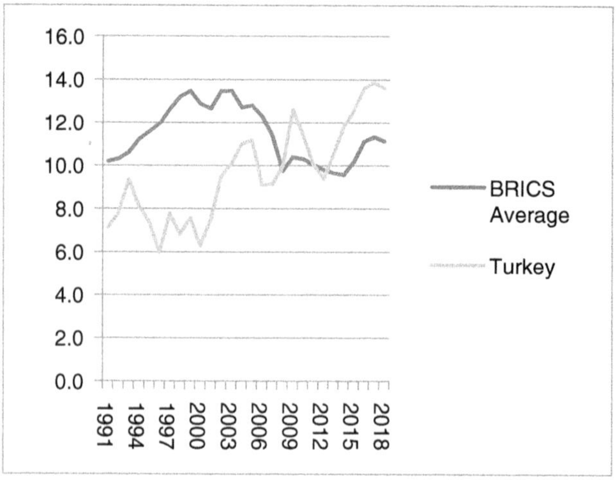

Figure 5.7 Unemployment Rate (F)
Source: World Bank Statistics, 31.12.2020

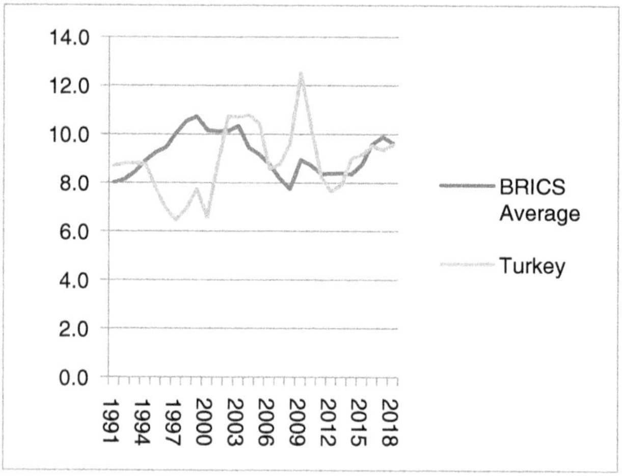

Figure 5.8 Unemployment Rate (M)
Source: World Bank Statistics, 31.12.2020

4 Empirical study

In this section, the BRICS countries and Turkey[1] will be examined with employment rate variables. An econometric model will be created, using the economic growth of these countries.

Many empirical studies based on gender inequality have been working on a global scale. These studies mostly compare developing and developed countries (Löfström, 2009: 10). Altunöz (2019) analyzed the relationship between the eurozone unemployment rate and economic growth between 2000 and 2012 in light of Okun's law. According to the result, the validity of Okun's law has been determined. In their studies Altuzarra et al. (2019) investigated EU-28 countries between 1990 and 2016 and found a U-shaped relationship between female employment and economic growth. Doğan and Akyüz (2017) tested economic growth and female labor force participation rate for the period 2000 to 2013. They applied ARDL model and found a long-term relationship between the variables. Lechman and Kaur (2015) analyzed whether there was a U-shaped relationship between the economic growth and female employment variables for 162 countries between 1990 and 2012. According to results, although this relationship doesn't happen in high-income countries, there is a U-shaped relationship between the two variables in low-income countries. Aydın and Erdem (2014) studied the relationship between competitiveness, economic growth and labor force participation rate for females in 11 countries between 1998 and 2008. They noted there is a positive relationship between female labor force participation rate and GDP growth. Moreover, while female labor force participation rate affects markets in countries with high competitiveness, there is no such relationship in countries with low competitiveness. Luci (2009) tested the relationship between female labor force participation rate and GDP between 1965 and 2004 using panel data analysis for 184 countries. She found a negative relationship between variables. In literature Desai and Joshi (2019), Verick (2018), Stuart et al. (2017). Saqib et al. (2016), Bhoganadam et al. (2014), Mujahid and Zafar (2012), Tsani et al. (2012), Erdem et al. (2016) and Mammen and Paxson (2000) examined the relationship between female employment and economic growth in their studies.

VAR (Vector Auto Regression) analysis is a model used in variables that are stationary at the same level in time or panel data series. VAR models are used without any restrictions on the structural model and do not require endogenous-exogenous separation in variables. However, since the lagged values of the dependent variables are included in the analysis, more robust predictions can be made for the future (Gacener, 2005: 109–110). The Likelihood Ratio (LR), Akaike Information Criterion (AIC), Schwarz Information Criterion (SIC), Final Prediction Error (FPR) and Hannan-Quinn Information Criterion (HQ) tests are generally used to determine the degree of the VAR model. The lag length that meets these criteria minimum is considered the best lag length (Tarı and Bakkal, 2017: 8). Granger causality test: if the lagged values of the independent variable are better than the lagged values of the independent variable, the independent variable is defined as the Granger cause of the dependent variable. Causality is expressed from the independent variable to the dependent variable after the accuracy of this statement is tested (Uluyol and Ekim, 2015: 70–71). If Granger causality analysis is established within the VAR model, Wald test statistics are practiced. Hypotheses based on whether each independent variable affects individually and collectively dependent variables are tested. Variance decomposition is expressed as separate shocks that affect a change in one of the exogenous variables that affect all exogenous variables. Thus, the variance decomposition process gives information about the dynamic structures of the systems. The main purpose of variance decomposition is to reveal the effect of each random shock on the error variance of the prediction for future periods (Sarı, 2008: 4). However, variance decomposition shows how much the percentage of each variable in the model changes, and the percentage of changes that occur in other variables.

In our model, all the variables show linear characteristics except the GDP variable (GDP variable is used by logarithmic form). We collected all data from World Bank statistics and applied E-views software program for econometric analysis.

According to Table 5.7 there is a cross-section dependency problem in variables. We should use the second generation unit root tests for model.

CADF (Cross Sectionally ADF) and CIPS (Cross Sectionally IPS) test statistics are given in Table 5.8. According to results, all variables do not have a unit root in their first difference.

The lag length selection for the female model was made according to the VAR model. Fourteen delays were determined according to the Akaike and the Schwarz criteria.

Table 5.7 Cross-Section Dependency Test

Test (Female)	*Statistics*	*Probability*
LM	26.06	0.0374
LM adj.	1.771	0.0765
LM CD	3.665	0.0002
Test (Male)	*Statistics*	*Probability*
LM	28.15	0.0207
LM adj.	5.409	0.0000
LM CD	0.6683	0.5039

Table 5.8 CADF Test

Variables (Female)	*t bar*	*%1 cv*	*%5 cv*	*%10 cv*	*Z[t bar]*	*P Value*
GDP	–2.065	–2.570	–2.330	–2.210	–0.769	0.221
Difference	–3.591*	–2.570	–2.330	–2.210	–4.624	0.000
Contributing Family Workers	–1.446	–2.570	–2.330	–2.210	0.793	0.786
Difference	–2.381*	–2.570	–2.330	–2.210	–4.624	0.000
Labor Force Participation Rate	–1.551	–2.570	–2.330	–2.210	0.527	0.701
Difference	–2.654*	–2.570	–2.330	–2.210	–2.258	0.012
Unemployment	–1.634	–2.570	–2.330	–2.210	0.317	0.624
Difference	–3.083*	–2.570	–2.330	–2.210	–3.340	0.000
Wage and Salaried Workers	–1.256	–2.570	–2.330	–2.210	1.274	0.899
Difference	–2.685*	–2.570	–2.330	–2.210	–2.336	0.010

Variables (Male)	*t bar*	*%1*	*%5*	*%10*	*Z[t bar]*	*P Value*
GDP	–2.046	–2.570	–2.330	–2.210	–0.721	0.235
Difference	–3.603	–2.570	–2.330	–2.210	–4.654	0.000
Contributing Family Workers	–1.559	–2.570	–2.330	–2.210	0.508	0.694
Difference	–2.680	–2.570	–2.330	–2.210	–2.324	0.010
Labor Force Participation Rate	–1.642	–2.570	–2.330	–2.210	0.297	0.617
Difference	–3.008	–2.570	–2.330	–2.210	–3.151	0.001
Unemployment	–2.188	–2.570	–2.330	–2.210	–1.082	0.140
Difference	–2.882	–2.570	–2.330	–2.210	–2.834	0.002
Wage and Salaried Workers	–1.228	–2.570	–2.330	–2.210	1.342	0.910
Difference	–3.253	–2.570	–2.330	–2.210	–3.769	0.000

Note: Critical values are from Pesaran (2007) Table II(b), respectively.

Table 5.9 CIPS Test

Variables (Female)	*Statistic*	*%1 cv*	*%5 cv*	*%10 cv*
Growth	–2.113	–2.570	–2.330	–2.210
Difference	–4.643*	–2.570	–2.330	–2.210
Contributing Family Workers	–1.657	–2.570	–2.330	–2.210
Difference	–3.781*	–2.570	–2.330	–2.210
Labor Force Participation Rate	–1.426	–2.570	–2.330	–2.210
Difference	–3.012*	–2.570	–2.330	–2.210
Unemployment	–1.075	–2.570	–2.330	–2.210
Difference	–3.440*	–2.570	–2.330	–2.210
Wage and Salary Workers	–1.007	–2.570	–2.330	–2.210
Difference	–3.328*	–2.570	–2.330	–2.210
Variables (Male)	*CIPS*	*%1 cv*	*%5 cv*	*%10 cv*
Growth	–2.103	–2.570	–2.330	–2.210
Difference	–4.643*	–2.570	–2.330	–2.210
Contributing Family Workers	–1.505	–2.570	–2.330	–2.210
Difference	–4.064*	–2.570	–2.330	–2.210
Labor Force Participation Rate	–1.644	–2.570	–2.330	–2.210
Difference	–3.612*	–2.570	–2.330	–2.210
Unemployment	–0.891	–2.570	–2.330	–2.210
Difference	–2.969*	–2.570	–2.330	–2.210
Wage and Salary Workers	–1.285	–2.570	–2.330	–2.210
Difference	–3.737*	–2.570	–2.330	–2.210

Note: Critical values are from Pesaran (2007) Table II(b).

Granger causality analysis performed from the VAR model is given in Table 5.11 for the female model. According to this table unemployment rate and labor force participation rate are the cause of GDP individually. In addition, all variables are totally the Granger cause of GDP.

All variables that in the model have Granger cause each other for individually case and in total case. The probability of this causality is at most 7%.

Finally, contributing family workers and wage and salaried workers variables are the Granger cause of the unemployment rate individually. However, all variables are totally the cause of the unemployment variable.

Variance decomposition analysis for female indicators is shown in Table 5.12. When we look at the 28-year period of employment indicators analyzed in the female population between 1991 and 2018, we can see that the growth rates are affected by their own changes. However, it should be noted that the labor force participation rate, which has been fluctuating over the years, is significant on growth. When the contributing family workers rate is analyzed, it is observed that it is affected by the changes in the growth variable more than its own changes during the period. Similar to this rate, the labor force participation rate is also affected by

Table 5.10 Lag Order Selection from VAR Model (Female)

VAR Lag Order Selection Criteria (Female)
Endogenous variables: DLNGDP DLFPR DCFW DWSW DU
Exogenous variables: C
Sample: 1991 2018
Included observations: 78

Lag	*LogL*	*LR*	*FPE*	*AIC*	*SC*	*HQ*
0	−357.1670	NA	0.007424	9.286332	9.437403	9.346809
1	−291.8947	120.5025	0.002647	8.253711	9.160138	8.616571
2	−263.9529	48.00264	0.002475	8.178280	9.840062	8.843522
3	−235.8643	44.65369	0.002333	8.099085	10.51622	9.066709
4	−202.2474	49.13246	0.001944	7.878137	11.05063	9.148144
5	−179.3201	30.56971	0.002186	7.931284	11.85913	9.503674
6	−147.0396	38.90208	0.002003	7.744606	12.42781	9.619378
7	−85.82836	65.91982	0.000916	6.816112	12.25467	8.993267
8	−39.01710	44.41069	0.000644	6.256849	12.45076	8.736386
9	27.82885	54.84795	0.000295	5.183876	12.13315	7.965796
10	85.79384	40.12961	0.000190	4.338620	12.04324	7.422922
11	145.3225	33.58025	0.000139	3.453270	11.91325	6.839956
12	240.7108	41.57954*	5.25e−05	1.648440	10.86378	5.337509
13	348.3154	33.10910	2.26e−05	−0.469626	9.501065	3.521825
14	**550.0463**	**36.20811**	**2.25e−06***	**−5.001188***	**5.724859***	**−0.707354***

Table 5.11 Granger Causality Test from VAR Model (Female)

VAR Granger Causality/Block ExogeneityWald Tests
Included observations: 78

Dependent variable: DLNGDP			
Excluded	**Chi-sq**	**df**	**Prob.**
DLFPR	26.11708	14	0.0250
DU	21.72405	14	0.0845
All	150.5953	56	0.0000
Dependent variable: DLFPR			
Excluded	**Chi-sq**	**df**	**Prob.**
DLNGDP	23.11256	14	0.0585
DCFW	35.96939	14	0.0011
DWSW	45.08554	14	0.0000
DU	29.54142	14	0.0088
All	224.9783	56	0.0000
Dependent variable: DCFW			
Excluded	**Chi-sq**	**df**	**Prob.**
DLNGDP	22.64545	14	0.0663
DLFPR	30.06039	14	0.0075
DWSW	44.48580	14	0.0000
DU	35.34183	14	0.0013
All	147.9374	56	0.0000
Dependent variable: DWSW			
Excluded	**Chi-sq**	**df**	**Prob.**
DLNGDP	43.37526	14	0.0001
DLFPR	45.06688	14	0.0000
DCFW	58.39647	14	0.0000
DU	65.68567	14	0.0000
All	402.5129	56	0.0000
Dependent variable: DU			
Excluded	**Chi-sq**	**df**	**Prob.**
DCFW	39.79762	14	0.0003
DWSW	34.20983	14	0.0019
All	222.9180	56	0.0000

changes in the growth rate more than its own changes. The unemployment rate is affected by the growth rate and the labor force participation rate more than its own changes in the 28-year period. The wage and salaried workers rate was affected by the labor force participation rate in the first 11 years and then the growth rate. In the following years, it was affected more by the growth rate and less by the labor force participation rate. It is later affected by its own changes.

Table 5.12 Variance Decomposition Model (Female)

DLNGDP

Period	*S.E.*	*DLNGDP*	*DCFW*	*DLFPR*	*DU*	*DWSW*
1	0.074231	100.0000	0.000000	0.000000	0.000000	0.000000
2	0.081617	85.87576	0.413164	11.66721	0.062911	1.980949
3	0.088662	84.43420	2.559287	11.21224	0.091873	1.702408
4	0.111185	64.75628	6.374179	22.36227	3.256425	3.250850
5	0.132575	67.86944	4.547470	22.51141	2.736721	2.334956
6	0.154680	68.24362	3.613997	19.84237	2.996313	5.303700
7	0.202422	64.92248	8.543080	16.26669	7.092557	3.175196
8	0.278111	41.43551	8.032969	38.17281	7.379633	4.979081
9	0.361613	58.55628	5.275892	27.85581	4.365276	3.946734
10	0.425025	53.73282	4.527504	31.75577	3.201604	6.782303
11	0.543104	58.93420	3.729487	28.41376	4.402791	4.519769
12	0.736766	54.89960	3.722412	32.39509	2.775915	6.206978
13	0.937997	63.72079	4.053139	25.38700	2.201599	4.637469
14	1.195151	56.77352	5.472309	29.58123	2.679123	5.493821
15	1.562265	61.62222	4.205385	27.18801	3.084553	3.899833
16	2.040180	61.92058	4.216641	26.67011	1.988315	5.204348
17	2.594368	66.14625	3.962943	23.63520	2.189143	4.066459
18	3.416063	61.03888	4.503321	27.36329	2.269591	4.824915
19	4.468207	63.95808	4.140666	25.54884	2.356001	3.996413
20	5.825530	62.65449	4.370635	26.28767	1.843105	4.844109
21	7.524160	63.79564	4.068524	25.80187	2.221250	4.112709
22	9.915162	61.35845	4.292435	27.63528	2.002556	4.711276
23	12.90042	63.54634	3.925573	26.31741	1.993390	4.217288
24	16.87545	62.33594	4.303669	26.83049	1.873215	4.656686
25	21.89962	62.98125	4.099452	26.58759	2.145518	4.186190
26	28.75187	62.37711	4.263283	26.89598	1.928887	4.534738
27	37.29567	63.39750	4.114766	26.24993	2.028533	4.209273
28	48.81776	62.69149	4.303770	26.61176	1.949227	4.443754

DCFW

Period	*S.E.*	*DLNGDP*	*DCFW*	*DLFPR*	*DU*	*DWSW*
1	0.293449	2.371599	97.62840	0.000000	0.000000	0.000000
2	0.389657	16.94372	77.08631	2.866655	2.314906	0.788407
3	0.402138	16.72037	74.94677	2.826789	4.595959	0.910117
4	0.479274	23.96082	58.55441	2.624669	13.82604	1.034059
5	0.488541	24.82803	56.88768	2.634099	13.75277	1.897420
6	0.524869	23.75726	54.64167	7.124564	12.11382	2.362683
7	0.552998	22.07998	50.23209	12.73969	12.51378	2.434466
8	0.652665	18.66161	41.57769	26.20640	9.794826	3.759481

DCFW						
Period	*S.E.*	*DLNGDP*	*DCFW*	*DLFPR*	*DU*	*DWSW*
9	0.783909	29.76526	35.08086	23.85187	7.260598	4.041416
10	0.809363	31.65683	33.81215	23.64901	6.891753	3.990251
11	0.868634	38.14475	29.35527	21.28975	7.736376	3.473848
12	1.065570	27.19247	26.57365	29.57770	14.02330	2.632883
13	1.407044	37.07896	23.37749	26.96075	10.42061	2.162189
14	1.771995	40.82838	19.70361	28.01128	7.666731	3.789996
15	2.097127	46.54211	16.28141	26.10179	7.536151	3.538537
16	2.737485	54.32786	10.07129	26.21257	5.172064	4.216213
17	3.507761	58.78198	6.194304	27.35236	3.448804	4.222551
18	4.539821	56.67202	5.753462	29.89154	2.528307	5.154667
19	6.101319	53.38944	5.684027	32.88481	3.530243	4.511482
20	8.167949	52.97863	5.488357	33.54516	3.111987	4.875864
21	10.56345	58.94174	5.204550	28.88482	2.492505	4.476382
22	13.46164	59.47822	4.671311	28.92219	2.365547	4.562732
23	17.49261	60.80906	4.349952	28.12182	2.596176	4.122987
24	23.12396	61.33865	4.679142	27.34682	2.278605	4.356780
25	30.09652	62.53970	4.602788	26.46806	2.210603	4.178842
26	39.27499	62.01394	4.723590	26.71521	2.204903	4.342358
27	51.14359	62.94813	4.299043	26.42325	2.160641	4.168933
28	66.81773	63.14857	4.180589	26.36320	1.955854	4.351788

DLFPR						
Period	*S.E.*	*DLNGDP*	*DCFW*	*DLFPR*	*DU*	*DWSW*
1	0.365940	0.000710	61.34189	38.65740	0.000000	0.000000
2	0.481842	32.05321	36.23850	25.72584	2.532861	3.449586
3	0.503781	36.38282	33.16096	23.61646	3.151056	3.688709
4	0.529158	38.29238	30.45936	24.53386	3.176720	3.537681
5	0.600989	30.59728	31.66070	27.04436	7.934452	2.763209
6	0.673483	37.22326	26.76631	26.99205	6.376272	2.642099
7	0.805443	44.85551	24.56951	22.23999	5.578412	2.756579
8	0.935487	42.20297	27.19837	21.78462	5.833263	2.980769
9	1.163643	53.38644	18.64610	20.80299	3.855061	3.309413
10	1.408362	57.40510	13.33843	22.25992	3.061935	3.934622
11	1.743175	61.49061	9.307187	23.00992	2.395688	3.796593
12	2.408380	60.61535	8.038057	24.87771	2.295005	4.173883
13	3.055104	53.12810	7.445534	31.72056	3.165347	4.540459
14	4.084695	60.33003	6.420544	26.57557	2.146249	4.527608
15	5.211042	59.81193	4.868827	28.36123	2.379045	4.578966
16	6.625835	61.91894	4.210879	27.31065	2.180848	4.378684
17	8.816385	63.43904	4.482448	25.77516	1.974116	4.329230

(*Continued*)

Table 5.12 (Continued)

DLFPR						
Period	*S.E.*	*DLNGDP*	*DCFW*	*DLFPR*	*DU*	*DWSW*
18	11.47245	62.08677	4.485522	26.98138	2.223341	4.222989
19	14.88719	62.05284	4.442399	27.01979	2.157832	4.327136
20	19.45275	63.45036	4.346237	25.89828	2.083493	4.221631
21	25.14054	63.06370	4.068620	26.50955	2.059719	4.298413
22	32.85735	63.69514	4.089357	25.99855	1.997488	4.219462
23	42.85004	62.66618	4.101396	26.86096	2.037280	4.334181
24	56.13749	62.72853	4.257003	26.66179	2.067982	4.284689
25	73.33249	62.41525	4.237029	26.94539	2.035778	4.366553
26	95.63976	63.04963	4.114245	26.56625	1.956359	4.313523
27	124.6011	62.83229	4.143327	26.69429	1.964523	4.365567
28	162.6388	63.04678	4.118147	26.56155	1.986682	4.286837

DU						
Period	*S.E.*	*DLNGDP*	*DCFW*	*DLFPR*	*DU*	*DWSW*
1	0.574118	27.25082	4.844893	31.30894	36.59535	0.000000
2	0.836139	16.30142	13.85617	44.88594	23.23423	1.722234
3	0.922832	19.14263	12.84959	43.65086	19.90155	4.455367
4	0.932239	20.23637	12.79522	42.77561	19.76226	4.430534
5	1.000037	19.00919	12.57178	44.10401	20.39566	3.919354
6	1.278371	24.93846	15.56752	38.82536	17.50567	3.162987
7	1.478437	29.09264	15.01037	38.30260	13.86463	3.729763
8	1.628895	37.55044	13.08476	33.71403	11.89868	3.752096
9	1.831771	40.52202	11.48999	31.79184	12.92398	3.272161
10	2.288785	52.68233	8.922245	26.72573	8.572611	3.097079
11	3.058076	59.70422	7.346467	24.14181	5.279931	3.527565
12	3.927389	51.33357	6.853013	31.93908	5.963461	3.910882
13	5.262010	49.49615	6.324528	34.54306	5.254866	4.381392
14	6.940799	54.73934	5.284542	31.72418	3.425230	4.826708
15	8.833749	58.20878	4.146112	30.41887	2.407330	4.818903
16	11.44597	57.31652	4.284420	31.12780	2.612371	4.658884
17	15.20249	56.63492	5.051306	30.88910	2.951338	4.473333
18	20.14252	59.42159	5.487366	28.12984	2.538412	4.422789
19	25.85014	60.77219	4.893006	27.60762	2.390750	4.336442
20	33.29088	61.74078	4.396611	27.30449	2.290220	4.267898
21	43.67332	62.78363	4.308423	26.53307	2.163420	4.211455
22	57.15298	63.19103	4.299989	26.23684	2.042506	4.229633
23	74.54881	62.91202	4.408967	26.33966	2.098237	4.241118
24	97.28755	62.34609	4.425512	26.76966	2.204058	4.254683
25	127.2757	62.59348	4.282029	26.73609	2.115130	4.273274
26	166.1131	62.82516	4.220125	26.63094	2.009064	4.314721
27	216.5179	62.63326	4.195451	26.83311	2.011616	4.326569
28	283.3588	62.54949	4.231547	26.85558	2.032022	4.331368

DWSW

Period	*S.E.*	*DLNGDP*	*DCFW*	*DLFPR*	*DU*	*DWSW*
1	0.359187	4.411660	0.879426	70.19366	0.774117	23.74114
2	0.423293	3.254707	20.15865	54.21383	1.241596	21.13122
3	0.588016	7.934097	26.15731	28.21218	21.59856	16.09785
4	0.724273	6.636477	37.10449	24.86424	19.39796	11.99683
5	0.809767	17.71058	29.77871	24.63516	18.16250	9.713060
6	0.902946	14.39240	27.18799	27.63571	21.68364	9.100259
7	0.933629	17.88507	26.56736	25.85145	20.45435	9.241768
8	1.255317	11.15076	14.73810	53.03973	11.40889	9.662524
9	1.492804	27.66337	12.23392	44.47733	8.083480	7.541893
10	1.734107	21.08502	10.76958	51.48336	7.122867	9.539175
11	1.967544	36.31635	8.578627	40.57297	6.990934	7.541119
12	2.179548	40.62640	6.994002	38.11335	5.720125	8.546120
13	2.536683	53.16812	6.416120	28.14117	5.526059	6.748536
14	3.342794	39.29132	15.37556	31.47624	7.019939	6.836940
15	4.319166	52.62837	13.06169	23.31823	6.833409	4.158300
16	5.330205	54.80838	9.569850	23.92453	4.508298	7.188944
17	6.369676	65.01875	6.720052	19.35944	3.790222	5.111534
18	8.252892	57.16973	4.454839	28.90579	2.498439	6.971206
19	10.76790	63.27656	3.386964	26.07169	2.530244	4.734539
20	14.43155	54.66182	5.791174	30.92536	2.075670	6.545972
21	18.60384	56.72731	5.362535	29.79840	3.456871	4.654881
22	24.57656	54.89687	5.372642	31.31952	2.456751	5.954215
23	31.19746	62.53345	4.095510	26.65687	2.159342	4.554826
24	40.62936	60.99748	4.458874	27.41923	1.750753	5.373661
25	52.38411	63.14512	4.010483	26.27643	2.378117	4.189850
26	69.54495	61.90974	4.664411	26.57647	1.909445	4.939939
27	89.30131	64.12839	4.240269	25.29186	2.227408	4.112077
28	116.7908	62.53758	4.504117	26.33816	1.961100	4.659040

The lag length selection for the male model was made according to the VAR model. Fourteen delays were determined according to the Akaike and Schwarz criteria.

Granger causality analysis from the VAR model is given in Table 5.14 for male model. According to this table, unemployment rate and wage and salaried workers variables are individually the Granger cause of GDP. Also, all variables are the Granger cause of GDP totally.

Labor force participation rate and unemployment rate variables are the Granger cause of contributing family workers variable individually. Also, all variables are the Granger cause of contributing family workers variable totally. Wage and

Table 5.13 Lag Order Selection from VAR Model (Male)

VAR Lag Order Selection Criteria
Endogenous variables: DLNGDP DCFW DLFPR DU DWSW
Exogenous variables: C
Sample: 1991 2018
Included observations: 78

Lag	*LogL*	*LR*	*FPE*	*AIC*	*SC*	*HQ*
0	−173.3459	NA	6.66e-05	4.572971	4.724042	4.633447
1	−125.8835	87.62289	3.75e-05	3.997012	4.903439	4.359871
2	−102.6954	39.83593	3.96e-05	4.043472	5.705253	4.708713
3	−75.70282	42.91127	3.84e-05	3.992380	6.409517	4.960004
4	−51.91108	34.77254	4.12e-05	4.023361	7.195854	5.293368
5	−21.96782	39.92435	3.87e-05	3.896611	7.824459	5.469000
6	14.61377	44.08550	3.17e-05	3.599647	8.282850	5.474419
7	37.49607	24.64248	3.88e-05	3.653947	9.092506	5.831102
8	82.64312	42.83182	2.84e-05	3.137356	9.331270	5.616893
9	127.9120	37.14370	2.26e-05	2.617641	9.566911	5.399561
10	163.6233	24.72321	2.58e-05	2.342992	10.04762	5.427295
11	298.7913	76.24860	2.72e-06	−0.481828	7.978153	2.904858
12	396.0054	42.37538*	9.79e-07	−2.333471	6.881865	1.355597
13	492.1472	29.58211	5.66e-07	−4.157621	5.813070	−0.166170
14	**636.0273**	**25.82462**	**2.49e-07***	**−7.205827***	**3.520219***	**−2.911994***

Table 5.14 Granger Causality Test from VAR Model (Male)

VAR Granger Causality/Block Exogeneity Wald Tests
Sample: 1991 2018
Included observations: 78

Dependent variable: DLNGDP			
Excluded	**Chi-sq**	**df**	**Prob.**
DU	35.32602	14	0.0013
DWSW	24.50768	14	0.0398
All	159.4519	56	0.0000
Dependent variable: DCFW			
Excluded	**Chi-sq**	**df**	**Prob.**
DLFPR	38.25869	14	0.0005
DU	39.37349	14	0.0003
All	149.6239	56	0.0000

Dependent variable: DLFPR			
Excluded	**Chi-sq**	**df**	**Prob.**
DWSW	32.28999	14	0.0036
All	168.0853	56	0.0000
Dependent variable: DU			
Excluded	**Chi-sq**	**df**	**Prob.**
DLFPR	48.00439	14	0.0000
DWSW	26.52031	14	0.0222
All	296.3422	56	0.0000
Dependent variable: DWSW			
Excluded	**Chi-sq**	**df**	**Prob.**
DLNGDP	28.93523	14	0.0107
DCFW	47.39039	14	0.0000
DLFPR	22.25046	14	0.0736
DU	81.71841	14	0.0000
All	354.5558	56	0.0000

salaried workers variable is the Granger cause of labor force participation rate variable individually. However, all variables are the Granger cause of labor force participation rate variable totally. Labor force participation rate and wage and salaried workers variables are the Granger cause of unemployment variable individually. In addition, all variables are totally the Granger cause of unemployment variable. Finally, all variables are the Granger cause of wage and salaried workers variable, both individually and totally. The probability value of the entire model is at 7% maximum.

Variance decomposition analysis for male indicators is shown in Table 5.15. The indicators of employment in the male population are examined between 1991 and 2018; it is observed that the growth rate is affected by the labor force participation rate and secondly from its own changes, and then it is affected by the contributing family workers rate. Contributing family workers rate is primarily affected by the growth rate, then affected by labor force participation rate and unemployment rate respectively. This variable is especially affected very little by its own changes after 1999. Although the labor force participation rate is affected by most of its own changes, it is later affected by the growth rate. Contributing family workers rate was effective in the first periods and then lost its effect. The unemployment rate is most affected by its own changes. This is followed by the growth rate and the labor force participation rate. Finally, the rate of wage and salaried workers is minimally affected by its change; labor force participation rate, growth rate, unemployment rate and contributing family workers rates explain this variable respectively.

Table 5.15 Variance Decomposition Model (Male)

DLNGDP

Period	*S.E.*	*DLNGDP*	*DCFW*	*DLFPR*	*DU*	*DWSW*
1	0.072229	100.0000	0.000000	0.000000	0.000000	0.000000
2	0.101226	52.97723	41.77909	2.195647	1.721344	1.326689
3	0.122118	38.71498	29.13822	26.19566	1.685596	4.265543
4	0.135114	38.07016	24.75596	27.76218	1.378628	8.033072
5	0.158634	27.62495	21.39505	32.08989	11.48149	7.408616
6	0.234102	29.97194	9.833441	20.02961	35.03401	5.131004
7	0.313464	31.26196	18.82207	17.64740	29.22681	3.041757
8	0.434285	26.85302	19.50946	30.99873	18.44499	4.193804
9	0.594701	31.11920	14.98023	34.85496	13.88913	5.156486
10	0.729099	28.48127	17.05356	41.42059	9.578269	3.466311
11	0.804386	23.41789	16.31697	43.55140	13.49806	3.215685
12	0.878173	23.41690	15.38616	36.64861	21.19331	3.355029
13	1.162831	26.99853	15.28408	26.31500	27.42590	3.976499
14	1.735925	29.48080	15.88386	23.38504	27.23606	4.014240
15	2.398701	28.89471	17.24825	30.19636	20.61185	3.048832
16	2.917719	26.80788	17.98359	38.16768	14.53207	2.508773
17	3.189884	23.84843	17.68640	43.83520	12.49552	2.134443
18	3.400795	22.31074	15.68746	41.15213	18.55069	2.298985
19	4.355704	24.54200	14.95211	27.56353	29.75436	3.187996
20	6.398821	26.96234	15.16371	25.55886	28.51685	3.798234
21	8.993789	27.54511	16.32233	29.73754	22.78759	3.607439
22	11.40479	25.96606	17.84686	35.98278	17.35305	2.851259
23	12.76259	23.75252	17.76285	42.26336	13.87168	2.349593
24	13.28774	21.92016	16.43157	42.77424	16.57145	2.302585
25	15.32853	22.58277	14.76116	32.75514	26.69693	3.204004
26	21.64856	26.00306	14.69977	24.49868	30.96407	3.834418
27	31.37648	26.93158	16.54695	26.50045	26.66369	3.357328
28	41.14579	26.40714	17.56332	32.46992	20.69100	2.868617

DCFW

Period	*S.E.*	*DLNGDP*	*DCFW*	*DLFPR*	*DU*	*DWSW*
1	0.116411	2.645318	97.35468	0.000000	0.000000	0.000000
2	0.180873	20.99393	59.10099	12.83745	7.018105	0.049524
3	0.187940	21.83094	55.18101	14.24027	6.644044	2.103739
4	0.199454	27.13588	48.99750	13.64859	6.356702	3.861333
5	0.243371	19.02817	40.83629	22.97895	13.80983	3.346769
6	0.347619	21.03723	20.37123	23.51945	33.40356	1.668538
7	0.440959	25.62972	28.53695	15.20239	29.56411	1.066832
8	0.652482	30.94295	24.04523	24.06676	18.13734	2.807727

DCFW

Period	*S.E.*	*DLNGDP*	*DCFW*	*DLFPR*	*DU*	*DWSW*
9	0.927741	34.49604	17.13604	30.33396	13.21846	4.815496
10	1.159035	29.60996	17.73532	40.78448	8.475102	3.395131
11	1.319759	22.99727	16.52562	46.81780	10.98332	2.675992
12	1.457083	22.31982	13.74126	39.79309	21.12320	3.022628
13	1.918051	25.68801	13.22002	26.15176	30.26601	4.674193
14	2.902115	29.93196	14.01210	23.58218	27.82603	4.647725
15	4.077772	30.16203	16.31728	30.59784	19.36763	3.555225
16	5.089079	27.31045	18.05332	38.34417	13.54593	2.746129
17	5.622384	24.36823	17.75631	44.29929	11.29369	2.282478
18	5.988546	22.42930	15.67367	42.14183	17.33330	2.421899
19	7.534885	25.10820	14.08146	28.18469	29.30260	3.323051
20	11.04052	28.12934	14.65643	24.06489	29.30501	3.844334
21	15.81059	28.26731	16.48177	28.45201	23.27292	3.525992
22	20.39299	26.31005	17.93437	35.59212	17.31485	2.848622
23	23.12027	24.02611	17.64987	42.42924	13.52403	2.370754
24	24.14764	22.02622	16.34981	43.85006	15.50647	2.267441
25	27.53729	22.74627	14.55653	33.99241	25.48845	3.216328
26	38.74731	25.92501	14.63670	25.10355	30.40614	3.928598
27	56.49181	26.81914	16.48804	26.94510	26.26247	3.485259
28	74.67065	26.30068	17.56908	32.73335	20.45066	2.946225

DLFPR

Period	*S.E.*	*DLNGDP*	*DCFW*	*DLFPR*	*DU*	*DWSW*
1	0.326538	3.911871	46.75636	49.33177	0.000000	0.000000
2	0.428658	11.78698	39.77946	45.31529	1.230336	1.887936
3	0.432034	12.09514	39.43428	44.96634	1.574393	1.929850
4	0.450271	16.51746	38.00220	41.39906	1.508043	2.573241
5	0.554094	23.17219	33.65648	39.21970	2.007309	1.944318
6	0.660009	22.45336	29.58099	42.33770	2.948983	2.678971
7	0.683982	24.03021	28.84718	40.71138	3.068451	3.342781
8	0.758804	19.70164	29.46183	43.79924	2.768767	4.268523
9	0.833756	19.55101	24.40576	40.12379	12.18263	3.736816
10	1.000474	19.35608	26.34954	30.78080	20.54111	2.972469
11	1.375976	25.66382	22.74620	26.66126	21.91693	3.011794
12	1.882764	31.60950	18.00088	28.11198	18.95431	3.323337
13	2.296966	25.80476	18.14614	37.75787	15.23640	3.054831
14	2.484681	24.23697	16.53490	43.11599	13.02140	3.090749
15	2.582618	22.43843	15.45510	42.32676	16.39297	3.386736
16	3.136490	24.02064	11.81620	28.91677	30.49311	4.753277
17	4.421503	25.67342	15.08395	23.04093	32.22999	3.971714

(*Continued*)

Table 5.15 (Continued)

DLFPR

Period	*S.E.*	*DLNGDP*	*DCFW*	*DLFPR*	*DU*	*DWSW*
18	6.226767	24.87105	16.51807	30.73778	24.47527	3.397831
19	8.024156	26.43784	15.68790	34.35599	20.09975	3.418512
20	9.312137	25.84970	16.89665	38.41853	16.16461	2.670510
21	9.877488	23.28809	16.15181	41.85834	16.24477	2.456982
22	10.77681	22.52622	14.79673	35.19538	24.92859	2.553083
23	13.91531	24.42180	14.69107	26.37619	31.15497	3.355970
24	20.31956	27.03759	15.20917	23.95391	30.04224	3.757093
25	28.22490	26.68223	17.13456	29.11307	24.01960	3.050543
26	34.39878	25.51714	17.61643	36.21553	18.03927	2.611631
27	37.44103	24.13149	17.12326	41.20072	15.23957	2.304956
28	38.99541	22.42730	15.80180	40.59053	18.74931	2.431064

DU

Period	*S.E.*	*DLNGDP*	*DCFW*	*DLFPR*	*DU*	*DWSW*
1	0.392676	4.814786	4.740262	0.767066	89.67789	0.000000
2	0.515534	23.66656	7.050408	2.442900	66.78280	0.057338
3	0.694077	34.70308	9.876976	10.09045	45.16680	0.162691
4	0.916095	37.44314	12.12950	19.67580	26.60245	4.149106
5	1.323570	30.26172	14.68696	39.55729	12.74458	2.749448
6	1.605385	21.90499	12.66039	48.72829	14.70308	2.003245
7	1.822253	20.79212	9.948275	40.29302	26.88423	2.082360
8	2.339029	28.30266	10.12086	26.99237	30.01572	4.568395
9	3.640784	30.19023	13.47339	25.43569	26.00518	4.895504
10	5.338243	29.30539	17.14644	31.20008	18.71628	3.631806
11	6.605133	27.59868	18.72407	38.09039	12.89118	2.695688
12	7.286537	24.74340	17.79340	44.08775	11.14583	2.229630
13	7.730826	23.13911	15.83458	41.65297	17.06511	2.308221
14	9.679434	26.01922	14.19810	27.87310	28.47635	3.433231
15	14.43879	28.76297	15.14077	22.45508	29.97984	3.661339
16	20.69157	29.32738	16.87416	27.35191	23.16670	3.279847
17	26.54018	27.15268	17.93071	35.14942	16.96563	2.801561
18	30.16870	24.58384	17.52269	42.34132	13.16814	2.384016
19	31.73209	22.22117	16.13796	44.20644	15.16523	2.269210
20	36.61023	22.99407	14.14362	33.38933	26.26983	3.203159
21	51.79852	26.06366	14.76259	24.81691	30.45797	3.898865
22	75.61524	27.07572	16.37826	27.36566	25.61431	3.566053
23	100.0364	26.48761	17.33555	33.24940	19.87387	3.053563
24	117.2164	25.14003	17.64189	39.30990	15.36723	2.540946
25	124.3711	23.09297	16.99637	43.13270	14.51458	2.263376
26	133.9832	22.11696	15.12487	37.57854	22.46108	2.718549
27	175.1079	24.52350	14.69638	26.14176	31.16943	3.468932
28	256.3302	26.63084	15.91398	24.72435	29.21812	3.512717

DWSW

Period	*S.E.*	*DLNGDP*	*DCFW*	*DLFPR*	*DU*	*DWSW*
1	0.247924	17.69684	4.026046	5.320052	41.20166	31.75540
2	0.400397	24.46856	11.86748	2.255074	47.70683	13.70206
3	0.492387	32.30141	17.56366	9.063246	31.97345	9.098231
4	0.562712	24.80944	16.02652	24.40182	26.27513	8.487078
5	0.618972	20.65802	13.30963	32.36595	23.89872	9.767678
6	0.744971	20.20538	9.990895	27.61097	33.72981	8.462940
7	1.160225	33.16063	5.012382	11.54124	42.69362	7.592123
8	1.848074	33.74612	16.15584	16.74327	28.86505	4.489714
9	2.727339	29.16746	19.85977	31.01317	16.61898	3.340620
10	3.478613	28.34841	17.98621	39.37005	11.17136	3.123959
11	3.889927	24.83222	17.70682	45.35733	9.583985	2.519639
12	4.173936	22.61511	15.43191	43.37497	15.52117	3.056848
13	5.321913	25.11400	13.67791	28.53612	28.66891	4.003069
14	7.842854	28.61578	15.78501	23.05483	28.48256	4.061825
15	11.36895	29.48907	17.44098	27.36872	22.44785	3.253390
16	14.60627	27.91195	18.08861	34.89758	16.36315	2.738720
17	16.64397	25.29969	17.97151	41.81850	12.61879	2.291512
18	17.57193	22.70114	16.55531	44.04449	14.54898	2.150086
19	20.32466	23.55161	14.57912	32.94824	26.01143	2.909597
20	29.05788	26.65873	15.49288	23.77715	30.60236	3.468878
21	42.36852	27.57821	16.45744	26.87144	25.59841	3.494503
22	56.32186	27.04314	17.00697	33.08084	19.70978	3.159275
23	66.50486	25.26478	17.64179	39.47843	15.01901	2.595990
24	70.97371	22.89495	16.95596	43.73469	14.12527	2.289132
25	76.51777	21.88031	15.18079	38.04042	22.20171	2.696763
26	99.90192	24.46955	14.74045	26.77422	30.46771	3.548058
27	146.4154	26.75224	15.71516	25.13791	28.74608	3.648614
28	202.4179	27.01214	16.91551	29.69646	23.18543	3.190457

5 Conclusions

The terms "production" and "consumption" have been crucial throughout human history. However, the secret word here is "employment". In one economy, if there are no individuals employed, neither production nor the goods and services resulting from this process can be mentioned. Even though employment is mostly used in a microeconomic meaning today, it can also mean whether all production factors are used in the macroeconomic field. Our study focused on the microeconomic meaning. The term "employment" started to be critical with the industrial revolution when countries began to transform into industrial economies. This situation allowed employment in industry to increase, mass production to increase and the capitalist doctrine to progress. Gender inequality and male-dominated employment in previous centuries largely ended after World War II. This was related to the United States's desire to spread the capitalist doctrine and women's need to gain economic independence. Also the decline of the male population after the war forced women to work in industrial sectors.

The increase in female employment in developing countries has not been the same in developed countries. This case is in favor of the male population in developing countries, and there were many reasons for this. One of the important reasons is the role of women in society; most of the women in these kinds of countries are employed as a contributing family worker. In addition, the low wage rates in these countries have paved the way for women to deal with family affairs rather than work.

In this study, Turkey is examined, along with emerging countries Brazil, Russia, India, China and South Africa. In an econometric model, the dependent and independent variables are respectively: GDP, unemployment rate, wage and salaried workers, contributing family workers and labor force participation rate. Almost all variables have causalities of each other. However, the female contributing family workers variable is negatively less effective on GDP than the male variable. Labor force participation rate variable is negatively more robust on GDP for females compared to males. Finally, the unemployment rate variable of males affects GDP more negatively than the unemployment variable of females. This result shows that women also affect economic growth, just as men do. For all countries, increasing female employment rate is essential for economic growth. This will bring a quantitative growth as well as a qualitative growth that will eliminate gender inequality.

The increase in the labor force participation rate of females will also affect women who are unemployed and will bring pressure for increasing labor force participation rates. This will alert policy makers to create new job fields. Also it will bring various solutions, such as micro credit. In recent years, especially in developed countries, researches that will provide positive discrimination of women in the economy, preparation of reports and even the emergence of new economy departments and thoughts are the result of these pressures.

It can be predicted that this increase in female employment in developed countries will gradually change the labor market structure of developing and underdeveloped countries. Especially after the 1970s, globalization, consumption, production and labor market structures have become more highly developed and diversified. This situation gradually eliminates gender discrimination in the economy. In the coming years, differentiation of human needs is expected with both monopolistic competition market structure and social media. This situation will bring an increase in consumption and production. Therefore, it can be predicted that female as well as male employment will increase. This situation is likely to occur especially in developing and underdeveloped countries where labor costs are cheap. Considered one of the most important developing country groups of the 21st century, BRICS will play a key role in this regard. However, many Middle East and Asian countries may be considered to benefit from this situation, too, even though some of them do not have formal cooperation. As a result, the term of wage reduction has different implications for the labor supply and the labor demand owners in the market.

Note

1 Turkey and BRICS countries have similarities with many macroeconomic indicators, especially foreign trade volume and foreign direct investment.

References

Ahiakpor, James C. W. (1997). Full Employment: A Classical Assumption or Keynes's Rhetorical Device? *Southern Economic Journal*, 64, July, 1–41.

Altunöz, Utku. (2019). The Relationship between Real Output (Real GDP) and Unemployment Rate: An Analysis of Okun's Law for Eurozone. *Sosyoekonomi*, 27(40), 197–210.

Altuzarra, Amaia, Galvez Galvez, Catalina and Gonzales-Flores, Ana. (2019). Economic Development and Female Labour Force Participation: The Case of European Union Countries. *Sustainability*, 11(7), 1962, 1–18.

Aydın, Fatma Fehime and Erdem, Ekrem. (2014). The Effect of Women's Employment on Competitiveness and Economic Growth: A Comparison of Turkey and The Most Competitive Countries. *Erciyes Üniversitesi İktisadi ve İdari Bilimler Fakültesi Dergisi*, (44), 59–71.

Bhoganadam, Syamala Devi, Malini, Hema and Rao, Dasaraju Srinivasa. (2014). Women's Empowerment and Economic Development. *EIJMMS*, 4(8), 100–107.

Chaudhry, Imran Sharif, Faridi, Muhammad Zahir and Gul, Ejaz (2011). The Classical-Keynesian Paradigm: Policy Debate in Contemporary Era. MPRA Paper No: 53920.

Cifre Eva, Vera Maria, Sánchez-Cardona Israel and de Cuyper, Nele. (2018). Sex, Gender Identity, and Perceived Employability among Spanish Employed and Unemployed Youngsters. *Frontiers Psychology*, 9(2467).

<data.worldbank.gov>, 10.11.2019.

Desai, Sonalde and Joshi, Omkar. (2019). The Paradox of Declining Female Work Participation in an Era of Economic Growth. *The Indian Journal of Labour Economics*, (62), 55–71.

Doğan, Buhari and Akyüz, Mürsel. (2017). Female Labor Force Participation Rate and Economic Growth in the Framework of Kuznets Curve: Evidence from Turkey. *Review of Economic and Business Studies*, 10(5), 33–54.

Duflo, Esther. (2012). Women Empowerment and Economic Development. *Journal of Economic Literature*, 50(4), 1051–1079.

Erdem, Ekrem, Yücel, Ali Gökhan and Köseoğlu, Ahmet. (2016). Female Labour Force Participation and Economic Growth: Theoretical and Empirical Evidence. *The Empirical Economics Letters*, 15(10), 985–991.

Eurofound (2016). *The Gender Employment Gap: Challenges and Solutions*. Publications Office of the European Union, Luxembourg.

Ewubare, Dennis Brown and Ogbuagu, Anuli Regina. (2017). Unemployment Rate, Gender Inequality and Economic Growth in Nigeria: A Short-Run Impact Analysis. *Global Journal of Human Resource Management*, 5(5), 12–41.

Gacener, Aydanur. (2005). Türkiye Açısından Wagner Kanunu'nun Geçerliliğinin Analizi. *Dokuz Eylül Üniversitesi İktisadi ve İdari Bilimler Fakültesi Dergisi*, 20(1), 103–122.

<https://ilostat.ilo.org/topics>, 01.08.2020.

Humpert, Stephan and Pfeifer, Christian. (2012). Explaining Age and Gender Differences in Employment Rates: A Labor Supply-Side Perspective. *Journal for Labour Market Research*, 46(1).

İnce Yenilmez, Meltem. (2017). Kadın Güçlendirmesi ve Toplumsal Cinsiyet Eşitsizliğinin Ölçülmesi: Türkiye Örneği. Manisa Celal Bayar University. *Journal of Management and Economy*, 24(2), 485–503.

İnce Yenilmez, Meltem. (2019). Female Employment and Care Economy in Turkey. *Sosyoloji Araştırmaları Dergisi*, 22(1), 69–95.

Kapucugil İkiz, Aysun. (2015). Dünya'da ve Türkiye'de İstatistiklerle Çalışan Anneler. Book Chapter in Çalış Anne, Editor: *Olca Sürgevil Dalkılıç*, 149–213, Ankara.

Klasen, Stephan and Lamanna, Francesca. (2009). The Impact of Gender Inequality in Education and Employment on Economic Growth: New Evidence for a Panel of Countries. *Feminist Economics*, 15(3), 91–132.

Klasen, Stephan and Minasyan, Anna. (2017). Gender Inequality and Growth in Europe. *Intereconomics*, 52(1), 17–23.

Lagarde, Christine. (2019). A Global Imperative. *Finance and Development*, 56(1). https://www.imf.org/external/pubs/ft/fandd/2019/03/pdf/fd0319.pdf [Accessed on 01 August 2020].

Lechman, Ewa and Kaur, Harleen. (2015). Economic Growth and Female Labor Force Participation: Verifying the U-Feminization Hypothesis: New Evidence for 162 Countries over the Period 1990–2012. *Economics and Sociology*, 8(1), 246–257.

Löfström, Asa. (2009). *Gender Equality, Economic Growth and Employment*. Swedish Ministry of Integration and Gender Equality, Sweden.

Luci, Angela. (2009). Female Labour Market Participation and Economic Growth. *International Journal of Innovation and Sustainable Development*, 4(2/3), 97–108.

Mammen, Kristin and Paxson, Christina. (2000). Women's Work and Economic Development. *The Journal of Economic Perspectives*, 14(4), 141–164.

Moyser, Melissa (2017). Women in Canada: A Gender-Based Statistical Report. Women and Paid Work. Statistics Canada, Catalogue No: 89-503-X.

Mujahid, Nooreen and Zafar, Naeem Uz. (2012). Economic Growth-Female Labour Force Participation Nexus: An Empirical Evidence for Pakistan. *The Pakistan Development Review*, 51(4), 565–586.

Otobe, Naoko. (2017). Gender Dimensions of Employment Trends and Future of Work: Where Would Women Work Next? International Labour Office, Employment Working Paper No: 222, Geneve.

Pesaran, Hashem. (2007). A Simple Panel Unit Root Test in the Presence of Cross-Section Dependence. *Journal of Applied Econometrics*, 22(2), 265–312.

Perron, Diane. (2009). Women and Gender Equity in Employment Patterns, Progress and Challenges. IES Working Paper No: 23.

Saqib, Najia, Aggarwal, Priyanka and Rashid, Saima. (2016). Women Empowerment and Economic Growth: Empirical Evidence from Saudi Arabia. *Advances in Management & Applied Economics*, 6(5), 79–92.

Sarı, Aydın. (2008). Parasalcı Görüşe Göre Türkiye'de Ödemeler Bilançosu Dengesinin Sağlanmasında Otomatik Denkleşme Mekanizmalarının Etkinliği. *Cumhuriyet Üniversitesi İktisadi ve İdari Bilimler Dergisi*, 9(2), 1–12.

Stirati, Antonella. (2012). Employment Theory in the History of Economic thought: An Overview. Roma Tre Universita Degli Studi, Working Paper: 148/2012.

Stuart, Sheila, Geny, Lydia Rosa, and Abdulkadri, Abdullahi. (2017). Advancing the Economic Empowerment and Autonomy of Women in the Caribbean through the 2030 Agenda for Sustainable Development. ECLAC – Studies and Perspectives Series – The Caribbean – No. 60.

Tarı, Recep and Bakkal, Hakan (2017). Türkiye'de İşsizliğin Belirleyicileri. *Kocaeli Üniversitesi Sosyal Bilimler Dergisi*, 33, 1–18.

Tsani, Stella, Paroussos, Leonidas, Fragiadakis, Costas, Charalambidis, Ioannis and Capros, Pantelis. (2012). Female Labour Force Participation and Economic Development in Southern Mediterranean Countries: What scenarios for 2030?, MEDPRO Technical Report No. 19.

Uluyol, Osman and Ekim, Samiye (2015). Bankacılık Sektörünün Karlılığı ile Mevduat Faiz Oranları Arasındaki İlişkinin Johansen Eşbütünleşme ve Granger Nedensellik Testi ile Araştırılması. *Journal of Economics, Finance & Accounting*, 2(1), 58–74.

UNDP. (2013). Humanity Divided: Confronting Inequality in Developing Countries. UNDP Report, USA.

Verick, Sher. (2018). Female Labor Force Participation and Development, IZA World of Labor, No: 87.

6 The relationship between minimum wages and youth employment in OECD countries

M. Akif Arvas

1 Introduction

It has long been understood that there must be labour market frictions and/or multiple equilibria for minimum wages to have beneficial effects (at least for the supply side of the market). Perhaps the strongest argument for the beneficial effects of government-imposed pay policies is the multiple equilibria case (see Van den Berg, 2003). Many labour market models show multiple equilibria, in the sense that a given set of primitive values of characteristics defining labour market structure can generate two or more labour market equilibria. Each equilibrium is proper in the sense that any agent in the equilibrium has no incentive to change its behaviour (Nash equilibrium). Wage policy, as one possible instrument among many, offers the possibility for the policymaker to select among equilibria, something that is not available to the economist or econometrician. Consider the simple case where two possible equilibria exist, and where both are associated with a unique equilibrium wage rate (Waldman, 2001). Now imagine that the two equilibria can be Pareto-ranked, meaning that in one equilibrium every agent is at least as well-off as in the other, with some being strictly better off, and that the preferred equilibrium is associated with the higher equilibrium wage rate. Then a minimum wage that surmounts or remains under the equilibrium market wage level results in disequilibrium for all labour market agents.

On the other hand, as pointed out in Stigler (1946), in a monopsonistic market the firm will optimally set employment below competitive equilibrium levels in order to pay a lower wage than the competitive one. In such a consideration, a positive minimum wage impact is expected, because it takes the ability to determine salaries out of the firm's control. Through eliminating the incentive to keep jobs 'artificially' low, the business will both pay the higher (mandated) wage and raise its level of employment – thus amounting to advantageous situation for the supply side of the market. The firm is worse off, of course, but it is still possible for it to earn positive profits depending the current level minimum wage.

The smaller the proportion of the economy left uncovered by the minimum wage law, the larger will be the proportion of diminished employment produced by that law that will be moved into the state of unemployment. The individuals who will be most antagonistically influenced by a legitimate the lowest pay permitted by law will be low-wage labourers. Therefore, low-wage workers are most intensively and most immediately touched by such laws. Low-wage workers who will be forced into second-best employment or into unemployment by minimum wage laws systematically include young people, minorities, the elderly, the handicapped, and those without skill (Rottenberg, 1981: 4).

The labour force or currently active population includes all individuals who meet the prerequisites for involvement in the workforce (the armed forces plus civil jobs) or the unemployed. Employees are described as those who work for pay or benefits for at least one hour a week, or who are employed but are temporarily out of work due to illness, leave or industrial action (OECD Employment Outlook, 2019).

A few decades ago, researches in the time series showed that a 10% increase in minimum wage would be correlated with a 1% to 3% drop in youth jobs (Brown, Gilroy, and Kohen, 1983). Because of the intrinsic challenges of drawing meanings from econometric studies, numerous ongoing examinations have used alternative methodologies to better determine the exact relationship between the both variables. Many studies assert that businesses, governments and sectors include varying ratios of workers whose wages are sensitive to any change in minimum wage policy (Currie and Fallick, 1996). Moreover, politicians generally advocate minimum wage policy in order to reduce poverty by raising income level of workers. Nevertheless, increases in some young workers' salaries owing to a minimum wage creates a disadvantageous case for others. Minimum wages reduce youth employment prospects and generate joblessness. Employees are missing out on work training programs that would equipped with high skills and also would have led to higher salaries later. Young people who cannot find jobs need to be helped by their families or the social welfare system. Late participation in the labour market limits young unskilled workers 'lifetime income levels' (Kalenkoski, 2016).

Since economic fluctuations and global crisis have worsened the business cycles and industrial production, more actions are seen to be done to provide youth with skills that meet the demands of firms in global competition and help them to have a good position in the labour market while seeking a prestigious career, in OECD countries.

The studies revealing the minimum wage impacts on employment date back almost a hundred years by the seminal work by Obenauer and Nienburg (1915). However, given this long past, researchers are critical of the [negative] impact of minimum wages on employment, specifically when researchers use datasets from different resources or apply newly developed empirical approaches. For these reasons, a negative relationship in a study can be accompanied by a positive relationship in another study. This study's contribution is to analyse the impact of minimum wage on youth employment rate for OECD countries, in which case adult employment rate is generally taken as a dependant variable for empirical purposes. As far as we know, this is the first study that takes youth employment rate as dependant variable and splits it up into three groups: (i) total youth employment, (ii) male youth employment and (ii) female youth employment, with an attempt to reveal any differences in the consequences of minimum wage level on genders.

2 Minimum wage issue in economic theory

In reality, first proposed by David Ricardo and other classical economists, wage theory was based on the Thomas Malthus population theory. The labour market price would always shift towards the minimum level of equilibrium, according to Malthus. If the supply of labour rose, the wage level declines, leading to a fall in the supply of labour. If the wage grew above the subsistence level, however, the population would rise until the greater labour-power would push wages down once again.

Mainstream Classical theory hypothesise that wages are equal to the marginal output of labour, i.e. the contribution of the additional labour input unit to total production. Therefore, any increase in jobs is generally associated with lower real wage levels, as employment increases. However, it is due to workers' refusal to accept the lower wages which corresponds to the decreasing marginal product of labour, and which results in persistence of unemployment.

Alternatively, Keynes specifically rejected the thesis that unemployment would disappear if workers accepted low wages enough. He regarded wage cuts to remedy unemployment as meaningless both from the theoretical and practical points of view. He considered such a step as highly anti-moral and anti-social. At their high time, Keynesian economist pioneered by Myrdal, Samuelson, Gunnar and Tobin were sceptical about the minimum wage. Tobin (in 1973), for instance, pointed out (www.econlib.org/archives/2011/03/keynesian_polit.html):

> I am against minimum wage legislation and have said so. It diminishes job opportunities, ceteris paribus, and it is an inefficient and haphazard tool for income maintenances or redistribution. At the same time, it does contribute to the existence of a Phillips trade-off, at least in the short run; this is because it makes for asymmetry in the response of wages to changes in demand and in rates of inflation.

What the Keynesians were critical about actually was the statement that workers who lack the capacity to live decently would not be satisfied or helped by minimum wages or trade union wage pressures. Therefore, basically, they argue that employment rate in an economy is essentially determined by effective demand but not by wage bargains between employers and workers.

The traditional Neoclassical theory postulates that when an increase in the minimum wage in a competitive market occurs then a firm will answer to it in two ways: first reducing the demand for jobs and, second, exchanging high skilled labour production for low skilled workers whose wages have increased.

Their economists emphasise that the conditions of the labour market are somewhat different. There are topics on the labour market with different market strength. Employers have a dominant position, primarily determined by greater market power and a higher level of information, and apply this when negotiating wages, in particular, whereas employees have disproportionately smaller market power and their information is imperfect. Only market power and information asymmetry describe imperfect competition on the labor market, whether it has a particular form of monopsony, oligopsony or monopsonic composition. Wages are often determined on a collective bargaining basis, which represents the governments, businesses and trade unions' decision making. Challenges to the current institutional framework change labour market outcomes: pay and employment. The definition of markets regulated by formal and informal sets of rules is set by employers, trade unions or the state to decide the hiring of jobs, the filling of vacancies, the recruitment of staff, relocations, temporary dismissals and or retirements has become the foundation of the theory of dual markets (Doeringer and Piore, 1985). Under conditions of imperfect information, asymmetric market power, conflict and non-cooperative strategies, one becomes under the control of institutions setting the rules, deforming markets and imposing barriers and restrictions on market agents' rational behaviour (Brozova, 2018: 31–32).

The main inference from the Neoclassical theory is that an upward movement in minimum wages lead to adverse employment effects, in other words, minimum wage increase drives employment rate to fall, which case is illustratively depicted in Figure 6.1.

In Figure 6.1, on the vertical axis the hourly wage for workers is presented, while on the horizontal axis employment is shown. Equilibrium condition in the labour market occurs where labour supply intersects labour demand at the point E (Equilibrium), at which market equilibrium wage is W^E and equilibrium employment level for labour input is L^E, without government intervention. Labour demand

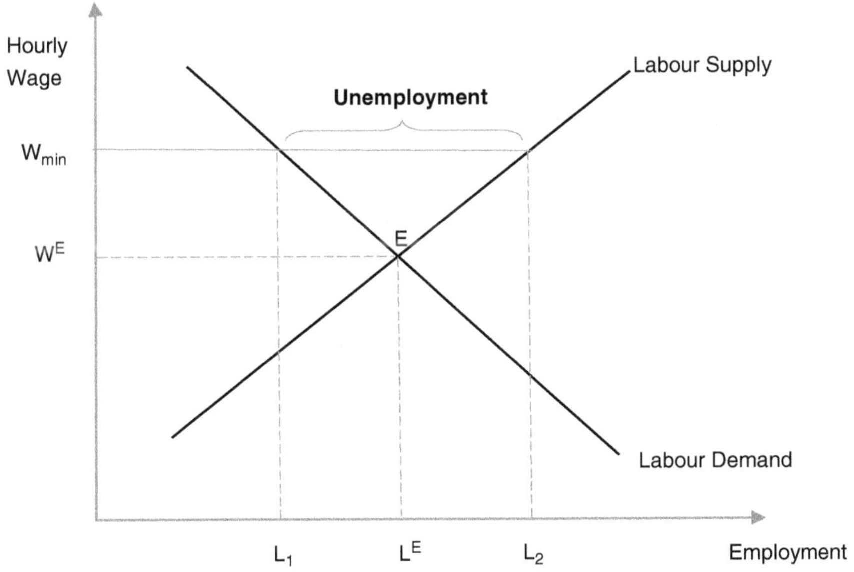

Figure 6.1 Minimum Wage and Employment Relationship

Source: Author's illustration

curve is downward sloping since at low level of wages firms are more willing to hire labour inputs, whereas labour supply curve is upward sleeping reflecting a positive connection between high level of wages and supply of labour, in which case higher hourly wage causes more workers to work more.

Now, assume that a minimum wage (W_{min}) is imposed by government on labour market aiming to boost workers' payoffs (on the horizontal line). Since minimum wage enforcement would increase the marginal cost per workers, firms will cut back on hiring workers. In this case, minimum wage surmounts the equilibrium wage, at which level labour demand shifts to left from the previous level of L^E to L_1, indicating that less jobs are now available, an amount of workers will no longer be in labour market, even though they are more satisfied at this new level of wage, the minimum wage. In effect, while at minimum wage the quantity of labour demand is L_1, the quantity of labour supply is L_2, reflecting an unemployment effect equivalent to L_1–L_2 distance.

3 Youth employment and wages in OECD area

The world's population is about 7.5 billion. China, by itself, accounts for 18,5% and India for 17,7%, respectively. In 2018, OECD members accounted for 17,3% of the world's population of 7.5 billion. Within the OECD, in 2018 (the most recent year), the United States accounted for 25% of the OECD total, followed by Japan (9,7%), Mexico (9,6%), Germany (6,3%) and Turkey (6,3%).

The UN defines those persons aged 15–24 as 'youth' and those aged 25 and over 'adults'. According the census data, there are over 1.2 billion persons at this group.[1] According to the estimations, 90% of this group live in developing countries and make up a large proportion of the population. Around 62% of youth live in Asia continental alone. In the OECD area, for the year 2018, the total population of OECD countries is 1.3 billion persons and the youth population is 162 million persons, whose cohort size (percentage of youth population) accounts for 12,4% of OECD population.

In Figure 6.2, the relative size of youth population (youth cohort size) to total OECD population is depicted. According to the data, the percentage of youth population in 2019 is 12,33 while this ratio was 12,45 in 2018, showing that there is a decrease in the size of youth population. It seems to be that this outcome will continue in the next years according to the OECD population projections. Based on this projection, the youth cohort size will drop to 11,6% in 2030, reflecting almost a 1% decrease in a 12-year period. It would not be hard to say that the OECD population is getting older, as the world does. On the other hand, this result has been worsened by fertility rate. Over the past few decades, it has been seen that total fertility rate in OECD member have declined dramatically, approximately decreasing from 2,7 in 1970 to 1,7 children per women in 2017.

In OECD countries, while the highest youth cohort rate belongs to Mexico (15%), the lowest rate belongs to Italy (8%). Among countries, it is the Turkey who experience the most dramatic drop in youth population rate from 16,3% in 2000 to 14% in 2018, following by Chile (14,3% to 12,7%) in two decades.

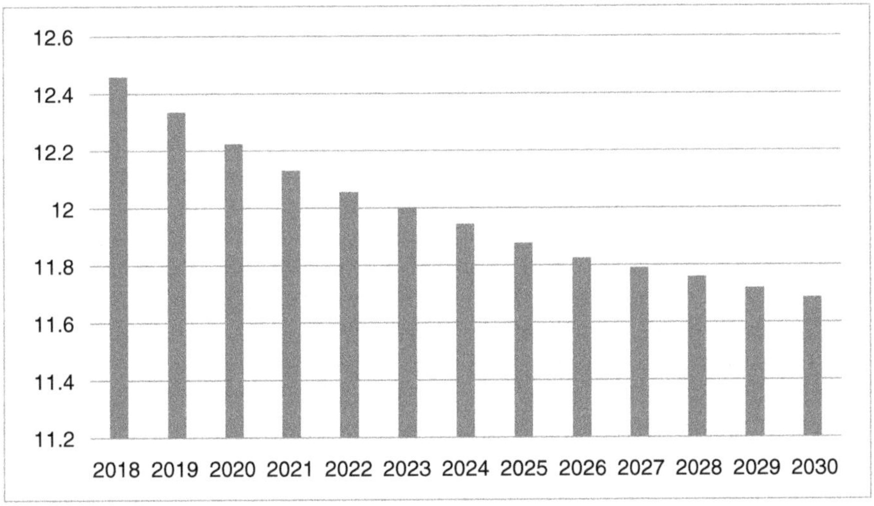

Figure 6.2 The Population Projections of Youth Cohort in OECD (2018–2030) (%)
Source: The author's estimation based on OECD data

However, this being the case, one should first take the life satisfaction and education, living, employment or unemployment conditions of youth population under consideration rather than the eldering population case. In this respect, governments need to take serious actions to tackle the problems that young people face. In the OECD Action Plan for Youth (2013), it has been pointed out that, globally, young people have been approximately threefold more likely to be unemployed as are adult workforce. Furthermore, this population has particularly been vulnerable to insecure and poorly paid jobs.

Globally, young people typically face significant barriers to participation to the labour market. Even though these barriers may differ from developed countries to developing or underdeveloped counterparts, they mark some common indications. The most important ones of these indications are

1 Mismatches between active jobs and job seekers
2 Mismatches between skills and experience demanded by job offers and those held by youth workforce
3 Less access to or difficulties in having financial services (credit), particularly in developing countries
4 Norms and cultural or religion barriers for specifically young women workforce
5 Living in a fragile or conflict-affected environment
6 Working conditions or low wage offers

In fact, the number or barriers that the youth experience are more than what are mentioned here, depending on country idiosyncratic factors such as political regime, economic stability/instability, union membership, geographic location and openness to trade, etc.

Henceforth, in the aftermath of the financial crisis of 2007–2008, politicians realised that more action needs to be taken to provide improved training to the youth population and to help them have a satisfying position in the labour market and have a good career. These actions can likely also reinforce their expectations for not being excluded from the labour force. This psychological exclusion is called 'discouraged labour force effect' in the literature.

In Figure 6.3, the OECD average of youth employment rate has been decreased by 3.1 for the 2000–2018 period. While this rate was 45.3 in 2000, it has dropped to 42.2 in 2018, the latest available year. In terms of a gender comparison, while OECD average men employment rate in that cohort has been decreased from 50 to 45.2 (by almost a 5-point decrease), women employment rate has showed a slight decrease from 40.6 to 39.1, by a 1.5-point drop for the period into consideration. Of course, the drop in total employment rate has been mainly led by the drop in youth men employment rate, rather than the drop in women cohort. In addition, when looking at the time-path of OECD youth employment rate, it is seen that decrease in total employment rate were more influenced by the 2008 crisis, leading approximately a dramatic three-point drop in 2009, the aftermath of this crisis. After this change in employment rate, a recovering in world economy has contributed a stability in employment rate, in which situation this rate has even gained a rise in the recent years. While this rate has significantly been lowered in member countries such as Italy, Czech Republic, Greece, Denmark and Czech Republic,

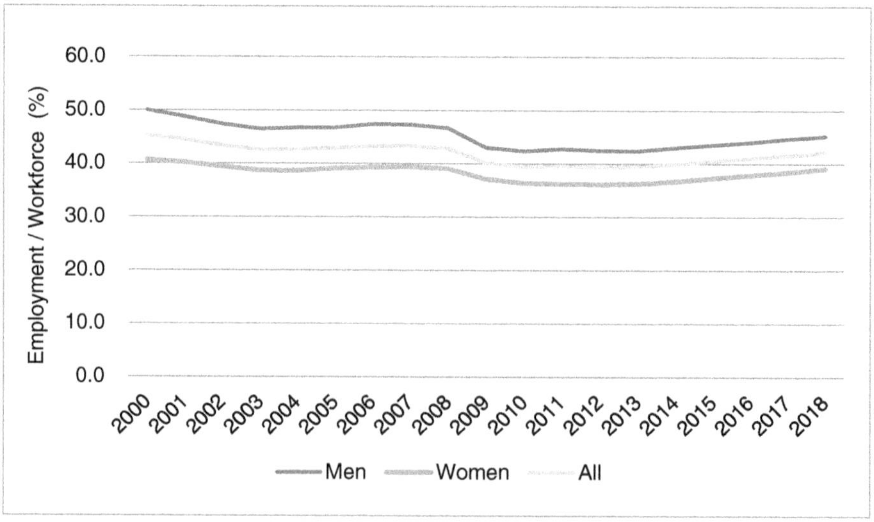

Figure 6.3 OECD Youth Employment Rate (2000–2018)

Source: The author's estimation based on OECD data

on the other hand it has shown a growth at various rates, for example, for Estonia, Finland, France, Iceland, Japan and Latvia. However, an overall slowdown in employment rate has been due to slowdown in main OECD member countries, which have proportionally bigger shares of population, labour force and economy, such as USA, United Kingdom, Germany and Spain.

As mentioned earlier, to create employment opportunities for youth is a key factor for reducing unemployment rate within OECD area. To do that, OECD ministers consented to take an extensive scope of measures at their meeting on 29–30 May 2013, as denoted in the OECD Youth Action Plan. The first goal of these initiatives is to address the ongoing high youth unemployment and under-employment situation. The second goal is to offer a good working environment to young people by equipping them with relevant skills and removing obstacles to their jobs in the longer run. Therefore, important actions of the OECD Action Plan for Youth (OECD, 2019) includes the following measures or actions (www.oecd.org/els/emp/Youth-Action-Plan.pdf, access date: November 28, 2019):

- Boosting job creation and addressing insufficient aggregate demand
- Providing adequate unemployed youth with income support, until labour market conditions improve
- Maintaining, and expanding active labour market measures that are cost-effective
- Addressing firm-oriented barriers to unskilled youth workers
- Encouraging firms to rise the quality of apprenticeship
- Preparing young workforce for business environment and strengthening the education system
- Assisting the transition within jobs
- Restructuring labour market policies and structures to promote employment opportunity and reduce exclusion by society

In addition to these actions, it was emphasised particular actions for the most disadvantageous groups consisting of low-skilled and migrant backgrounds or marginalised persons from labour markets.

In economic theory, it has been well known that minimum wage has a significant effect on employment rate, in a clear term; a rise in minimum wage leads a drop in employment rate, showing an inverse relationship between two macroeconomic entities. Therefore, the aim of imposing a minimum wage rate by the authorities is to raise incomes of workers. However, this policy comes at a cost to firms since the level of this wage rises the amount of variable costs, because of which job providers are less willing to offers new jobs.

In the cross-sectional studies, minimum wage statistics are additionally provided with an alternative measurement of minimum wages related to common income, i.e. the rate of minimum wages to full-time median incomes. Instead of mean earnings, median incomes are seen a more reliable proxy for global evaluations because they account for changes in the dispersal of incomes through nations. Nevertheless, although median fundamental incomes of full-time employees remain

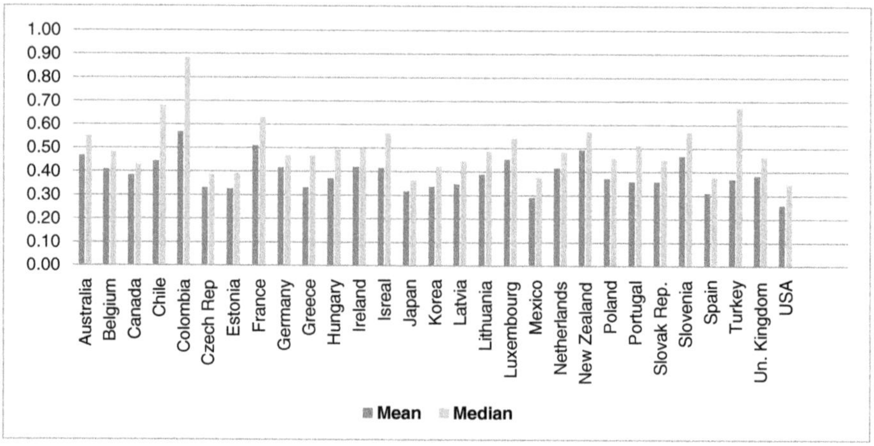

Figure 6.4 Minimum Wage Relative to Average Wages of Full-Time Workers (Average of 2000–2018)

Source: The author's estimation based on OECD data

ideally the favoured indicator of common earnings for worldwide minimum-to-median incomes comparisons, they cannot be applied to some countries. With this respect, in Figure 6.4, the minimum income related to the average earnings of full-time employees of OECD average is illustrated. In this illustration, firstly, using the OECD data, the rate of minimum wage (in current price) to average wage for each member country is averaged for the 2000–2018 period,[2] in terms of mean and median relative wages. In the vertical axis, the ratio of minimum wage to average wage is depicted. The maximum of this rate equals 1, indicating there is no difference between minimum and average wages, on the contrary a low level shows a significant gap, reflecting an inequality in the payment system in the labour markets. For this respect, on the median ratio basis, it is seen on average that almost for all members, the ratio of minimum wage to average wage is approximately 50%, ranging usually from 35% to 88% of the median wage.

That could be the case of developing countries since relatively low paid workers earn median wage. Therefore, the daily wants and necessities of workers and their families often lead to higher minimum wage levels. For example, Figure 6.4 indicates that minimum wages in France are relatively high, which could mean that it also has greater effects on labour costs than in other countries. Nonetheless, to some degree the burden of minimum wages in France is mitigated by lowering social security contributions for employers employing minimum wage workers.

4 Literature review

Although wage policy is meant to confirm a lowest commonplace of living, serving to poor and low-income families earn enough cash, it will increase input prices for corporations. During this case, it should discourage corporations to demand less labour input, leading to a scale back in a job. That is, if a rise in minimum wage ends up in larger turnover of workers, then firms' marginal costs rise as well, and also marginal profit of additional worker could also be lessened. For this reason, in many countries, researchers have conducted studies on the effect of a minimum wage policy on employment rate. Even though, a majority of these studies have significantly revealed the negative affect of minimum wages on employment rate, there are some studies supporting a positive effect, vice versa. The fact that much of literature focus on adult labour market, just few studies have estimated the possible hazards and effects of minimum wage on employment pattern. Therefore, literature review specifically includes those studies who estimate the effect of minimum wage on youth employment rather than adult cohort. Though much of the new studies attempt to capture the cross-sectional variation on the theme, early approaches have focused on state-specific effects.

One of the preliminary studies is done by Neumark and Wascher (2004), benefiting from a pooled cross section time series data set comprising 17 OECD countries for the years 1975–2000, the authors estimate the possible impact of changes in national minimum wage on employment status of labour force. Based on estimation results, they find that employment losses are essentially driven by minimum wage policy among youths. In particular, the adverse effect of minimum wages on unemployment situation seems to be smaller in countries that have precautions for youth when average market equilibrium wage is below the minimum wage. The outcomes of the study also indicate that if labour market regulations more restrictive and union density or union power is though, coverage strengthen the unemployment effects of minimum wages are forceful. However, laws on the protection of employment and active labour market policies aimed at bringing unemployed people into the workforce help to compensate for these effects. Overall, the impact of minimum wages on unemployment are greatest in those countries where labour markets are weakly protected.

On the other hand, Campolieti, Fang, and Gunderson (2005), benefiting from Master File of Survey for the period 1993–99, estimate minimum wage influences on youth employment transitions for Canada. Methodologically, they employee longitudinal panel data, and the results show that minimum wage increases have generally resulted in an increase of around 4 to 8 percentage points in the transition from employment to non-employment for the at-risk group of low-wage youth. They also estimate minimum wage elasticity varying from -0.3 to -0.5. percentage points. Their findings are consistent with the results previously obtained by Baker (2003), verifying that minimum wage rises in Canada might bring about a decrease in total youth employment. Interestingly, findings of the study by Yuen (2003) indicate that rises in the minimum wage has a strong adverse effect on low wage jobs when high wage workers are included in the control group. However, when this group of workers are excluded, this effect turns out to be insignificant.

The study by Chuang (2006), using Taiwan's quarterly time series data on 30 industries for the years of 1973–2004, investigates the effect of minimum wage on youth employment and unemployment. In the study, the Kaitz index is used as a widely adopted minimum wage proxy, however, due to data limitation and availability, the independent variable consists of the adult male employment rate. According to the findings, a 10 percent rise in the minimum wage will raise the rate of youth employment and the rate of youth labour participation by 0.47 percent, although no substantial impact for youth unemployment has been found.

In another study utilising the OECD data for the period 1970 to 2008, Addison and Ozturk (2012) examine the impact of minimum wage policy on women in jobs. Using panel methods to evaluate minimum wage effects among adolescents and young adults, their results are consistent with Neumark and Wascher (2004) results so that minimum wage rises are translated into lower women's work and participation levels. However, it is pointed out that their results for employment are found somewhat less transparent, specifically because of labour market withdrawal.

Sabia, Burkhauser, and Hansen (2012) investigate whether the impacts of minimum wage increase are always small, and provide further data of sample research of New York State. Applying data described from the 2004 and 2006 Current Population Survey, they use difference-in-difference estimates, one of popular approaches in labour from a case study of New York state. As a dependent variable, they use minimum wage increase per hour, while the employment ratio of 16- to 29-year-old individuals who do not have a high school qualification. Their estimates indicate that NYS minimum wage rise is linked with a 20,2% to 21,8% decrease in the employment of less-skilled, less-educated employees, with the highest impacts on those aged 16 to 24. It is apparent that minimum wage policy has a more adverse effect on the employment rate of low-skilled workers rather than on high-skilled ones.

Dickens, Riley, and Wilkinson (2014) estimate the effect of the UK minimum wage on 22 years of age, rather than on a broad young group. Their aim is to the impact of the legislated wage rise on the possibility of being in paid work for those turning 22 years of age. They use data from the UK Labour Force Survey (LFS) and pool all observations. Utilising from regression discontinuity methodology, one of the approaches grown recently, they find a 3–4% point increase occurred in the employment rate of low skilled individuals when a minimum wage increases legislated. This outcome shows that minimum wage policy has disadvantageous effect of the employment of high skilled individuals, this is because (i) their reservation price is over the offer wage and (ii) firms are more prone to hire workers at considerably low skilled workers since their reservation price is floating at minimum wages. They also report that this effect is bigger among men than women at 22. Another study (Wadsworth, 2010) has further shown that national minimum wages not also affect employment pattern of the UK but also UK prices, especially in the four years immediately after the introduction of the minimum wage.

In the one of latest study on the OECD case by Marimpi and Koning (2018), the authors employee a cross-country analysis of the impact of specific youth minimum wage levels on the performance of young people on the labour market. Their results indicate that in countries with youth minimum wages, the relative employment rates of young people under the age of 25 are close to those in countries with no minimum wages at all compared to older workers. As a result, rises in the rates of youth minimum wages have a significant negative impact on young people's employment rate.

As seen earlier, these and other studies not mentioned here, generally find a negative impact of minimum wage increases on youth employment rate. Studies further indicate that this impact is worsened among men individuals. The difference among studies is just the varying amounts of impact of minimum wages on employment. This slight difference resource from the econometric approach they use.

5 Data and model specification

The data set for 35 OECD countries are derived from databases and OECD publications over the period 2000–2018. The sample is an unbalanced panel and covers 28 OECD countries.[3] Because of data unavailability on minimum wage, seven countries (Austria, Denmark, Finland, Germany, Ireland, Italy and Norway) are excluded from the sample. Data on labour market indicators, including the employment to population ratio, minimum and median wages, adult unemployment rate, youth cohort size, replacement rate and union density are gathered from OECD Statistics Database. Youth cohort size is derived from World Population Prospects 2019 by United Nations Population Division. The dependent variable is the log of employment rates for both men and women at ages 15–24. The main independent variable is the minimum wage relative to average wages of full-time workers. For cross-country comparisons, data on minimum wage is proxied as the rate of minimum wages to median incomes of full-time employees. Median rather than mean wages present a more reliable source for global evaluations as it accounts for changes in wage dispersion across countries. As for control variables; adult unemployment rate, cohort size (the ratio of youth population over total), replacement rates in unemployment[4] and union density (a proxy for the strength of collective bargaining power of union members) are included in equations to be estimated.

To test for the impact of minimum wages on youth employment, this chapter follows the approach by Totty (2017), Neumark and Wascher (1992). In order to control the time trends and country idiosyncratic factors, time and country dummies are included in the models.

The estimated equation is given by

$$E = f\left(\begin{array}{l} MW,\ Pop,\ Adult\ Unemployment,\ Youth\ cohort\ size, \\ replacement\ rate,\ Union\ Density,\ Time\ and\ Country\ Dummies \end{array}\right) \tag{1}$$

Henceforth, the empirical panel data model for estimating the effect of minimum wages on employment is presented here, such as;

$$\begin{aligned} \ln(E_{it}) = {} & \varphi_1 + \varphi_2 \ln(MW_{it}) + \varphi_3 UNEMP_{it} + \varphi_4 COHORT_{it} + \varphi_5 REP_{it} \\ & + \varphi_6 UNION_{it} + \theta_{it} + \gamma_{it} + \varepsilon_{it} \end{aligned} \tag{2}$$

where E represents youth employment rate (employment/population) and MW is the log of minimum wages measured both in average and hourly wages. θ_{it} and γ_{it}

stand for country and time fixed effects, respectively. In addition, ε_{it} is the error term where $\varepsilon_{i,t} \sim IIN(0, \sigma^2) and\ Cov(x_{i,t}, \varepsilon_{i,t}) = 0$. Other control variables are *UNEMP* (adult unemployment rate, as a business cycle control), *COHORT* (relative size of youth population over total, as a supply side control), *REP* (unemployment benefit replacement rate, as a proxy for institutional labor market characteristics). Sub-indices *i* and *t* stand for country and time dimensions. Time fixed effects (γ_{it}) are included to control for common time shocks across countries, while country fixed effects (θ_{it}) are added to remove time-invariant heterogeneity between countries (country idiosyncratic factors), in order to estimate the net impact of regressors on regressand.

The identification theory is that minimum wage change is uncorrelated with the wrong term ϵit, conditioned on the two-way fixed impacts and additional controls.

A priori, the expected sign of the coefficient of minimum wage is negative, since a rise in minimum wages will shift the employment rate down. As for the control variables; the expected signs of coefficients of UNEMP, REP are negative, however those for COHORT and UNION are positive, respectively.

Since the sample consists of 28 cross-section units (n = 28) and 19 time periods (T = 19), it is called short panel (n > 28). STATA 16 statistics software is used for estimations. Descriptive statistics are shown in Table 6.1.

In Table 6.1, the variation in women employment rate is bigger than the variation in male employment rate. For example, while minimum and maximum rates of women employment are 9.1 and 77.7 percentage points, they are found, respectively, 14.6 and 76.6 percentage points for male employment among youth labour force. This shows that young women workforce is likely less employed than its male counterpart for some countries.

The scatterplots of dependant variable for cross-sections are depicted in Figure 6.5, where youth employment rate reflects a big variation across units (Iceland and Greece are two distinct examples).

Table 6.1 Descriptive Statistics of the Variables

Variable	*Obs.*	*Mean*	*Std. Dev.*	*Min.*	*Max.*
Male Youth Employment	532	41.64887	14.08387	14.6	76.6
Female Youth Employment	532	36.46579	16.17003	9.1	77.7
Total Employment Rate	532	39.09267	14.67437	11.8	77.1
Minimum Wage (Mean)	520	.3801346	.0678643	.23	.59
Minimum Wage (Median)	515	.4894951	.1012516	.29	.74
Adult Unemployment (Male)	532	6.394361	3.931912	1	23.8
Adult Unemployment (Female)	532	7.373308	4.59966	1.6	30.9
Adul Unemployment (Total)	532	6.81485	4.097322	1.3	26.9
Cohort Size	532	.117469	.0171566	.08	.16
Replacement Rate	446	53.65471	17.67591	6	134
Union Density	460	24.99523	19.68154	4.3	92.5

Source: Author's presentation

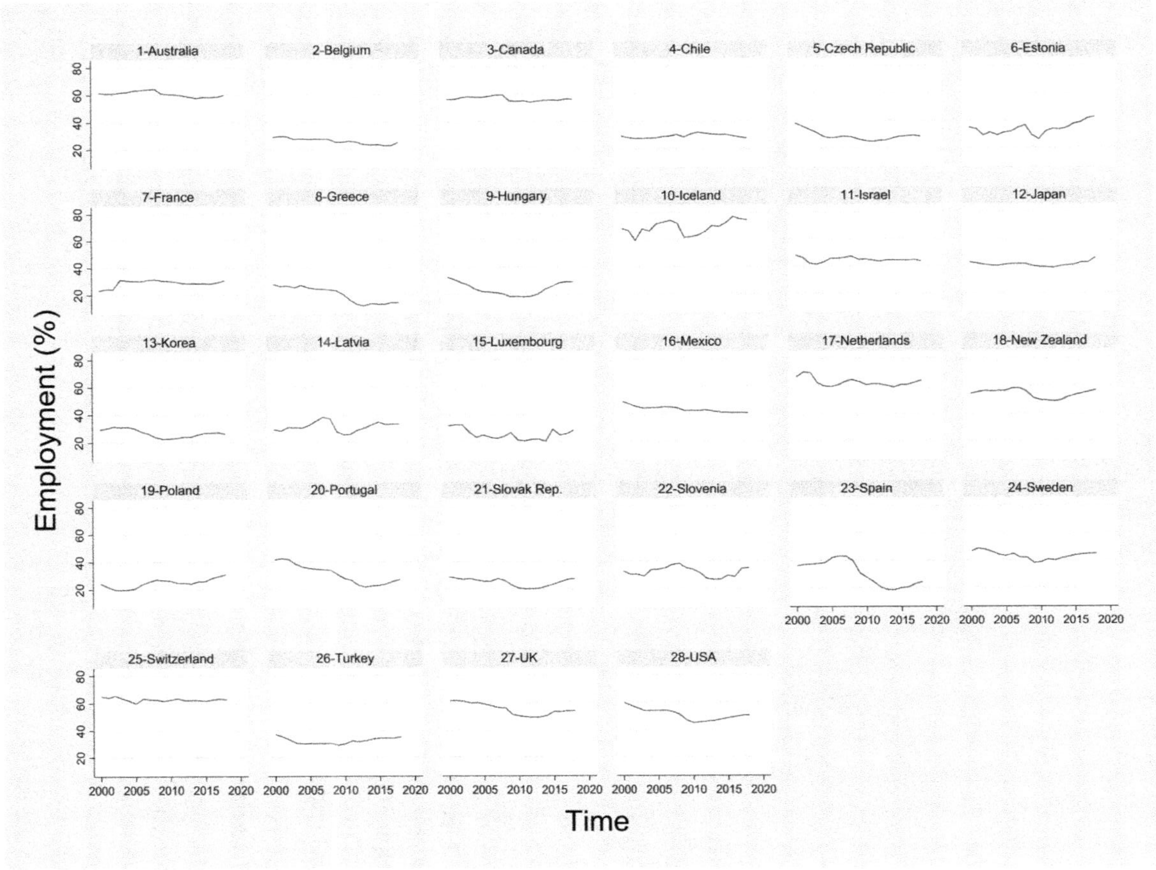

Figure 6.5 The View of Dependant Variable for Countries

Source: Author's presentation

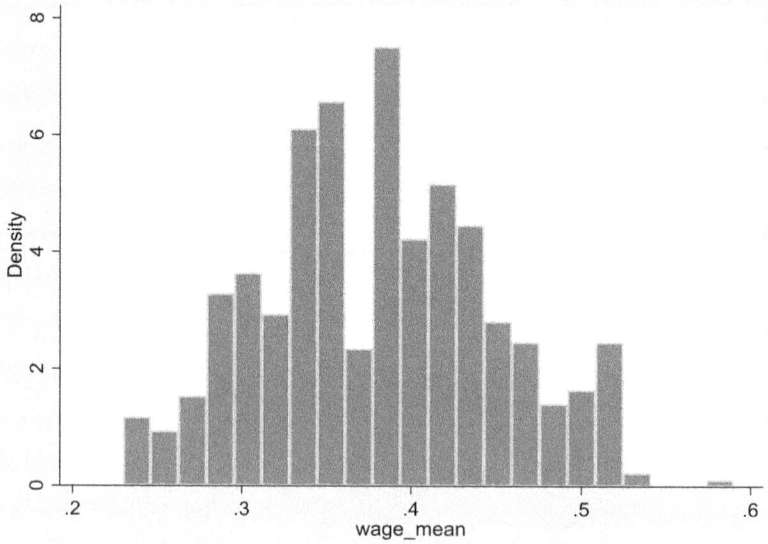

Figure 6.6 Histogram of Minimum-to-Mean Wage Ratios (2000–2018)

Source: Author's estimation

Beginning in 2008, the economic recession brought about a substantial decline in the employment ratios in many countries. According to the data, youth employment ratios (41%) has been much lower than those of adults (70%). This is mostly occurred since young cohorts has been enrolled in higher education, thus not participating in the labour force. In addition, during the sample period 2000 to 2018, the minimum-to-mean wage ratio fell significantly in some countries, varying from 23% to 59% of the mean wage, with an average value of 38% across countries (see Figure 6.6).

6 Estimation results

While this study does not provide a clear theoretical model in this work, empirical research may be observed as an empirical contribution to labour market studies, especially those based on the effect of minimum wages on the structure of jobs.

As far as empirical validation is concerned, the study employees testing the hypothesis of stationary of the variables using Im-Pesaran-Shin IPS (2003) unit root test statistic, which hypothesis that all the panels comprise a unit root. IPS (2003) established a set of tests that relaxed the assumption of a common parameter for auto regression. In addition, the IPS test does not need balanced datasets, although there are no gaps within a panel. They also assume that the error term for all i and t is distributed independently as normal, and they allow the error term to have heterogeneous panel variances. According to test statistic, while replacement rate and each of three minimum wages (total, men and women) variables are found to be stationary at the level (*I(0)*), remaining variables are found to be stationary only after taking their first differences (*I(1)*). Statistics are not reported here.

The first multiple regression outcomes are given in Table 6.2 for the total youth employment-to-population rate. OLS outcomes given in the first column of the table excludes country fixed effects, year fixed effects and country specific time trends. According to the OLS regression result, there is statistically a significant relation between minimum wage (wage) variable and youth employment rate, according to which a rise in minimum wage results in a decrease in employment rate (the coefficient is significant at 5% level). In addition, the sign of the coefficient of wage variable is turned out to be negative, an outcome consistent with the much of literature. The same relationship has been found on the coefficients of replacement rate (rep) and adult unemployment rate (unemp) variables. However, only cohort size variable is not found statistically significant. Union density is found to be statistically significant at 10% level of significance, according to

Table 6.2 Panel Estimation Results for Total Youth Employment (Model 1)

	(1)	*(2)*	*(3)*
	OLS	*FE*	*RE*
D.wage	−99.04**	24.36***	24.26***
	(41.77)	(8.18)	(8.28)
D.unemp	−0.05	−0.25**	−0.25**
	(0.56)	(0.12)	(0.12)
cohort	83.46	−91.02*	−90.02*
	(56.01)	(53.27)	(53.17)
rep	−0.10**	−0.05*	−0.05*
	(0.04)	(0.03)	(0.03)
D.un	0.95*	0.05	0.05
	(0.57)	(0.09)	(0.09)
Constant	37.02***	613.27**	76.61***
	(7.26)	(289.09)	(6.67)
Country fixed effects	No	Yes	Yes
Year fixed effects	No	Yes	Yes
Country spec. time trends	No	Yes	Yes
N	393	393	393
r2	0.37	0.83	
chi2			661.6047
p			0.0000
Hausman test			1.12
(p-values)			(0.9526)

Hausman test assumes RE is fully efficient under null hypothesis.

which there is a positive relationship between the union power and employment opportunity for youth.

Turning to the results in second column of Table 6.2, where a panel fixed effects method is applied, the coefficient estimate for the minimum wage variable is found statistically important, however the sign is positive and contradicts the former as previously found in the OLS regression. However, though its coefficient is positive and significant at 1% level of significance, the absolute value of its estimated coefficient is smaller than that in OLS outcome. In the second column, just the coefficient of union is not found significant. And finally in the third column where individual effects (random effects) are allowed, the results are almost the same as in column 1 and 2, reflecting once again, a statistically significant and positive relationship between minimum wage and employment rate.

The second and third columns contain fixed results by country, fixed results by year, and country-specific time bents.

Now we turn to case where dependant variable is the male youth employment, aiming at to find significant relation between minimum wage and employment rate when sex matters.

A possible influence of minimum wage on male youth employment rate is estimated in Table 6.3. As in the first model, the second model reflects a

Table 6.3 Panel Estimation Results for Male Youth Employment (Model 2)

	(1)	*(2)*	*(3)*
	OLS	*FE*	*RE*
D.wage	–96.02**	24.37***	24.17***
	(38.32)	(8.99)	(7.99)
D.unemp	–0.23	–0.43***	–0.42***
	(0.50)	(0.13)	(0.13)
cohort	120.61**	–70.93	–69.93
	(50.09)	(58.56)	(57.56)
rep	–0.08**	–0.06*	–0.06*
	(0.04)	(0.03)	(0.04)
D.un	0.82	0.05	0.05
	(0.52)	(0.10)	(0.10)
Constant	33.38***	58.19**	75.30***
	(6.53)	(317.79)	(7.33)
Country fixed effects	No	Yes	Yes
Year fixed effects	No	Yes	Yes
Country spec. time trends	No	Yes	Yes
N	393	393	393
r2	0.50	0.73	
chi2			183.3866
p			0.0000

statistically important relation between male employment and wage. Even though the negative sign in OLS method, the wage coefficients in fixed and random effects models turned out to be positive. Unemployment (only in OLS method) and union density (in the second and the third model) are found to be insignificant. As for adult unemployment, for example, a one-unit increase in adult unemployment rate leads to 0.45 points decrease in male youth employment. The similar impact is found in two other models. On the other hand, it is obvious that as union density increases in a country, the more people could possibly be employed.

Finally, in Table 6.4, the impact of minimum wage on female youth employment rate is analysed. As it is found in the previous two models, once again a statistically significant relationship (inverse relationship in OLS method) is found between two variables under consideration. In the fixed and random effects models the signs of the minimum wage coefficients are found statistically significant (at 1% level), reflecting a positive relationship between wage and youth employment. Furthermore, while adult unemployment rate, cohort size and replacement rate have negative and statistically significant impact on employment, union density have positive but insignificant effects, vice versa.

Table 6.4 Panel Estimation Results for Female Youth Employment (Model 3)

	(1)	*(2)*	*(3)*
	OLS	*FE*	*RE*
D.wage	−103.18**	23.97***	23.97***
	(46.37)	(7.99)	(7.99)
D.unemp	0.14	−0.07	−0.07
	(0.63)	(0.12)	(0.12)
cohort	47.43	−110.44**	−110.44**
	(64.76)	(52.05)	(52.05)
Rep	−0.12**	−0.04	−0.04
	(0.05)	(0.03)	(0.03)
D.un	1.09*	0.06	0.06
	(0.63)	(0.09)	(0.09)
Constant	33.22***	25.17	62.37***
	(4.87)	(22.10)	(6.69)
Country fixed effects	No	Yes	Yes
Year fixed effects	No	Yes	Yes
Country spec. time trends	No	Yes	Yes
N	393	393	393
r2	0.40	0.66	
chi2			484.0490
P	0.0000	0.0000	0.0000

7 Conclusion

In our modern world, younger individuals are the most educated generation ever. However, they experience varying degrees of problems in participating and remaining in the labour market. On one hand, while these problems exist, on the other hand it poses a handicap when young people cannot find jobs matching to their skills and capabilities. The public and private sectors, as major job providers, have both a crucial function for young individuals to participate in the quest for more and better works. From this point of view, enterprises on the local and national level by governments, firms and employers' associations are flourishing in several nations. These enterprises are inevitably varied, depending on the socio-economic, political, religious and institutional context, the challenges of youth employment and the needs and opportunities of the marketing community in a remarkable country.

Over the past decade, labour market circumstances have been worsened specially for young individuals who have less education. Therefore this group will likely be either out of work, underemployed or low-paid if in work. These changes are unlikely to be the short-lived product of the economic downturn, which raises significant policy challenges for the years to come. From a gender perspective, in several countries, the number of jobless or underemployed male workers has been rose in the recent years. Nevertheless, the joblessness remains more widespread among female workforce, who are also more likely to involve in low-paid jobs (OECD Employment Outlook, 2019: 19).

According to common economic system, it is predicted that minimum wages will decrease employment and raise unemployment. This occurs when minimum wage outrages the wage determined under market condition by supply and demand sides of labour input. Since imposition of the minimum wage policy increases the cost per labour input, firms would likely cut back on hiring labour input. Most of the empirical literature found an adverse correlation between the minimum wage and the employment rate. Nevertheless, fever studies have aimed to find any influence of wages on youth employment and generally they just have found negative impacts. This study also purposes to investigate the connection between two factors including some main control variables, for the OECD case. The case is tested in three models, where total youth employment, male youth employment and female youth employment rates are taken as dependant variable, respectively. For three models, three econometric methods are used: Pooled OLS, panel fixed effects and panel random effects. According to the results, apart from the results of OLS regression, a positive and statistically meaningful relationship was found between the minimum wage and youth employment rate in general, which contradicts the standard economic theory. Of course, this result can give us information about the total employment influences of the minimum wages that we require to collect employment earnings and losses between firms. We hope to find some negative and some positive employment effects for companies that increase wages from the old minimum wage to the new minimum wage unless the increase in the minimum wage is very large.

The problem conjointly happens since theoretical model assumes that completely different firms can reply to changes within the salary in numerous ways that, while this strategy indirectly suppose that all companies can reply in the same way. Such a methodology is only wise when the competitive model is correct. Bias is likely to be directed towards finding an indirect correlation between wage and employment increase, which is a notable giant if it concentrates on lower-wage companies. Given this, it is surprising that Katz and Krueger (1992) and Card and Krueger (1994) do not inquire such an impression, and there is the potential to debate that the positive influence of wages on employment can be underestimated by their results.

Notes

1 Encompassing the ages of 10–24, adolescents and youth are referred to as "young people". The adolescents group includes those aged between 10–19 and accounts for approximately 17% of world population. Together with youth, the population of young group accounts for 25% of world population.
2 Because of data unavailability, for some countries such as Chile, Columbia, Germany, Slovenia and Costa Rica, this ratio was calculated for the fewer years, for example, a five-year period for Germany. For the German case the wage data just consist of a five-year observation. Not all data points are available for all years for all countries.
3 Australia, Belgium, Canada, Chile, Czech Republic, Estonia, France, Greece, Hungary, Iceland, Israel, Japan, Korea, Latvia, Luxembourg, Mexico, Netherlands, New Zealand, Poland, Portugal, Slovak Republic, Slovenia, Spain, Sweden, Switzerland, Turkey, UK and USA.
4 According to the OECD definition, Net Replacement Rates in unemployment measure the proportion of previous in-work income that is maintained after 1, 2, . . ., T months of unemployment.

References

Addison, J. T. and Ozturk, O. D. (2012). Minimum wages, labor market institutions, and female employment: A cross country analysis. *ILR Review*, 65(4): 779–809.

Baker, M. (2003). *Minimum Wages and Human Capital Investments of Young Workers: Work Related Training and School Enrolment*. Mimeo: University of Toronto.

Brown, C., Gilroy, G. and Kohen, A. (1983). Time-series evidence of the effects of the minimum wage on youth employment and unemployment. *Journal of Human Resources*, 18(1): 3–31.

Brozova, D. (2018). The minimum wage in the neoclassical and the behavioural labour market theory. *Acta Oeconomica Pragensia, University of Economics, Prague*, 2018 (4): 30–41.

Campolieti, M., Fang, T. and Gunderson, M. (2005). Minimum wage impacts on youth employment transitions. *The Canadian Journal of Economics*, 38(1): 81–104.

Card, D. and Krueger, A. B. (1994). Minimum wages and employment: A case study of the fast food industry in New Jersey and Pennsylvania. *The American Economic Review*, 84(4): 772–793.

Chuang, Y. C. (2006). The effect of minimum wage on youth employment and unemployment in Taiwan. *Hitotsubashi Journal of Economics*, 47: 155–167.

Currie, J. and Fallick, B. (1996). The minimum wage and the employment of youth evidence from the NLSY. *Journal of Human Resources*, 31(2): 404–428.
Dickens, R., Riley, R. and Wilkinson, D. (2014). The UK minimum wage at 22 years of age: A regression discontinuity approach. *Journal of the Royal Statistical Society*, 177(1): 95–114.
Doeringer, P. B. and Piore, M. J. (1985). *Internal Labor Markets and Manpower Analysis*. London: Routledge.
Im, K. S., Pesaran, M. and Shin, Y. (2003). Testing for unit roots in heterogeneous panels. *Journal of Econometrics*, 115(1): 53–74.
Kalenkoski, C. M. (2016). The effects of minimum wages on youth employment and income. *IZA World of Labor*: 243.
Katz, L. F. and Krueger, A. B. (1992). The effect of the minimum wage on the fast-food industry. *ILR Review*, 46(1): 6–21.
Marimpi, M. and Koning, P. (2018). Youth minimum wages and youth employment. *IZA J Labor Policy*, 7: 5, doi:10.1186/s40173-018-0098-4.
Neumark, D. and Wascher, W. (1992). Employment effects of minimum wages and subminimum wages: Panel data on state minimum wage laws. *Industrial and Labor Relations Review*, 46(1): 55–81.
Neumark, D. and Wascher, W. (2004). Minimum wages, labor market institutions and youth employment: A cross-national analysis. *Industrial and Labor Relations Review*, 57: 2.
Obenauer, M. L. and Nienburg, B. M. (1915). *Effect of Minimum-Wage Determinantions in Oregon*. Washington, DC: U. S. Government Printing Office.
OECD (2013). OECD Action Plan for Youth, www.oecd.org/els/emp/Youth-Action-Plan.pdf.
OECD (2019). *OECD Employment Outlook 2019: The Future of Work*. Paris: OECD Publishing, https://doi.org/10.1787/9ee00155-en.
Rottenberg, S. (1981). *The Economics of Legal Minimum Wages*. Washington, DC: AEI Press, American Enterprise Institute.
Sabia, J., Burkhauser, R. V. and Hansen, B. (2012). Are the effects of minimum wage increases always small? New evidence from a case study of New York State. *ILR Review*, 65(2): 350–376.
Stigler, G. (1946). The economics of minimum wage legislation. *American Economic Review*, 36(3): 358–365.
Totty, E. (2017). The effect of minimum wages on employment: A factor model approach. *Economic Inquiry*, 55(4): 1712–1737.
Van Den Berg, G. (2003). Multiple equilibria and minimum wages in labor markets with informational frictions and heterogenous production technologies. *International Economic Review*, 44(4): 1337–1357.
Wadsworth, J. (2010). Did the national minimum wage affect UK prices? *Fiscal Studies*, 31(1): 81–120.
Waldman, O. L. (2001). *The Case of the Minimum Wage: Competing Policy Models*. Albany, USA: State University of New York Press.
Yuen, T. (2003). The effect of minimum wages on youth employment in Canada: A panel study. *The Journal of Human Resources*, 38(3): 647–672.

Internet sources

www.econlib.org/archives/2011/03/keynesian_polit.html (access date: 24.12.2019).

7 Gender gap in the labour market

A comparative view for youth and adults

Fatma Didin Sönmez and Yasemin Özerkek

1 Introduction

There are considerable gender differences in many aspects throughout the world. Some of the prominent gender gaps occur in labour markets. Labour economists have long tried to investigate these differences. Many countries have gender-based inequality problems in their labour markets. Gender equality is an important phenomenon for an efficient labour market and economic environment to achieve sustainable development.

There exist several studies analysing the labour market outcomes such as employment and unemployment by age and/or gender in the literature (O'Higgins, 1997, 2003, 2012, 2015; Korenman and Neumark, 1997; Blau and Kahn, 2000; Blanchflower and Freeman, 2000; Breen, 2005; Pastore, 2018; Tåhlin and Westerman, 2020, among others). In his studies with European countries, O'Higgins (1997, 2015) and Bell and Blanchflower (2011) (with the cases of United States and United Kingdom) report that youth unemployment rates of young people are higher than those of adults and variations in youth unemployment have a close relationship with the variations in adult unemployment.[1]

Besides the bulk of the literature investigating age and gender differentials, many studies focus on the gender gap in unemployment and employment (Albanesi and Şahin, 2013; Bičáková, 2014; Baussola, Mussida, Jenkins and Penfold, 2015; Dauth, 2016, among others) Niemi (1974) points out three factors accounting for the relatively high unemployment rate of females:

> a high level of frictional unemployment because of movement in and out of the labour force; a relative lack of training, particularly specific training, and consequently a susceptibility to cyclical layoffs and unemployment; and occupational and geographic immobility, resulting in a high level of structural unemployment.
>
> (p. 331)

In addition, Niemi (1974) mentions one other factor which lowers the female unemployment rates relative to male rates. Since the industrial distribution of the male and female labour forces differ (i.e., some industries employ mostly male workers), this leads to causing men to suffer the most from the economic recession (Niemi, 1974; Şahin, Hobijn and Song, 2009; Albanesi and Şahin, 2017).

Albanesi and Şahin (2017) analyse gender differences in unemployment for a group of OECD countries in view of the female and male labour force attachment. Azmat, Güell and Manning (2006)'s findings show that the unemployment rates of males and females are close for some OECD countries, while especially for Mediterranean countries, the gap is large in favour of men. They also analyse the gaps in employment and unemployment flows. They point out that the rise in labour market attachment is just some part of the explanation for the changes in the gender unemployment gap. Labour market institutions, by changing the effect of human capital differences on unemployment rates, are likely to account for the gaps (Azmat, Güell and Manning, 2006). In a recent paper, Tåhlin and Westerman (2020) study on the causes of declining youth employment by using data for a group of European countries. They suggest that the structural change of skill in the form of skill upgrading and skill mismatch affects young people's employment opportunities inversely.

This study includes two main strands of work. First, some facts emerged from descriptive evidence for the labour market gender gaps by age groups are delineated. Second, the empirical part analyses the sensitivity of the gender unemployment gap to the level of the unemployment rate for different age groups and investigates the relationship between the gender unemployment gap, gross domestic product (GDP) and inflation.

Considering factors such as unemployment rate, relative cohort size, employment rate, and labour force participation, descriptive part of the study aims to reveal main findings for gender-based inequalities in the labour market for a group of European countries. The study examines the gender disparities also by taking the age groups into account. Thus, the results will enable us to understand how these gender gaps differ for the youth (ages 15–24) and adults (ages 25–64). Employing annual labour force data available in Eurostat Database (2019), descriptive analysis summarises countries' gender gap performance.

The empirical part also highlights the fact of the unequal representation of women in different sectors. Adult and youth employment rates for different sectors including agriculture, manufacturing and services, point to gendered employment distribution in many countries. In fact, employment distribution across sectors is gender-biased; females are less represented in the manufacturing sector and more in the service sector. In the second part of the descriptive analysis, employment data for different age groups are used to reveal the key findings on the gender employment gap and the differences between youth and adult employment by sectors.

The first part of the empirical analysis explores the linkage between gender unemployment gap and the unemployment rate. To this end, the elasticity of the gender unemployment gap with respect to unemployment is estimated for the two age categories separately. The last part of the study presents models estimated by panel vector auto-regression (VAR) to illustrate the relationship between the gender unemployment gap and two basic macroeconomic variables, namely GDP per capita and inflation. These macroeconomic indicators are ultimate determinants of total demand and supply, human capital accumulation and labour market. Therefore, the unemployment rate is expected to be influenced mainly by economic activities. However, economic activities may have a disproportional effect and enlarge the gender-based inequalities in the labour market. Hence, the study aims to investigate whether the economic activities are able to generate the expected positive employment effect in terms of gender-based point of view. Besides, the model estimations for two different age groups allow comparing how this relationship differs for youth and adults.

The structure of this chapter is as follows. Section 2 discusses some gendered employment facts observed from the descriptive analysis for youth and adults. It comprises of four different subsections; unemployment, labour force participation, employment and sectoral gendered employment. Section 3 includes the gender unemployment gap sensitivity to the unemployment level. The model specification and estimation results for the relationship between the gender unemployment gap and the main macroeconomic variables are presented in Section 4. Finally, Section 5 concludes.

2 Descriptive analysis and some gendered facts in labour market

Using different age groups, descriptive evidence in this part displays gender inequalities for both youth and adults. Annual data of 27 European countries from Eurostat Database (2019) is used. Table 7.1 lists the countries included in the sample. The table also shows the country's performance in the Global Gender Gap Index provided by World Bank (2020). Measuring gaps rather than levels, this index ranks 149 countries based on four major parameters; economic participation and opportunity, educational attainment, health and survival, and political empowerment. Thus, the Global Gender Gap Index is not an index focusing on only economic variables. Also, the economic dimension considers the participation (labour force participation) gap, the remuneration (wage, income) and advancement (occupation). Index score measures how much of the gender gap is closed. It takes a range of values from 0 to 1. The high value of index performance means greater gender equality based on the aforementioned categories in the countries.

Global Gender Gap Index is available for the period 2006–2018, except for 2017. To track the country's progress on gender equality performance, Table 7.1 shows index score and rankings for the initial year and the last two years. Iceland ranks first in the index, followed by Norway, Sweden and Finland. These countries consistently occupy as top four in 2006, 2016 and 2018. Hungary, Slovakia, Czechia and Italy have the lowest level of scores across the European countries reported in the table. Moreover, among those listed countries, France and Slovenia are the countries making the greatest progress. France increased 58 places (from 70 in 2006 to 12 in 2018) and Slovenia raised 40 places (from 51 in 2006 to 11 in 2018) in the index. Table 7.1 reveals the fact that 11 out of 27 countries have closed

Table 7.1 Global Gender Gap Index Performance of Countries

Country	*Country Code*	*2006 Index Score*	*2006 Index Rank*	*2016 Index Score*	*2016 Index Rank*	*2018 Index Score*	*2018 Index Rank*
Austria	AUT	0.6986	27	0.716	52	0.718	53
Belgium	BEL	0.7078	20	0.745	24	0.738	32
Bulgaria	BGR	0.687	37	0.726	41	0.756	18
Croatia	HRV	0.7145	16	0.7	68	0.712	59
Czechia	CZE	0.6712	53	0.69	77	0.693	82
Denmark	DNK	0.7462	8	0.754	19	0.778	13
Estonia	EST	0.6944	29	0.747	22	0.734	33
Finland	**FIN**	**0.7958**	**3**	**0.845**	**2**	**0.821**	**4**
France	FRA	0.652	70	0.755	17	0.779	12
Germany	DEU	0.7524	5	0.766	13	0.776	14
Hungary	HUN	0.6698	55	0.669	101	0.674	102
Iceland	**ISL**	**0.7813**	**4**	**0.874**	**1**	**0.858**	**1**
Ireland	IRL	0.7335	10	0.797	6	0.796	9
Italy	ITA	0.6456	77	0.719	50	0.706	70
Latvia	LVA	0.7091	19	0.755	18	0.758	17
Lithuania	LTU	0.7077	21	0.744	25	0.749	24
Luxembourg	LUX	0.6671	56	0.734	34	0.712	61
Netherlands	NLD	0.7250	12	0.756	16	0.747	27
Norway	**NOR**	**0.7994**	**2**	**0.842**	**3**	**0.835**	**2**
Poland	POL	0.6802	44	0.727	38	0.728	42
Portugal	PRT	0.6922	33	0.737	31	0.732	37
Slovakia	SVK	0.6757	50	0.679	94	0.693	83
Slovenia	SVN	0.6745	51	0.786	8	0.784	11
Spain	ESP	0.7319	11	0.738	29	0.746	29
Sweden	**SWE**	**0.8133**	**1**	**0.815**	**4**	**0.822**	**3**
Switzerland	CHE	0.6997	26	0.776	11	0.755	20
United Kingdom	GBR	0.7365	9	0.752	20	0.774	15

Source: World Bank (2020)

between 67 per cent and 74 per cent of gender gaps in their countries, whilst 16 countries have closed between 75 per cent and 86 per cent.

Country's scores and rankings in the Global Gender Gap Index allow a comparison of countries in different aspects such as economic participation and opportunity, educational attainment, health and survival and political empowerment. Thus, Table 7.1 provides a helpful list to rank countries based on their gender gap performances in different categories. However, this part of the study concentrates on economic issues, specifically on gender gaps in unemployment, employment and labour force participation. The selected countries in the analysis have some similarities and also disparities based on the labour market issues discussed in the following subsections.

2.1 Unemployment

Figure 7.1 shows the evolution of youth and adult unemployment rates for 27 European countries. The most obvious striking characteristic of the figure is that youth unemployment rates are higher than adult unemployment rates in all countries during 1995–2018.[2] Italy, Croatia and Spain among the others, are the countries that suffer the most from very high youth unemployment. Figure 7.1 also illustrates that both rates generally move together. The correlation between these rates (0.87) is pretty high. The lowest correlations are in Sweden (0.39) and Austria (0.37).

In some countries, for low levels of unemployment rates, the gap between youth and adults is narrow. One observes this pattern, especially in Switzerland, Germany and Austria. The gap between adult and youth unemployment rates are remarkably larger in Poland, Croatia, Italy and Spain.

The response of youth unemployment to economic fluctuations is remarkably higher than that of adults. The youth rates rise more in downturns and recovering more rapidly during expansions (O'Higgins, 1997). This observation is true across several countries. As is seen in Figure 7.1, the unemployment rates appear to increase in response to the 2008 economic crisis, particularly affecting youth rates more than do adult rates. In Bulgaria, Croatia, Czechia, Denmark, Estonia, Hungary, Iceland, Ireland, Italy, Latvia, Lithuania, Slovakia, Slovenia, Portugal, Poland, Spain and the United Kingdom, the gap between adult and youth unemployment enlarges due to the economic crisis.

Figure 7.2 provides the coefficient of variation[3] showing the extent of unemployment variability across the countries for the period between 1995 and 2018. The lower the coefficient of variation, the smaller the unemployment dispersion around the mean for a specific year. For both adults and the young, there is a sharp increase in female and male unemployment variations across countries from 1999 through 2001. Starting in 2002, both female and male unemployment variations decline significantly, before following an increasing trend. As is depicted in the figure, youth and adult unemployment variations follow a similar pattern.

However, it should be noted that variation in adult male unemployment is decreasing while the variation in adult female unemployment is increasing after 2010. In recent years, unemployment variation across countries is relatively high for females and the young. Figure 7.2 also indicates that since the effect of the global economic crisis on unemployment varies significantly across countries, the coefficient of variations during economic downturn periods display higher values.

Based on the different trends in the coefficient of variations over the time period, the whole period is separated into specific time intervals as shown by the vertical lines (Figure 7.2). Table 7.2 highlights the other important aspects of unemployment over three different time periods; 1995–2001, 2002–2008 and 2009–2018. Table 7.2 presents the average unemployment rates of youth and adults by gender. Compared to 1995–2001 numbers, the average rates of unemployment declines in the 2002–2008 period, and increases even more in the 2009–2018 period. This is the case for all young people and adults regardless of gender. Figure 7.1 and Table 7.2 together reveal the fact that during the period where the dispersion of unemployment across countries is falling, unemployment rates are declining on average as well.

It is also prominent that youth rates and adult rates are moving apart. Female and male youth unemployment rates are higher than their counterparts for adults.

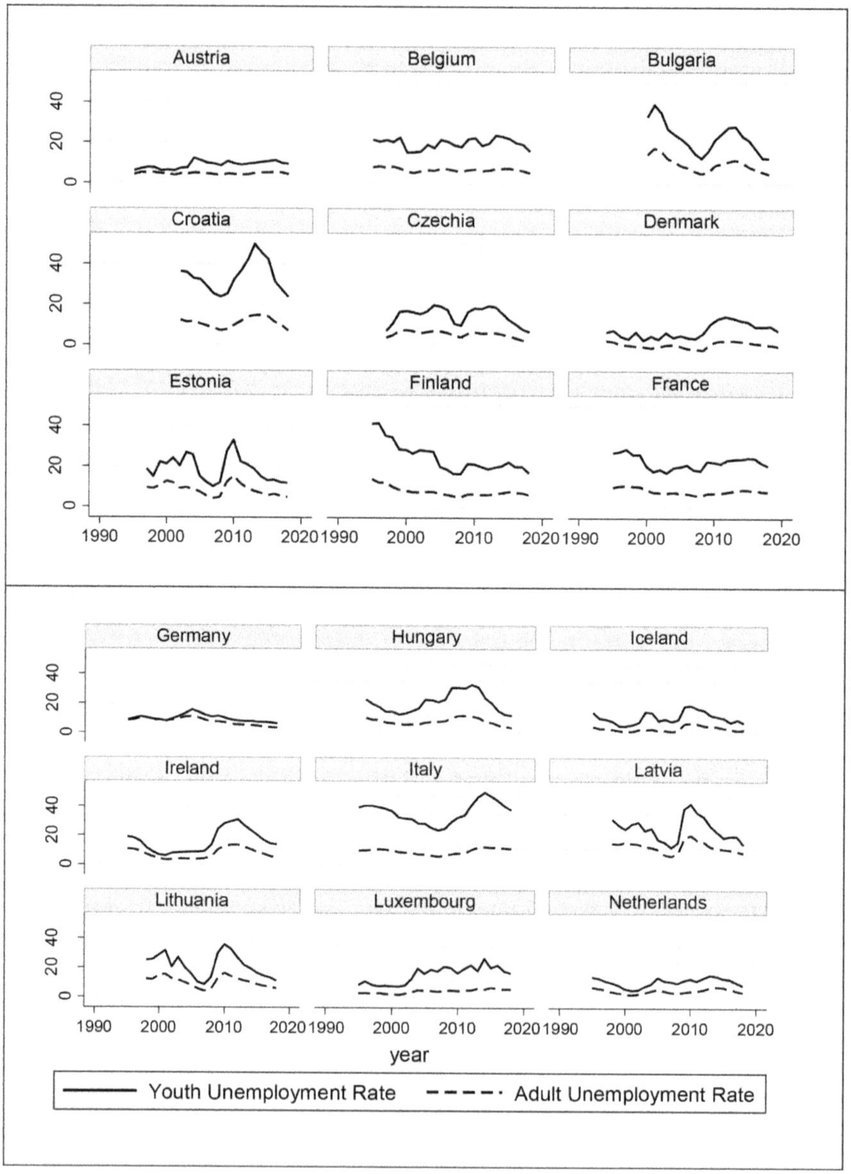

Figure 7.1 Youth and Adult Unemployment Rates by Country

Source: Eurostat Database (2019)

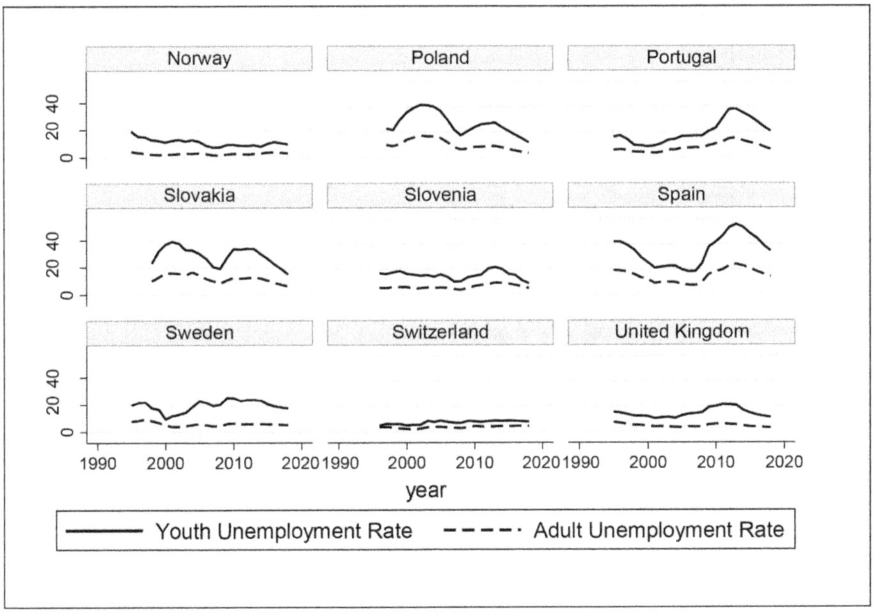

Figure 7.1 (Continued)

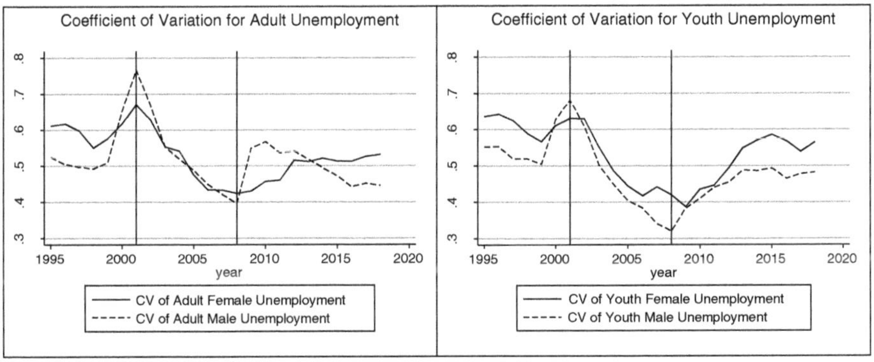

Figure 7.2 Variations in Unemployment Across Countries (1995–2018)

Source: Authors' own calculations

The unemployment rates for females and males are synchronised most of the time. The intensity of this co-movement increases from 1995–2001 to 2002–2008 and from 2002–2008 to 2009–2018.[4]

In countries like Italy, Croatia, Slovakia and Spain, youth unemployment rates are persistently high. Considering three different time spans, Bulgaria and Finland make remarkable progress in reducing youth unemployment that reached very high levels in the first period, whilst Italy and Spain show a retrograde movement.

Table 7.2 Unemployment Rates for the Young and Adults by Gender (%)

Country	*Young*						*Adult*					
	1995–2001		*2002–2008*		*2009–2018*		*1995–2001*		*2002–2008*		*2009–2018*	
	Male	*Female*	*Male*	*Female*	*Male*	*Female*	*Male*	*Female*	*Male*	*Female*	*Male*	*Female*
Austria	6.7	6.5	9.6	9.1	10.3	9.6	4.5	4.7	4.3	4.5	4.9	4.4
Belgium	17.5	22.0	18.0	19.5	21.4	19.9	5.8	9.2	5.8	7.3	6.7	6.5
Bulgaria	39.5	32.5	23.4	21.1	21.6	19.6	16.4	15.7	9.7	9.7	9.2	7.9
Croatia	n.a*	n.a*	28.3	34.1	34.8	36.8	n.a*	n.a*	8.6	11.8	10.8	12.2
Czechia	13.2	13.9	15.7	15.6	14.1	15.0	4.8	7.8	4.5	7.7	4.0	6.0
Denmark	7.6	9.9	8.7	7.9	15.2	12.3	4.0	5.8	3.5	4.3	5.6	5.8
Estonia	20.1	20.1	17.0	18.3	20.7	16.4	11.6	9.7	7.8	6.1	9.3	7.7
Finland	33.2	34.4	22.5	21.9	22.1	18.4	10.3	10.5	6.5	6.6	7.2	6.3
France	22.8	27.4	18.6	20.0	23.6	22.7	8.3	11.8	6.3	7.7	8.0	8.2
Germany	10.1	8.0	13.6	10.5	8.8	7.1	8.1	9.6	9.3	9.2	5.3	4.6
Hungary	16.0	12.4	16.4	16.4	20.8	20.2	7.3	6.1	5.8	6.0	7.1	7.3
Iceland	11.8	10.0	10.4	7.9	13.0	8.9	3.1	2.7	1.9	1.9	4.1	3.8
Ireland	12.8	11.6	10.2	7.9	27.1	18.1	7.2	6.8	4.3	3.6	11.0	8.6
Italy	28.9	37.4	20.9	27.5	33.0	36.8	6.5	12.2	4.8	8.3	8.3	10.1
Latvia	24.8	22.5	15.2	20.0	24.4	22.3	13.5	12.3	9.5	8.4	13.4	10.3
Lithuania	31.1	23.0	16.7	18.5	24.0	19.6	15.1	12.1	7.9	8.1	12.2	8.9
Luxembourg	6.7	7.9	11.7	16.7	18.3	15.5	1.5	3.1	2.7	4.5	4.2	5.4
Netherlands	8.0	8.9	8.6	8.2	11.1	10.3	3.0	5.1	2.8	4.2	4.3	5.2
Norway	14.2	13.8	11.1	9.7	10.7	8.0	2.7	2.7	2.7	2.4	3.2	2.6
Poland	28.0	31.8	31.3	34.3	20.3	22.7	10.1	13.3	12.3	13.9	6.4	7.2

Portugal	9.8	14.4	12.7	17.6	27.6	30.1	4.1	5.3	5.4	7.4	10.7	11.2
Slovakia	35.3	29.8	29.2	27.6	27.3	27.7	13.4	13.9	12.0	14.2	9.7	11.2
Slovenia	15.8	18.1	11.9	15.7	15.5	16.2	5.5	5.4	4.4	5.5	6.8	7.9
Spain	27.8	40.0	18.0	24.7	46.1	44.2	11.1	21.6	6.5	11.8	18.1	20.1
Sweden	17.8	15.8	18.8	18.2	22.9	20.6	7.7	6.2	4.9	4.6	5.9	5.5
Switzerland	6.1	5.3	7.6	7.3	8.4	8.3	2.5	3.5	2.8	3.9	4.0	4.5
United Kingdom	15.0	10.8	14.3	10.9	19.0	14.8	6.3	4.5	4.0	3.4	4.9	4.5
Average	**18.5**	**18.8**	**16.3**	**17.3**	**20.8**	**19.3**	**7.5**	**8.5**	**6.0**	**6.9**	**7.6**	**7.5**

Source: Eurostat Database (2019)

* Not available

There are many countries with high unemployment rates for the young over the time periods mentioned in Table 7.2. The shares of the countries having 20 per cent and over youth unemployment rates are 30 per cent, 26 per cent, and 52 per cent in consequent time periods.[5] In the first period, 63 per cent of these countries with the youth unemployment rate of 20 per cent and over, have higher female rates than male rates. For the second and the third periods, the corresponding rates are 57 per cent and 36 per cent. These results indicate that in these countries, the disadvantage of young females in the form of relatively high rates compared with males is gradually decreasing.

The link between gender unemployment gap, defined as the difference between male and female unemployment rate, and real GDP per capita for youth and adults is depicted in Figure 7.3. In the figure, the average values of the variables are plotted for the period 1995–2018. The negative relationship for the variables is observed for both age groups. In addition, for youth, unemployment gaps are more dispersed in the scatter diagram compared to those of adults. Majority of the countries are positioned in the same way, suggesting that the gender unemployment gaps for youth and adults are showing a similar pattern. Unemployment gaps vary between −6 per cent and 4.7 per cent for youth and −5.5 per cent and 3 per cent for adults. The number of countries with negative gender unemployment gaps (i.e. female unemployment is higher than male unemployment) is 16 for adults and 9 for youth out of 27 countries. Although female adults have relatively higher unemployment rates than male adults in many countries, the gap is not reaching that much high values as in the case of youth.

Figure 7.4 provides evidence on the relationship between the average gender unemployment gap and relative cohort size for youth and adults. Relative cohort size is measured as the ratio of the female labour force by the male labour force. Reference lines show the average level of relative cohort size and zero unemployment gap for youth and adults. All countries have relative cohort size smaller than 1, suggesting that the male labour force is greater than the female labour force,

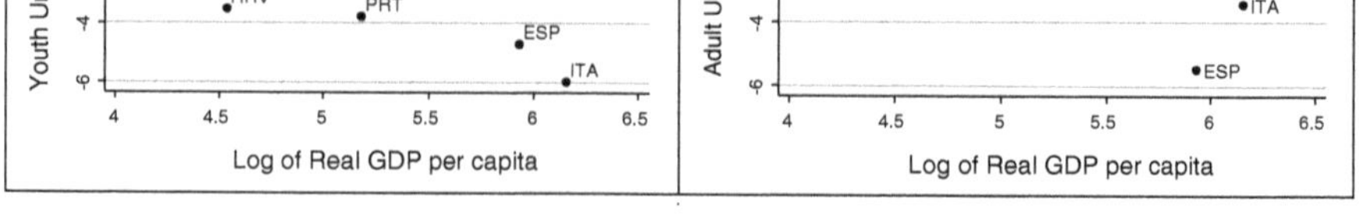

Figure 7.3 Unemployment Gap Versus Real GDP Per Capita (1995–2018)

Source: Eurostat Database (2019)

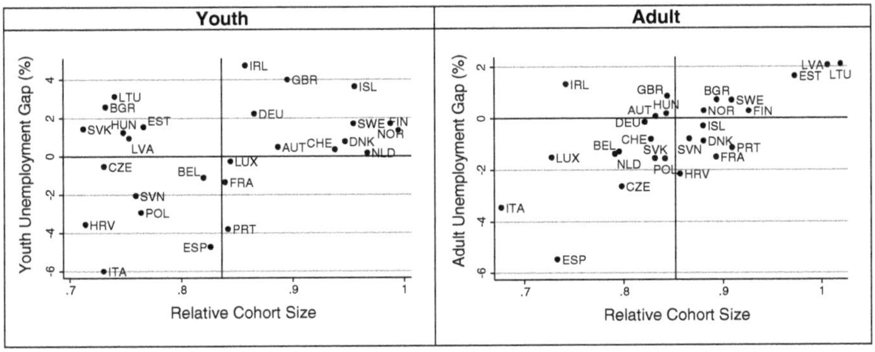

Figure 7.4 Unemployment Gap Versus Relative Cohort Size (1995–2018)
Source: Eurostat Database (2019)

with only exceptions of Lithuania and Latvia for adults. The adult female labour force is slightly above the adult male labour force in these countries. Estonia has also a ratio closed to 1. On the contrary, the young female labour force is quite lower relative to the young male labour force in Lithuania, Latvia and Estonia. Italy, Spain, Luxemburg and Ireland have the lowest relative cohort size for adults. As illustrated in Figure 7.4, adult unemployment gap values are mostly concentrated around the intersection of two reference lines, whereas for young people, the values of gender unemployment gap and relative cohort size are widely spread.

2.2 *Labour force participation*

Figure 7.5 illustrates the average level of female and male labour force participation (LFP) rates by age for the period 2014–2018. The 45-degree line is used to investigate whether a gender-biased distribution exists for LFP. It is a striking fact that male LFP rates are considerably higher than those of female for adults. Youth LFP rates display a similar gendered distribution at relatively low levels while the difference between male and female rates shrinks at high rates of LFP for the young. Adult LFP rates range from 78 per cent (Croatia) to 94 per cent for male (Iceland) and from 61 per cent (Italy) to 86 per cent (Iceland) for female, respectively. Figure 7.5 reveals more dispersion in LFP for youth than adults. Among the reported European countries, the maximum level of youth LFP is observed in Iceland (82 per cent for female and 80 per cent for male), followed by Switzerland (almost 68 per cent for female and male) and the Netherlands (69 per cent for female and 67 per cent for male).

Figure 7.6 depicts the average gender gaps in unemployment and LFP by age for the period 2014–2018. The fitted line with a negative slope portrays a negative relationship between the gender unemployment gap and gender LFP gap for both youth and adults. Generally, higher values of LFP gaps tend to be associated with

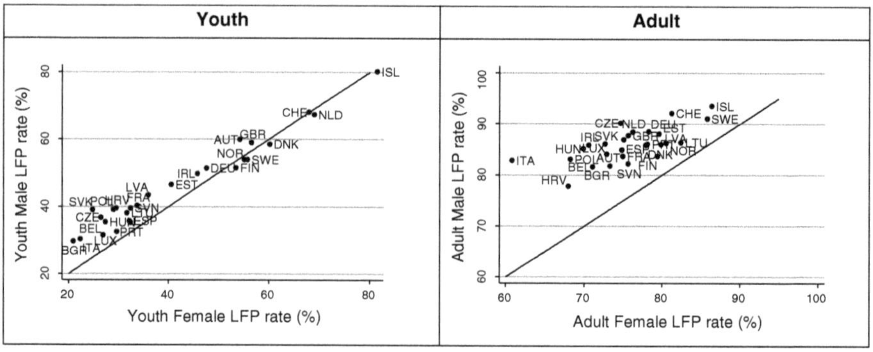

Figure 7.5 Adult and Youth LFP Rates (%) by Country (2014–2018)
Source: Eurostat Database (2019)

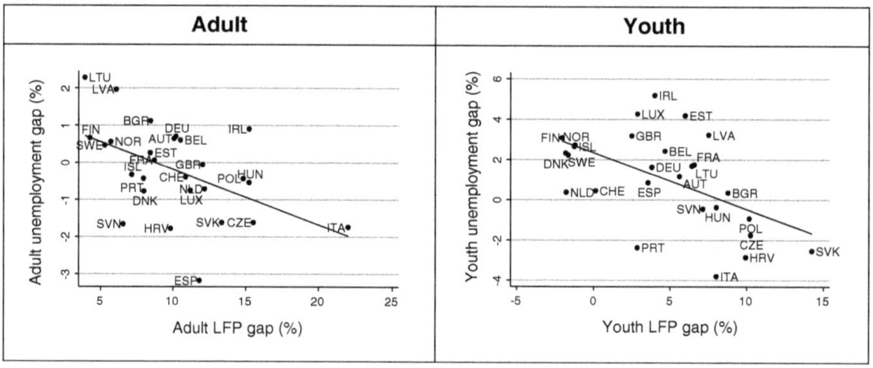

Figure 7.6 Gender Unemployment Gap and Gender LFP Gap (%) by Country (2014–2018)
Source: Eurostat Database (2019)

lower levels of gender unemployment gap. The figure implies that notably, all countries display a positive adult gender gap in LFP,[6] meaning that adult female LFP rate is less than male in the European countries plotted. Most of the countries have also positive gender LFP gap for youth while only 7 out of 27 countries, namely Switzerland, Netherlands, Sweden, Denmark, Iceland, Norway and Finland have a negative one.

2.3 *Employment*

The gender employment gap is defined as the difference between the employment rates of males and females. The employment rate is computed by dividing the number of persons in employment by the total population of the same age group.

Eurostat calculates the gender employment gap for the 20–64 age group. In this study, the rates are computed for 15–24 and 25–64 age groups by using the same methodology as Eurostat used.

The gender gap in employment rates for youth and adults are plotted for the last five-year averages in Figure 7.7. Reference lines are representing average values. The average gender employment gap is positive for adults in all countries, indicating that the adult female employment rate is smaller than the males. As for the case of young people, gender gaps are negative for seven countries (Norway, Finland, Sweden, Denmark, Iceland, the Netherlands and Czechia). Put differently, females are more advantageous than males with their greater employment rates in these countries. Indeed, gender gaps have the smallest values in Denmark, Iceland, Sweden and Finland. Although the employment gender gap for adults has very low levels in Lithuania and Latvia, young females have lower employment rates than young males. On the other hand, both the youth and adult gender employment gaps are apparently high in Italy, Hungary, Poland and Slovakia. In addition, Ireland, Spain, the United Kingdom, Czechia and Luxemburg have relatively large (between 10 per cent and 15 per cent) gender employment gaps for adults, but corresponding rates for young people is quite low (even negative for some).

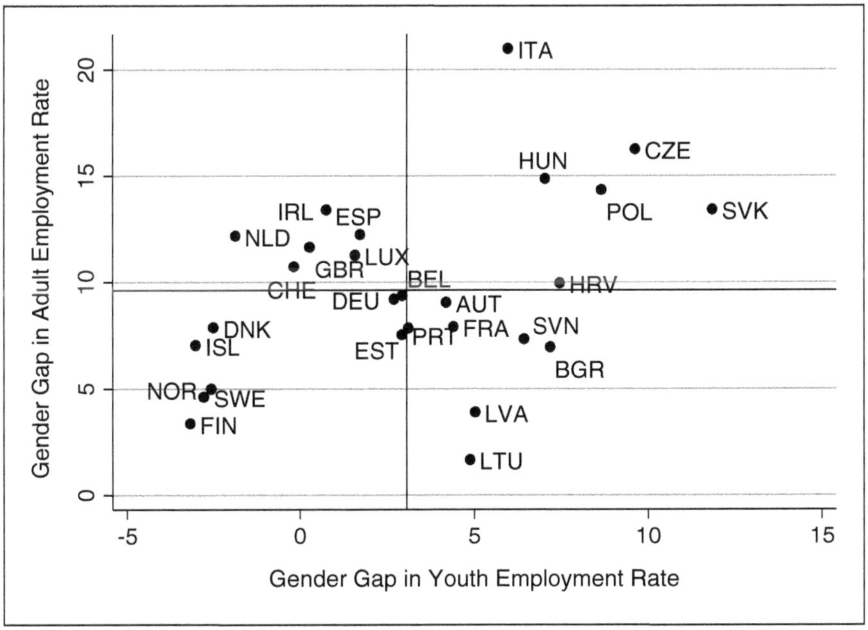

Figure 7.7 Gender Gap Employment Rate by Country (2014–2018)

Source: Eurostat Database (2019)

2.4 Sectoral employment

This part of the study reveals the main findings regarding employment distribution by sex, age, and economic activity for 27 European countries. Sectoral employment data for agriculture, manufacturing and service provided by Eurostat database is used to scrutinise whether there is a gender-biased employment distribution for adults and the young. Figure 7.8 shows the average male and female

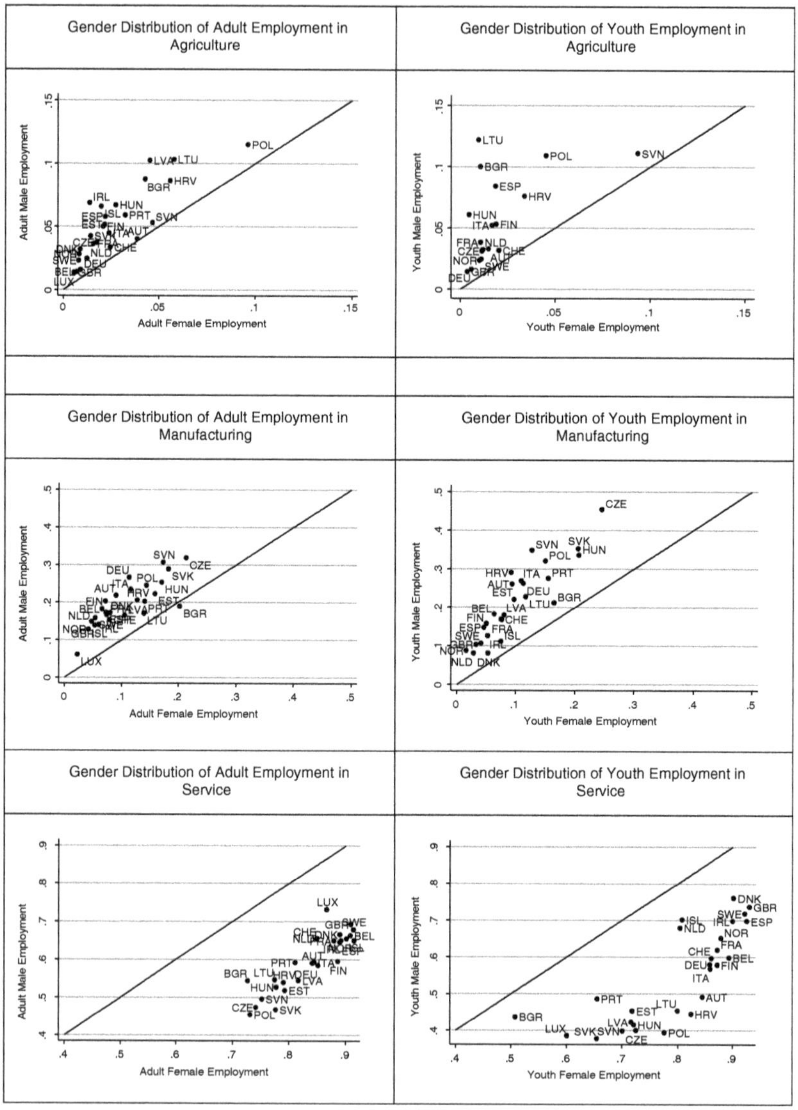

Figure 7.8 Gender Employment Distribution Across Sectors by Country (2014–2018)
Source: Eurostat Database (2019)

employment shares[7] by age groups in different sectors for the period 2014–2018. It also includes a 45-degree solid line to point out a gendered employment distribution across sectors. The left part of the line demonstrates the countries having a higher level of male employment share than that of the female. The right part of the line shows the countries with a higher level of female employment share than a male has for a specific sector.

Figure 7.8 shows that agricultural employment shares for both male and female are very low compared with employment shares in the manufacturing and service sectors in the countries. Approximately, on average only 2 per cent of female employees and 5 per cent of male employees are working in the agriculture sector. The maximum levels of employment shares are 12 per cent for males (Lithuania and Poland) and 9 per cent for females (Slovenia and Poland). Also, there is a positive strong correlation between youth and adult male employment share in agriculture while this correlation is moderate for females.[8]

The average female employment share in the manufacturing sector is roughly half that for male. On average, 20 per cent of total male employees and 10 per cent of total female employees are working in this sector. Czechia has the maximum shares of youth and adult employment in the manufacturing sector, (i.e. 45 per cent and 31 per cent for males, 25 per cent and 21 per cent for females, respectively). For both females and males, there is a strong relationship between the proportions of the young and adults employed in the manufacturing sector.[9]

In the service sector, both female and male employment proportions in total employment are remarkably high in comparison to the other sectors (Figure 7.8). Moreover, employment proportions vary considerably for adults and youth in the service sector, although these rates change relatively less in the manufacturing and agricultural sectors. Male employment shares range from 38 per cent (Slovakia) to 76 per cent (Denmark) for youth and from 45 per cent (Poland) to 73 per cent (Luxembourg) for adults. Corresponding shares for females range from 51 per cent (Bulgaria) to 93 per cent (United Kingdom) for the young and from 73 per cent (Bulgaria) to almost 92 per cent (Norway and Sweden) for adults. The link between adult and youth employment is not as strong in the service sector as it is in the manufacturing sector.[10]

It is apparently observed that regardless of the age group, agriculture and manufacturing sectors mainly employ males while service sector employs relatively more females. Almost every country analysed in this study, has higher employment shares of males than females in manufacturing and agriculture, with a disproportionally large share of female workers in the service sector. Briefly, women are more likely than men to be represented in the service sector and among the young and adults similar disparities exist.

3 The gender unemployment gap sensitivity to unemployment level

It is generally accepted that if aggregate unemployment rates are high, both females and males are less likely to be employed. An increase in the unemployment rate for a specific age group may create high unemployment levels for both male and females but the relative effect in terms of gendered unemployment may differ. In order to examine the existence of such a disproportional effect, this part of the study focuses on the sensitivity of the gender gap in unemployment to the level of unemployment for youth and adults.

There are several studies investigating the elasticity of youth unemployment with respect to relative cohort size and adult unemployment.[11] This study contributes to the literature by jointly employing the variables with gender and age aspects. The models to gauge the elasticity of gender unemployment gap with respect to the unemployment rate are as follows.

$$\begin{aligned} \text{Ln}\left(\text{adult\_ungap}\right)_{\text{it}} &= \alpha + \beta_1 \text{Ln}\left(\text{cohort\_adult}\right)_{\text{it}} \\ &\quad + \beta_2 \text{Ln}\left(\text{adult\_un}\right)_{\text{it}} + \varepsilon_{\text{it}} \end{aligned} \tag{1}$$

$$\begin{aligned} \text{Ln}\left(\text{youth\_ungap}\right)_{\text{it}} &= \alpha + \S_1 \, \text{Ln}\left(\text{cohort\_youth}\right)_{\text{it}} \\ &\quad + \S_2 \, \text{Ln}\left(\text{youth\_un}\right)_{\text{it}} + \varepsilon_{\text{it}} \end{aligned} \tag{2}$$

where youth_un, adult_un, youth_ungap and adult_ungap are the unemployment rates and the gender unemployment gaps (calculated as the male unemployment rate minus the female unemployment rate) for youth and adults. The variables of cohort_youth and cohort_adult stand for the relative cohort sizes, defined as the female labour force divided by the male labour force for youth and adults, correspondingly. Ln indicates the natural logarithm.

The preceding two models are estimated by the fixed effect estimation method, which incorporates the time-invariant factors. Table 7.3 reports the estimated results of the models. An increase in the unemployment rates shows similar effects on gender unemployment gap for both youth and adults, suggesting that a 1 per cent increase in the unemployment rate will raise gender unemployment gap by around 0.83 per cent. An elasticity of unemployment gender gap with respect to the unemployment rate of less than one implies that as unemployment rates increase, unemployment gender gap also increases but less than proportionately. This implies that change in male unemployment is more than female. It is a well-known fact that some sectors have more male workers than female workers (e.g. the manufacturing sector). If male-dominated sectors are more affected by unfavourable economic conditions (say, in terms of high unemployment), this situation is expected to generate a disproportionate change against male workers. Likewise, in the presence of favourable economic conditions with declining unemployment rates, new job opportunities seem to benefit males in those gender-biased sectors more.

An increase in the relative cohort size of 1 per cent for young people will raise the youth gender unemployment gap by around 2.2 per cent. In other words, as the ratio of the young female labour force to the young male labour force increases, young males become disproportionally more unemployed than females. However,

Table 7.3 The Elasticity of Gender Unemployment Gap with Respect to Unemployment

Model 1		*Model 2*	
Dependent Variable: Ln(adult_ungap)		*Dependent Variable: Ln(youth_ungap)*	
Ln(cohort_adult)	2.893	Ln(cohort_youth)	2.265**
	(1.909)		(1.017)
Ln(adult_un)	0.825***	Ln(youth_un)	0.833***
	(0.220)		(0.260)
Constant	−1.335**	Constant	−1.306*
	(0.541)		(0.733)

Source: Authors' own calculations. Robust standard errors in parentheses.

*** $p<0.01$, ** $p<0.05$, * $p<0.1$

the corresponding elasticity coefficient for the adults in Model 1 is not significant. That is, the relative cohort size does not have significant implications on the gender unemployment gap for adults. Thus, the relative (male and female) youth unemployment rates of young people are sensitive to the ratio of female to the male labour force. In addition, although the youth unemployment rate has a significant effect on the gender unemployment gap in youth, relative cohort size has a more important influence.

4 Gender unemployment gap, GDP and inflation

From an empirical point of view, the linkage between unemployment, GDP and inflation is explained by Okun's Law and Phillips Curve. There are enormous empirical studies checking the validity of Okun's Law which states a negative relationship between changes in unemployment and real output. It is possible to say that there is no unique result in the literature. Results are highly sensitive to country-specific factors, time periods and the samples selected but generally consistent with Okun's Law for developed countries.[12] Some of those studies focused on European countries. Hutengs and Stadtmann (2013) explore Okun's Law relation for a sample of European countries for different age groups. They find that young unemployment rate is responding more to economic growth.[13] Considering both age and gender, Dunsch (2017) indicates that unemployment sensitivity to business cycles is higher for youth but gender does not matter in Central and Eastern European countries. By analysing a panel of European countries, Brincikova and Darmo (2015) show that the effect of economic growth on unemployment is higher for males and sensitivity of gender-specific unemployment is higher for the countries with a lower level of economic activities. Hence, it is worth studying both age and gender aspects in the analysis.

The unemployment rate is also linked to inflation by the Phillips Curve which stresses the existence of a trade-off relationship between inflation and short term unemployment fluctuations. A low level of unemployment is expected as inflation increases because of expansions in economic activities which provide new job opportunities. Thus, unemployment, inflation and GDP are highly interdependent variables.

Our study contributes to the literature by considering the bi-directional relationship between gender unemployment gap, real GDP and inflation. Comparing with existing literature, this study analyses the link between these variables for a group of European countries, by using a different model specification which jointly takes age and gender into account.

4.1 Model specification

As is stated by Okun's Law and Phillips Curve, inflation and GDP per capita are closely linked to unemployment. Focusing on disproportional gendered unemployment, this part of the study examines the interaction between gender unemployment gap and two basic macroeconomic variables, namely inflation and GDP per capita. In the analysis, annual data of inflation measured by consumer price index (CPI), real GDP per capita, male and female unemployment rates for 27 European countries for the period 1995–2018 are used.[14] Unemployment gap is calculated as the difference between male and female unemployment rates for adults aged 25 to 64 and the young aged 15 to 24.

Because of the possibility of multidirectional interactions of these variables, panel vector auto-regression (VAR) model is used. This methodology including a system of equations allows us to enter all variables as endogenous. It also derives the impulse-response functions representing the dynamic response of an endogenous variable to a shock in another variable in the model.

The following regression model was used for VAR analysis including three endogenous variables:

$$un\_gap_{i,t} = \alpha_{1j} + \sum_{j=1}^{p} \beta_{1j} GDP_{i,t-j} + \sum_{j=1}^{p} \delta_{1j} inf_{i,t-j} + \sum_{j=1}^{p} \lambda_{1j} un\_gap_{i,t-j} + \omega_{1i} + e_{1t} \tag{3}$$

$$GDP_{i,t} = \alpha_{2j} + \sum_{j=1}^{p} \beta_{2j} un\_gap_{i,t-j} + \sum_{j=1}^{p} \delta_{2j} inf_{i,t-j} + \sum_{j=1}^{p} \lambda_{2j} GDP_{i,t-j} + \omega_{2i} + e_{2t} \tag{4}$$

$$inf_{i,t} = \alpha_{3j} + \sum_{j=1}^{p} \beta_{3j} un\_gap_{i,t-j} + \sum_{j=1}^{p} \delta_{3j} GDP_{i,t-j} + \sum_{j=1}^{p} \lambda_{3j} inf_{i,t-j} + \omega_{3i} + e_{3t} \tag{5}$$

where *un_gap* is the gender unemployment gap computed as the difference between male and female unemployment rates, *GDP* is the log real GDP per capita, *inf* is the inflation measured by CPI, *wi* and e_i are panel fixed-effects and idiosyncratic

Table 7.4 MBIC, MAIC and MQIC Information Criteria

lag	*Model 1*			*Model 2*		
	MBIC	*MAIC*	*MQIC*	*MBIC*	*MAIC*	*MQIC*
1	−179.008	−32.7956	−90.5360	−38.1464	−6.4137	−19.2696
2	−149.726	−40.0662	−83.3715	−21.4061	−0.2510	−8.8215
3	−101.109	−28.0030	−56.8732	−8.5518	2.0258	−2.2595

Source: Authors' own calculations

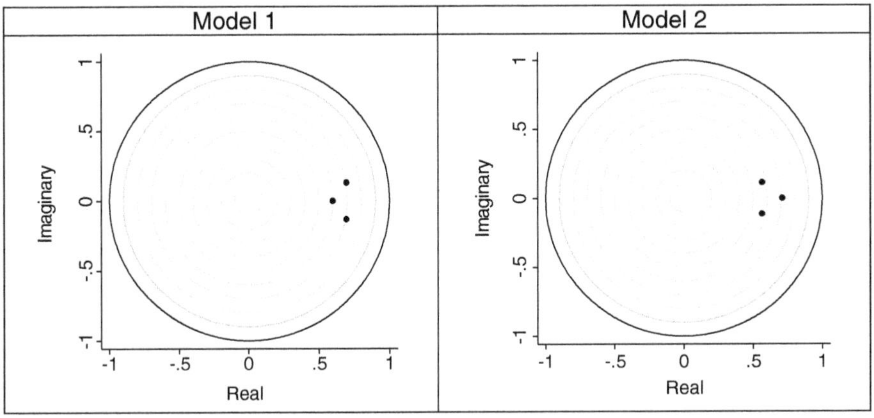

Figure 7.9 Roots of the Companion Matrix

Source: Authors' own calculations

error terms, respectively. The preceding equations are estimated for both adult and youth unemployment in Model 1 and Model 2 correspondingly.

For the analysis, the panel VAR method in the study of Abrigo and Love (2016) is employed.[15] Lag order selection is made by using MBIC, MAIC and MQIC[16] information criteria presented in Table 7.4 (Andrews and Lu, 2001). The appropriate lag length which gives the smallest value of information criteria is determined as 1 for both Model 1 and Model 2.

The eigenvalues of three different endogenous variables in the model are calculated. Figure 7.9 shows that all the eigenvalues are smaller than one in modulus and lie inside the unit circle. In other words, all moduli of the companion matrix are less than one. Thus, the constructed panel VAR models satisfy the necessary and sufficient conditions for stability (Abrigo and Love, 2016).

4.2 *Results*

The estimation results are reported in Table 7.5. All variables in the models are positively affected by their lagged values for both youth and adults. There is highly

Table 7.5 Estimation Results

VARIABLES	*Model 1: Adult*[17]			*Model 2: Youth*[18]		
	(1)	*(2)*	*(3)*	*(1)*	*(2)*	*(3)*
	un_gap	*GDP*	*inf*	*un_gap*	*GDP*	*inf*
L.un_gap	0.857***	–0.00305***	–0.133	0.687***	–0.00281***	–0.0739
	(0.0770)	(0.00118)	(0.111)	(0.135)	(0.000872)	(0.0575)
L.GDP	20.02***	0.516***	–15.47**	14.53	0.466***	-9.511
	(4.270)	(0.0650)	(7.367)	(9.013)	(0.0848)	(7.422)
L.inf	0.0305	–0.00131**	0.614***	–0.0766	–0.00139*	0.684***
	(0.0397)	(0.000618)	(0.0703)	(0.107)	(0.000718)	(0.0771)

Source: Authors' own calculations. Standard errors in parentheses.

*** p<0.01, ** p<0.05, * p<0.1

significant bi-directional causality between adult gender unemployment gap and real GDP per capita (Model 1). However, for the young, there exists only one-way causality from the gender unemployment gap to real GDP per capita (Model 2). Both adult and youth gender gaps in unemployment affect real GDP per capita inversely, whereas real GDP per capita has a positive impact on the gender unemployment gap for adults but not for youth. Inflation is found to be insignificant in determining adult and youth gender unemployment gaps. Table 7.5 also signifies a negative bi-directional causality between real GDP and inflation for Model 1 and one-way causality from inflation to real GDP per capita for Model 2.

Stability of estimated panel VAR analysis allows driving impulse-response functions. Figure 7.10 illustrates the impulse-response functions and confidence intervals (i.e. the shadowed area) calculated by using Monte Carlo simulations with 500 iterations. Each function in the figure demonstrates the reaction of an endogenous variable which is normalised by one standard deviation to one standard deviation exogenous shock in another variable in the dynamic systems of equations over the step horizon specified as ten periods. Since there is no statistically significant relationship between inflation and the gender unemployment gap, related impulse-response functions are not reported.

The functions estimated for Model 1 and Model 2 imply that a positive shock to real GDP per capita has a statistically significant positive impact on the adult gender unemployment gap as well as a negative effect on inflation. However, this exogenous shock does not have any statistically significant effect on the youth gender unemployment gap.[19] The maximum effect is experienced in two periods and it lasts in seven periods for the adult gender unemployment gap. Moreover, a positive exogenous shock in youth and the adult gender unemployment gap creates a negative impact on real GDP per capita. This effect peaks in two periods and lasts approximately in five periods. The results also suggest that adult gender unemployment gap has a larger impact on real GDP per capita in comparison to the youth gender unemployment gap.

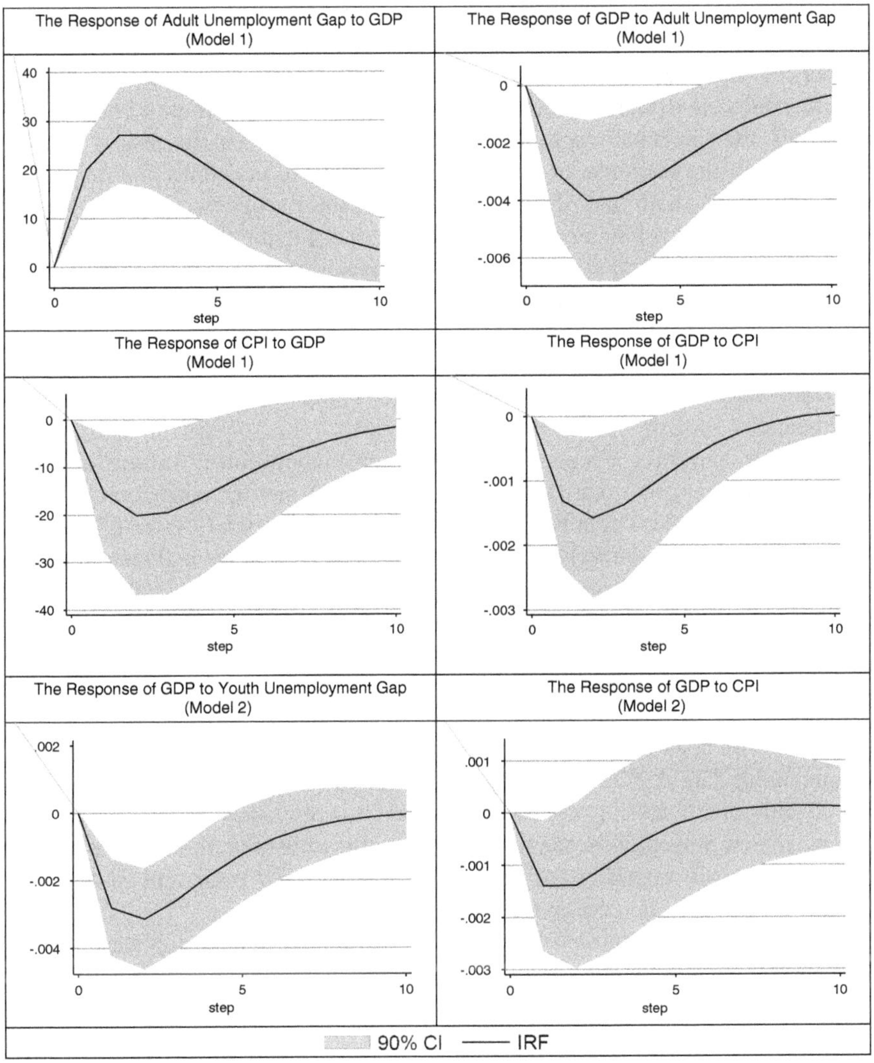

Figure 7.10 Impulse-Response Functions

Source: Authors' own calculations

5 Conclusion

This study concentrates on gender gaps which exist in the labour market in a comparative view for different ages and the relationship among gender unemployment gap, GDP and inflation. Descriptive analysis part presents some gendered labour market facts observed, specifically for unemployment, employment and labour force participation.

The most obvious fact is that youth unemployment rates are higher than adult unemployment rates in all countries and some of those countries are suffering persistently very high youth unemployment. The shares of the countries having 20 per cent and over youth unemployment rates are increasing over time. Although female adults have relatively higher unemployment rates than male adults in many countries, the gap is not reaching that much high values as in the case of youth.

Moreover, the response of youth unemployment to economic fluctuations is distinctly higher than that of adults. In most of the European countries, the gap between adult and youth unemployment enlarges due to the economic crisis. Since the effect of the global economic crisis on unemployment varies significantly, greater unemployment variations exist across countries during economic downturn periods. On the contrary, when the unemployment rates are declining, the variations in unemployment across countries are falling as well. Also, unemployment variation across countries is relatively high for females and the young for the last five years.

The male labour force is greater than the female labour force in almost all countries. It is another important fact that adult male LFP rates are considerably higher than those of female. Youth LFP rates display a similar gender-biased distribution across countries at relatively low levels, while the difference between male and female rates tends to close at high rates of LFP for the young. It is also observed that higher LFP gaps mostly are associated with lower levels of gender unemployment gap for both youth and adults.

In addition, all countries have positive employment gaps indicating smaller adult female employment rate than male employment for adults. Only seven exceptions out of 27 with negative gender gaps are observed for youth employment. Sectoral employment data demonstrate very low employment shares in agriculture compared with manufacturing and service sectors. It is obviously observed that males are mostly employed in the manufacturing sector, whilst females are employed in the service sector regardless of age group. Thus for both youth and adult similar gender-biased sectoral employment distribution exist.

Additionally, an empirical investigation of unemployment gap sensitivity to changes in unemployment level finds an inelastic unemployment gap with a positive sign. This implies that change in unemployment rate enlarges gap but less than proportionately and varies male unemployment more.

Finally, the relationship between unemployment gaps for different age groups and two main macroeconomic variables is analysed. Panel VAR models are employed to investigate whether multidirectional interactions exist among those variables. The estimation results are different for young and adult labour force. Highly significant bi-directional causality between the gender unemployment gap and real GDP per capita is found for adults. On the other hand, there is only one-way causality from the gender unemployment gap to real GDP per capita for youth.

It is important to highlight that regardless of age group, a greater level of gender unemployment gap is associated with a lower level of GDP per capita. This implies that if relatively more males tend to be unemployed then GDP per capita declines. This result is not surprising considering the gender employment gap, labour force participation gap and gender-biased distribution of sectoral employment. Relatively smaller female employment and labour force participation compared to males in most countries suggests relatively less active female labour force in the labour market. The economy having male-dominated labour market contracts if men become more unemployed. Moreover, since males are mostly employed in the manufacturing sector which is a key sector to support the economy, relatively high male unemployment may indicate a lower level of GDP.

The results of the analysis also suggest a positive significant effect of real GDP per capita on the gender unemployment gap for adults, but no significant effect for youth. This indicates that if the economy is expanding, the adult male unemployment rate decreases less than adult female unemployment does (assuming that real GDP and unemployment are inversely related). Also, lower GDP per capita is associated with a relatively larger increase in adult female unemployment. As a result, the change in real GDP per capita creates a gender-biased effect on adult unemployment, thereby affecting female unemployment rates more.

Notes

1 O'Higgins (1997) explains the reasons of these facts based on aggregate demand, size of the youth labour force and wages.
2 The only exception is for some years before 2002 in Germany.
3 Coefficient of variation is calculated as the standard deviation of unemployment rate across countries divided by the average unemployment rate for a given year.
4 The correlation coefficients between average young male and female unemployment rates for all countries in Table 7.2 are 0.90, 0.92 and 0.96 for 1995–2001, 2002–2008 and 2009–2018, respectively. Corresponding rates for adults are 0.80, 0.88, 0.92.
5 The countries having 20 per cent and over youth unemployment rates are as follows: 1995–2001 period: Bulgaria, Finland, France, Italy, Lithuania, Poland, Slovakia, Spain; 2002–2008 period: Bulgaria, Croatia, Finland, Italy, Poland, Slovakia, Spain; 2009–2018 period: Belgium, Bulgaria, Croatia, France, Hungary, Ireland, Italy, Latvia, Lithuania, Poland, Portugal, Slovakia, Spain, Sweden.
6 LFP gap equals to male LFP rate minus female LFP rate.
7 Female employment share is calculated as the ratio of female employment in a specific sector to total female employment, and male employment share is calculated as the ratio of male employment in a specific sector to total male employment.
8 The correlation coefficients between youth and adults are 0.84 for males and 0.53 females in the agricultural sector.
9 The correlation coefficients between the young and adults are 0.91 for males and 0.93 females in the manufacturing sector.
10 The correlation coefficients between the young and adults are 0.75 for males and 0.72 females in the service sector.
11 See Korenman and Neumark (1997) and O'Higgins (1997, 2001, 2003).
12 Perman, Stephan and Tavera (2015) covers the related literature testing Okun's Law for different groups of countries in its meta analysis.
13 Banerji, Saksonovs, Lin and Blavy (2014) also present a statistical analysis which points out three times more sensitive youth unemployment rate in comparison to adult unemployment rate.
14 In order to detect whether variables have unit roots, panel unit root tests of ADF-Fisher (Maddala and Wu, 1999), IPS (Im, Pesaran and Shin, 2003) and LLC (Levin, Lin and Chu, 2002) are performed. CPI and gender unemployment gap (both for youth and

adults) exhibit stationary characteristics in levels. On the other hand, GDP per capita has a unit root, therefore it is detrended by applying Hodrick-Prescott filter.

15 Stata 14 statistical package program is used in the analysis.

16 MAIC: Modified value of Akaike information criteria (Akaike, 1969); MBIC: Modified value of Bayesian information criteria (Schwarz, 1978; Rissanen, 1978; Akaike, 1977); MQIC: Modified value of Hannan–Quinn information criteria (HQIC) (Hannan and Quinn, 1979).

17 To test overidentifying restriction, Hansen's J test is used and p-value is 0.328 for Model 1 (Hansen, 1982).

18 Hansen's J test p-value is 0.163 for Model 2.

19 Since it is not statistically significant, impulse-response function is not reported.

References

Abrigo, M. and Love, I. (2016). Estimation of panel vector autoregression in Stata. *Stata Journal*, 16 (3), 778–804.

Akaike, H. (1969). Fitting autoregressive models for prediction. *Annals of the Institute of Statistical Mathematics*, 21, 243–247.

Akaike, H. (1977). On entropy maximization principle. In P.R. Krishnaiah (eds.), *Applications of Statistics*, Amsterdam: North-Holland, 27–41.

Albanesi, S. and Şahin, A. (2013). *The gender unemployment gap*. Federal Reserve Bank of New York Staff Report No. 613.

Albanesi, S. and Şahin, A. (2017). *The gender unemployment gap*. NBER Working Paper No. 23743.

Andrews, D.W.K. and Lu, B. (2001). Consistent model and moment selection procedures for GMM estimation with application to dynamic panel data models. *Journal of Econometrics*, 101 (1), 123–164.

Azmat, G., Güell, M., and Manning, A. (2006). Gender gaps in unemployment rates in OECD countries. *Journal of Labor Economics*, 24 (1), 1–37.

Banerji, A., Saksonovs, S., Lin, H., and Blavy, R. (2014). *Youth unemployment in advanced economies in Europe: Searching for solutions*. IMF Staff Discussion Note 14/11. Washington: International Monetary Fund.

Baussola, M., Mussida, C., Jenkins, J., and Penfold, M. (2015). Determinants of the gender unemployment gap in Italy and the United Kingdom: A comparative investigation. *International Labour Review*, 154 (4), 537–562.

Blanchflower, D.G. and Freeman, R.B. (2000). The declining economic status of young workers in OECD countries. In D.G. Blanchflower and R.B. Freeman (eds.), *Youth Employment and Joblessness in Advanced Countries*, Chicago: Chicago University Press/NBER, 19–55.

Blau, F.D. and Kahn, L. (2000). Gender and youth employment outcomes (The United States and West Germany, 1984–1991). In D.G. Blanchflower and R.B. Freeman (eds.), *Youth Employment and Joblessness in Advanced Countries*, Chicago: Chicago University Press/NBER, 107–168.

Bell, D. and Blanchflower, D. (2011). Young people and the great recession. *Oxford Review of Economic Policy*, 27, 241–267.

Bičáková, A. (2014). *Selection into selection into labor force and gender unemployment gaps*. CERGE-EI Discussion Paper Series, 513.

Breen, R. (2005). Explaining cros-national variation in youth unemployment. *European Sociological Review*, 21 (2), 125–134.

Brincikova, Z. and Darmo, L. (2015). The impact of economic growth on gender specific unemployment in the EU. *Scientific Annals of the "Alexandru Ioan Cuza", University of Iaşi Economic Sciences*, 62, 383–390.

Dauth, C. (2016). *Gender gaps of the unemployed-what drives diverging labor market outcomes?* IAB Discussion Paper No. 27.

Dunsch, S. (2017). Age-and gender-specific unemployment and Okun's law in CEE countries. *Eastern European Economics*, 55, 377–393.

Eurostat Database (2019). Retrieved January 10, 2020, from https://ec.europa.eu/eurostat/data/database

Hannan, E.J. and Quinn, B.G. (1979). The determination of the order of an autoregression. *Journal of the Royal Statistical Society*, Series B 41, 190–195.

Hansen, L.P. (1982). Large sample properties of generalized method of moments estimators. *Econometrica*, 50 (4), 1029–1054.

Hutengs, O. and Stadtmann, G. (2013). Age effects in Okun's law within the Eurozone. *Applied Economics Letters*, 20 (9), 821–825.

Im, K.S., Pesaran, M.H., and Shin, Y. (2003). Testing for unit roots in heterogeneous panels. *Journal of Econometrics*, 115 (1), 53–74.

Korenman, S. and Neumark, D. (1997). *Cohort crowding and youth labor markets: A cross-national analysis*. NBER Working Paper No. 6031. Cambridge, MA.

Levin, A., Lin, C.F., and Chu, C.S.J. (2002). Unit root test in panel data: Asymptotic and finite sample properties. *Journal of Econometrics*, 108 (1), 1–24.

Maddala, G.S. and Wu, S. (1999). A comparative study of unit root tests with panel data and a new simple test. *Oxford Bulletin of Economics and Statistics*, 631–652.

Niemi, B. (1974). The female-male differential in unemployment rates. *Industrial and Labor Relations Review*, 27, 331–350.

O'Higgins, N. (1997). *The challenge of youth unemployment*. Employment and Training Papers No. 7. Geneva: Employment and Training Department, ILO.

O'Higgins, N. (2001). *Youth Unemployment and Employment Policy: A Global Perspective*. Geneva: ILO.

O'Higgins, N. (2003). *Trends in the youth labour market in developing and transition countries*. World Bank Social Protection Discussion Paper Series No. 0321.

O'Higgins, N. (2012). *This time it's different? Youth labour markets during 'The Great Recession'*. IZA DP No. 6434.

O'Higgins, N. (2015). *Youth unemployment*. IZA Policy Paper No. 103.

Pastore, F. (2018). *Why is youth unemployment so high and different across countries?* IZA World of Labor, 420.

Perman, R., Stephan, G., and Tavera, C. (2015). Okun's law: A meta analysis. *The Manchester School*, 83(1), 101–126.

Rissanen, J. (1978). Modeling by shortest data description. *Automatica*, 14, 465–471.

Şahin, A., Hobijn, B., and Song, J. (2009). The unemployment gender gap during the current recession. *Current Issues in Economics and Finance*, 16 (2), 1–7.

Schwarz, G. (1978). Estimating the dimension of a model. *Annals of Statistics*, 6, 461–464.

Tåhlin, M. and Westerman, J. (2020). Youth employment decline and the structural change of skill. *European Societies*, 22 (1), 47–76.

World Bank (2020). Overall Global Gender Gap Index. Retrieved January 10, 2020, from https://tcdata360.worldbank.org/indicators/af52ebe9?country=BRA&indicator=27959&viz=line_chart&years=2006,2018

8 An assessment of the gender (in)equality in education

Gül S. Huyugüzel Kişla and Tarık Kişla

1 Introduction

Whether a country is specified as developed, developing or less-developed, education is accepted as the cornerstone of economic and social development. Education helps people to develop skills and knowledge, along with improving their lives, thus improving human capital. High levels of education contribute to better living, earnings, health and life satisfaction (Organization for Economic Cooperation and Development, 2011). An educated person is a key factor for economies, in terms of social and political stability and sustainability. In this manner, the education of girls, with the same rights as boys, and an efficient role of gender equality are very crucial in reaching the sustainable development goals.

The importance of gender equality in education has emerged over time. In this respect, countries have run many national educational programs in line with international education policies. Due to its importance, we first aim to discuss gender equality in education for the selected country groups. In this respect, some regions are selected in order to make comparisons. In addition, same perspectives are maintained for the Turkish education system. Therefore, in the first part of the chapter, we discuss the concept of gender equality in education. Afterwards, we make some comparisons that include the European Union (EU), sub-Saharan Africa (SSA), South Asia (SA), Latin America and Caribbean (LAC), Middle East and North Africa (MENA), East Asia and Pacific (EAP) countries. For this reason, we discuss the enrollment rates, literacy rates and the teachers' and academicians' positions of both sexes. After discussing the selected country groups, we consider the Turkish education system. Herein, data for the enrollment rates, literacy rates and the teachers and academicians are analyzed in the context of gender equality. Finally, we conclude the study with a general assessment of gender equality in education.

2 Gender equality in education

2.1 Major concepts

Gender equality is not a new or simple concept, and it needs to be discussed in a more detail for every country. Equality between women and men has been seen as an important branch of human rights, and in 1948 its importance was pronounced in the Universal Declaration of Human Rights. Equality between women and men has also been supported in international agreements such as the 1979 Convention on the Elimination of All Forms of Discrimination against Women (CEDAW) and the 1995 Beijing Declaration and Platform for Action.

Since the 1970s, many declarations, action plans and projects have been proposed and applied globally (Aragones-Gonzalez, Rosser-Liminana, & Gil-Gonzales, 2020). Especially, in the international era, discrimination against women has been discussed and many efforts have been targeted for the elimination of such discrimination. In particular, a big concern centered on gender inequality in education. From this point, specific initiatives have been made at different time periods. For instance, in 1990, representatives from 155 countries and from 150 organizations agreed in the World Conference on Education for All (EFA) to "universalize primary education" and "reduce illiteracy by the end of the decade". However, this was not an easy task for countries, and, in 2000, the international community met again in Dakar with 164 countries. The ultimate target in this platform was the achievement of Education for All (EFA) by the year of 2015. Six EFA goals were proposed. The first one was about expanding early childhood care and education. The second goal was providing free and obligatory primary education for all. The third goal was promoting various skills for young people and adults. The fourth goal was increasing adult literacy by 50%, and the other goals were including the achievement of gender parity and gender equality. Lastly, this global movement supported the quality of education totally.

Besides, the United Nation (UN) made vigorous efforts and proposed crucial development goals, namely the Millennium Development Goals (MDGs) in 2000 and Sustainable Development Goals (SDGs)[1] in 2015. In the SDGs, there are two important goals that are related to education and gender. The goal of gender equality includes the *achievement of the gender equality and empowerment of all women and girls*. The goal of quality education denotes *the ensurance of inclusive and equitable quality education and promoting lifelong learning opportunities for all*. The reason behind these efforts was quite obvious. Education itself preserves an impetus for economic growth and social development and hence educating girls has many positive outcomes from such an effort. According to UN (1995), education is a human right and achieves the purposes of equality, development and peace, though it has an essential place in people's lives. In addition, equalization of education among boys and girls can contribute to a more equal relationship between women and men. Also, gender–justice issues can be addressed by education. These issues have direct inclusions or implications within the formal education system. According to Klein, Ortman, and Friedman (2002), some of those gender–justice issues can be listed as:

- Women's health and reproductive rights
- Women in the workplace
- Women's impact on culture, literature, the arts, and history
- Women in politics and other leadership roles

- Women in sports area
- Global women's issues (such as marital and property rights, women's economic freedom)
- Family roles for both females and males

Moreover, the United Nations Educational, Scientific and Cultural Organization (UNESCO) supports the idea of gender equality in and through education. According to UNESCO (2019) Global Education Monitoring (GEM) report, girls must be part of the overall education system; they must remain in schools and benefit from the same opportunities as the boys have. Beyond the inclusion of the education system, girls need to have access to specific areas – like science and technology. Hence, the relationship between education and gender issues cannot be ignored. There are some important concepts regarding gender–education relationships. For example, gender equality and gender equity can be thought as the interchangeable concepts but there is no consensus for the exact difference between them (Aikman, Halai, & Rubagiza, 2011). According to United Nation Population Fund, *gender equity* concerns the fairness of treatment for women and men. On the other hand, *gender equality* implies equal satisfaction of socially valued goods, opportunities, resources and rewards for both women and men. More clearly, people are not the same, but their rights, responsibilities and opportunities won't depend on whether they were born female or male. They can totally participate in daily life and can be productive equally. In case of gender inequality, women generally have been over a barrel in taking decisions and having access to overall resources (UNFPA, 2019). Even though there have been some improvements for gender equality in education, some studies reveal that persistent inequalities still exist between women and men or girls and boys in all levels or types of education. From this point, we will discuss gender (in)equality in education more specifically in the next section.

2.2 Comparison of gender equality in education: some statistical facts

Basically we have some markers that might be used for indication of the gender (in)equality in education. According to World Atlas of UNESCO (2012), adult and youth literacy, enrollment rates for primary education, enrollment rates for secondary education and enrollment rates for tertiary education, and teachers' and/or professors' situations have been proposed for reflecting gender equality in overall education.[2]

- **Literacy rates:** This indicator shows the total number of literate people in a given age group. With the great efforts on the education system, the adult (people ages 15 and above) literacy rate of the world has been increased from 74.4% in 1990 to 86.3% in 2018. In case of adult females, this ratio was 67.5% in 1990 and increased to 82.8% in 2018. On the other hand, the literacy rate for adult males was 80.7% in 1990 and 89.8% in 2018. Literacy rates for youth (people ages 15–24) are much better for both females and males. For instance, the literacy rate for female youth was 78.9% in 1990 and surged to 90.4% in 2018. In addition, the literacy rate for male youth was 87.4% in 1990 and raised to 92.9% in 2018. These numbers reveal that there is a noticeable improvement in the literacy rates of females. The gap between females and males has narrowed in the past 20 years. However, literacy rates for all countries are not the same; there are still significant differences between developed countries and developing or less-developed countries. Figures 8.1 and 8.2 present the literacy rates for youth and adults for selected country groups.

According to Figures 8.1 and 8.2, there is a positive trend for literacy rates in the last 30 years, but regional and gender disparities still exist. Especially, literacy rates for South Asia and sub-Sahara Africa remained under the level of

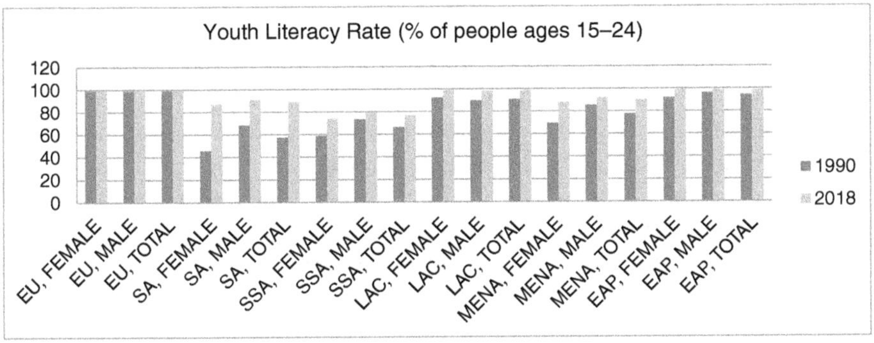

Figure 8.1 Youth Literacy Rates (Female, Male, Total)

Source: Thomson Reuters Datastream

Note: EU: European Union, SA: South Asia, SSA: sub-Saharan Africa, LAC: Latin America and Caribbean, MENA: Middle East and North Africa, EAP: East Asia and Pacific.

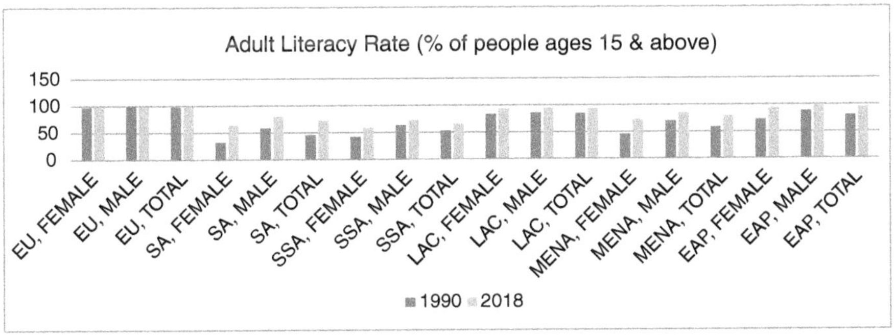

Figure 8.2 Adult Literacy Rates (Female, Male, Total)

Source: Thomson Reuters Datastream

Note: EU: European Union, SA: South Asia, SSA: sub-Saharan Africa, LAC: Latin America and Caribbean, MENA: Middle East and North Africa, EAP: East Asia and Pacific.

80% and disparities between women and men are quite high compared to the other regions.

- **Enrollment rates:** This indicator can be defined as the number of boys and girls of the age of a particular level of education (like preprimary, primary, secondary and so on) that are enrolled in that level of education, expressed as a percentage of the total population in that age group.[3] According to World Bank World Development Indicators (WDI), four kinds of enrollment rates are considered, namely *preprimary, primary, secondary and tertiary. Preprimary education* refers to programs at the initial stage of organized instruction. A school-type environment is introduced to very young children for the purpose of providing a bridge between home and school. *Primary education* provides students with fundamental skills in reading, writing and mathematics. At this stage, they also develop an elementary understanding of history, geography, social science, art and music. *Secondary education* follows the primary education; at this stage, students (up to the age of 16 or 18) intend to learn an intermediate level of complexity. According to International Standard Classification of Education (ISCED), there are two phases of secondary education, lower secondary education and upper secondary education. Lastly, *tertiary education* requires a completion of secondary education and mostly it is accepted as the academic or vocational or professional education. In this respect, Figure 8.3 to Figure 8.6 represent the selected periods for the enrollment rates in country groups.[4]

According to Figure 8.3, even though the disparities between female and male students have not been observed, there are still remarkable disparities between the regions. Although the European Union emphasized preprimary education, South Asian countries, sub-Saharan countries and Middle East and North African countries are the ones whose preprimary education levels are quite low, under the level

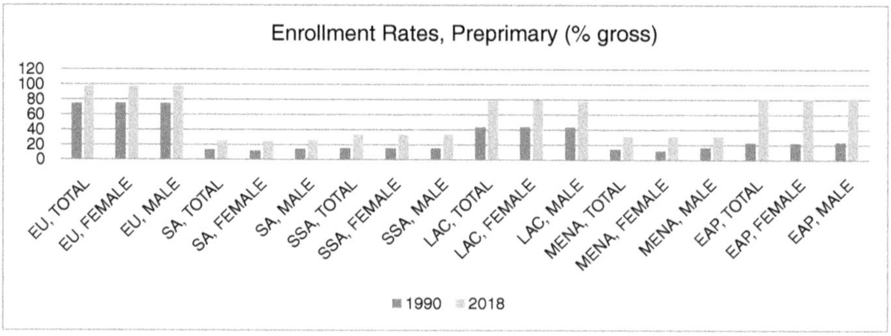

Figure 8.3 Enrollment Rates for Preprimary Education (Total, Female, Male)

Source: Thomson Reuters Datastream

Note: EU: European Union, SA: South Asia, SSA: sub-Saharan Africa, LAC: Latin America and Caribbean, MENA: Middle East and North Africa, EAP: East Asia and Pacific.

of 40%. On the other hand, enrollment rates in this category have increased as a result of the overall awareness on this issue.[5]

Contrary to Figure 8.3, the primary enrollment rates shown in Figure 8.4 are quite similar except for the rates of sub-Saharan Africa. The primary enrollment rates of the European Union, Latin America and Caribbean, and East Asia and Pacific are relatively higher than the other country groups. Also, it can be observed that the gender gaps in primary enrollment rates have narrowed in the last 20 years. While Figure 8.4 shows that countries give importance to primary education, Figure 8.5 indicates that some country groups like South Asia and sub-Saharan Africa lag behind the other countries in case of the secondary education. However,

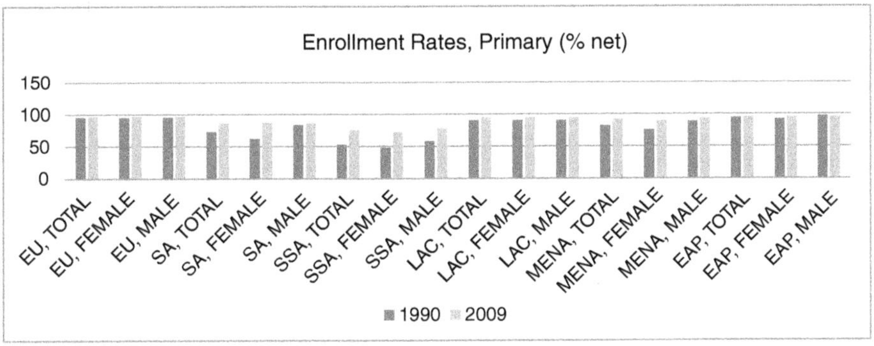

Figure 8.4 Enrollment Rates for Primary Education (Total, Female, Male)[1]

Source: Thomson Reuters Datastream

Note: EU: European Union, SA: South Asia, SSA: sub-Saharan Africa, LAC: Latin America and Caribbean, MENA: Middle East and North Africa, EAP: East Asia and Pacific.

[1] Data for some country groups ends in 2009, therefore we decide to take the last 20 years for the comparisons. The latest data for the other country groups have not changed between the years of 2009–2018.

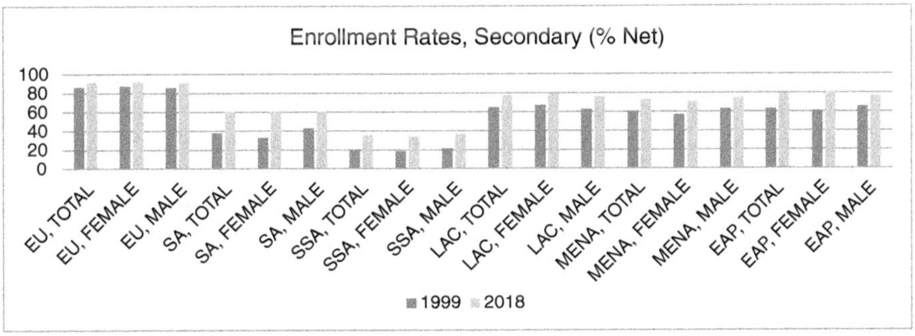

Figure 8.5 Enrollment Rates for Secondary Education (Total, Female, Male)[6]

Source: Thomson Reuters Datastream

Note: EU: European Union, SA: South Asia, SSA: sub-Saharan Africa, LAC: Latin America and Caribbean, MENA: Middle East and North Africa, EAP: East Asia and Pacific.

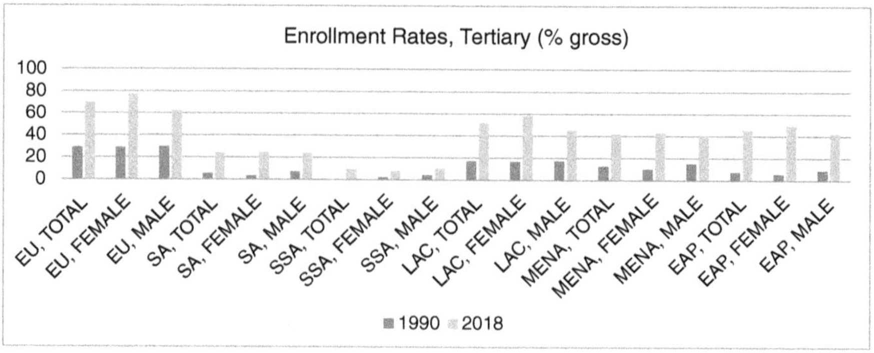

Figure 8.6 Enrollment Rates for Tertiary Education (Total, Female, Male)

Source: Thomson Reuters Datastream

Note: EU: European Union, SA: South Asia, SSA: sub-Saharan Africa, LAC: Latin America and Caribbean, MENA: Middle East and North Africa, EAP: East Asia and Pacific.

improvement in enrollment between 1999 and 2018 has been observed, and the gender gaps have narrowed for all the country groups.

Because the development of girls' education has recognized with the help of many attempts and the Education for All (EFA) agenda, primary and secondary enrollment rates have noticeably increased all over the world. On the other hand, enrollment rates for tertiary education have been relatively lower compared to the other education levels. The lowest rates are observed in sub-Saharan Africa with a rate of 3% in 1990 and 9.39% in 2018, but there is an interesting point that must be considered. Although the female enrollment rates for tertiary education were lower than the male enrollment rates in 1990, these ratios surged to higher levels and in fact they came up in the male enrollment rates in 2018 for the European Union, Latin America and Caribbean, Middle East and North Africa, East Asia and Pacific.

- **Teachers' and/or professors' situation:** Apart from the schooling situation, gender (in)equality can be monitored in the female teachers' in primary and secondary education[7] and female academic staff. Underlining the role of teachers in every child's educational journey, we represent some statistical facts about the female teachers in education. Figure 8.7 and Figure 8.8 show the aforementioned ratios between the years 1990 and 2018, and Figure 8.9 shows the ratio of female academic staff respectively.

While there is an increasing trend in the number of female teachers in primary education for South Asia, sub-Saharan Africa, Middle East and North Africa, East Asia and Pacific, the female teachers' ratio is nearly stable for the European countries and Latin America countries. However, those two regions have the highest female teachers' ratio compared to the other regions, with a ratio of nearly 80%. Also, there is a convergence between the regions in terms of the female teachers' ratio

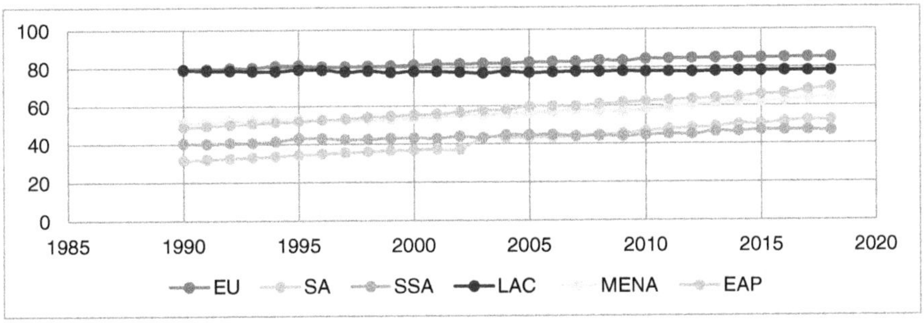

Figure 8.7 Female Teachers in Primary Education (%)

Source: Thomson Reuters Datastream

Note: EU: European Union, SA: South Asia, SSA: sub-Saharan Africa, LAC: Latin America and Caribbean, MENA: Middle East and North Africa, EAP: East Asia and Pacific.

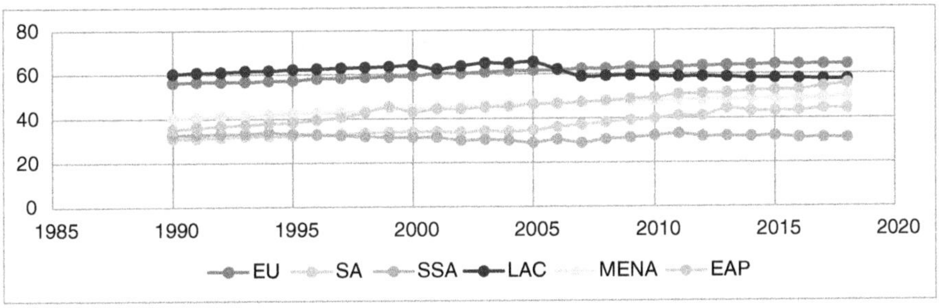

Figure 8.8 Female Teachers in Secondary Education (%)

Source: Thomson Reuters Datastream

Note: EU: European Union, SA: South Asia, SSA: sub-Saharan Africa, LAC: Latin America and Caribbean, MENA: Middle East and North Africa, EAP: East Asia and Pacific.

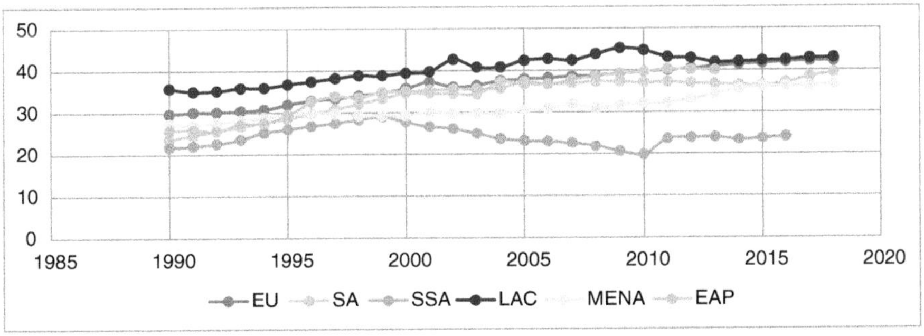

Figure 8.9 Female Academic Staff in Tertiary Education (%)

Source: Thomson Reuters Datastream

Note: EU: European Union, SA: South Asia, SSA: sub-Saharan Africa, LAC: Latin America and Caribbean, MENA: Middle East and North Africa, EAP: East Asia and Pacific.

in the last 30 years. Especially, the female teachers' ratio has increased between 1990 and 2018 in South Asia (from 31% to 52%), Middle East and North Africa (from 51% to 64%), East Asia and Pacific (from 48% to 69%).

The highest levels of female teachers in secondary education still exist in the European Union and Latin America and Caribbean countries. However, the percentage of female teachers in all of the country groups is found to be lower than primary education teachers. It might be a proof of the selection of female teachers whether they found a job or employment opportunities in primary education or secondary education. Especially, there is a little momentum for sub-Saharan Africa in case of reducing the gender disparities in teachers' ratios in secondary education. In particular, the female teachers' ratio is persistent in the level of 30–33% considering the SSA.

According to David (2007), the increasing involvement of women as students and academics has led to the expansion of the higher education. Figure 8.9 presents the share of female academic staff in tertiary education for the selected country groups.

According to Figure 8.9, the number of female academics has increased in the last 30 years. The biggest improvements in the number of female academics have occurred in South Asia, East Asia and Pacific, and the European Union. However, the majority of the academics are still composed of the male counterparts. Therefore, it can be said that there is still room for improvement of gender equality in academia, especially promoting women academics' careers.

3 A closer look inside the Turkish education system

Education is one of the most important factors affecting the future of a country as well as that of a person. For this reason, countries work diligently to organize their education systems and to create better systems. In the Turkish education system, the Ministry of National Education (MoNE) carries out processes such as determining education policies, directing education, managing the workforce in the field and organizing all educational activities. The framework of the Turkish education system is determined by the National Education Basic Law No. 1739. In Turkey, the Ministry of Education organizes the activities of formal and non-formal education to meet the individual educational needs.

Formal education can be defined as the education provided by private and public schools that are in line with the specific instructional plan and targets for the individuals who are at the same age. Non-formal education includes educational activities other than formal education in accordance with the general objectives of national education.

3.1 Formal education

In Turkey, formal education basically consists of four levels: *preschool (or preprimary)*, *primary education (primary and secondary school)*, *secondary education (high school)* and *higher education*. Primary education consists of eight years, four

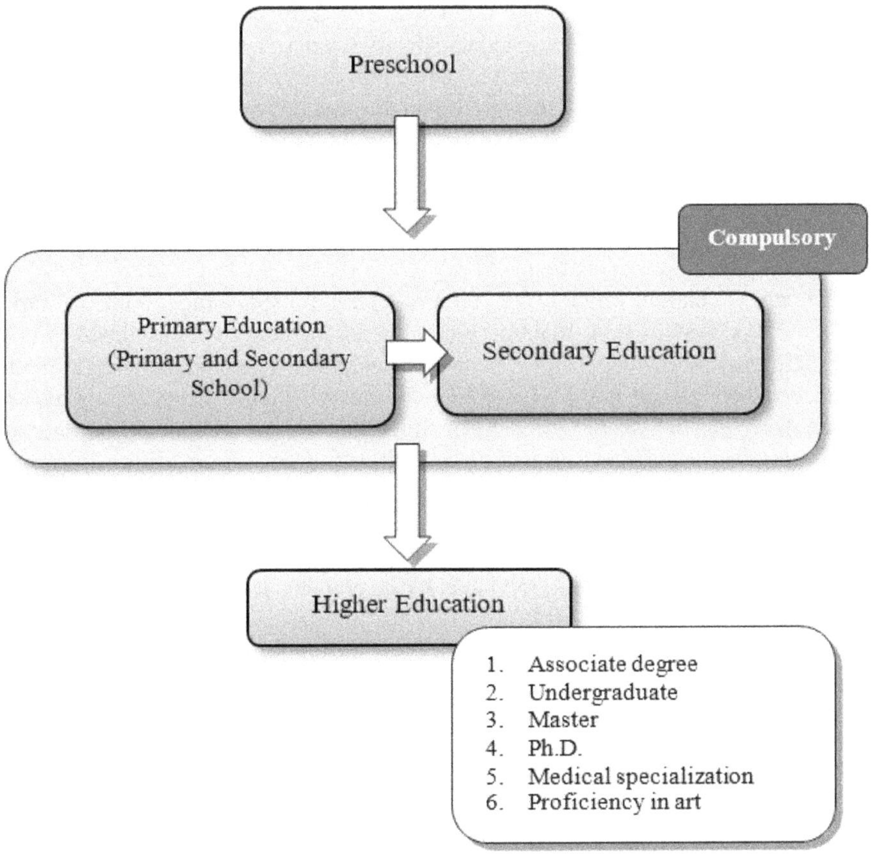

Figure 8.10 The General Structure of the Formal Education System

years primary school and four years secondary school, whereas secondary education, namely high school education, is arranged to last four years. In preschool education, the duration of the kindergarten level varies according to the student's starting time, and the kindergarten consists of one year. After the necessary infrastructure is established, it is planned to include compulsory five-year-old early childhood education within the scope of compulsory education. In the Turkish education system, 12-year education, including primary and secondary education, is compulsory as of now.

Preschool education can be defined as the process of development and education, covering children between birth and six years and laying the foundations for a child's later educational life, shaping the personality of the child. This period is also called early childhood. Children's psycho-motor, social-emotional, mental and language development are supported with help of the education offered in early childhood. In this context, children can express themselves, develop their problem-solving skills, be creative, realize that they are individuals in the society, and reveal their talents and skills in the best way. In recent years, the importance of preschool education has emerged and positive outcomes of the early childhood education can be observed. Preschool education is carried out in the independent kindergartens and in the nursery classes that are opened within the formal and non-formal educational institutions. While kindergartens provide education for children at the ages of 36–66 months, nursery classes give education for the children at the ages of 48–66 months. Because of the importance of preschool education in Turkey, MoNE provides mobile class services for children who have problems in continuing preschool education.

Primary education, which is the first level of compulsory education in the Turkish education system, aims to prepare students for the next education level by giving them basic knowledge, skills, behavior and habits. There are two stages in the primary education: primary schools and secondary schools. Primary schools are compulsory and consist of four years of education, whereas secondary schools are also compulsory and also four years of education but allow students to choose different types of programs such as normal or imam-hatip secondary schools. In order to participate in primary education, students must be at least 66 months of age. At the secondary education level, several trainings are offered toward the students' skills. For this reason, there are also elective courses according to the abilities, development and preferences of the students in order to establish the infrastructure of high school education. Open education secondary schools are provided for those students who cannot complete their educations at any secondary level for any reason. Thus, equal opportunities in education are promoted in this way.

Four-year compulsory secondary education, which comes after eight years of primary education, consists of general, vocational and technical high schools providing formal and non-formal education. The aim of secondary education is to prepare students for higher education or business life by increasing their knowledge, skills and general culture levels. There are secondary education institutions that implement various programs at the secondary level and offer education in different categories. These can be listed as follows:

- General high schools are educational institutions that accept students without any conditions.
- Vocational high schools are the educational institutions that aim to provide students with knowledge and skills for the profession, which were established to prepare students for business life. Vocational high schools focus on areas like technical, trade, communication, health, hospitality and tourism, teacher, maritime etc.
- Fine arts high schools are high schools that are opened to raise children with special interests and skills in fine arts from a young age.
- Imam hatip high schools are educational institutions established with the aim of training the staff in charge of performing religious services.
- Anatolian high schools are institutions where foreign language courses are more intense than general high schools and students are required to take an entrance exam.

- Science high schools are high schools that accept students with an entrance exam; for students who have a special interest and ability in science and technology.

Private high schools, which have unique admission conditions and provide paid education are generally educational institutions that offer foreign language education.

Similarly to primary education, there are also open education high schools and vocational open education high schools at the secondary education level so that individuals who are out of the system can continue their educations.

In the Turkish education system, an individual who graduates from a secondary education institution has to take a selection examination and get enough points in order to continue higher education. There is at least two years of education in higher education. The main purpose of higher education is to educate individuals with the knowledge, skill behavior and general culture of the professions they choose based on their interests and abilities. Higher education institutions are universities, faculties, colleges, institutes, conservatories, vocational schools, practice and research centers. There are three kinds of learning: daytime education, evening education and open learning. Degrees that are taken from higher education can be listed as follows:

- An associate degree is generally given by vocational schools. These colleges are generally aimed at vocational high school graduates and generally provide two years of education. Students who are entitled to receive an associate degree can continue their educations in educational institutions that give an undergraduate degree if they wish.
- A bachelor's degree is a degree given by universities that provide education for at least four years.
- A master's degree is a higher education degree conducted with two different structures, with and without thesis, in which undergraduate graduates are admitted with a decentralized election.
- The doctorate degree is the highest degree of higher education that students with a bachelor's or master's degree can apply and are accepted with a decentralized choice.
- The degree of specialization in medicine is the equivalent degree of doctorate for individuals with a medical education. In order to achieve this degree, candidates must be successful in a central examination and prepare a thesis.
- The degree of proficiency in art is the degree of higher education equivalent to a doctorate for an individual trained in an art.

In the Turkish education system, individual or institutional education is also provided for individuals who need special education. These services are provided through inclusion/integration practices or in public/private education schools and institutions according to the individual's needs in each training level mentioned previously. For students who cannot benefit from the services provided in educational institutions for any reason, education services are provided at home or in the hospital. Guidance research centers in almost every district provide educational assessment and diagnostic services for special education. In addition to these, trainings are provided through science and art centers to develop talent without disrupting the educations of gifted individuals.

3.2 Non-formal education

Non-formal education institutions serve to meet the basic education needs of individuals who have somehow been out of the system or who want to gain knowledge and skills to develop themselves in certain subjects. These institutions offer trainings in order to prepare continuous training opportunities, to provide opportunities for individuals to acquire professions, to improve the professional skills of employees, and to adapt to the requirements of the age. Non-formal education institutions in the Turkish education system are open schools, public education centers, practical art schools, technical education centers and maturation institutes. Courses are organized by these institutions for individuals of all ages and all educational levels.

4 Gender equality in the Turkish education system

Nowadays, learning and information acquisition resources and possibilities have increased and diversified with the possibilities offered by technology. The quality of the education that a society will provide to its individuals is of great importance in that it covers all segments of the society. Education is an important factor in meeting the needs of the individual to survive, improve herself/himself, become a member of the society and live in harmony with the society. In addition, education is extremely important for the individual to know and exercise her/his rights. This situation raises the need and the right of every person to be educated (Özaydınlık, 2014).

The concept of "equal opportunities in education" is defined as the ability of everyone to benefit from education in equal conditions, according to their abilities and desires. In order to say that there is equality of opportunity in education in a society, the basic parameters should not have any determination on the access to education process (Ferreira & Gignoux, 2010). One of the most important parameters of equal opportunity in education is gender equality. Various problems and obstacles may be encountered in society regarding the right to education. Gender inequality and sexist attitudes (Forbes, Öhrn, & Weiner, 2011) are among the most important of these obstacles. Today, significant improvements have been made in terms of gender equality in education systems. However, in the Turkish education system, as in most parts of the world, although there is a decreasing trend in gender inequality, the gap between women and men has not been fully closed. Access to the right to education for girls and women is still an important problem, although it is often due to income level and class position. Two-thirds of illiterate individuals in the world are unfortunately women, and this rate is found in almost all levels of education (UNESCO, 2016). The released data and the studies in the literature provide that although governments have taken various measures to prevent economic, social and cultural conditions threatening equal opportunities in education, they are not very successful in this regard.

It can be said that gender equality has two dimensions in education. The first is related to the opportunities offered by the education and school system regardless of gender. To this point, access to education, continuing, completion, etc., factors become important. Another dimension concerns the content of education and the process that takes place at school. The indicators listed here are used to determine gender equality status in education (UNGEI, 2012):

- The number of women and men enrolled in the education system
- The number of men and women who continue their education regularly
- The number of women and men who repeat the class
- Average school attendance of women and men
- The number of men and women who completed the training
- Literacy rates for women and men
- Number of male and female teachers
- Female and male manager rates
- Recruitment rates of men and women at the end of the training or education

Gender equality in education in Turkey, has become one of the main topics with the establishment of the national education system following the declaration of the republic. The legal basis of gender equality in education in Turkey is defined in the Constitution and the Fundamental Law of Education (Sayılan, 2012). Turkey's policy of equal opportunities in education is based on equal opportunities and responsibilities to be given to individuals regardless of gender. In Turkey, all individuals have equal rights in terms of access to schools at all levels of education since the founding of the republic. Beyond the Constitution and national education basic law, Turkey has also signed international conventions that support gender equality in education, for example, "All Kinds of the Convention on the Elimination of Discrimination against UN Women" (CEDAW), the "Beijing Declaration", "Convention on the Rights of the Child", and "EU National Report". In addition, action plans and decisions are included in Turkey's development plans in order to support gender equality in education. At this point, education policies are focused more on increasing the schooling rates of girls, reducing school dropouts and increasing the literacy rate of women. For this purpose, the Ministry of National Education has carried out various campaigns with the support of various non-governmental organizations, European Union and UNICEF. From this point, Figure 8.11, Figure 8.12 and Figure 8.13 present the Turkish education situation by making comparisons among women and men within the selected periods.

Figure 8.11 shows the literacy rates for adults and yuth considering females and males separately. Although there is a big difference between the literacy rates of adult females and males in 1990, this discrepancy has decreased in 2017; in

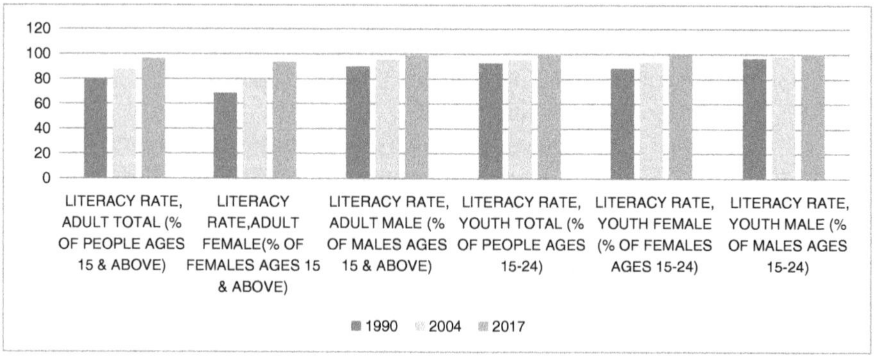

Figure 8.11 Literacy Rates in Turkey
Source: Thomson Reuters Datastream

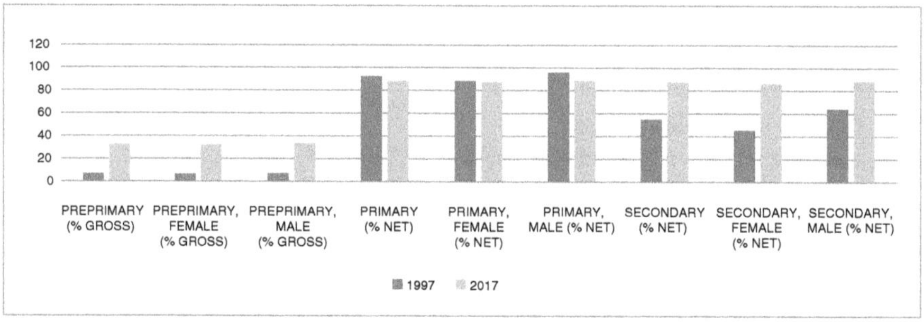

Figure 8.12 School Enrollment Rates in Turkey
Source: Thomson Reuters Datastream

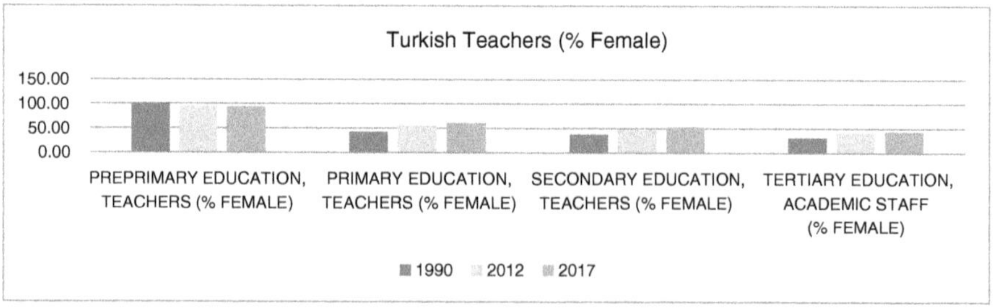

Figure 8.13 Female Teachers in Turkey
Source: Thomson Reuters Datastream

other words, the number of literate women and men converged to the same levels. Literacy rates for young people are getting much better compared to adult literacy. Especially, female literacy rates of young people, which have been above the level of 88% for the last 30 years.

According to Figure 8.12, while preprimary school enrollment rates in the last 20 years have increased considerably, primary education ratios seemed to be decreased in 2017, but this is not because of the worsening of the education system. It is because of changing the calculation method.[8] In case of the secondary education, the number of students enrolled in the secondary education has increased between the period of 1997 and 2017, whereas the gender disparity has narrowed in 2017 compared to 1997.[9]

Data on the enrollment rates and the literacy rates show that gender gaps between female and male students has narrowed in the last 30 years. Gender equality can also be monitored by looking at the teachers' situation (Figure 8.13). In other words, the ratio of the female teachers' can be used for comparisons. In this manner, we represent the female teachers' ratio in preprimary, primary, secondary and tertiary education. Whereas most of the teachers are female in the preprimary education, more than half of the primary teachers are female after the year of 2012. The ratio of the female teachers in secondary education resembles the primary education case. Half of the teachers in secondary education are female in 2017. The proportion of female teachers changes when tertiary education is considered. The number of female academics have been getting higher since 1990, but the majority of the academics in tertiary education are still male. Despite all of the efforts and initiatives that are taken, the Turkish education system still needs some improvements in achieving gender equality in education. Especially after compulsory education, a situation occurs in favor of men in the indicators of gender equality in education. Although the ratio of girls and boys in general secondary education converges, the traditional gender-based characteristics are still maintained in vocational technical schools in secondary education. In addition, the distribution of enrollment in tertiary education has evolved over time. Figure 8.14 shows the tertiary enrollments according to field of study.

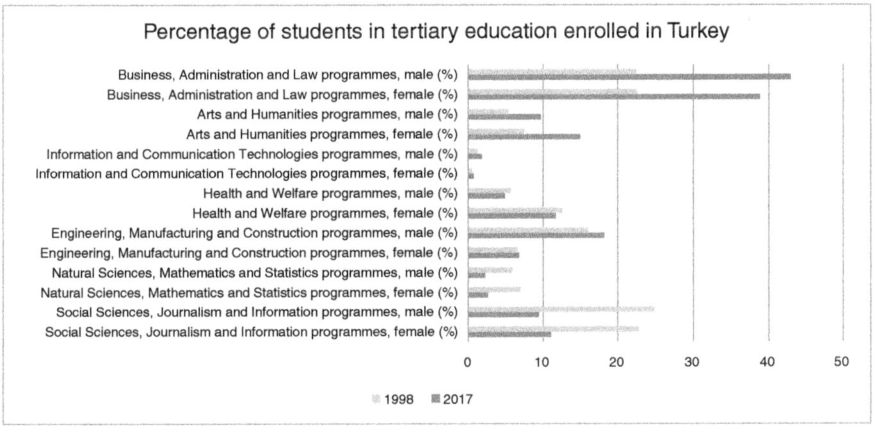

Figure 8.14 Enrollment Rates in Tertiary Education by Field of Study

Source: UNESCO Education Statistics (http://data.uis.unesco.org/)

According to Figure 8.14, students basically have tended toward business administration and law programs; art and humanities programs; and engineering, manufacturing and construction programs. The number of students in those fields have increased substantially. While the enrollment rates of both sexes seem to be similar in business administration and law programs, female enrollment rates in art and humanities programs are higher than the male enrollment rates. However, in engineering, manufacturing and construction programs, more male students enrolled than female students. The gap between the female and male students didn't narrow in this program. Contrary to those aforementioned programs, the enrollment rates of both sexes in health and welfare programmes, natural sciences, mathematics and statistics programs and in social sciences, journalism and information programs have decreased in the last 20 years. Even though there is a slight decrease in the enrollment rates in health and welfare programs, female students are still choosing this program more than male students. In addition, female enrollment rates in social science, journalism and information programs are higher than their counterparts in 2017.[10]

5 Conclusion

Achieving gender equality has a non-negligible importance in the international era, especially in case of economic and sustainable development. Equal access to education, healthcare and protecting human rights and freedom has been discussed in many studies. Since the Universal Declaration of Human Rights in the year of 1948, there have been many attempts and campaigns focusing on gender equality in education carried out by UN, UNESCO, Organization for Economic Cooperation and Development (OECD) and EU. According to OECD (2011), education is vital for enhancing human capital through improving the individuals' knowledge and skills. Generally, high education levels can lead to higher earnings, and higher productivities in turn improve countries' economic and social development. As of its importance, this chapter aims to analyze the gender equality in education from different perspectives. Thereby, there are two kinds of assessments of gender equality in education: comparisons of the country groups and the Turkish education system. In discussing gender equality in education, we basically focus on enrollment rates, literacy rates and the teachers' situation. In other words, we try to understand whether students are gender equal in reaching education and whether teaching staff are gender equal or not. In this respect, with the help of the many initiatives and governmental programs aimed at the improvement of education, it is obvious that literacy rates and enrollment rates have increased in the last 30 years. However, when considering literacy rates, the gender gap between the female and male still exists in some country groups like South Asia, sub-Saharan Africa, and Middle East and North Africa. On the other hand, enrollment rates of all the country groups has gotten better in the aforesaid period. In particular, there is progress in reducing the gender gaps in primary education, secondary education and tertiary education. In addition, gender equality can be monitored by looking at the female teachers' ratio. In this respect, most of the female teachers are found to be employed in preprimary and primary education. On the other hand, the number of female academicians are unfortunately lagging behind the male academicians. The reason behind this situation can be explained by some potential obstacles which are generally coming from responsibilities such as being a mom, maternal leaves and other societal roles that women must take on.

As a developing country, Turkey has made remarkable progress in expanding to education. Specifically, the enrollment rates and the literacy rates are getting higher year by year. This result may be coming from compulsory education that takes 12 years. On the other hand, gender gaps still exist in some areas like choosing tertiary education fields. For example, in engineering, manufacturing and construction programs, male students enrolled more than female students. Notably, the female teachers' ratio has increased in the last 30 years. Particularly, the female teachers' ratio is very high in preprimary education whereas this ratio stayed at the level of 50–60% in primary and secondary education. The foregone facts about the female academicians discussed previously are also compatible with the Turkish female academicians. Nearly 44% of the academicians are female and the rest of the academicians are male. This ratio is quite good when we compare it with the European Union where the female academician ratio was 42% in 2017.

Various attempts and the programs focusing on gender discrepancies in education are essential. The result of such efforts will not only be an improvement of educational status but also of the individuals' health; living conditions will also benefit from this improvement. These efforts made for gender equality in education will also lead to a decrease in the number of earlier marriages or pregnancies. Lastly, it would be good to integrate gender equality in education into economic, social and political policies. So, the power of women can be transformed into sustainable development via education (UNESCO, 2012).

Notes

1 An interested reader can look at the other SDGs on the website of https://sustainabledevelopment.un.org/?menu=1300.

2 Gender parity which is calculated by dividing female to male value for a specific category is the reflection of "formal" equality" in terms of access to and participation in education. In some cases, gender parity index can be used for the comparisons but it is a static measure and it doesn't conform to a wider definition of equality (Subrahmanian, 2005). According to Unterhalter (2015), it is a narrow measurement and does not give extra information about the dimensions of the gender equality. Therefore, we don't include the gender parity indices for the comparisons.

3 This definition is taken from Eurostat website of https://ec.europa.eu/eurostat/statistics-explained/index.php/Glossary:Net_enrolment_rate.

4 The interpretation of the school enrollment rates can be complex. There are two kinds of enrollment rates, namely gross enrollment rates and net enrollment rates. According to UNESCO's definition, gross enrollment ratio is calculated as the number of students enrolled in a level of schooling, regardless of age, expressed as a percentage of the school-age population that officially corresponds to that level. Net enrollment rate can be given as the total number of school-age students enrolled, expressed as a percentage of the total population in that age group. In some cases, net enrollment rates can be more preferable (Psaki, McCarthy, & Mench, 2018). However, we will represent both kinds of

enrollment rates based on the data availability. We collect data from Thomson Reuters Datastream who retrieves the relevant data from the Database of World Bank WDI.

5 Data for secondary enrollment rates in sub-Saharan Africa and Latin America and Caribbean start at the year of 1999. Therefore, we made the comparisons according to data availability.

6 Data for secondary enrollment rates in sub-Saharan Africa and Latin America and Caribbean start at the year of 1999. Therefore, we made the comparisons according to data availability.

7 This ratio shows the female teachers as of total primary education teachers.

8 In the former calculations, foreign students were including into the calculation, but after 2016–2017 period, they are excluded from the calculations Turkish Statistical Institute (TSI).

9 In WDI and UNESCO database, the gross enrollment rates of both sexes (female and male) are unfortunately missing after the year of 2000. While the female enrollment ratio of tertiary education has increased from 8.81% in 1990 to 18.98% in 1999; the male enrollment ratio of tertiary education has increased from 17.51% in 1990 to 28.72% in 1999. According to TSI statistics, the female enrollment rate was 33.6% whereas male enrollment rate 42.6% in 2007–2008. However, the enrollment rates of both sexes raised up to 100% in 2018–2019. It can be said that gender gap between male and female students has narrowed after 2016–2017 period.

10 Even though women and men have equal rights to education in Turkey, they may not have the same opportunities in finding a job after completing an education. For the sake of simplicity, we may leave the issue of gender equality in employment to the chapters in this book respectively.

References

Aikman, S., Halai, A., & Rubagiza, J. (2011). Conceptualiding Gender Equality in Research Education Quality. *Comparative Education*, 46–60.

Aragones-Gonzalez, M., Rosser-Liminana, A., & Gil-Gonzales, D. (2020). Coeducation and Gender Equality in Education Systems: A Scoping Review. *Children and Youth Services Review*, *111*, 104837.

David, M. E. (2007). Personal Learning on Professional Doctorates: Feminist and Women's Contribution to Higher Education. In M. A. Sagaria (Eds.), *Women, Universities and Change: Gender Equality in the European Union and the United States*. New York: Palgrave Macmillan.

Ferreira, F. H., & Gignoux, J. (2010). *Eğitimde Fırsat Eşitsizliği: Türkiye Örneği*. Ankara: DPT-Dünya Bankası Çalışma Raporu. Retrieved from http://siteresources.worldbank.org/INTTURKEYINTURKISH/147254-1269017398324/22764932/EgitimdeFirsatEsitsizligi.pdf

Forbes, J., Öhrn, E., & Weiner, G. (2011). Slippage and/or Symbolism: Gender, Policy and Educational Governance in Scotland and Sweden. *Gender and Education*, *23*(6), 761–776.

Klein, S., Ortman, P., & Friedman, B. (2002). What Is the Field of Gender Equity in Education? In J. Koch & B. Irby (Eds.), *Defining and Redefining Gender Equity in Education* (pp. 3–27). Greenwich, CT: Information Age Publishing.

Organization for Economic Co-operation and Development (2011). *Report on the Gender Initiative: Gender Equality in Education, Employment and Entrepreneurship*. Retrieved from https://www.oecd.org/social/48111145.pdf

Özaydınlık, K. (2014). Toplumsal Cinsiyet Temelinde Türkiye'de Kadın ve Eğitim. *Sosyal Politika Çalışmaları Dergisi*, *33*, 93–112.

Psaki, S. R., McCarthy, K. J., & Mench, B. S. (2018). Measuring Gender Equality in Education: Lessons from Trends in 43 Countries. *Population and Development Review*, *44*(1), 117–142.

Sayılan, F. (2012). *Toplumsal Cinsiyet ve Eğitim: Olanaklar ve Sınırlar*. Ankara: Dipnot Yayınevi.

Schultz, T. P. (2002). Why Government Should Invest More to Educate Girls. *World Development*, *30*(2), 207–225.

Subrahmanian, R. (2005). Gender Equality in Education: Definitions and Measurements. *International Journal of Educational Development*, *25*, 395–407.

UN. (1995). Summary of the Beijing Declaration and Platform for Action Adopted by the United Nations Fourth World Conference on Women. New York.

UNESCO. (2012). *World Atlas of Gender Equality in Education*. Paris: UNESCO.

UNESCO. (2016). *Global Education Monitoring Report (GEM Report)*. Retrieved from http://unesdoc.unesco.org/images/0024/002462/246230E.pdf

UNESCO. (2019). *Global Education Monitoring Report*. Paris. Retrieved from https://en.unesco.org/gem-report/2019genderreport

UNFPA. (2019). *Gender Equality Strategy 2018–2021*. Retrieved from https://www.unfpa.org/publications/unfpa-gender-equality-strategy

UNGEI. (2012). *Gender Analysis in Education*. Retrieved from www.ungei.org/files/Gender_Analysis_in_Education.pdf

Unterhalter, E. (2015). *Measuring Gender Inequality and Equality in Education*. Retrieved from www.researchgate.net/publication/283084293_Measuring_Gender_inequality_and_equality_in_education

9 Intersectional challenges in the labor market

The case of Roma women*

Meral Uzunöz and Aslıhan Yurdakul

1 Introduction

The labor market is one of the fields where gender inequality is most extreme. Gender-based segregation of labor leads to discriminatory practices starting from the recruitment process. However, gender inequality is solely one of the power imbalances in society, and individuals face various inequalities based on different power relations. The theory of intersectionality, introduced by black feminist Kimberlé Crenshaw (1989) at the end of the last century, precisely addresses this issue, namely the situation of being at the intersection of various inequalities. According to this approach; there are different factors that aggravate gender based inequality, such as race, ethnicity, religion, sexual orientation, class, age and disability. This intersectionality exists also in labor markets; that is, in our case, women who have different ethnicities may face different types of discrimination in labor market participation even if they have the same qualifications. Therefore, in addition to the gap between men and women, there is an intra-categorical gap between different groups of women, as well.

This study aims to shed light on the challenges Roma women face in Turkish labor market through an intersectional lens, and draw attention to the necessity of making intersectional policies for women. Roma women, who are members of an ethnic minority, are discriminated against due to both their ethnic identity and gender. In other words, ethnic discrimination is added to the existing disadvantages that stem from gender roles, social values, cultural habits, patterns and traditions. Thus the inequality faced by Roma women is different from the one faced by female members of mainstream society.

Another issue is the concentration in informal labor and ethnic niche jobs. The continuous reconstruction of negative stereotypes towards the Roma leads this ethnic group to move away from the formal labor market, pushing them to become cheap and temporary labor in the informal labor market. In the meantime, traditional roles assigned to women cause them to concentrate in certain occupations and not be able to go beyond them. As we evaluate this situation in the case of the Roma, the link between ethnic identity and the labor market also comes into play and it is found that Roma women work at low wages in the occupations which are specifically called ethnic niche.

To thoroughly investigate Roma women's intersectionality in Turkish labor market, we will first introduce the theory of intersectionality and we will remark the necessity of its use in labor market research. In the following sections we outline the overall labor market participation of Roma women in Turkey and the three specific challenges they face: discrimination, lack of education and dependence on social transfers.

2 What is intersectionality?

Emergence of the intersectionality theory is related to the criticism black feminists direct to mainstream feminism. Black feminists have criticized that white women, and specifically white middle class women, do not include blacks in their feminist ideals. First coined by Kimberlé Crenshaw (1989), the term intersectionality is a conceptualization of this criticism. According to Crenshaw, "black women can experience discrimination in any number of ways and that the contradiction arises from our assumptions that their claims of exclusion must be unidirectional" (1989:149). Put differently, Crenshaw's conception of intersectionality underscores the "multidimensionality" of marginalized subjects' lived experiences and implies that a focus on the most privileged members of the society marginalizes those who are multiply burdened and obscures claims that cannot be understood as resulting from discrete sources of discrimination (1989:139–140). Accordingly, any type of single axis analysis will connote a concentration on the experiences of the "otherwise privileged" within one single group (McBride et al., 2015:5).

Emphasizing the vulnerability caused by different disadvantages, intersectionality theory has been transformed and reinterpreted many times after Crenshaw's groundbreaking work. Although it emerged in the axis of race and gender, the intersectionality theory was actually a response to one-dimensional analysis, and "a methodological caution against over-generalization" (McBride et al., 2015:5). Therefore, its influence has been wider than discrimination analysis based on race and gender. In this regard, building on the first step on theorizing intersectionality, Patricia Hill Collins (2015) defined the race, class, gender, sexuality, age, ability, nation, ethnicity and similar categories of analysis to be best analyzed and understood in relational terms rather than in isolation from one another. According to Collins (2015:14), these mutually constructing categories underlie and shape intersecting systems of power which catalyze social formations of complex social inequalities that are organized via unequal realities and distinctive social experiences for people who live with them.

Afore-cited critique of conventional feminism emphasizes the disconnect between feminism's claims to speak for all women and feminism's perennial inattention to racial, ethnic, class and sexual differences (Nash, 2008:3). The complex network of different categories is called "intersection" (McCall, 2005). One of the most significant contributions of intersectionality theory to the literature was the emphasis it puts on the difference of the experiences of women in the intersection. There are different power relations in the society. Gender is just one of these and there are many others, such as race, ethnicity, sexual orientation and social class. Oppression caused by more than one of the power relations in question and experienced by marginalized groups, was conceptualized in such ways as double disadvantage, triple oppression until Crenshaw's (1989) conceptualization of intersectionality. And this was the reason for a misconception that oppression of power relations increases additively. However, what the theory of intersection argues is that the disadvantage of multiple power relationships cannot be called double or triple oppression, but rather that oppression will be different from racism or sexism alone. Thus, although initially proposed by black feminists to understand the different experiences of black women from whites, today, intersectionality studies include a wider range of intra-categorical differences based on power relations in the society.

2.1 *Intersectionality in the labor market*

Since its proposal, from political science to psychology, various fields of social sciences have drawn on intersectionality theory, and various scholars have drawn attention to the need for intersectional approach in labor market studies (Browne & Misra, 2003; Mulinari & Selberg, 2013; Tomaskovic-Devey, 2014; McBride et al., 2015). When evaluated in the context of labor market studies, the intersectionality theory argues that women are not a homogeneous group, and therefore their working life experiences differ from one another on the basis of their sub-groups. The contribution of the concept to labor market studies is twofold. While the first draws attention to the limits of generalization of women's experiences, the second is that individuals who are at the intersection of more than one category will experience different experiences than individuals having only one category. McBride et al. (2015:8) therefore emphasizes the necessity of intersectionality theory in labor market research.

Intersectional approach assumes that employers make decisions about hiring, promotions, training and wages based on the combination of a worker's race and gender (Weber, 2001), or any other social categories they belong to. In other words, it states that there are different variables in contrast to neoclassical economic theory based on human capital in labor market participation, so only education, ability or experience are not decisive in this context (Browne & Misra, 2003:506). The power relations, which are the determining factor of the mentioned variables caused by the power relations we explained in the previous section, indicates not only inequality in the labor market, but also the invisible norms, values and attitudes that construct some people as different, deviant and subordinate (De los Reyes, 2017:1).

On the other hand, Paulina De los Reyes (2017) argues that intersectionality is not only related to the discrimination mechanisms based on different types of oppression but also to different perceptions of labor arising from the accumulation of capital in the current capitalist order. Accordingly, while the current capitalist order provides the privileged with new consumption opportunities, it brings new forms of exploitation, and therefore tasks in the workplace are determined not only by skills and qualifications but also by other power relations such as class, age, gender, sexuality and nationality (De los Reyes, 2017:4).

This view also explains the economic stratification. Domestic work, one of the clearest examples of economic stratification, has been historically carried out by ethnic minorities and immigrants and informal working conditions as well as the idea that chores are the natural female work result in precarity for workers (Browne & Misra, 2003:502). Evelyn Nakano Glenn (1992) argues that to raise their living standards, white middle class women depend on the exploitation of minority women. Intersectionality theory draws attention to this point in labor market research; despite the gains of mainstream feminism in the labor market, the position of women who stay at the intersection have mostly been ignored.

3 Case of Roma women in Turkey

The intersectional examination of the challenges that Roma women face in access to labor market and the intersectional policies to be applied in this direction can be clearly concretized when supported by statistics and field studies. Statistical data on ethnicity-based labor market dynamics is not available in Turkey. Thus, the challenges Roma women face in labor market will be explained with the data obtained through surveys and interviews in the fieldwork.

3.1 Methods and data

Mixed method of qualitative and quantitative techniques have been employed in the research. In this context, the research was built on questionnaires, in-depth interviews and focus group studies. Before applying these techniques, the provinces and districts where the research will be carried out were determined. Two criteria were taken into consideration in the determination of the provinces: the cities where the Roma population is dense and the regional distribution of the population. The research was carried out in 12 provinces – Istanbul, Ankara, Izmir, Antalya, Eskişehir, Diyarbakır, Kocaeli, Edirne, Çanakkale, Samsun, Hatay and Muğla – where the Roma live at the highest rate, selected from the NUTS-2 subregions, each linked to NUTS-1 region. The fieldwork of the research was based on questionnaires, in-depth interviews and focus group studies. A total of 1568 households were surveyed; 120 people were interviewed in depth and 26 focus group studies were conducted. In the research, 593 women were interviewed face to face.

The interviews focused on the personal experiences of Roma. The background of general and quantitative data obtained in the questionnaires was tried to reach and qualitative information complementing the quantitative data have been received. In this context, the adaptation processes in the working life arising from the identity of women, the treatment they are exposed to in work life, work motivations, working disciplines, education levels, etc., were tried to be determined from the point of view of the interviewed Roma.

3.2 Roma women's participation in labor market

There is a large body of research focusing on the Roma's participation in labor market. Some have so far highlighted that unemployment rates are significantly higher among the Roma than majority (non-Roma) communities (Ringold et al., 2005; UNDP, 2005). However, lack of necessary data results in lack of gender-based analysis of the Roma's labor market performance. Even so, despite some recent studies on gender-based analysis of the Roma's employment (Tóth, 2005; UNDP, 2006; Kóczé, 2009; Drydakis, 2011; Kahanec, 2014; Blazevski et al., 2018; Dincă & Luches, 2018; Lawton et al., 2018), the amount of the research based on intersectional approach is highly limited. As noted by Kóczé and Popa (2009) although there are remarkable theoretical literature and persuasive arguments in this regard, intersectionality has been limitedly studied in the studies focusing on the Roma and the Roma women.

The female labor force participation rate in Turkish labor market is 34.8%; while it is 73.0% for men (TSI, 2019b). According to the OECD, the female labor force participation rate was 52.5% for 2018 (OECD, 2019). However the gender gap is bigger in the case of the Roma in Turkey. According to the results of our research, conducted in 12 provinces in Turkey, the participation rate of labor market for Roma women is 24.9%, while it is 72.2% for men. In the light of these data, it is clear that Roma women are more vulnerable to becoming unemployed than their counterparts in general population of Turkey.

Information of gender gap in employment is of particular importance to understand the existing structural problems in ethnic groups. Rauh (2018) concluded that Roma communities faced lower employment and thus higher unemployment levels than non-Roma. He emphasizes that ethnic and gender employment gaps occur among the Roma, with the possibility of women being employed less than men, and that the literacy rates results in improvements for the community.

Numerous economic and sociological reasons underlie the gender gap in employment. Social values, cultural codes and patterns play an extremely important role in this context. In our field of research, the following statements of a participant reflect this fact:

> Doms[1] do not approve women's employment, in general. They judge me because I let my daughter works in a cafe. But I have nothing to do. I don't have a husband, I'm a widow. I and my children will necessarily work and make our living. We need to do these in order not to rely on anybody.
>
> (F. G., Diyarbakır: Woman)

Andersen and Muriel (2007) state that women in the disadvantaged groups generally prefer to be employed in informal sectors. According to our results, 36.9% of the employed Roma in Turkey work in the formal labor market. The rate of those who find employment opportunities in the informal sectors is 63.1%, while this goes up to 70.78% for women. According to 2018 data, rate of informal employment is 33% for general population, and 41.5% for women (TSI, 2019b). The main reason for women being more inclined to be employed in informal sectors is, according to Öztürk and Başar (2018), related to the invisible labor women are responsible for. This is the case especially in developing countries. Furthermore,

OECD (2019) report implies that women receive lower wages than men in the informal sectors.

There is a relationship between marital status of Roma women and employment. In such cases as divorce, death of the spouse, living separately with the spouse, it is observed that women who were not in the workforce before, enter labor markets and especially informal areas.

Literacy is also an intersectional problem for Roma women. Participation in education is generally low in the Roma community. However, considering the pattern of girls not being sent to school, we can say that Roma women are disadvantageous in a deeper way than men. We have found that 90% of illiterate women work in informal sectors. As the level of education increases, the number of women who find employment opportunities in formal markets increases. These findings support the fact that education is one of the basic conditions for the Roma to be able to take place in formal employment. With the increase in the level of education of the Roma, the probability of being visible in formal sectors increases linearly. However, our findings imply that 70% of women who find employment opportunities in the formal sectors are primary and secondary school graduates and still do not work in the qualified jobs.

Our study results indicate that among Roma women, the rate of those who have annual household income between 0 and 15 000 TL[2] is 22%; those who have income between 15 001 and 30 000 TL 39.5%; those between 30 001 TL and 45 000 TL have a rate of 20.2%. The remaining 18.3% portion has an annual income of 45 001 TL and above. According to the Income and Living Conditions Survey (2018) prepared by TUIK; According to the household members' income in Turkey average annual income is 30 748 TL (TSI, 2019a). Considering the annual household income of the Roma, it is observed that the proportion of those living below the poverty line is 85%. Establishing a link between poverty and informal employment will not be wrong. It cannot be denied that women's living in poor families is an obstacle to conveying them from the informal sector to the formal sector. As Öztürk and Başar (2018) stated, women are willing to work in informal sectors especially when they are in poverty, which results in a vicious cycle. The reason for poor women to choose to work in informal sectors is mainly their domestic responsibilities, since they cannot afford time to work in formal labor market.

For Roma women, another important issue is the concentration in informal labor and ethnic niche jobs. Ethnic niche (ethnic labor market intensity) is a concept that defines ethnic division in the labor market (Kushnirovich, 2015) and indicates that an ethnic group has a dominant number of major business lines (Wang & Pandit, 2007; Zhou, 2013). The continuous reconstruction of negative stereotypes towards the Roma leads this ethnic group to move away from the formal labor market, pushing them to become cheap and temporary labor in the informal labor market. In the meantime, traditional roles assigned to women cause them to concentrate in certain occupations and not be able to go beyond them. As we evaluate this situation in the case of the Roma, the link between ethnic identity and the labor market also comes into play and it is found that Roma women work at low wages in the occupations which are specifically called ethnic niche. Drydakis (2011) examines that Roma women are overrepresented in blue-collar jobs and in the private sector, which are the low-paid jobs in Athens sample. The highest wage gaps are estimated for blue-collar occupations, followed by service jobs and white-collar jobs.

Our results imply that albeit the differences based on the regions, Roma women are concentrated in similar professional groups across Turkey. They work extensively in unqualified jobs such as unauthorized hunting, cleaning jobs, babysitting, garbage collecting, jobs in factories or textile ateliers (insured), basketry, nursing and hawking. Agricultural working is very low, and usually limited to daily works on a seasonal basis. Apart from domestic cleaning jobs, they also work as cleaners in shopping malls. Again, there are women who are engaged in activities such as fortune telling and musicians. Some women work formally in the textile sector, insured at minimum wage. Some Roma women work from home and do handcraft like wreaths. Some of them sell handcrafts that they bought from other provinces to women in non-Roma neighborhoods as dowry, and thus they often travel as part of their work.

According to our findings; there are two main reasons for the Roma to concentrate in such professions: The first one arises from the Roma themselves. As a significant part of the Roma are not accustomed to the hard work discipline, they do not want to work in formal jobs (salaried and insured), which require regularity and stability. This results in more concentration in temporary informal jobs. The other one emerges as a result of discrimination against the Roma. As a result of widespread discrimination, it is clearly observed that the Roma have to live in certain neighborhoods and mostly in ghettos as a closed community, which leads to a mismatch between the work and their neighborhoods.

We have found that provinces where Roma women have the highest formal employment rate are Antalya and Edirne. Antalya is a city in which the tourism sector is dense and women work in this sector or other sectors that are related to this sector with salary and formal employment. In Edirne, we encounter a completely different situation. Municipalities, Roma associations and vocational training organizations throughout the province make a special effort to provide Roma women with insured jobs. In other words, both private and state institutions implement intersectional policies across the city and as a result, the formal employment rates of Roma women are positively affected by these policies. Another reason for the positive cases in Antalya and Edirne provinces is that discrimination against the Roma in these provinces is less than that in the others. Eskişehir is the other province where we observe intersectional policies towards employment of Roma women. Municipality employs Roma women in recycling sector.

3.3 Challenges in access to labor market

We have discussed in the preceding section that Roma women generally work in fields that nobody else does or no one wants to do. In addition, factors such as the need to obtain permission from their spouses, fathers and brothers to work outside the home (FSG/ERCC, 2010), low education rates and domestic responsibilities explain the intersectional challenges Roma women experience in participating in the labor market.

The Roma living in spatially isolated and separated areas have a closed lifestyle, limited networks for job opportunities, and therefore less opportunity to participate in formal sectors (WB, 2002). Nevertheless, the Roma with high unemployment levels face barriers in access to labor market due to their legal status, low level of education, high illiteracy rates and, accordingly, prejudices and discrimination in the labor market. Having low skills and irregular work habits they are mostly dependent on social transfers (EMPL, 2008).

3.3.1 Discrimination in labor market

Discrimination is a barrier in access to labor market for Roma women. Some of Roma women prefer to hide their identity because they would like to avoid discrimination. In their study carried out on behalf World Bank, Divna et al. (2004) imply that there is official proof indicating Roma people have been discriminated against. In addition, they highlights that employers consider the name, surname and nationality of jobseekers, when deciding to employ an employee and The European Council determines and implies "in case one Roma and one non Roma person would apply for a same job, the Roma person would not get it".

Roma communities face a lot of prejudices, exclusion and discrimination in society. Roma women experience this problem differently and deeply due to both gender and ethnic identity they possess and thus they are bound to maintain their disadvantaged positions in society. They are exposed to a higher risk of social exclusion and poverty than Roma men and a greater risk of gender-based exclusion than majority women. Angéla Kóczé expresses the exclusion and discrimination suffered by Roma women through her own feelings. In their study (Kóczé & Popa, 2009) on "Roma women and labor market", Angéla Kóczé highlights:

> This paper grew out of my background as a Romani woman, a seasoned political activist for Roma rights, a scholar, and a feminist. Many Romani women, including myself, harbor countless, unspoken stories of discrimination, exclusion, and violence. Over the years, I have had many encounters during which I felt that I was the target of discrimination, exclusion, and calculated attacks. I am sure that many times, these attacks were not directed at me, personally. But, they do reflect specific intersections of ethnicity, gender, and class. I have come to see my own subject position as a Romani woman as a site where multiple forms of power and hierarchy are enacted.

Discrimination against Roma women emerges simultaneously from inside and outside of their own communities. Intersectional forms of discrimination based on ethnic origin and gender operate in interrelated ways and intensify social exclusion (ILO, 2016). Kóczé and Popa (2009) specify that their research finding addresses "the interaction between ethnicity and gender" in poverty and concludes that "the interaction between gender and race creates a double disadvantage for Roma women". Tóth (2005) put forward that based on indirect evidence – like wage gaps between Roma and non-Roma women or between Roma women and men – we have reasons to believe that Roma women face a more severe discrimination on the labor market. Yet if Roma women manage to gain formal employment despite discrimination and other disadvantages, their families' potential for escaping poverty increases substantially. At the same time, Cukrowska and Kóczé (2013) argue that the summary statistics on employment patterns and wages by ethnicity and gender have confirmed that Romani women tend to suffer from labor market marginalization which is both due to ethnicity as well as gender.

We can better understand the discrimination and exclusion experienced by Roma women, especially in terms of access to the labor market, through their feelings and expressions. A 65-year-old woman living in Ankara said,

> We are definitely discriminated. When we send the children to school, they always regard us as thieves. They don't make friends with our children. They don't want to live in the same neighborhood as us. Those who understand that we are the Roma do not even give a job.

Another woman (46) from Zeytinköy, Antalya who states that they are discriminated against because of the negative image attributed to them, expressed the following;

> Yes, unfortunately, we have a very negative image. This image comes from the exclusion of Zeytinköy as Gypsy. If you are from Zeytinköy, nobody will give you a job. They exclude you. Therefore, Zeytinköy is closed into itself and turned into a wide open air prison.

Behavior patterns of other people towards Roma in labor market become very injurious. If a woman's physical characteristics such as clothing style, appearance etc. indicate ethnic belonging, when it comes to Roma women discrimination can be an obstacle for her to access the labor market (Kóczé, 2009). The participants indicated that their applications for jobs are accepted during the phone interviews, but when they have a face to face interview, they cannot get the jobs because of their appearance, and clothing styles. Similarly, in their study, Uzpeder et al. (2008) state that the Roma's job applications are not accepted when they write their addresses, known as Roma neighborhoods, in the forms. As a result, it is stated that the Roma participants have to misinform about their addresses in order to increase their chances of finding a job. Some Roma even lose their jobs due to the emergence of their ethnicity. Blazevski et al. (2018) imply that the stories are of people saying that they could not get a job due to their ethnicity, such as the that of a 25- to 29-year-old woman from the former Yugoslav Republic of Macedonia: "I have been unemployed for 5 years now. I have a secondary school diploma to be a radiology technician, but I can't get a job because of my look and ethnicity".

Inequalities between Roma women and men as well as between Roma women and the majority women cannot be clarified only by the lower education level of Roma women. It is clear that an important part of inequality is due to discrimination based on ethnicity of gender. Here, of course, multidimensional inequality plays an important role (Schiek & Chege, 2009). Spatial segregation and ghettoization cause women to stay away from many social, economic and cultural activities. Regarding this problem, Tóth (2005) puts forward that; the segregation problem is not restricted to the ghettos concern: an increasing number of Roma live in areas where Roma are outnumbering, but they are not categorized as ghettos. All types of segregated life unfavorably affects include educational potential, availability and diversity of jobs, job opportunities, living and housing standards, social networks, health indicators, etc. On the other hand, Schiek & Chege (2009:258) emphasized there are the relationship between ghettoized locality and relatively high unemployment levels and dependency on social transfers.

3.3.2 Lack of education, skills or opportunities

Lack of employment opportunities is generally related to low education levels for Roma women. In the report prepared by EUMAP/ERRC (2004), remote and inaccessible housing, and lack of education are among the reasons of low employment for Roma women. The report also emphasizes that another significant obstacle for Roma women in participation in the labor market is their taking on the responsibility for all the domestic work and childcare.

Literacy rates are an indicator of the multiple disadvantages Roma women face. The gap in literacy rates for Roma women is not only based on gender, yet on ethnicity, as well. In some countries in Europe, most Roma women do not complete secondary education; across Europe, a very small minority pursue higher education (college, university, or graduate studies) (Kóczé & Popa, 2009), which, according to our results, is also the case in Turkey. Tóth (2005) found that at least a vocational training or secondary school education is a must access in labor market. As they lack in education and necessary qualifications required by the labor market, the Roma are among the first who lose their jobs, without any chances to be re-employed (WB, 2004).

From the interviews and in-depth observations with Roma women in the research, it would not be wrong to state that they could not take place in positions they want to be in the labor market. One of the important reasons for us to reach this judgment can be stated as having early children and early marriages and consequently lack of educational opportunities. A.Ç., who lives in Çanakkale (62 years old), draws attention to the fact that girls get married at an early age:

> We send the children to school, but they cannot continue because they marry young. Girls deliver babies when they are just children. We were like this in the past, there has been no change. So they can't find good jobs. They always work in uninsured jobs.

Another Roma woman S.Y. (22 years old, lives in Gallipoli) says that

> Our biggest problem is unemployment, poverty and lack of education. Children leave school at an early age and cannot find work in jobs that require

> education afterwards. I got married very young and I regret a lot. If I knew then what I know now, I would have finished at least high school.

One of our interviewees who works as a specialist sociologist for SODAM (Social Solidarity Center), an organization in Edirne, where Roma women are trained, provided with professional skills, and directed to employment opportunities, indicates that

> Through our organization, we can offer vocational courses, job opportunities, and personal development opportunities. We provide trainings especially for women. Roma women who lack formal and vocational education are provided with courses on hairdressing, cooking, sewing-embroidery, handicrafts etc. We provide training in such fields and we help them move towards formal labor markets where they can work with insurance.

A 35-year-old Roma woman (F.G.) living in Diyarbakır Bismil said,

> Dom children cannot continue their education because they do not have a role model. For example, I have a college graduate nephew but sells oranges in the market. He couldn't get any job because he couldn't find a job. Being educated doesn't work if you are a Dom. We are facing unemployment for two reasons. Firstly, in a place like Bismil, unemployment is generally experienced as industry and trade are not developed much. Secondly, because we are Doms, we are discriminated against, so we cannot find a job.

3.3.3 Dependence on social transfers

It is known that Roma communities need state aids, especially because of their vulnerabilities and disadvantages they have. They even see this situation as a mechanism for coping with life and survival. However, in some regions, Roma men either do not work or work in the fields of informal labor, with the fear that the transfers and benefits they receive from the state will be cut off. Therefore, it results in women working in unqualified jobs.

A Roma woman living in Ankara, Kale Region, 22 years old expresses:

> Men are used to make women work in this region. They do not want to work in insured jobs to avoid the reduction in the state aids they receive.

Another woman (45 years old), who lives in the same region, said,

> In this region, Roma women are engaged in unauthorized hunting and suitcase trading, selling to Baku, Azerbaijan. The desire of men to marry young is directly related to women earning good money from unauthorized hunting. Men are forcing women to work and they want them to do unauthorized hunting. Women also go to clean shopping malls.

At the same time, these women state that they go to other cities to sell dowry to holidaymakers who come to the summer resorts. However, Blazevski and Keskine (2018) in their study observe the majority of the Roma people reveal a desire to work and not relying on social benefits. Some discourse of Roma people reflects a sense of tiredness or resignation and relief in relying on benefits as a way of escaping from the risks and hardships of informality.

4 Conclusion

The participation of ethnic minority women in the labor market cannot be analyzed without an intersectional approach. In addition, each community needs to be evaluated within itself, because each has its own characteristics.

The inability of Roma women to attend education due to early marriage results in the inability to find employment in the qualified and formal labor market. As a result, women who have to work in the informal labor market work in unregistered, uninsured and precarious jobs, and consequently, they experience a constantly reproductive intersectional cycle. Another challenge experienced by Roma women is discrimination. Women who cannot access mainstream labor market due to their lack of education and discrimination, work precariously in jobs known as ethnic niches. On the other hand, we encounter a very specific situation of the Roma community in participation in the labor market: dependence on social transfers. Since social transfers are given only to unemployed individuals in Turkey, the Roma tend to work in unregistered and uninsured jobs in order not to be deprived of these benefits, and this is a situation that reproduces their disadvantage.

Based on all these, it would be appropriate to draw attention to the necessity of intersectional policies. Indeed, in some provinces of Turkey, intersectional policies of institutions focusing especially on Roma women prove to be effective and consequently Roma women can participate in formal employment. This type of intersectional activities addressing specifically Roma women must be increased. Also, it is urgently needed to prevent early marriages in Roma community. Early marriages are the main reason for dropouts from school, and for the women being stuck in informal labor market. Gender-based poverty in Roma community reproduces itself mainly due to the women's participation in informal sectors. In order to be informed about various job opportunities, Roma women living in enclaves must be provided with access to necessary social networks. In addition, the criteria for social transfers must not be whether there is a registered employee in the family. Since the fear of social transfers being cut off pushes women to work in unregistered and precarious jobs, more convenient criteria is needed to be developed.

Finally, we must add that all policies implemented on behalf of the Roma must integrate gender equality and must avoid any provisions based on gender stereotypes. Labor market participation of Roma women is an intersectional question, thus policies on the Roma must consider the intersectionality of gender, class and ethnic identity of Roma women.

Notes

* This study was funded and supported under the project "The Roma in Turkey: An Identity Economy" with the number 116R050 under the scope of "Scientific and Technological Research Projects Support Program-1001" of TUBITAK.

1 An ethnic group that is sub-branch of the Roma. Their language is Domari, different from that of the Roma. They generally have similar socio-economic and cultural characteristics as the Roma. They live in the east of Turkey.

2 1 USD was equal to 4,81 Turkish Liras in 2018 (Ministry of Treasury, 2018. Budget Analysis Reports).

Bibliography

Andersen, L.E. & Muriel, B. (2007). Informality and Productivity in Bolivia: A Gender Differentiated Empirical Analysis. *Development Research Working Paper Series*. Institute for Advanced Development Studies.

Blazevski, N.M.S. & Keskine, I. (2018). The Position of Roma Women and Men in the Labor Markets of the Western Balkans: Micronarratives Report.

Browne, I. & Misra, J. (2003). 'The Intersection of Gender and Race in Labor Market', *Annual Review of Sociology*, 29, 487–513.

Crenshaw, K. (1989). 'Demarginalizing the Intersection of Race and Sex: A Black Feminist Critique of Antidiscrimination Doctrine, Feminist Theory and Antiracist Politics', *University of Chicago Legal Forum*, 8, 1–20.

Cukrowska, E. & Kóczé, A. (2013). Interplay between Gender and Ethnicity: Exposing Structural Disparities of Romani Women: Analysis of the UNDP/World Bank/EC Regional Roma Survey Data. *Roma Inclusion Working Papers*. UNDP Europe and the CIS, Bratislava Regional Centre.

De los Reyes, P. (2017). 'Working Life Inequalities, Do We Need Intersectionality?', *Society, Health and Vulnerability*, 8, 2, 1–5.

Dincă, M. & Luches, D. (2018). 'Work Integration of the Roma: Between Family and Labor Market', *Sustainability*, 10, 1495, doi:10.3390/su10051495

Divna, L., Memedov, Z., & Demir, L. (2004). *Needs Assessment for the Roma Education Fund*. Macedonia: World Bank, http://documents.worldbank.org/curated/en/828981468086050099/pdf/352070MK0NA0Report.pdf (accessed on 25.12.2019).

Drydakis, N. (2011). Roma Women in Athenian Firms: Do They Face Wage Bias? *Discussion Paper Series, IZA DP No. 5732*. Germany.

EMPL (2008). *The Social Situation of the Roma and Their Improved Access to the Labour Market in the EU*. Policy Department Economic and Scientific Policy, IP/A/EMPL/ST/2008-02, Erişim: 10.03.2018.

EUMAP/ERRC (2004). Shadow Report on the Situation of Sinti and Roma Women and Girls in Germany. EU Monitoring and Advocacy Program/European Roma Rights Center Shadow Report.

FSG (Fundación Secretariado Gitano), ERCC (Avrupa Roman Hakları Merkezi), Edirne Roman Derneği (2010). *Türkiye'de Romanların Durumu Türkiye'de Çalışma ve Insana Yakışır İş Koşulları Sorunları*, http://www.errc.org/uploads/upload_en/file/turkey-understanding-employment-and-decent-work-challenges-in-turkey-december-2010-turkish.pdf.

Hill Collins, P. (2015). 'Intersectionality's Definitional Dilemma', *Annual Review of Sociology*, 41, 1, 1–20.

ILO (2016). *Promoting Decent Work Opportunities for Roma Youth in Central and Eastern Europe: An ILO Resource Guide/International Labor Office*. Geneva: Decent Work Technical Support Team and Country Office for Central and Eastern Europe.

Kahanec, M. (2014). 'Roma Integration in European Labor Markets', *IZA World of Labor*, 39, doi:10.15185/izawol.39

Kóczé, A. & Popa, E. (2009). *Missing Intersectionality Race/Ethnicity, Gender, and Class in Current Research and Policies on Romani Women in Europe*. Budapest: Center for Policy Studies Central European University.

Kushnirovich, N. (2015). 'Immigrants' Integration: Do Ethnic Niches Matter?', www.surrey.ac.uk/cronem/files/conf2009papers/Kushnirovich.pdf Son erişimtarihi (accessed on 10.03.2018).

Lawton, N., Bari, J., & Gilchrist, K. (2018). *Roma Women and The World of Work in Republic of Moldova*. Moldova: International Labor Organization.

McBride, A., Hebson, G., & Holgate, V.J. (2015). 'Intersectionality: Are We Taking Enough Notice in the Field of Work and Employment Relations?', *Work, Employment and Society*, 29, 2, 331–341.

McCall, L. (2005). 'The Complexity of Intersectionality', *Signs*, 30, 3, 1771–1800.

Ministry of Treasury (2018). *Budget Analysis Reports*. Ankara: Republic of Turkey, Ministry of Treasury.

Mulinari, P. & Selberg, R. (2013). 'Intersectional Directions in Working Life Research: A Proposal', *Nordic Journal of Working Life Studies*, 3, 3, 81–98.

Nakano Glenn, E. (1992). 'From Servitude to Service Work: Historical Continuities in the Racial Division of Paid Reproductive Labor', *The University of Chicago Press Journals*, 18, 1, 1–43.

Nash, J.C. (2008). 'Re-Thinking Intersectionality', *Feminist Review*, 89, 1–15.

OECD (2019). *Employment: Labor Force Participation Rate, by Sex and Age Group*, https://stats.oecd.org/index.aspx?queryid=54741# (accessed on 05.01.2020).

Öztürk, S. & Başar, D. (2018). 'Women's Preferences in Labor Market in Turkey: An Analysis with a Focus on Informal Sector', *Journal of Social Security*, 8, 2, 41–58.

Rauh, C. (2018). 'Decomposing Gaps Between Roma and Non-Roma in Romania', *Journal of Demographic Economics*, 84, 2, 209–229.

Ringold, D., Orenstein, M.A., & Wilkens, E. (2005). *Roma in an Expanding Europe: Breaking the Poverty Cycle*. Washington, DC: The World Bank.

Schiek, D. & Chege, V. (2009). *Multidimensional Equality in the Czech and Slovak Republics: European Union Non-Discrimination Law: Comparative Perspectives on Multidimensional Equality Law*. Abingdon: Routledge.

Tomaskovic-Devey, D. (2014). 'The Relational Generation of Workplace Inequalities', *Social Currents*, 1, 1, 51–73.

Tóth, H. (2005). *Romani Women's Unemployment in Hungary Research*. Budapest: Center for Policy Studies, Central European University.

TSI (2019a). *Gelir Dağılımı ve Yaşam Koşulları İstatistikleri*, www.tuik.gov.tr/PreTablo.do?alt_id=1011 (accessed on 12.01.2020).

TSI (2019b). *İşgücü İstatistikleri*, www.tuik.gov.tr/PreHaberBultenleri.do?id=33777 (accessed on 12.01.2020).

UNDP (2005). *Faces of Poverty, Faces of Hope: Vulnerability Profiles for Decade of Roma Inclusion Countries*. Bratislava: Regional Bureau for Europe and the Commonwealth of Independent States, United Nations Development Programme.

UNDP (2006). *At Risk: Roma and the Displaced in Southeast Europe*. Bratislava: Europe and the CIS Bratislava Regional Centre, United Nations Development Programme.

Uzpeder, E., Danova, S., Özçelik, S., & Gökçen, S. (eds.) (2008). *We Are Here! Discriminatory Exclusion & Struggle for Rights of Roma in Turkey*. İstanbul: Edirne Roma Association, European Roma Rights Centre, and Helsinki Citizens' Assembly.

Wang, Q. & Pandit, K. (2007). 'Measuring Ethnic Labour Market Concentration and Segmentation', *Journal of Ethnic and Migration Studies*, 33, 8, 1227–1252.

WB (2002). *Poverty and Welfare of Roma in Slovak Republic*. The World Bank Foundation, INEKO the Open Society Institute.

Weber, L. (2001). *Understanding Race, Class, Gender, and Sexuality: A Conceptual Framework*. Boston: McGrow Hill.

Zhou, M. (2013). 'Ethnic Enclaves and Niches', *The Encyclopedia of Global Human Migration*.

10 What makes labor markets inaccessible for women migrants? From "triple disadvantage" to multiple challenges

Mehmet Gökay Özerim and Elif Çetin

Introduction

While most of the public, policy and scholarly debates around migratory flows still revolve around "young male migration", women are also significant agents involved in contemporary migrations as almost half of the immigrant populations are composed of women. As a result, it has become both relevant and important endeavor to provide further visibility to experiences of women and have in-depth discussions regarding the consequences of the ongoing "feminization of migration" in migration research. The first dimension of this feminization is quantitative and connected to the share of immigrant and refugee women within the total number of immigrants and refugees around the globe. Yet, as highlighted by Marinucci (2007), focusing only on numbers does not deliver a full understanding of feminization and increasing visibility of women in social and economic structures, which emanate from the transformation of women's roles in contemporary societies, constitutes a second and an equally an essential dimension of this issue.

The third aspect of feminization discusses the "qualitative" value of women-based initiatives, policies and practices during the migratory processes, where it is recognized that women actively seek to pursue their agency by being involved in decision-making processes, instead of just remaining as passive dependents. As a result of this growing awareness, the number of academic studies taking women as a subject of analysis and the number of initiatives addressing women as the target group in migration-related policies and practices have been on the rise.

Although these studies and initiatives might have diverse approaches and methodologies, they confirm and reach to a consensus on one certain reality about the place of women in migratory flows: Women have more disadvantages and an additional challenge than men during migratory processes.

Some of these challenges are highly related to the perceptions about the role of women in origin or destination countries and communities, while some of them are the direct outcomes and side effects of constructed relations between men and women. As confirmed by the relevant reports and studies, in all cases, women migrants have lower employment rates than migrant men and other women in their new communities. Women migrants, who achieve to find a job, mostly can find part-time recruitment opportunities instead of full-time positions.

Moreover, longitudinal analyses show that full labor market integration does not happen very quickly, and its completion would often require several years. Therefore, the major question of whether migration supports women's empowerment remains unanswered. In the case of voluntary migration, which is economically motivated, this empowerment might be possible, especially if the socio-economic status of women increases because of such migration. Nevertheless, in the case of those who are forced to migrate, the answer is more complicated and darker. Several studies demonstrate that forced migration mostly causes women to lose social and economic status by posing several new challenges to their lives. They would have a vulnerable position in terms of having access to certain rights, including the social and economic ones (Rudnick, 2009). This may result in status deprivation and pave the way for some other related problems, such as discrimination, which, most of the time becomes more intricate due to the gender-based biases of host communities.

Within this framework, this chapter will investigate the challenges that women migrants encounter in the labor market and the linkages of these challenges with structural problems in the employment market of the host countries. As to provide more concrete examples, the study is based on the significant remarks from the literature and also provides insights from the case of women migrants in Italy and Turkey; two countries from different sides of the Mediterranean with different backgrounds as countries of immigration but quite comparable in terms of being relatively recent countries of immigration; their strategic positioning within global migratory routes; the great diversity of migrants and also the growing share of migrant women they receive.

Women migrants and integration

International Organization for Migration (IOM) emphasizes that gender is one of the issues, which should be considered in the center of debates for any contemporary migratory flows (IOM, 2019). The primary reason to attach such a value to the gender issues in migration is twofold. One reason is related to the quantitative increase and visibility of women in contemporary migration flows at both global and national levels. The second one is originated from the remarkable power of gender as a factor, which shapes the post-migration process of individuals in destination countries.

The first reason is more self-evident within the light of the migration statistics. According to the 2016 report of the UN Secretary General, almost half of 244 million migrants and half of the 19.6 million refugees worldwide are women. Women migrants constitute around 48% of the international migrant stock, and except East Asia and Pacific, the ratio of female migrants has been in rising since 1990 in all regions of the world (UN DESA, 2019; World Bank, 2019). While the ratio of female migrants is still lower than male migrants at the global level, it has some slight superiority to the number of male migrants in some regions. For instance, according to the data of the Population Division of the United Nations Department of Economic and Social Affairs (UN DESA), female migrants outnumbered male migrants in Northern America and Europe in 2019. Consequently, these two regions became the leading regions, also in the numbers of female migrant workers since they represent 66% of all female migrant workers around the world (UN DESA, 2019).

Beneria et al. (2013: 49) point out the following as the key factors that have given rise to the numbers of female migrants globally: lack of opportunities to engage in paid work and life options; divorce or separation; women's desire for greater autonomy (e.g., fleeing abusive marriages and patriarchal traditions); decrease in social restrictions on women's mobility and knowledge of employment opportunities in receiving countries.

Beyond these numbers, migration studies discuss the increasing role of women from the perspective of two particular processes. These are the decision-making, which refers to the process before the start of mobility and integration, which refers to the process in destination countries. Integration might be defined as "the process of settlement, interaction with the host society, and social change that follows immigration" (Penninx and Garcés-Mascareñas, 2016). Migrant integration is a multidimensional and multi-stakeholder process. Employment and integration into the labor market are the major components by representing a domain of integration process, which is also entitled as "economic integration".

Economic integration means both entrance to the labor market and remaining stably inside it, formally or informally. It is also an important parameter of integration by providing access to the other domains (such as accommodation, social integration, etc.) while the level of access to the other domains can also influence it. For instance, the level of integration into the education system or access to language courses might be an essential factor for a migrant to find a proper job in the employment market. On the other hand, economic integration opens the necessary gates for migrants to be in contact with the host society as to develop formal and informal ties and to feel a part of the society that already arrived. Therefore, employment might be considered both a result and a factor in the integration process. Consequently, this process related to accessing the job market is also entitled as "integration through employment" on the way to "structural integration".

Notably, Boyd and Grieco (2003) highlight three elements that affect integration outcomes within these processes. These are (1) the impact of entry status on the ability to integrate and settle, (2) patterns of incorporation into the labor market and (3) the impact of migration on the status of women and men. These three elements are interlinked and provides basis to explain exclusion of women migrants. If the system defines women migrants as only "male dependent", they might easily face deprivation of status and discrimination in the destination societies. While voluntary and economically motivated migration movement of women to a destination society might empower women, in particular, after being accepted by a job with a higher status than the origin country, other types of migratory flows, including forced migration, might endanger the status of women. Even, family reunification might expose women migrants with in a passive and dependent position.

Therefore, the same questions on whether migratory processes empower the women remain in the center of the debates regarding the migratory processes of women. Despite these endemic barriers and limitations, women migrants constitute a significant bulk of workers in certain sectors, such as household jobs. For instance, "11.5 million (17.2%) of the world's 67.1 million domestic workers are international migrants – meaning roughly 'every sixth domestic worker in the world is an international migrant'; and 8.4 million (73.4%) of migrant domestic workers are women or adolescent girls" (ILO, 2015). In addition to domestic workers, increasing numbers of professionals, such as teachers, nurses, scientists, technicians and business owners, are also composed of female migrants many of whom go through difficulties while trying to integrate themselves to the employment market of the host countries.

More importantly, the increase of female migrants does not equally represent itself within the numbers related to the women migrant workers, and they are still underrepresented in the labor markets. International Labour Organization (ILO) reports that 96 million migrant workers are men, while only 68 million are women (ILO, 2019). The difference between labor force participation of migrant men and non-migrant men is not significant at the global level (only 0.3%), while the difference between the labor force participation of migrant women and non-migrant women is remarkably high (around 18%) (ILO, 2018: 12). Although they have specific professional capabilities and educational backgrounds, woman migrants might be excluded from the job market of the host country due to the lack of proper status (such as citizenship and or work permit), language skills, or country-specific requirements of a particular profession. Most of the studies show that female migrants are more disadvantaged in accommodating these gaps when they are compared to male migrants. In the reminder of this chapter, the factors that cause these disadvantages will be discussed.

Integration of women migrants into the employment market: multiple challenges

The UN's 2030 Agenda for Sustainable Development Goals, adopted by all the UN Member States in 2015, sets out a list of commitments for achieving global peace and prosperity, some of which have relevance for improved labor market integration of women migrants. In particular, specific targeted actions listed under "Goal 8: Promote sustained, inclusive and sustainable economic growth, full and productive employment and decent work for all" carry the potential for achieving improved access to proper job opportunities for women migrants (UN, 2015). For instance, one of these targets involves achieving full and productive employment and decent work for all women and men (target 8.5; UN, 2015). Yet, in most cases, refugees face limitations while trying to have access to opportunities in the legal job market in their host countries.

Among many others, Liebig and Tronstad's report, which was published as part of the Organization for Economic Cooperation and Development (OECD) Social, Employment and Migration Working Papers is worth to highlight (Liebig and

Tronstad, 2018). In their report, Liebig and Tronstad identify the challenges faced by women, and argue that women experience "triple disadvantage". Accordingly, they classify these disadvantages under three main headings: (1) the level of education, (2) health conditions and (3) labor market integration. In a similar vein, the United Nations Refugee Agency, UNHCR lists its Commitments for Refugee Women under five key headings that provide insightful hints regarding the labor market challenges that women migrants go through (UNHCR, 2001). These areas of commitments are (1) encouragement of women for meaningful participation in all structures, (2) ensuring basic rights through individual registration and documentation, (3) management and distribution of food and non-food items, (4) economic empowerment and (5) prevention of and response to sexual and gender-based violence.

The situation of women migrants regarding labor market integration stands at the intersection of all of these issues and challenges. Therefore, while all the disadvantages are equally important, the labor market integration is a significant issue since it is directly related to the survival of women migrants in their new destinations by providing to earn a decent livelihood, meeting their own and family members' needs, and consequently by determining their social status.

Based on the dynamics of the contemporary labor markets and employment systems of the European Union member countries, the reports of the European Commission argue that the level of integration support in terms of language training and other skills acquisition programs are significantly below the required levels. The reports published by the European Commission's European Economic and Social Committee (EESC) underline those migrant women are far from being a monolithic group of people. Instead, these migrant women have a diverse background, and the primary source of motivation for them to leave their hometowns varies. For instance, while some of them migrate to seek asylum, some others are on the move by economic motivations or due to the reasons like family reunification. Ultimately, different groups of women migrants motivated by various factors in their migratory journeys, also have their unique experiences.

Consequently, we can discuss the challenges for women migrants on the way to the employment market from two different perspectives. The first one is related to limitations for entrance to the job market, and the second one is the challenges after entering the job market. Within both of the processes, one challenge that obstructs the insertion of women migrants into the employment market and/or worsens employment conditions of women migrants is the structure of the economy in host countries. Contrary to the expectations and general wisdom, this problem is observable even in the western and north European countries due to the derogation of the welfare systems in many of these countries due to the financial and economic crises within the last decades. A European scale research (FEMIPOL – Integration of Female Immigrants in Labor Market and Society. Policy Assessment and Policy Recommendations) confirms this challenge by claiming that welfare state system derogation of the European countries creates multiple challenges for women migrants' integration to the employment market (Kontos, 2009). Accordingly, this derogation has been increasing their financial burden for childcare and getting them into a dilemma between working or taking responsibility of their own children (Kontos, 2009: 8). Moreover, flexibilization in the job market directly affects women migrants adversely and restrains them with short term – low wage jobs (Kontos, 2009: 8). Gender-based labor market opportunities also determine the gender profile of migrants that a country will predominantly receive. For instance, countries with higher demand for physically demanding labor will more likely receive male migrant workers, whereas countries that have a particular demand for domestic workers, teachers and nurses will attract higher numbers of migrant women (Hondagneu-Sotelo, 2003).

Another challenge to the integration of women migrants into the employment market is "occupational concentration" (Pedraza, 1991), which restrain them both before and after the entrance to the job market. Mostly, women migrants are deemed worthy only for some particular job sectors in host societies due to some distinctive reasons, such as the lack of skills and competences and/or stereotypes that are matching migrants just with low qualified jobs. As a result, migrant women might experience "deskilling or be confined to 'feminine' jobs, often paid or valued less than other work" (O'Neil et al., 2016: 4). The UN's 2030 Agenda for Sustainable Development Goals' another prominent target addresses to protecting labor rights and promoting safe and secure working environments for all workers and those in precarious employment, including migrant women (target 8.8; UN, 2015). This target is significant by having implications for equal labor market involvement of female migrants. While protection of labor rights is highly essential for migrants in general, migrant women and children are at a higher risk of exploitation and abuse, and are also "frequently isolated and therefore more vulnerable to exploitation, violence and abuse" (O'Neil et al., 2016: 4). Men tend to be overrepresented in mining, industry, transport, trade, construction industries and in management positions due to being seen as stronger and more able to perform physically demanding jobs (O'Neil et al., 2016: 5–6). Yet, migrant women are pushed towards performing stereotypically feminine roles related to care (e.g., health, teaching, cleaning, cooking, service industries) or entertainment, or in factory positions that "prefer workers to be 'nimble' or meticulous" (ILO, 2015; de Villard and Dey de Pryck, 2010; Ghosh, 2009; UNFPA, 2006; IOM, 2009, 2011; quoted in O'Neil et al., 2016: 6).

On the other hand, occupational concentration provides also networking of migrant workers in some particular sectors, and after a while, this network might make these sectors more accessible for migrant workers and facilitates their insertion into these jobs. These sectors mostly include domestic servants/housework, garment industry, nursing and care work, agriculture, catering and general hospitality services (Pedraza, 1991). However, these are the sectors also where the rates of informal working and flexibility are generally high. The concrete outcome of this informality is the exploitation of women migrants' work by lower wages, discrimination, long working hours and lack of social security. Therefore, "occupational concentration" of women migrants and "informality" are highly interrelated with each other. The demand for informality influences experiences of women migrants (Kontos, 2009: 22). For instance, Kindler and Szulecka state that informal economy market of Poland as one of the significant structural barriers for the entrance of Ukrainian and Vietnamese women migrants to the employment market (Kindler and Szulecka, 2013).

Another noteworthy challenge is related to the problems that women migrants have while their qualifications are recognized in the destination countries (UN, 2005: 63). Even though the lack of clear criteria for the assessment of qualifications and skills of migrants constitutes a significant barrier to employment for both men and women, women and girls, and in particular, refugee women and girls are the most disadvantaged groups (Wong, 2018). For instance, according to the 2014 European Labour Force Survey, less than half of refugee women in Europe are employed, which is 17 percentage points lower than refugee men (Dumont et al., 2016) do. Low level of education and low labor market participation appear as two key factors creating this situation. Refugee women with low education suffer higher rates of unemployment when compared with refugee men and highly educated foreign-born women from non-EU countries, where less than one in three would be in employment (30%) (ibid.). Refugee women in Europe also tend to have relatively low level of economic activity when compared with other non-EU born migrant women (61%) and the native-born women (66%) (ibid.).[1]

Nevertheless, the limitations and challenges for women migrants in the labor market is not always developed by the regulations, structure and rules of hosting state or society. The origin culture of women migrants might have restrictive attitudes for women by casting a role for them in the scope of their spousal relationships, family and childcare and/or religious limitations. Therefore, there is still an ongoing debate about the contribution of employment for women migrant's empowerment and liberation. A significant distinction should be noted here again about the women who migrated voluntarily and who migrated due to the forced reasons since forced migration mostly results with status deprivation of women migrants. For instance, based on a field study, Pedraza (1991: 313) argues that work represents an opportunity for Cuban women migrants to contribute their families rather than self-actualization, which means "employment without liberation". Moreover, growing numbers of female migrants taking part in labor markets led to a shift in the caretaker role performed by women from the local population to migrant women. In return, migrant women, who leave their homes to take up jobs in the care sector abroad, leave their own children and other dependents to other female members of their families, such as grandmothers and sisters. In some instances, some of these migrant women would earn sufficient to hire lower-income domestic workers to help them manage their own households (UNFPA, 2006: 25). These shifting caretaker roles from one woman to another is referred to as "global chains of care" (Hochschild, 2000; Ehrenreich and Hochschild, 2002). While global chains of care help with migrant women to become economically active, these women would also feel heavy psychological and emotional pressures emanating from traditional gender roles where they carry a disproportionate amount of responsibility to sustain their families. Therefore, as Nermin Abadan-Unat (1977: 55) noted, while migration promotes the emancipation of women, it also creates a "false climate of liberation, which actually does not surpass increased purchasing power, thus resulting only in pseudo-emancipation".

While discussing discrimination as another challenge to the economic integration of women migrants, gender is listed as one of the major reasons, which exposes women migrants to inequalities in the job market together with race, ethnicity, class and status (Lacroix et al., 2017: 422). The inequalities that women migrants encounter is discussed within the context of integration and social integration by referring to the concept of "intersectionality" (Bürkner, 2011). Intersectionality might be considered as the basis of challenges that we entitle as "triple disadvantage" in this study, and this challenge is not particularly observed only in economic integration but also in all integration domains of women migrants. Notably, the International Labour Organization discusses six domains where women migrant workers are discriminated (ILO, 2020). These are (1) sex; (2) race, color, ethnicity; (3) occupation; (4) wages; (5) nationality and (6) migration status.

Finally, another general factor that multiplies the challenges of women migrants is the mental health problem. They fled their countries due to forced reasons and studies confirm that women refugees encounter the risks of anxiety, depression and post-traumatic stress disorder (PTSD), which are the serious problems that might be escalated by the pressure of childcare and family responsibilities and by the lack of necessary social support. Having a decent and secure job is an element that shapes the mental health situation of the women migrants (Shishehgar et al., 2017: 960).

Discussing the challenges for women migrants through case analysis: Italy and Turkey

After juxtaposing the major discussions, insights and challenges related to women migrants' integration into the employment markets by relying on the academic literature and reports in the previous sections, the last section of this chapter will discuss the situation of women migrants based on the examples of Italy and Turkey as two distinctive case countries. Italy and Turkey are selected as the case countries since these countries have been major destinations for several migrants within the Mediterranean route, in particular with an increasing rate of arrivals from the Middle East and North African (MENA) region by the beginning of the 2000s. More importantly, these countries are precious examples to discuss the challenges regarding the economic integration from both the migrants and states' perspectives due to the velocity, irregularity and intensity of migratory flows that they encountered during the last decade.

Case one: women migrants in Italian labor market

Similar to some other Mediterranean front line countries of immigration within the European Union (EU), Italy was a latecomer country of immigration, where it started to experience a positive migration balance during the mid-1970s (Martiniello, 1992; Papademetriou and Hamilton, 1996; Zincone and Caponio, 2005). The fact that a trend to replace labor migration policies by stricter controls in several Western European countries, such as France, Belgium and Germany, also played a role in increasing the numbers of migrant arrivals to Italy during that time period (Geddes, 2006; Pastore 2004; Zincone 1995, 1998).

One of the particular characteristics of migration policies in Italy is the relatively slow emergence of policy responses toward managing this phenomenon in the country. The very first all-encompassing immigration law document was introduced only in 1990, the so-called Martelli Law, which also introduced annual labor migration quotas in response to the calls made by the Italian business elites for the introduction of an active labor migration management scheme (Menz, 2009: 233).

The time lag between migration realities on the ground and policy responses indicates, at least to a certain extent that, there was some resistance in Italian policy makers' mindset to acknowledge that the country had turned into a country of immigration, and was not solely a migrant-sending country anymore. While the 1990s marked an increased pace of migrant arrivals to Italy, it was also the time period during which populist right-wing parties started to rise in the country's political scenery. These new political players did not hesitate, to scapegoat migrants, including refugees, for those things that did not go well in the country, including the political turmoil and economic instability.

Since Italy has become a country of immigration, the dominant political rhetoric and policies towards immigrants and refugees have always been characterized by that of an emergency logic where political approaches are guided by short-term, reactionary measures treating migrants as sources of imminent threat. For instance, there has never been any active labor recruitment program, even though there is a demand for foreign labor in Italian economy. As a result, those migrants who arrive in Italy irregularly, or who are undocumented usually search for space in the county's extensive black-market economy and most of the time find one for themselves relatively easily, which would often pave the way for these migrants to disappear within the system. Instead of creating legal entry channels, Italian governments, independent from where they are located on the political spectrum, have been narrowing down the legal entry channels. Amnesties that grant legal status to these irregular and undocumented migrants have turned into a defining feature of the Italian migration management system from the late 1980s onwards. Providing only temporary solutions, these regularization campaigns are far from addressing any of the structural factors (re)generating irregularities (Boswell, 2003), and thus constitute a striking example for the country's short-term, reactionary policy approaches.

Although migrants are needed in the Italian economy, they are not always "welcomed" by the society (Zolberg, 1987). Political authorities' inability to target the sources of irregular and undocumented migratory arrivals mixed with anti-immigrant rhetoric of populist parties, to whom a certain cohort of the media also join from time to time, further increases public feelings of insecurity and hostility toward immigrants. Despite these anti-immigrant sentiments, the foreign population keeps on rising in Italy.

The Italian economy is marked by a dual structure which involves "high tech islands and seas of low-skill assembly" (Menz, 2009: 236) meaning that small and medium-sized enterprises are the "pivotal sources of economic activity" in the country (ibid.: 238), and Italy's economy has a particular dependence on unskilled and low-skilled labor. As a result, there is not much incentive for employers to be in search for highly skilled migrants, and most of the public and political concerns appear to be concentrated on the public order and security implications of immigration with a disregard for its potential to contribute to the Italian economy.

While the Italian labor market does not provide any significant opportunities for being integrated into the job market, attempts of assimilation and exclusionary approach of the host community constitutes two of the major obstacles that migrant women in Italy face. Lack of Italian language fluency appears to be a key factor that hinders migrant women's orientation within Italian society and pushes them to a marginalized position (Chiappelli and Cabral, 2006: 16). As discussed previous sections of this chapter, one of the pressing problems when it comes to migrant women's integration into their host society's labor markets is going through de-skilling, and this applies to migrant women in Italy too. Referring to the experiences of migrant women within Italian society in general, and in the employment market, in particular, Ambrosini et al. (1995) introduced the concept of "subordinated integration", which primarily argues that because of the jobs usually performed by migrant women, they end up having limited social capital, and as a result remain at the margins of Italian society (cited in Chiappelli and Cabral, 2006: 16). In fact, more recent empirical research data, unfortunately, reveals that subordinated integration still very much continues to be experienced by many migrant women in the employment market, especially by the unskilled and relatively low-skilled ones. For instance, Chiappelli and Cabral (2006: 17) note domestic workers experience discrimination, harassment, and sometimes violence at work where:

> the work and living conditions that migrant women experience in domestic work lead to a general situation of vulnerability, overexploitation, withdrawal of personal and private space, and great difficulties in developing relationships outside of work.

Because of such negative experiences lack of equal treatment, even though migrant women might be employed in the job market, this does not automatically mean they are accepted by the society and lead to their better integration into Italian society.

A particularly difficult case of labor market integration concerns that of trafficked women. While reintegrating these individuals to employment market is of crucial importance, finding decent job alternatives often prove to be a highly challenging task to be fulfilled due to "erosion of self-esteem . . ., their difficulty in perceiving themselves as capable of building positive relationships, and lack of education" (Chiappelli and Cabral, 2006: 28). The general difficulty posed by the Italian job market, which tends to offer limited space to foreigners in low skilled and/or low-paid labor constitute a further diminishes trafficked women's chances for achieving full job market integration. Female victims of human trafficking usually find themselves space in the Italian economy either through internships that are later on transformed into contract-based jobs, or through entrepreneurship. Still, their employment chances would be most of the time-limited to "small handicrafts industry (leather goods, clothes, and ceramics) and the tertiary service sector (the hotel industry, cleaning services, domestic work, and care assistance)" (ibid.).

To sum up, the main guiding logic of Italian migration policies concentrates on limiting undocumented and irregular migrant entries, and creating a pool of low-skilled and, as a result, low-paid, foreign labor force, for Italian employers (Chaloff, 2005: 11). This results in Italy neither being able to attract much of highly skilled women migrant labor force nor offering them the right opportunity structures for their proper integration into the domestic labor market. In that sense, despite its peculiarities in terms of how immigration is (mis)-managed, Italy emerges as another case carrying some of the endemic problems that block the integration of migrant women and girls into job markets of their receiving countries.

Case 2: women migrants in Turkish labor market

Turkey had undertaken a prominent role for the irregular immigration of Iraqi, Iranian, Afghan asylum seekers between 1980s and 2000s. After being entitled as an emigration and transit country for long years, consequently it became a leading immigration country by 2000s due to the increased conflicts and wars in its neighborhood. The escalation of the civil war in Syria by 2011 added Syrian asylum seekers into the group of people, who seek refuge in Turkey. Because of Turkey's open-door policy during the first years of the conflict, the country became the leading destination for Syrians and the number of Syrians in Turkey reached around 3.6 million by 2020. Together with Syrians, it is estimated that the total number of foreigners, who seek international protection in Turkey is more than 4 million (IOM Turkey, 2020).

However, this number does not correspond directly to the number of the people who are granted internationally recognized refugee status by Turkey. Due to its geographical limitation to the Convention Relating to the Status of Refugees, also known as the 1951 Refugee Convention, Turkey admits to providing refugee status only for those fleeing as a result of events occurring in Europe. Therefore, Turkish government decided on granting temporary protection for Syrians by considering as an alternative to refugee status and due to the emergency of the situation for responding rapidly to the mass influx of Syrians towards Turkey's borders. Temporary Protection Regulation was published in 2014 by the Council of Ministers Decision, within the framework of Law on Foreigners and International Protection (No. 6458) and became functional for Syrians in Turkey.

The temporary protection status, which provides basic provisions for Syrians' access to residence permit, health facilities, education was enriched by the right to apply for a work permit in 2016 by the Regulation on Work Permit for Foreigners under Temporary Protection, which regulates the procedures for the work permit process of Syrians under temporary protection. Based on this regulation, Syrians may file an application for a work permit in Turkey after six months receiving their temporary protection status.

In this regard, Syrian women in Turkey is a worthy example and case to discuss the situation of women migrants, in particular, who fled their country due to the forced reasons rather than economic motivations. Nevertheless, the number of the work permit beneficiary Syrians is still less than 35 000 by 2020 and it still falls short when it is compared to the number of working age Syrians already living in Turkey. So, the estimations indicate that the number of Syrians in informal employment is around 1.5 million while noting that Syrians in seasonal agriculture or husbandry are exempt from work permit regulation.

Syrian women constitute 46% of all Syrians under temporary protection in Turkey. Only 10% of Syrian women have an occupation (EU, 2020). According to a large-scale field research about Syrian Women in Turkey, which was coordinated by United Nations Women Turkey, only 15% of Syrian women work in wage-earning employment (UNWOMEN, 2018). Aygül and Kaba claim that a major barrier to the integration of Syrian women into employment market in Turkey is "human capital accumulation" (Aygül and Kaba, 2019: 1267). Accordingly, this accumulation identifies educational level, language competency and professional experience. Seventy percent of Syrian women expressed that they do not have Turkish language competency. While only 8% of Syrian women obtained any kind of vocational training in Syria, the proportion of university graduates remains at around 5% (UN WOMEN, 2018). The overall employment rate of Syrian women in Turkey is around 20%, and only 10% of Syrian women define their employment in Turkey as a "proper and decent job". It is worth to note that 85% of Syrian women also indicated that they were not working and/or unemployed while they were living in Syria (UN WOMEN, 2018: 45).

Leghtas lists the significant barriers to the economic integration of women migrants in Turkey as childcare and housework responsibilities of women together with the limited financial and social opportunities for women migrants to provide care assistance for their own children, gender roles and cultural restrictions (Leghtas, 2019: 17). Among others, the argument on "cultural restrictions" underlines that a high number of Syrian women express that they are not looking for a job. The primary two reasons for this voluntary disengagement of Syrian women from the employment market reveal as their childcare responsibilities and the reluctance of their spouses. These two particular reasons might be considered highly associated with the role of women and traditions in Syrian culture. International Labour Organization (ILO) reports explain this situation as "cultural distance to working" among Syrian women (ILO, 2019) and argue that traditional measures for women's access to the employment market might not be the related stakeholders not address enough if the cultural distance to working is as a major problem.

However, low level of economic integration among Syrian women in Turkey might not be solely explained by individual competences and culture. Occupational concentration, which is discussed as a challenge to the women migrants' economic integration in the academic literature and explained within the previous sections of this chapter, is observable also in the employment experience of Syrian women in Turkey. Syrian women in the Turkish job market are more disadvantaged when compared with Syrian men, and they are directly or indirectly restrained by some sectors such as textile, services and domestic work (Aygül and Kaba, 2019). Both public bodies and civil society organizations design and implement vocational training programs for Syrian women in different cities of Turkey. However, the impact of "occupational concentration" might reveal itself again about the types of these courses, since these courses are mostly concentrated on jobs, which are traditionally considered for women such as hairdressing, cookery and handicraft. More importantly, completion of this training process with a successful insertion into the employment market cannot always be possible due to the low levels of human labor demand in Turkish job market by these job sectors.

The increasing flexibility of Turkish labor market since the beginning of the 2000s is another factor and challenge that enhances the vulnerability of women migrants (Tören, 2018: 26). Beyond their childcare and family responsibilities, the structural problems of the Turkish economy might be listed as a factor that transforms Syrian women into "flexible laborer". On the one hand, it should also be noted that the labor force participation of Syrians in Turkey is low for both men and women. On the other hand, Syrians' women participation rate to the labor force is much lower than that of Syrian men and Turkish women (ILO, 2019). However, an observation in ILO report is interesting by claiming that Syrian women's labor participation rate increased in Turkey when it is compared that of in Syria, and this result is partly justified by the status change of women who became the head of household due to the loss of husbands due to war and conflict (ILO, 2019: 48).

Conclusion

Although the numbers of female migrants have been increasing globally since the 1980s, specific challenges and risks, such as the trauma and stress that they endure due to family separation, gender-based violence, exploitation and particular health problems such as the ones experienced by pregnant women have long been ignored, both at the research and policy-making levels. It is important to note that migrant women and girls are often referred to as "vulnerable" groups, a label that is used in most policy and legal documents which, with a total disregard of their potential and capabilities as individuals imply that these women and girls constitute a "special needs" group and discriminates them further (Khan and Laurie, 2017). Instead, there is an urgent need for most countries to redesign their political and legal frameworks so that migrant women and girls would no longer be viewed as personally vulnerable but as individuals who are forced to experience conditions that involve human rights abuses, limitations, and are thus put under a vulnerable position. Some of these limitations emanate from culturally rooted gender-biases that often attach women socially dependent roles: lack of proper educational opportunities that are necessary for improving their living conditions and their ability for exercising their agency; limited access to proper employment conditions (Women's Refugee Commission, 2017).

In addition to the general analysis of the literature, two specific cases including Italy and Turkey also demonstrate that the challenges are common for women migrants even in different countries, in particular, within the process regarding economic integration and insertion into the employment market. Providing migrant women equal opportunities to have access to jobs that will be in line with their skills and professional qualifications will improve workplace productivity and will lead to better recognition of the social and economic value of the work they perform.

Furthermore, due to isolation in the workplace and economic precariousness, unskilled migrant women exhibit limited or no knowledge about the legal rights they possess. As a result, despite the existence of these legal rights, they may not be enforced simply because of migrant women's disempowerment resulting from the gender segregation of labor and the feminization of certain jobs, such as care and household-related work (Garcia-Retamero and López-Zafra, 2006). For real change to happen, toxic masculinity (re)generating gender stereotypes needs to be addressed systematically and globally.

Note

1 In addition to high unemployment, refugee women and girls are also often the target of systematic sexual and gender-based violence in conflict and post-conflict situations which involves "rape as a method of control of community and family destruction, rape of women as a punishment for men in a community, sexual assault, sexual torture, sexual slavery trafficking, corrective rape of LGBTI identifying women, early and forced marriage, female genital mutilation, and domestic violence" (Pittaway, 2008, 2010; UNHCR, 2011)

Bibliography

Abadan-Unat, Nermin. (1977). 'Implications of Migration on Emancipation and Pseudo-Emancipation of Turkish Women', *The International Migration Review* 11(1): 31–57.

Ambrosini, Maurizio, Rosangela Lodigiani and Sara Zandrini. (1995). 'L'integrazione subalterna. Peruviani, eritrei e filippini nel mercato del lavoro milanese [Dependent Integration. Peruvians, Eritreans and Filipinos in the Milanese Labour Market]', *Quaderni ISMU* 3.

Aygül, Hasan Hüseyin, and Emine Merve Kaba. (2019). 'Suriyeli Kadınların İşgücüne Katılımı ve Deneyimleri: İstanbul-Sultanbeyli', *Social Sciences* 14(4): 1255–1275.

Beneria, Lourdes, Carmen Diana Deere and Naila Kabeer. (2013). 'Gender and International Migration: Globalization, Development and Governance', in L. Oso and N. Ribas-Mateos (eds.), *The International Handbook on Gender, Migration and Transnationalism: Global and Development Perspectives*. Northampton, MA: Edward Elgar Publishing, pp. 45–68.

Boswell, Cristina. (2003). *European Migration Policies in Flux: Changing Patterns of Inclusion and Exclusion*. London: Royal Institute of International Affairs.

Boyd, M. and E. Grieco. (2003). 'Women and Migration: Incorporating Gender Into International Migration Theory', *Migration Information Source* 1(35): 28.

Bürkner, Hans-Joachim. (2011). 'Intersectionality: How Gender Studies Might Inspire the Analysis of Social Inequality Among Migrants', *Population, Space and Place* 18(2): 181–195.

Chiappelli, Tiziana and Ilundi Cabral. (2006). 'Analysis of Policy Formation and Policy Implementation: The Italian Case', *Integration of Female Immigrants in Labour Market and Society: Policy Assessment and Policy Recommendations*. A Specific Targeted Research Project of the 6th Framework Programme of the European Commission. Available at <www.femipol.uni-frankfurt.de/docs/working_papers/wp2/Italy.pdf> [Accessed 22 January 2020].

de Villard, Soline and Dey de Pryck, Jennie. (2010). *Making Migration Work for Women and Men in Rural Labour Markets*, Gender and Rural Employment Policy Brief #6. Food and Agriculture Organization of the United Nations (FAO), International Fund for Agricultural Development (IFAD), International Labour Office (ILO). Available at <www.fao.org/docrep/013/i2008e/i2008e06.pdf> [Accessed 20 October 2020].

Dumont, Jean-Christophe, Thomas Liebig, Jorg Peschner, Filip Tanay and Theodora Xenogiani. (2016). *How Are Refugees Faring on the Labour Market in Europe?*. A First Evaluation Based on the 2014 EU Labour Force Survey adhoc module Working Paper 1/2016. Available at <https://ec.europa.eu/social/BlobServlet?docId=16130&langId=en> [Accessed 15 January 2020].

Ehrenreich, B. and Arlie Russell Hochschild. (2002). *Global Woman: Nannies, Maids and Sex Workers in the New Economy*. New York: Henry Holt.

Garcia-Retamero, Rocio and Esther López-Zafra. (2006). 'Prejudice Against Women in Male-congenial Environments: Perceptions of Gender Role Congruity in Leadership', *Sex Roles* 55: 51–61.

Geddes, Andrew. (2006). *The Politics of Migration and Immigration in Europe*. London: Sage.

Ghosh, Jayati. (2009). *Migration and Gender Empowerment: Recent Trends and Emerging Issues*, Human Development Research Paper 04. New York: United Nations Development Programme. Available at <https://mpra.ub.uni-muenchen.de/19181/1/MPRA_paper_19181.pdf> [Accessed 01 November 2020].

Hochschild, Arlie Russell. (2000). 'Global Care Chains and Emotional Surplus Value', in W. Hutton and A. Giddens (eds.), *On the Edge: Living with Global Capitalism*. New York: Free Press, pp. 130–146.

Hondagneu-Sotelo, Pierrette. (ed.). (2003). *Gender and US Immigration: Contemporary Trends*. Berkeley and Los Angeles: University of California Press.

International Labour Organization (ILO). (2015). *ILO Global Estimates on Migrant Workers: Results and Methodology: Special Focus on Migrant Domestic Workers*. Geneva: International Labour Office.

International Labour Organization (ILO). (2018). *ILO Global Estimates on Migrant Workers: Results and Methodology* (2nd ed.). Geneva: International Labour Office.

International Labour Organization (ILO). (2019). *Labour Migration: New ILO Figures Show 164 Million People Are Migrants Workers*. Available at <www.ilo.org/global/about-the-ilo/newsroom/news/WCMS_652106/lang-en/index.htm> [Accessed 10 January 2020].

IOM. (2009). *Gender and Labour Migration in Asia*. Available at <https://publications.iom.int/system/files/pdf/gender_and_labour_migration_asia.pdf?language=en> [Accessed 30 October 2020].

IOM. (2011). *Thailand Migration Report 2011. Migration for Development in Thailand: Overview and Tools for Policymakers*. Bangkok: International Organization for

Migration. Available at <http://publications.iom.int/system/files/pdf/tmr_2011.pdf> [Accessed 28 October 2020].

IOM. (2019). *Gender and Migration*. Available at <www.iom.int/gender-and-migration> [Accessed 05 January 2020].

IOM Turkey. (2020). *Migration in Turkey*. Available at <https://turkey.iom.int/migration-turkey> [Accessed 25 January 2020].

Khan, Rimi and Timothy Laurie. (2017). 'The Concept of Minority for the Study of Culture', *Continuum: Journal of Media and Cultural Studies* 31(1): 92–103.

Kindler, M. and M. Szulecka. (2013). The Economic Integration of Ukrainian and Vietnamese Migrant Women in the Polish Labour Market. *Journal of Ethnic and Migration Studies* 39(4): 649–671.

Kontos, M. (2009). 'Integration of Female Immigrants in Labour Market and Society', *A Comparative Analysis: Summary, Results and Recommendations*. Frankfurt am Main: Institute of Social Research, The Goethe University.

Lacroix, J., A. Gagnon and V. Lortie. (2017). 'At the Intersection of Gender and National Origin: The Career Trajectories of Selected Immigrants in Quebec', *Population* 72(3): 419–444.

Leghtas, İ. (2019). 'Türkiye'deki Mülteciler için Güvensiz Bir Gelecek: Zorla Geri Gönderme ve Yasal İş İmkanlarına Erişimdeki Zorluklar', *Refugees International Saha Araştırması Raporu*. Eylül.

Liebig, T. and K. Tronstad. (2018). 'Triple Disadvantage? A First Overview of the Integration of Refugee Women', *OECD Social, Employment and Migration Working Papers, No. 216*. Paris: OECD Publishing.

Marinucci, R. (2007). 'Feminization of Migration?', *REMHU-Revista Interdisciplinar da Mobilidade Humana* 15(29): 5–22.

Martiniello, Marco. (1992). 'Italy: The Late Discovery of Immigration', in D. Thraenhardt (ed.), *Europe: A New Immigration Continent: Policies and Politics in Comparative Perspective*. Hamburg: Lit.

Menz, Georg. (2009). *The Political Economy of Managed Migration: Nonstate Actors, Europeanization, and the Politics of Designing Migration Policies*. New York: Oxford University Press.

O'Neil, Tam, Anjali Fleury and Marta Foresti. (2016). *Women on the Move Migration, Gender Equality and the 2030 Agenda for Sustainable Development*. ODI Policy Brief. Available at <www.odi.org/publications/10476-women-move-migration-gender-equality-and-2030-agenda-sustainable-development> [Accessed 07 January 2020].

Papademetriou, Demetrious G. and Kimberly A. Hamilton. (1996). *Converging Paths to Restriction: French, Italian and British Responses to Immigration*. Washington, DC: Carnegie Endowment for International Peace.

Pastore, Ferrucio. (2004). 'A Community Out of Balance: Nationality Law and Migration Politics in the History of Post-Unification Italy', *Journal of Modern Italian Studies* 9(1): 27–48.

Pedraza, S. (1991). 'Women and Migration: The Social Consequences of Gender', *Annual Review of Sociology* 17(1): 303–325.

Penninx, R. and B. Garcés-Mascareñas. (2016). 'The Concept of Integration as an Analytical Tool and as a Policy Concept', in *Integration Processes and Policies in Europe*. Cham: Springer, pp. 11–29.

Pittaway, Eileen. (2008). 'The Rohingya Refugees in Bangladesh: A Failure of the International Protection Regime', in H. Adelman (ed.), *Protracted Displacement in Asia: No Place to Call Home*. London and New York: Routledge, pp. 83–105.

Pittaway, Eileen. (2010). *Making Mainstreaming a Reality: Gender and the UNHCR Policy on Refugee Protection and Solutions in Urban Areas: A Refugee Perspective*. Available at <http//www.unhcr.org/4b0b83f9.pdf> [Accessed 19 January 2020].

Rudnick, A.M. (2009). *Working Gendered Boundaries: Temporary Migration Experiences of Bangladeshi Women in the Malaysian Export Industry from a Multi-Sited Perspective*. Amsterdam: Vossiuspers UvA and Amsterdam University Press.

Shishehgar, S., L. Gholizadeh, M. DiGiacomo, A. Green and P.M. Davidson. (2017). 'Health and Socio-Cultural Experiences of Refugee Women: An Integrative Review', *Journal of Immigrant and Minority Health* 19(4): 959–973.

Tӧren, T. (2018). *Documentation Report: Syrian Refugees in the Turkish Labour Market* (Vol. 22). Kassel: Kassel University Press GmbH.

UN. (2005). *2004 World Survey on the Role of Women in Development: Women and International Migration* (A/59/287/Add.1, ST/ESA/294). New York: Division for the Advancement of Women, Department of Economic and Social Affairs. Available at <www.un.org/womenwatch/daw/public/WorldSurvey2004-Women&Migration.pdf> [Accessed 10 January 2020].

UN. (2015). *Sustainable Development Goals*. Available at <https://sustainable development.un.org/?menu=1300> [Accessed 19 January 2020].

UN DESA. (2019). *Immigration and Emigration Statistics: Gender and Migration*. Available at https://migrationdataportal.org/themes/gender [Accessed 10 January 2020].

UNFPA. (2006). *A Passage to Hope: Women and International Migration*. Available at <www.unfpa.org/sites/default/files/pub-pdf/sowp06-en.pdf> [Accessed 01 February 2020].

UNHCR. (2001). *UNHCR's Commitments to Refugee Women*. Available at <www.refworld.org/docid/479f3b2a2.html>.

UNHCR. (2011). *Survivors, Protectors, Providers: Refugee Women Speak Out*. Available at <www.refworld.org/docid/4f310baa2.html> [Accessd 10 January 2020].

UNWOMEN. (2018). *Need Assessment of Syrian Women and Girls Under Temporary Protection Status in Turkey*. Available at <https://eca.unwomen.org/en/digital-library/publications/2018/08/needs-assessment-of-syrian-women-and-girls-under-temporary-protection-status-in-turkey> [Accessd 05 January 2020].

Women's Refugee Commission. (2017). *Making the Global Compact on Refugees Work for All Women and Girls Recommendations*. Advocacy Brief. Available at <www.womensrefugeecommission.org/general-resources/1522-making-global-compact-on-refugees-work-for-all-women-girlsrecommendation> [Accessed 20 January 2020].

Wong, Lorraine. (2018). *Challenges and Opportunities in the Labour Market Integration of Asylum Populations*. Agenda for International Development (A-id) blog entry. Available at <www.a-id.org/2018/07/30/challenges-and-opportunities-in-the-labour-market-integration-of-asylum-populations/> [Accessed 18 January 2020].

World Bank. (2019). *Women and Migration: Exploring the Data*. Available at <http://blogs.worldbank.org/opendata/women-and-migration-exploring-data> [Accessed 15 January 2020].

Zincone, Giovanna. (1995). 'Immigration to Italy: Data and Policies', in F. Heckmann and W. Bosswick (eds.), *Migration Policies: A Comparative Perspective*. Stuttgart: Euke, pp. 137–156.

Zincone, Giovanna. (1998). 'Illegality, Enlightenment and Ambiguity: A Hot Italian Recipe', *South European Society and Politics* 3(3): 45–82.

Zincone, Giovanna and Tiziana Caponio. (2005). *Immigrant and Immigration Policy-Making: The Case of Italy*, IMISCOE [International Migration, Integration and Social Cohesion in Europe] Research Network Working Paper: Country Report. Rotterdam: IMISCOE.

Zolberg, Aristide. (1987). 'Wanted but Not Welcome: Alien Labor in Western Development', in W. Alonso (ed.), *Population in an Interacting World*. Cambridge, MA: Harvard University Press, pp. 37–73.

11 Femvertising

A new concept for female empowerment in advertising

Emel Yarimoğlu

1 Introduction

After the foundation of the Republic of Turkey in 1923, the traditional situations of women in the society changed and modernization movements started in Turkish society. A decade beyond the foundation of the Republic of Turkey, under the leadership of Mustafa Kemal Atatürk, the founder of the Republic of Turkey, women had their national voting rights. Women started to participate in social and economic life more than ever with the help of winning the suffrage. Women are key actors in the modernization of societies. Women are active participants in social and economic development; women's participation in the labor market and rising employment enable sustainable development in societies. This sustainable development allows women to have higher participation levels to economic life, have more share in growth, and have stronger positions in family life.

Women have been represented in advertising campaigns with stereotypes such as domestic, housewife, embarrassed, and dependent for years. An evolution was needed in order to deny stereotyping and objectifying women and their bodies in advertising and it began in 2004 with a campaign called the Real Beauty, released by Dove. After this campaign, many companies all over the world used women's empowerment activities in advertising, and the purpose was to increase women's empowerment in society with the help of advertising campaigns.

After Dove's empowerment activities, empowerment campaigns from other companies, such as Nike, Always, Kotex, Under Armour, and Pantene, have continued to increase, and, in 2015, SheKnows Media (now She Media) represented the term "femvertising" for the first time in a contest. This media agency managed a contest with the hashtag femvertising (#femvertising) in order to honor brands that use female empowerment messages, images, and stories in their advertising campaigns. Under these developments, the term femvertising has entered into marketing literature.

There have been many previous studies that searched about femvertising and the effects of femvertising campaigns on both social and economic life, however the term femvertising has been launched lately. Some qualitative studies and quantitative studies were conducted in order to explore a better understanding of femvertising and to analyze its impacts on some particularly marketing-based variables such as brand loyalty, consumers' attitudes, and customers' buying decisions (Jalakas, 2016; Drake, 2017; Akestam et al., 2017; Sternadori and Abitbol, 2019; Champlin et al., 2019; Abitbol and Sternadori, 2019).

The aim of this chapter is to analyze women's empowerment activities in advertising campaigns and show the companies' implementations regarding femvertising, especially in Turkey. Within this aim, literature is reviewed in detail; the situation of women in the labor market is explained with numbers; and women's rights, feminism, women's representations in advertising (stereotypes and gender roles), and women's empowerment activities in advertising are examined widely. Then, the concept of femvertising is introduced, and the femvertising implementations of Nike, Always, Orkid, and Dove are investigated. Lastly, the importance of female empowerment in advertising and its effects on society are discussed.

2 Women's situations in the labor market

In order to understand women's economic situation in the labor market in Turkey, some data taken from Turkish Statistical Institute (Turkstat) are analyzed first. According to Turkstat (2020a) data that show labor participation rates of both women and men, between 15 and 64 years old, the men's labor participation rate was 78.6% whereas the women's participation in labor was 38.3% in 2018. It meant every 38 women among 100 women were working officially in the labor market, whereas every 79 men were working at the same time. Women's participation in the labor market was dramatically less than nearly half of men's participation.

After labor participation, the unemployment rated of both women and men were analyzed (Turkstat, 2020b). It was found that the unemployment rate among men was 9,2% in 2014 and 9,7% in 2018. It increased only 0,5% in four years. However, the unemployment rate among women was 12,2% in 2014 and increased to 14,2% in 2018. It raised 2%, which is a huge rise compared to men. According to the OECD (2018a), some unemployment rates of both men and women in 2018 were as follows: men 4,0% and women 3,9% in the United States, men 4,3% and women 4,2% in the United Kingdom, men 6,5% and women 6,4% in Sweden, men 10% and women 11,9% in Italy, men 10,9% and women 14,0% in Brazil (non-OECD), and men 25,3% and women 29,3% in South Africa (non-OECD).

Lastly, annual average gross earnings by sex and education were investigated for the Turkish labor market. According to data (Turkstat, 2020c), men who graduated from university were earning 55.633 Turkish liras, whereas women who were graduated from university were earning 45.483 Turkish liras annually (1 United States dollar equaled 2.2 Turkish lira) in 2014. These data all showed that women's situation in the Turkish labor market was worse than men's situation.

Besides the poor situation of women in the Turkish labor market, in Europe the situation was the same and women's participation in the labor market has remained insufficient. Even if the women's employment rate has been increasing over time, it is still lagging behind men. In part-time jobs, usually, women were selected to work more than men, whereas men were selected for more prestigious full-time jobs. Moreover, women were paid less than men even in the same job, and this put forward subjects such as the glass ceiling, mobbing in work life, and sex discrimination in professional life. The European Commission (2019a) clarified that 67% of women were employed, whereas men's employment rate was at 79%. It meant that there was a gender employment gap of 12% in Europe, and more than 40% in Turkey (Turkstat, 2020a).

Just as in Turkey, there has been a gender gap in earnings in Europe. In Europe, women earned 39,6% less than men in 2014 (European Commission, 2014). In 2017, the gender pay gap across European Union countries was 16%, which meant that men earn 16% more than women. The countries that had the smallest gender pay gap were Romania (3,5%), Luxembourg (5%), and Italy (5%), and the countries that had the highest gender pay gap were Estonia (25,6%), Czechia (21,2%), and Germany (21%) (European Commission, 2019b). Besides Europe, according to the report of World Economic Forum (2018), there have been gender gaps globally all over the world, and the countries that have the least gender gaps were Iceland, Norway, and Sweden, whereas the countries that have the highest gender gaps were Yemen, Pakistan, and Iraq. Burgess (2003) found out that there were differences in earnings of women and men in managerial positions in accounting and hospitality industries in the United Kingdom.

The reasons for a gender pay gap can be explained as follows (European Commission, 2019c; European Institute for Gender Equality, 2019): (1) Low level education of women. (2) Women spend more time in unpaid work such as housework and cooking than men. In Turkey, men's paid work was 358.3 minutes per day, and unpaid work was 67.6 minutes per day; however women's paid work was 133.9 minutes per day and unpaid work was 305 minutes per day (OECD, 2018b). (3) Women work part-time more than men; only 8.7% of men worked in part-time jobs, compared to 31.3% of women in 2017. (4) Glass ceiling implementations against women cause lower ratios of women in managerial positions. In Turkey, the ratio of female CEOs in Turkish companies remained low in 2018. Only 4% of the companies (13 companies) appointed a female as the CEO, however 40% of the companies (164 companies) appointed a male as the CEO, and 56% of the companies (226 companies) did not appoint a board member as the CEO (IWDP, 2018). (5) Sectoral segregation leads to women working in low-paying industries such as caring and education. (6) Discrimination decreases women's earnings less than men in equal jobs. (7) Women who have child/children are the primary carers and this leads to lower employment of mothers compared to fathers. In European Union countries 15% of women were inactive for caring children, compared to only 1,4% of men in 2017. (8) Women have non-standard and temporary work contracts, which result in lower pay.

European Commission developed some activities in order to fight against the gender pay gap and to promote work-life balance (European Commission, 2019d, 2019e). Within this context, some legislative actions such as maternity leave (minimum of 14 weeks), paternity leave (at least ten working days around the birth), parental leave (minimum four months), carers leave (five working days per year), and flexible working arrangements (working parents of children up to at least eight years have a right to request flexible working arrangements) were undertaken. Beyond these legislative actions, some non-legislative actions such as launching studies and organizing seminars for increasing the labor market participation of women and addressing the high gender pay gap were performed. Outside Europe, some countries' maternity leaves are as follows: Turkey 16 weeks, Canada 17 weeks, Ireland 42 weeks, Japan 14 weeks, Sweden 19.9 weeks, and the United Kingdom 52 weeks (OECD, 2016).

Beyond the gender pay gap, women's economic participation and opportunity were other important criteria that should be analyzed while investigating women's situation in an economy. In the global report of World Economic Forum (2018), the 149 countries were ranked by economic participation and opportunity sub-index. Selected countries and their rankings were as follows respectively: Lao PDR 1st, Sweden 9th, United States 19th, Canada 27th, Russian Federation 31st, Germany 36th, Australia 46th, United Kingdom 52nd, France 63rd, Brazil 92nd, Japan 117th, Turkey 131st, India 142nd, Pakistan 146th, and Iraq 149th. Unfortunately, Turkey was ranked as the 131st among 149 countries, which was nearly at the end of the list.

3 Feminism and women's representations in advertising

3.1 Women's rights and feminism

Feminism includes issues such as the liberation of women, legitimacy of their rights, and having equal rights with men (Tas, 2016). The feminism movement started as the suffrage movement, later called the first wave of feminism. There have been some waves in feminism and the first wave almost included the years 1800s and the early of 1900s. It occurred in the United States between 1848 and 1920, which is the year that American women got their right to vote (Rowe-Finkbeiner, 2004). As in the world, women tried to get rights for voting in this era in Turkey as well. A decade after the foundation of the republic in Turkey (1923), Turkish women achieved voting rights in the elections on 5th November 1934 under the leadership of Mustafa Kemal Atatürk, who is the founder of the Turkish Republic. Women's rights for voting, both to elect and to be elected, is one of Atatürk's Revolutions in social life. Before getting full suffrage in 1934, Turkish women achieved voting rights in 1930 in local elections. Women's getting voting rights was the most important reform to advanc the place of women in society and also made women more visible in the society (Ince, 2015). With the help of the empowerment role of Mustafa Kemal Atatürk, the day that women's getting voting rights was announced as Women's Rights Day in Turkey. This first wave of feminism was the first organized movement that shifted the place of women, especially in politics, and provided them an equal and sustainable opportunity (Hunt, 2017).

After the early years of the 1900s, the second wave of feminism began. In the world, particularly in the United States, the years between the 1960s and 1980s were known as the second wave of feminism, which enabled women to seek their rights in equal pay, equal opportunities, and gender discrimination (Rowe-Finkbeiner,

2004; Harrold, 2014). The main topics during these years were to get equal rights in education, work, and even at home, and women wanted to destroy the restrictive stereotype of the housewife (Paglia, 2008). According to Hunt (2017), the second wave picked up around the 1960s and women were inspired to find equality in both political and socio-cultural life. Many feminist theorists criticized second wave feminism because it was just addressed to white, college-educated, and upper-middle class women (Beail and Goren, 2009; Hunt, 2017).

As feminism evolved in the world, the third wave of feminism began around the 1990s. The main characteristics of the third wave of feminism were: many relations with pop culture, it celebrates women's choices that are unique and special for every woman, and it promotes telling women's stories that enlighten the movement for equality (Hunt, 2017). These characteristics specified individualism and localization, which are the core of third wave feminism. Since second wave feminism was seen as it was for educated and upper-middle class white women, many women viewed it as judgmental, divisive, and rigid (Snyder-Hall, 2010). On the contrary, third wave feminism rejected a uniform and universal perception of femininity and suggested to deal with women individually in the universal platform, and to focus on more individual sides of each woman in terms of race, religion, ethnicity, gender identity, and sexual orientation. It was tailored in order to adapt to women's needs (Harrold, 2014). Beail and Goren (2009) claimed that third wave feminism was the challenge of colored women to white feminism, it inspired "girly culture" and returned back to high heels, Barbie dolls, fashion, and makeup; moreover it rejected the idea that feminist women should have masculine norms instead of feminine ones. As a result of the third wave of feminism, lipstick feminism was born, which aimed to emphasize that feminist women may be girly and possess femininity and sexual power (Harrold, 2014). Lastly, third wave feminism denied judgmentalness and represented sexual liberation for gender equality (Snyder-Hall, 2010).

3.2 Women's representations in advertising: stereotypes and gender roles

Different types of advertising campaigns, such as substantial, persuasive, informative, or reminder, can influence people, although many people are not aware of this. Cohan (2001) said that advertising, which is the most efficient way of socialization in a society, could change the values of a majority and switch attitudes, values, and behaviors of people. Advertising campaigns and media images have strong powerful effects on forming society's ideas toward gender images and changing perspectives regarding gender equality (Rajagopal and Gales, 2002). Women are embodied in advertisements by stereotypes and generalizations that only focus on women's appearance and damage their unique and individual innate differences. It was proven that the advertising industry is an effective medium that affects society's request, forms people's wants and needs, and changes their buying behaviors with the help of languages, images, and representations used in advertisements (Hunt, 2017). However, these images are from the perspectives of producers, marketers, and advertisers, and stand for their own views rather than the views of society or reality since they want to sell the product in this shape.

It was found out in many previous studies that advertisers objectified the parts of women's bodies that associated with men's desires and it was proven that many times women were shown as passive characters in advertisements (Kilbourne, 1999; Andersen, 2002; Shields and Heinecken, 2002; Hunt, 2017). Sullivan and O'Connor (1988) showed that imaginary/unrealistic images of women have been drawn in advertisements and they only showed how women's perfect bodies should be. Because of these images of perfect bodies that stereotyped women's bodies, many women feel themselves as ugly and sense insecurities about themselves. Besides this, in many advertising campaigns, women are shown in supporting roles, needing the help of men and waiting at home where they care, clean, and cook, whereas men were shown in leading roles, looking directly into the camera (Matlin, 1987; Sullivan and O'Connor, 1988; Rajagopal and Gales, 2002). Women feel themselves less attractive when they are imaged with beautiful female models in advertisements (Matlin, 1987; Rajagopal and Gales, 2002).

Gill (2008) analyzed representations of women in advertising and suggested new empowerment styles in contemporary advertising by describing new figures of women represented in advertising, such as active heterosexual "midriff" women, sexy "vengeful" women who punish their male partners, and lesbian "hot" women who hold their female partners. This showed that representation of women in advertising has started to change from passive, unintelligent, embraced women to smart, powerful, and beautiful women. Cohan (2001) discussed three ethical concerns regarding women representation in advertising. The first concern was the description of sex stereotypes and women's presentations as needy, easily manipulated, vulnerable, ashamed, contradictory, and submissive. The second issue was advertising creates perfection and unrealistic beauty standard that is hard to accomplish. The third one was the sexuality of women, which was displayed in advertisements showing women's bodies as sexual objects.

3.3 Women's empowerment in advertising

United Nations Women carried out the Unstereotype Alliance in Turkey in December 2019 in order to fight against gender stereotypes in advertisements. United Nations Women, the United Nations entity for Gender Equality, the Unstereotype Alliance, and partners came together and tried to find solutions for positive changes in the advertising industry all over the world. The main aim of the Unstereotype Alliance was to empower women from all races, classes, ages, ethnicities, religions, and education levels and to eliminate harmful masculinities to create a gender equal world (Unstereotype Alliance, 2019). According to the United Nations report, in Turkey, women's bodies were used as an object of desire in advertisements and the images of strong women did not take place in advertising campaigns; so Turkey was selected as a pilot country by United Nations in order to develop women's empowerment campaigns, especially, in advertising (Gulersoyler, 2019).

Companies' involvement in women's empowerment issues were explained by two important reasons: (1) feminism and harmful use of women bodies in advertising, (2) women's participation in the labor market and their increasing purchasing power (Sener, 2019). Nowadays, women work in different types of marketing activities, such as producing, selling, distributing, and promoting goods and services. Especially in advertising activities, as one of the important types of promotion activities, women can be not only leaders who manage the advertising campaigns but also people who play a role in the advertising campaigns. In particular, in developing countries like Turkey, women who played a role in television advertisement were asked to perform as if they were shy, sexy, embarrassed, devoted, and passive characters. However, within the help of women's empowerment implementations and research studies, the view in the advertising industry has been changed and the era of strong women has just started. Today, women are asked to play more aggressive, strong, active, self-confident, and powerful characters in advertisements instead of shy, quite, maternal, and adaptable characters.

The developments regarding female empowerment in advertisements enable women to feel stronger and more confident. They started to behave as more self-confident and independent. Female empowerment in advertisements strengthen the image of women in the society and make them happier than ever before because of this new image of women. In this new image, women can be or do anything that they want to be or do, not only in their daily lives but also in their work lives. They can work in managerial positions, they can get equal earning with men, and they can care for their children as well as they can work outside the home. Because of the positive effects on society of female empowerment in advertising, the numbers of women in both economic and political environments have started to increase nowadays because they believed they could achieve.

4 Femvertising

4.1 The concept of femvertising

Many studies regarding the representation of women in advertising showed that women's bodies were idealized and used as objects for sex or desire in advertisements (Bati, 2010; Aydin, 2014; Gudekli and Celik, 2014; Sener, 2019). Besides this, in advertisements, women were represented in traditional roles such as wife, mother, and housewife, whereas men were represented as businessmen in public places (Bal, 2014; Senkal, 2016; Sener, 2019). Cankaya (2013) found out that, in Turkey, advertisements conserved traditional gender stereotypes, such as women are romantic, subordinate, emotional characters without control over situations, whereas men were characterized as dominant, powerful, and with limited emotional disclosure.

In the new decade, the 2020s, femvertising that shows female empowerment in advertising is a growing trend in marketing. It was mentioned for the first time in 2015 by She Media (formerly SheKnows Media), which is a digital media company for women. Femvertising referred to the advertising campaigns that use pro-female messages, images, and talents in order to empower women. SheKnows Media started a contest with the hashtag femvertising (*#femvertising*) in 2015 to honor brands that were challenging gender norms by eliminating stereotypes, supporting female empowerment messages, and putting images related to them into these advertisements (Femvertising Awards, 2020). The president of SheKnows Media, Samantha Skey, said that the femvertising contest forced the advertising industry to focus on gender issues and the panel was organized by SheKnows Media in order to see how pro-female campaigns enable brands to build more meaningful connections with women and push them to present different portrayals of women compared to stereotypes (Business Wire, 2016). SheKnows Media (2014) conducted a survey with women about what they thought about pro-female messages and femvertising campaigns. The results suggested that a majority of women (92%) were aware of at least one femvertising campaign, more than half of them (52%) bought a product because they just liked the pro-female message, close to half of them (45%) shared the campaign because it included femvertising campaign, and half of them (51%) liked the campaign because it focused on gender issues.

Femvertising that also fits advertising literature could be an effective advertising strategy for brands and advertising agencies (Sternadori and Abitbol, 2019). However, female empowerment advertisements were not common in the years before 2017; their messages were well understood, especially by women (Drake, 2017). Becker-Herby (2016) defined the main aims of femvertising as using different female talents, giving pro-female messages, eliminating gender stereotypes, ignoring sexuality, and representing women authentically. One of the most important aims of femvertising campaigns was to present various female portrayals in different parts of lives instead of just one female stereotype. Stereotyping of gender is common in advertising, however women were 1.5 to 4 times more stereotyped than men (Eisend, 2010).

Besides destroying stereotypes in advertisements, advertisers also consider to promote the fit between brands and social issues, which is called brand-cause fit, and femvertising campaigns create a link between brand and gender equality, as a social issue (Champlin et al., 2019). Abitbol and Sternadori (2019) showed that femvertising campaigns could be a good corporate social responsibility activity for a firm that supports women's empowerment causes. Besides these societal effects of femvertising campaigns, there have been some commercial effects. It was expected that femvertising campaigns would increase the sales of firms that respect women, because women generally asked themselves why they would buy from a firm that did not respect them. It was found that women have more positive attitudes toward the product that uses femvertising features in its advertising campaigns rather than traditional messages and female stereotypes, and so they have high purchase intentions to buy this product (Drake, 2017). In previous studies, research was conducted with only females in order to see how femvertising campaigns affect them (Akestam et al., 2017; Drake, 2017). However, males should be included in the sample as they are one of the components of empowering women studies (Jacobson et al., 2018; Sternadori and Abitbol, 2019). Sternadori and Abitbol (2019) conducted research with both women and men and found out that consumers' evaluations about femvertising advertisements will be affected positively by attitudes toward femvertising, consumers' evaluations about femvertising advertisements will positively affect attitudes towards brand, and women's attitudes are more positive than men's toward femvertising messages.

From the perspective of advertising agencies, femvertising was seen as a shift in how advertisers speak to women (Becker-Herby, 2016). In femvertising advertisements, the message, created by advertising agencies, can be more narrative self-referencing that absorbs people in a story instead of analytical self-referencing that provides cognitive details since femvertising campaigns are focused on people (Sternadori and Abitbol, 2019; Escalas, 2007). Hunt (2017) mentioned that the concept "sex sells" has been used for a long time by advertising agencies; however, objectifying women's bodies in advertisements brought too many ethical issues. The online survey conducted in 2016 searched about the attitudes towards femvertising campaigns that involve gender equality messages and images, and the results showed that advertisements affect how society views women, and more than half of men (65%) and the majority of women (90%) believe that representing women as sex symbols in advertisements has bad effects on society (Business Wire, 2016).

Doing femvertising right is the most important issue in implementation that brands experience. Brands should have femvertising points of view holistically. If a company/brand has stereotyped or objectified women's bodies, it would not help to create the most successful femvertising campaign, because women do not believe that this company is sincere. SheKnows (2014) showed the brands that women believe have been producing right femvertising campaigns, such as Dove, Nike, Always, Under Armour, Pantene, and Olay. Besides these companies, companies such as Under Armour and Verizon launched campaigns that promote women to display their "masculine" features, such as ambition, athleticism, courage, and decisiveness (Abitbol and Sternadori, 2016).

4.2 Famous implementations of femvertising campaigns

Dove was the first company that used female empowerment in its advertisement campaign, in a campaign called Real Beauty, in 2004. The research conducted in 2001 about the self-esteem and body positivity among women showed that only 2% of women have seen themselves as beautiful (Hunt, 2017). After this result, the company decided to launch a campaign that changed beauty standards related to skin color, wrinkles, weight, and height. They used some slogans in their advertisements, such as "Dove Firming. As tested on real curves", "withered? or wonderful?", "flawed? or flawless?" (Simmons, 2018). Beauty was redefined with the Real Beauty campaign, and nowadays the stereotypes are collapsed in the world and beauty has no stereotypes such as being skinny or flawless. Wang (2018) stressed that Dove achieved to show that mothers are still beautiful despite their ages, and emphasized that the Real Beauty campaign also aimed at changing the directions of women to have plastic surgery in order to reach perfect beauty with the taglines "tell your mom she is beautiful" and "what's your beauty legacy".

Although many advertising campaigns were still focused on stereotypes, Dove connected with real women in real lives (Drake, 2017). In 2004, within the Real Beauty campaign, the company preferred to use real women with different ages, shapes, and ethnicities instead of celebrities or models in the company's advertising strategy. This campaign was extremely successful, generating the attention of target markets and raising sales (Taylor et al., 2016). Dove's campaign especially focused on the insecurities of women and resisted one dominant beauty ideology. It used various women in its campaign in order to show everyone has her own beauty, even if she was overweight and of varying shapes and sizes, or had wrinkles on her face. Because it was the first femvertising implementation, Dove's Real Beauty campaign was analyzed frequently in marketing literature. Many scholars researched the effectiveness of the Real Beauty campaign and found that the campaign was successful and affected the society positively, especially in terms of women's empowerment and loving women themselves (Patton and Vasquez, 2008; Morel, 2009; Jalakas, 2016; Abitbol and Sternadori, 2016).

After Dove, many companies started to use a femvertising strategy in their advertisements. Some famous global femvertising campaigns include Like a Girl by Always in 2014; Labels Against Women by Pantene in the Philippines in 2013, which became viral globally; I will What I Want by Under Armour in the United States in 2014; This Girl Can by Sport England in the Great Britain in 2015; Doesn't Stop Me by Kotex in 2017; A Run with the Girls Shouldn't Hurt the Girls by Nike in 2014; and Dream with Us by Nike in 2019 (Akestam et al., 2017; Case, 2019).

There were many femvertising campaigns created after Dove's Real Beauty campaign. In global markets, Always, which sells menstrual and hygienic pads, is one of the global brands of Procter and Gamble, and it released Like a Girl campaign to encourage girls to be more confident and increase girl power in society. In the United States, the first release of Like a Girl campaign was during the 2015 Super Bowl. Since the campaign attracted attention, it revealed many different types of advertisements such as print, video, outdoor, and internet, particularly social media content (Hunt, 2017). The campaign emphasized that girls' self-esteem dropped during puberty, and the use of negative words will affect and underestimate a girl's power.

In the Like a Girl video campaign (Always, 2014), the young women and men were asked "what it looks like to run like a girl" and all the participants ran slowly and acted feminine, code of behavior in order to show representations of the phrase "like a girl". Then, the same question was asked to the little girls around ten years old and they ran as fast as they could. Then, the second question was asked to the little girl – "what does it mean to you when I say run like a girl?" – and she answers "it means run as fast as you can". Lastly, another little girl was asked "is 'like a girl' a good thing?" and she answers "it sounds like you are trying to humiliate someone". In the video, the little girls proved that they were much stronger and tougher than they were assumed to be when they ran as fast as they could in response to the first question. Always targeted these young girls because they are of the age to use Always's feminine products. The video (Always, 2014) aimed to encourage young girls and keep them never quit to meet the expectations of other people (Wang, 2018).

In Turkey, Orkid, which is the same company as Always and belongs to Procter and Gamble as well, broadcasted the same campaign (Orkid, 2014). The same video was released in Turkey in 2014. Based on the findings taken from Orkid Self-Confidence and Adolescence Research, 72% of girls thought that they were restricted by the society about what they should do or should not do (Marketing Turkiye, 2016). Since the self-confidence levels of young girls declines at the beginning of puberty with the first menstruation, their self-confidence levels would be easily affected by harmful words that humiliate and underestimate them such as "like a girl". Girls, who were insulted by these words, will be hurt deeply since they are in puberty, which is a delicate period, and it will have a huge negative impact on the development of their self-confidence.

Orkid reached over 90 million people with the Like a Girl campaign; then it released a second video as the continuance of the first campaign with the name Unstoppable Like a Girl in 2015. The company aimed to turn the negative perception of the phrase "Like a Girl" into a positive perception with the name of the new campaign "Unstoppable Like a Girl" (Halkla Iliskiler, 2015). The company wanted to break down the thoughts such as "girls cannot dare" and "girls are powerless". Always released the same femvertising campaign across the world. Alkan (2016) stated that the brand has repositioned itself by rewriting the rules of femininity and empowering women.

Lately, Orkid (2019) has developed another country-specific advertisement for empowering Turkish women with the hashtag "uncover the shame" (#uncovertheshame), which remarked violence against women in Turkey. The company made new packaging that consists of news about women's violence, gender inequality, and discrimination, then wrapped the product with it due to period stigma and said that "we covered Orkid to uncover the shame" (Orkid, 2019). The aim of the campaign was to show that people should be ashamed of the news covering the pads instead of being ashamed of the sanitary pads. The company also emphasized inequalities between women and men by covering sanitary pads with newspapers consisting of the news regarding violence, discrimination, and unfairness toward women.

Besides Orkid and Dove, Nike is one of the most successful companies in the world to implement successful well-known femvertising campaigns. Nike started women's empowerment activities, in particular sports contests, almost three decades ago. In the 1990s, Nike started to create various women's empowerment features in advertisements that eliminated the differences between genders. In those years, especially in sports contests, there have been lots of gender discrimination issues, for example, it was just "basketball tournament" for men whereas it was "women's basketball tournament" for women, and also men athletes that participated in the tournaments were called with their last names and were also referred to as "men" or "young men", however women who joined the tournaments were called by their first names and also referred to as "girls" or "young ladies" (Grow and Wolburg, 2006). The first empowerment campaign was launched in

1990 with the aim of encouraging women to reject traditional patterns and making them a part of an empowered community (Grow and Wolburg, 2006). The company released the campaign called List. The printed advertisement listed various things that create pressures on women and continued with the slogan as "Self-support from Nike. Just do it" (Grow and Wolburg, 2006; Nike News, 2015).

Recently, Nike (2019a) released Dream with Us campaign and it provided ultimate messages of female empowerment. Nike promoted girls' powers, especially in sports, in this campaign and also focused on encouraging women to keep trying even if they experience failure. In the video advertisement, amateur and professional athletes are shown and some provoking questions are asked, such as "Do you want to be a bigger athlete than Serena Williams? Or do you want to be the first girl to play for the Yankees? Can you be the generation that ends gender inequality?" (Soccer Today, 2019). After releasing the Dream with Us campaign, Nike (2019b) released Dream Crazier, which showed strong links with femvertising. The video advertisement ended with the narrative "If they want to call you crazy? Fine, show them what crazy can do" (McCaffrey, 2019).

Lastly, like Orkid, Nike also released a country-specific femvertising campaign for Turkey in 2017 called This Is Us. Nike Women Turkey broadcasted the video advertisement (Nike, 2017). The campaign emphasized the importance of destroying the cliches in society and showed the girls that they can break stereotypes and redefine themselves. The advertisement showed the contrast between what society thought girls are and what girls actually are. In the advertisement, at first, the women appeared as if they were doing what society expected of them but suddenly they turned into rule breakers, for example one turned into a successful athlete. One woman said "Did I mention we love gold?" when she left the jewelry store, and added "It suits us well" when she wore a gold medal that showed a championship in a tournament. Wang (2018) said that the campaign empowered women, broke stereotypes, and showed that women are stronger than the society thought. Nike tried to inspire more women to get physically active within this campaign (Nike News, 2017).

Conclusion

In Turkey, the labor participation of women and women's participation in the economy were too low, and the unemployment rate of women and gender pay gap were too high. Both in the world and in Turkey, women's participation in the labor market was not at a sufficient level. Iqbal (2015) said that many women and young girls were encouraged to work in STEM-based jobs, which consist of jobs in science, technology, engineering, and math, that women barely participated in. For example, just one of seven women has worked in these roles in the United Kingdom.

Improving gender equality in work life and women's gaining economic power were the most important issues in women's empowerment and these linked women to a better status (Cueva Beteta, 2006). Because of its strong effects on political and economic environments, women's empowerment usually was taken as a part of international development policies generated by particular international organizations such as Organisation for Economic Co-operation and Development (OECD) and United Nations (UN). Women's empowerment was seen as a process, conceptualized in literature with qualitative and quantitative methods, new measures were found out, and most studies compared the women who lived in developed countries and the women who lived in underdeveloped or developing countries (Schuler et al., 1994; Mason and Smith, 2003; Malhotra and Schuler, 2005; Cueva Beteta, 2006; Schuler et al., 2010).

Women's empowerment relates to women gaining power and so controlling their lives with the help of building self-confidence, raising awareness, expanding choices, and increasing access to resources (Zheng, 2015). The principles of women's empowerment were to establish corporate leadership for gender equality; behave fairly to women and men at work; provide safety, well-being, and health of women and men at work; support training, education, and professional developments for women; perform business functions to empower women; promote equality; and test ongoing progress to achieve equality (UN Women, 2011). The five main components of women's empowerment were explained in the glossary of European Institute for Gender Equality (2020): women's sense of self-worth, women's rights to choose, women's rights to access to resources, women's rights to have power and control over their lives, and women's impact on their social changes in both social and economic areas.

Advertising campaigns have effects on society (Rajagopal and Gales, 2002). The images used in advertisements affect people's behaviors, thoughts, and emotions. Since advertisements and campaigns have impacts on society's life, they need to be investigated as a part of social life. The advertising industry should pay attention to issues such as stereotypes, generalizations of women's bodies, and female empowerment. Byrne (2004) reported five female stereotypes often used in advertisements, such as perfect mum, great granny, alpha female, beauty bunny, and fashionista. Becker-Herby (2016) categorized prevalent gender stereotypes in advertisements under six main categories: (1) mode of presentation (the way in which the figure is represented – visually, visually with voice, visually with music), (2) credibility of the source (figure's knowledge about the product–user, authority), (3) role of the figure in the advertisement (office worker, career, spouse), (4) age of the figure (young, middle-aged, or old), (5) product type in advertisement (clothing, food and beverage, leisure), and (6) setting of advertisement (inside the house, private residence). In addition to these, stereotypes can be classified into two parts: traditional, which shows women in family and men in business, and non-traditional, which shows women in business and men at home (Zawisza and Cinnirella, 2010; Knoll et al., 2011; Becker-Herby, 2016).

Today, the representation of women in advertisements has started to change; more powerful, active, and strong representations, and women who love their bodies, have high self-confidence, have economic power, and manage their lives have started to be represented in advertisements through the agency of femvertising implementations (Sener, 2019). Gill (2008) clarified the reasons behind this change in the representation of women in advertisements. The first reason for women's representations in advertisements as more powerful and strong was that women became the target market for new products since they had their economic power. In addition, the second reason advertising agencies have changed their representations is that women became angry at them because these agencies demonstrated them as objects of sex or desire in past advertisements. For these reasons, femvertising campaigns and female empowerment activities are expected to increase in the near future.

In Turkey, gender stereotypes and sexism may be destroyed through education. Advertisements also provide this education. The numbers of companies that use femvertising should increase, femvertising campaigns should be extended, and people should be educated through these campaigns. Advertisements should be seen as one of the activities that raise awareness of society and educate people. This education should break down stereotypes, sexism, objectifying of women's bodies, and gender inequalities. The education through advertisements should increase the self-confidence of girls, eliminate the objectifying of women's bodies, and provide gender equality in both social and economic life.

References

Abitbol, A., & Sternadori, M. (2016). You Act Like a Girl: An Examination of Consumer Perceptions of 'Femvertising'. *Quarterly Review of Business Disciplines*, 3(2), 117–128.

Abitbol, A., & Sternadori, M. (2019). Championing Women's Empowerment as a Catalyst for Purchase Intentions: Testing the Mediating Roles of OPRs and Brand Loyalty in the Context of Femvertising. *International Journal of Strategic Communication*, 13(1), 22–41.

Akestam, N., Rosengren, S., & Dahlen, M. (2017). Advertising 'Like a Girl': Toward a Better Understanding of 'Femvertising' and Its Effects. *Psychology & Marketing*, 34(8), 795–806.

Alkan, N. (2016). New Trends in the Representation of Women in Contemporary Media Culture: A Critical Analysis of Three Women Empowering Advertising Campaigns. *Iletisim*, (24), 119–143.

Always (2014). Like a Girl Video Advertisement, Accessed: 10.11.2019, Retrieved from www.youtube.com/watch?v=XjJQBjWYDTs&t=59s

Andersen, R. (2002). The Thrill Is Gone: Advertising, Gender Representation, and the Loss of Desire. In Meehan, E. R. and Riordan, E. (Eds.), *Sex and Money: Feminism and Political Economy in the Media* (pp. 223–239). Minneapolis, MN: University of Minnesota Press.

Aydin, G. A. (2014). Reklamlarda beden temsili üzerine karşılaştırmalı bir inceleme: Cosmopolitan ve Ala Dergileri örneginde. *Akdeniz Iletisim*, 22, 41–59.

Bal, S. (2014). Reklamların Eskimeyen Yüzü 'Muhteşem Annelik': Anneler Günü Reklamları Örneği. *Ankara Universitesi Ilef Dergisi*, 1(2), 59–85.

Bati, U. (2010). Reklamcılıkta Retorik Bir Unsur Olarak Kadın Bedeni Temsilleri. *Kültür ve Iletişim*, 13(1), 103–134.

Beail, L., & Goren, L. J. (2009). Introduction: Feminism, Front and Center. In Goren L. J. (Ed.), *You've Come a Long Way, Baby: Women, Politics, and Popular Culture* (pp. 1–12). Lexington, KY: University Press of Kentucky.

Becker-Herby, E. (2016). The Rise of Femvertising: Authentically Reaching Female Consumers. The University of Minnesota School of Journalism and Mass Communication, Master Program, Capstone Project. Twin Cities: University of Minnesota.

Byrne, C. (2004). Five Cliches of Woman (as Portrayed by Advertisers), Accessed: 27.01.2020, Retrieved from www.independent.co.uk/news/media/five-clichatildecopys-of-woman-as-portrayed-by-advertisers-5351917.html

Burgess, C. (2003). Gender and Salaries in Hotel Financial Management: Tt's still a Man's World. *Women in Management Review*, 18(1/2), 50–59.

Business Wire (2016). SheKnows Media to Reveal New Research on #Femvertising and Announce Winners of the 2016 #Femvertising Awards at Advertising Week 2016, Accessed: 10.01.2020, Retrieved from www.businesswire.com/news/home/20160921005572/en/SheKnows-Media-Reveal-Research-Femvertising-Announce-Winners

Cankaya, M. (2013). Traditional? Modern? or both? Representation of Gender in Turkish TV Commercials. *Journal of Social Sciences*, 30, 279–295.

Case, L. M. (2019). From Femininity to Feminism: A Visual Analysis of Advertisements before and after the Femvertising Movement. *Elon Journal of Undergraduate Research in Communications*, 10(1), 35–45.

Champlin, S., Sterbenk, Y., Windels, K., & Poteet, M. (2019). How Brand-Cause Fit Shapes Real World Advertising Messages: A Qualitative Exploration of 'Femvertising'. *International Journal of Advertising*, 38(8), 1240–1263.

Cohan, J. A. (2001). Towards a New Paradigm in the Ethics of Women's Advertising. *Journal of Business Ethics*, 33(4), 323–337.

Cueva Beteta, H. (2006). What Is Missing in Measures of Women's Empowerment? *Journal of Human Development*, 7(2), 221–241.

Drake, V. E. (2017). The Impact of Female Empowerment in Advertising (Femvertising). *Journal of Research in Marketing*, 7(3), 593–599.

Eisend, M. (2010). A MetaAnalysis of Gender Roles in Advertising. *Journal of the Academy of Marketing Science*, 38(4), 418–440.

Escalas, J. E. (2007). Self-Referencing and Persuasion: Narrative Transportation versus Analytical Elaboration. *Journal of Consumer Research*, 33(4), 421–429.

European Commission (2014). The Gender Pay Gap Situation in the EU, Accessed: 22.01.2020, Retrieved from https://ec.europa.eu/info/policies/justice-and-fundamental-rights/gender-equality/equal-pay/gender-pay-gap-situation-eu_en

European Commission (2019a). Women's Situation in the Labour Market, Accessed: 22.01.2020, Retrieved from https://ec.europa.eu/info/policies/justice-and-fundamental-rights/gender-equality/women-labour-market-work-life-balance/womens-situation-labour-market_en

European Commission (2019b). Factsheet on the Gender Pay Gap 2019, Accessed: 20.01.2020, Retrieved from https://ec.europa.eu/info/sites/info/files/factsheet-gender_pay_gap-2019.pdf

European Commission (2019c). The Gender Pay Gap Situation in the EU, Accessed: 20.01.2020, Retrieved from https://ec.europa.eu/info/policies/justice-and-fundamental-rights/gender-equality/equal-pay/gender-pay-gap-situation-eu_en

European Commission (2019d). EU Action to Promote Work-Life Balance, Accessed: 20.01.2020, Retrieved from https://ec.europa.eu/info/policies/justice-and-fundamental-rights/gender-equality/women-labour-market-work-life-balance/eu-action-promote-work-life-balance_en

European Commission (2019e). EU Rights to Work-Life Balance, Accessed: 20.01.2020, Retrieved from https://ec.europa.eu/info/policies/justice-and-fundamental-rights/gender-equality/women-labour-market-work-life-balance/eu-rights-work-life-balance_en#right-to-maternity-leave

European Institute for Gender Equality (2019). What Lies behind the Gender Pay Gap?, Accessed: 20.01.2020, Retrieved from https://eige.europa.eu/gender-statistics/dgs/data-talks/what-lies-behind-gender-pay-gap

European Institute for Gender Equality (2020). Empowerment of Women, Accessed: 15.01.2020, Retrieved from https://eige.europa.eu/thesaurus/terms/1102

Femvertising Awards (2020). Which Brands Will Win?, Accessed: 10.01.2020, Retrieved from www.femvertisingawards.com/

Gill, R. (2008). Empowerment/Sexism: Figuring Female Sexual Agency in Contemporary Advertising. *Feminism & Psychology*, 18(1), 35–60.

Grow, J. M., & Wolburg, J. M. (2006). Selling Truth: How Nike's Advertising to Women Claimed a Contested Reality. *Advertising & Society Review*, 7(2), 55–79.

Gudekli, I. A., & Celik, I. (2014). Using Woman in Advertisement as a Symbol of Sex: Cosmopolitan Magazine Example. *Journal of Yasar University*, 35(9), 6129–6137.

Gulersoyler, S. (2019). Cinsiyet algılarını reklamlarla yıkacaklar. Sozcu Newspaper, Accessed: 10.01.2020, Retrieved from www.sozcu.com.tr/2019/gundem/cinsiyet-algilarini-reklamlarla-yikacaklar-5509267/

Halkla Iliskiler (2015). Orkid'den #KızGibi Kampanya, Accessed: 08.01.2020, Retrieved from www.halklailiskiler.com.tr/Orkidten_KizGibi_kampanya.php

Harrold, M. L. (2014). Lipstick and Granola: Perceptions of Feminism. *PURE Insights*, 3(1), 1–7.

Hunt, A. R. (2017). Selling Empowerment: A Critical Analysis of Femvertising. *Doctoral Dissertation in Boston College, College of Arts and Sciences*. Advisor: Dr. Michael Serazio, Boston College Senior Communication Honors Thesis.

Ince, G. B. (2015). The Depiction of Women's Suffrage in Turkey in the Editorial Cartoons of the Era. *Journal of Yasar University*, 10(37), 6381–6477.

Iqbal, N. (2015). Femvertising: How Advertisers Are Selling #Empowerment to Women. *The Guardian*, Accessed: 21.01.2020, Retrieved from www.theguardian.com/lifeandstyle/2015/oct/12/femvertising-branded-feminism

IWDP (Independent Woman Directors Project) (2018). Corporate Governance Forum of Turkey Sabanci University: 6th Annual Report Women on Board, Accessed: 20.01.2020, Retrieved from https://iwdturkey.sabanciuniv.edu/sites/iwdturkey.sabanciuniv.edu/files/2018wobturkeyreport.pdf

Jacobson, C., Katalin Abdallah, L., Liasse, D., & Lund, E. (2018). Femvertising and Its Effects on Brand Image: A Study of Men's Attitude towards Brands Pursuing Brand Activism in Their Advertising. *LBMG Strategic Brand Management-Masters Paper Series*. Sweden: Lund School of Economics and Management.

Jalakas, L. D. (2016). The Ambivalence of Femvertising. *Master Thesis in the Media and Communication Studies Lund University*, Advisor: Assoc. Prof. Magnus Andersson.

Kilbourne, J. (1999). *Deadly Persuasion: Why Women and Girls must Fight the Addictive Power of Advertising*. New York, NY: Free Press.

Knoll, S., Eisend, M., & Steinhagen, J. (2011). Gender Roles in Advertising: Measuring and Comparing Gender Stereotyping on Public and Private TV Channels in Germany. *International Journal of Advertising*, 30(5), 867.

Malhotra, A., & Schuler, S. R. (2005). Women's Empowerment as a Variable in International Development. *Measuring Empowerment: Cross-Disciplinary Perspectives*, 1(1), 71–88.

Marketing Turkiye (2016). Kız çocuklarının yüzde 72'si toplum tarafından kısıtlandığını söylüyor!, Accessed: 27.01.2020, Retrieved from www.marketingturkiye.com.tr/haberler/kiz-cocuklarinin-yuzde-72si-toplum-tarafindan-kisitlandigini-soyluyor/

Mason, K. O., & Smith, H. L. (2003). Women's Empowerment and Social Context: Results from Five Asian Countries. *Gender and Development Group*. Washington, DC: World Bank.

Matlin, M. W. (1987). *The Psychology of Women*. New York, NY: Holt, Rinehart & Winston.

McCaffrey, O. (2019). Nike's Newest Spot Highlights Women's Athletics. *Ad Age*, Accessed: 22.11.2019, Retrieved from https://adage.com/article/cmo-strategy/nikes-newest-spot-highlights-womens-athletics/2170601

Morel, L. (2009). The Effectiveness of the Dove Campaign for Real Beauty in Terms of Society and the Brand. *Syracuse University Honors Program Capstone Projects 480*. New York, NY: Syracuse University.

Nike (2017). This Is Us Video Advertisement, Accessed: 22.11.2019, Retrieved from www.youtube.com/watch?v=1OYi2pbNK_4

Nike (2019a). Dream with Us Video Advertisement, Accessed: 22.11.2019, Retrieved from www.youtube.com/watch?v=IHcWPVbDArU

Nike (2019b). Dream Crazier Video Advertisement, Accessed: 22.11.2019, Retrieved from www.youtube.com/watch?v=whpJ19RJ4JY

Nike News (2015). Nike Puts Women Front and Center for 40 Years and Counting, Accessed: 28.01.2020, Retrieved from https://news.nike.com/news/nike-women-advertising-a-40-year-journey

Nike News (2017). 'This Is Us' Celebrates Beautiful Duality of Turkish Women, Accessed 29.01.2020, Retrieved from https://news.nike.com/news/p73a428a64bdfcfe108dca4082e84a7a8/sneak_peek

OECD (2016). Employment: Length of Maternity Leave, Parental Leave, and Paid Father-Specific Leave, Accessed: 20.01.2020, Retrieved from https://stats.oecd.org/Index.aspx?DataSetCode=TIME_USE#

OECD (2018a). Employment: Unemployment Rate, by Sex and Age Group, Accessed: 20.01.2020, Retrieved from https://stats.oecd.org/Index.aspx?DataSetCode=TIME_USE#

OECD (2018b). Paid and Unpaid Hours by Sex, Accessed: 20.01.2020, Retrieved from https://stats.oecd.org/Index.aspx?datasetcode=TIME_USE#

Orkid (2014). Kız Gibi Video Advertisement, Accessed: 28.11.2019, Retrieved from www.youtube.com/watch?v=Qv_jwegGtvY

Orkid (2019). Uncover the Shame Video Advertisement, Accessed: 28.11.2019, Retrieved from www.youtube.com/watch?v=cuwZQti3lU0

Paglia, C. (2008). Feminism Past and Present: Ideology, Action, and Reform. *Arion: A Journal of Humanities and the Classics*, 16(1), 1–18.

Patton, C. R., & Vasquez, R. (2008). Dove's Campaign for Real Beauty: A Case Analysis. In Oglesby, R.A. & Adams, M. G. (Eds.), *Business Research Yearbook: Global Business Perspectives* (Vol. 15, pp. 856–861). Florida, FL: International Academy of Business Disciplines.

Rajagopal, I., & Gales, J. (2002). It's the Image That Is Imperfect: Advertising and Its Impact on Women. *Economic and Political Weekly*, 37(32), 3333–3337.

Rowe-Finkbeiner, K. (2004). *The F-Word: Feminism in Jeopardy: Women, Politics, and the Future*. Emeryville, CA: Seal Press.

Senkal, Y. (2016). Feminist kuramlar bağlamında reklamda kadın imgesine bakış. *Anadolu Bil Meslek Yüksekokulu Dergisi*, 42, 91–114.

Schuler, S. R., & Hashemi, S. M. (1994). Credit Programs, Women's Empowerment, and Contraceptive Use in Rural Bangladesh. *Studies in Family Planning*, 65–76.

Schuler, S. R., Islam, F., & Rottach, E. (2010). Women's Empowerment Revisited: A Case Study from Bangladesh. *Development in Practice*, 20(7), 840–854.

Sener, G. (2019). Metalaşmış Feminizm Kadınları Güçlendirir mi? 8 Mart Dünya Emekçi Kadınlar Günü Reklamlarının Feminist Eleştirel Söylem Analizi. *Kültür ve Iletişim*, 22(44), 146–172.

SheKnows (2014). SheKnows Survey Finds That When It Comes to Advertising, Women Are Leading the Charge, Accessed: 25.01.2020, Retrieved from www.sheknows.com/living/articles/1056821/sheknows-unveilsresults-of-its-fem-vertising-survey-infographic

Shields, V. R., & Heinecken, D. (2002). What Do Ads Teach Us about Gender? In *Measuring Up: How Advertising Affects Self-Image* (pp. 35–62). Philadelphia: University of Pennsylvania Press.

Simmons, K. (2018). The Campaign of a Century: Dove's 'Real Beauty', Accessed: 20.11.2019, Retrieved from https://stmuhistorymedia.org/the-campaign-of-a-century-doves-real-beauty/

Snyder-Hall, R. C. (2010). Third-Wave Feminism and the Defense of 'Choice'. *Perspectives on Politics*, 8(1), 255–261.

Soccer Today (2019). Nike's Dream with Us: Having a Dream Won't Change the World Sharing One Will #Justdoit, Accessed: 05.01.2020, Retrieved from www.soccertoday.com/nikes-dream-with-us-shines-spotlight-on-female-athletes-and-surf-soccer/

Sternadori, M., & Abitbol, A. (2019). Support for Women's Rights and Feminist Self-Identification as Antecedents of Attitude toward Femvertising. *Journal of Consumer Marketing*, 36(6), 740–750.

Sullivan, G. L., & O'Connor, P. J. (1988). Women's Role Portrayals in Magazine Advertising: 1958–1983. *Sex Roles*, 18(3–4), 181–188.

Tas, G. (2016). Feminizm üzerine genel bir değerlendirme: Kavramsal analizi, tarihsel süreçleri ve dönüşümleri. *Akademik Hassasiyetler*, 3(5), 163–175.

Taylor, J., Johnston, J., & Whitehead, K. (2016). A Corporation in Feminist Clothing? Young Women Discuss the Dove 'Real Beauty' Campaign. *Critical Sociology*, 42(1), 123–144.

Turkstat (2020a). Labor Participation Rate of Women and Men, Accessed: 20.01.2020, Retrieved from https://biruni.tuik.gov.tr/medas/?kn=72&locale=tr

Turkstat (2020b). Unemployment Rate of Women and Men, Accessed: 20.01.2020, Retrieved from https://biruni.tuik.gov.tr/medas/?kn=72&locale=en

Turkstat (2020c). Annual Earnings of Women and Men, Accessed: 20.01.2020, Retrieved from https://biruni.tuik.gov.tr/medas/?locale=tr

UN Women (2011). Women Empowerment Principles: Equality Means Business, Accessed: 10.01.2020, Retrieved from www.unwomen.org/-/media/headquarters/attachments/sections/library/publications/2011/10/women-s-empowerment-principles_en%20pdf.pdf?la=en&vs=1504

Unstereotype Alliance (2019). We Have a Vision of an Unstereotyped World, Accessed: 19.01.2020, Retrieved from www.unstereotypealliance.org/en

Wang, S. (2018). Empowering Women through Advertising: A Content Analysis on 'Femvertising' Campaigns. *Master Thesis in the Department of Mass Communication and*

Media Arts, Graduate School Southern Illinois University Carbondale. Advisor: Dr. Kavita Karan.

World Economic Forum (2018). The Global Gender Gap Report 2018, Accessed: 20.01.2020, Retrieved from www3.weforum.org/docs/WEF_GGGR_2018.pdf

Zawisza, M., & Cinnirella, M. (2010). What Matters MoreBreaking Tradition or Stereotype Content? Envious and Paternalistic Gender Stereotypes and Advertising Effectiveness. *Journal of Applied Social Psychology*, 40(7), 1767–1797.

Zheng, S. (2015). Empowerment of Women and Girls, United Nations Statistics, Accessed: 15.01.2020, Retrieved from https://unstats.un.org/unsd/genderstatmanual/Glossary.ashx

12 Evaluation of labor market issues in sport and exercise environment in Turkey

Gözde Ersöz

Introduction

Sports has become an extremely attractive economic activity in the service sector due to its properties that protect, support and improve personal and public health, and in the consumption sector as a show and entertainment activity that intensely excites the masses because it is a profitable advertising medium under the influence of mass media (Gündoğdu & Devecioğlu, 2008; İyem, 2013; Oflaz, 2013). The contribution of sports to social capital in the early periods when it emerged as a physical activity has left its place to the desire to make economic profit in time and it was redefined as an economic activity due to its growth trend on a global scale (Desbordes & Richelieu, 2012; Çırka, 2017). Globalization of sports played an important role in strengthening of sports economics. According to Andreff (2008), globalization process of sports is defined around three main developments: (1) extension of holiday periods, (2) television broadcasts, (3) emergence of new information and communication technologies.

International sports organizations, revenues from broadcast rights, sponsorship agreements, and tourism revenues based on sports have constantly developed global sports economics, and consequently, sports has become a political tool as well as a social and economic one (Inal, 2008; Bairner & Molnar, 2010). In this context, almost every country in the world uses international sports organizations due to their contribution to the country's economy, and to maintain or increase their diplomatic visibility at an international level. In this context, when the countries shape their sports policy, they focus on the potential international prestige brought by successful athletes' representation as well as its contribution to social capital (Leeds, Von Allmen, & Matheson, 2018).

Sports industry is the name of the market that offers sports, fitness, recreation, leisure activities and related products, services, people, places, and thoughts to consumers (Devecioğlu, 2005). This diversity in the sports industry has led to diversification of people working in this field (Murathan, 2019). Considered as a profession due to its social, economic, and political aspects at the present time, sports can be done individually or collectively at leisure or as a full-time profession, and has a high employment ratio (İyem, 2013). As it involves numerous activities and cooperates with overly employed institutions such as media organizations, labor supply in sports industry is increasing every passing day. This increase in employment rates is considered as one of the most important indicators for the development of an industry (Sage, 2015). Employment ratio is particularly high in big international sports activities (such as Olympics, European Championships, World Championships). At this point, it is possible to say that the sports industry has a positive effect on the entire economy due to its added value in terms of providing employment opportunities (Sivrikaya & Demir, 2019; Çakmak, İşlek, & Keskin, 2017).

It is important to reveal the general structure and current state of labor markets for development of countries. Analysis of the labor market is of vital importance when examining the macroeconomic structure of a country due to its direct connection with employment and unemployment which are critical indicators of a sound economy. The reviews suggest that it is necessary to develop challenging policies that would lead to positive development in labor markets so that economic development, economic welfare, and social development are ensured (Taks & Schubert, 2016).

The "sine qua non" condition of economic development is to use production factors as high and productive as possible. Analysis of the labor force, which is one of the production factors, is necessary for economic development. Analysis of human capital in terms of qualities and quantities on a sectoral basis, how efficient and effective this resource is used and discussing the factors affecting this productivity will contribute to the development of that sector. In this context, in this part of the book, information about the workforce in the sports sector is given and the factors affecting the workforce are discussed. However, the contribution of living physically active or dealing with regular exercise to labor productivity is also discussed in this section.

1 Labor market in professional sports

Sports that have the characteristics of games and professional sports were differentiated in time as sports games are commercialized. In sports branches organized with a commercial understanding where billions of dollars are at stake, sports has become a product and fans have become consumers. It has created results that allow athletes to transform their talents into commodities and to establish an economic market where physical talents can be traded (Talimciler, 2008). Being the basic actors of the dealings in professional sports, athletes work very hard physically and psychologically and as the sports is accepted as an entertainment and show, they have begun to be perceived as the stars of sports. Athletes who are employees, workers and products in the sports sector have numerous roles in business life as employees, entrepreneurs, products, stars and statistical factors differently from the employees of other sectors (Aydın, 2007). The labor market of athletes differs in terms of the popularity of sports branches and earnings. Since football is the most popular professional sports in Turkey, information regarding this sports branch are discussed under a separate heading (Talimciler, 2002).

2 Labor market in football

Football was only a sports branch by the end of 1980s, but it underwent a change in historic process and has become a commercial business followed by millions in 1990s under the influence of globalization (Akşar, 2005). England has played an important role in the development of football industry with establishment of British Football Association in 1863. The British Football Association was initially in opposition to transition from amateurism to professionalism in football (Ülker, 2019), but as a result of the secret payments made to the players and pressure of the clubs in 1880s, it had to legitimize professionalism in 1885 (Şahin & Tunçkol, 2010). Consequently, the first professional football league in the world was established by the British Football Association in 1888 with participation of 12 sports clubs. After being commercialized in 1980s, football was industrialized in 1995 after the "Bosman Ruling" decision by European Court of Justice. As a result of Bosman Ruling, footballers have gained the right to move freely in Europe and the restriction on the number of European Union (EU) national footballers in a football team is removed. This ruling accelerated transfer of European players in all clubs (Boniface, 2007; Çınarlı & Ersöz, 2007).

3 Wages in sports sector

Football players playing in professional football leagues are described as sports workers in the football labor market. Being the human capital of football industry due to their qualities and talents, the footballers are purchased and sold sometimes by managers and sometimes by their own will as any commodity passes from hand to hand in business world as a factor of production who are paid for their labor (Ataçocuğu, 2012; Wang, Cheng, & Jane, 2014). As in many other industries, employment levels and positions of the employees in football industry also differentiate and their wages vary. As the wages of workers in any industry vary from business to business, the wages of footballers playing in football leagues may vary depending on the clubs they play for and classification of the leagues their clubs play in (Ataçocuğu & Zelyurt, 2016).

Many factors affect the valuation of footballers such as criteria like performance, position, physical properties, experience and talents such as assisting, scoring a goal, good defensing and good shooting, and factors that would increase the capital such as enabling the club to sell more tickets and merchandise, bringing in advertisement and sponsorship revenues and increasing recognition along with other factors which are not related to football (Horasan & Keleş, 2017; Ataçocuğu & Zelyurt, 2016; Battre, Deutscher, & Frick, 2008). Position of footballers (goalkeeper, striker, defense etc.) is another factor that affects their wages. According to Frick (2007), although the goalkeepers are the most specialized players, they are underpaid as they play only in one position. Although the midfield players are the least specialized ones, they are paid more as they can play both in defense and offense. In recent years, capital has become another factor that affects the transfer of footballers. For example, the footballers transferred from far east can be a factor that increase the sale of the team's merchandise in that region, and this plays an important role in preference of players (Bryson, Rossi, & Simmons, 2014).

Footballers are employees and the financiers they face are the executives of the clubs. In other words, footballers and executives reflect the employee-employer relationship in football. Footballers intend to make maximum profit through transfers and contracts and club management intends to earn maximum profit to capitalize (Ataçocuğu & Zelyurt, 2016). The "equal pay for equal work" mentality does not work for football and all wages are negotiable. "Hourly fee" or "piece rate" seen in other industries is applied as "contract duration-fee" relationship in football. Contract duration is one of the determinants of transfer fee in the footballers' labor market. When a footballer signs a three-year contract, he may request a different amount for each year depending on his contract with the club. Footballers with high bargaining power can sign advantageous contracts. Clubs may also prefer to sign a long-term contract with promising players and gain both sportive and commercial advantages from the player. Transfer fees in Turkish labor market for footballers are the highest transfer fees in higher divisions in Europe even though there are big differences among the leagues. Although Turkish football clubs are in financial difficulties, transfer fees are rather high and Iyibozkurt (1999) explains this as follows: "Transfer fees in Turkey are paid out of the pocket of clubs' executives and the executives who make easy money transfer money to football clubs to gain reputation and benefit from tax reduction or tax exemption." In addition to transfer fees, clubs also pay premiums to footballers for matches they win as a motivation tool. Sometimes, footballers place a condition on their contracts to get paid by the number of goals they score in a season and goalkeepers place the same condition on to get paid if the number of goals they concede is less than a certain number (Ataçocuğu, 2012).

4 Performance-wage correlation in sports

Some studies conducted on the correlation between the total fees paid to the athletes and team performance reveal that the correlation between wage and performance in North American leagues is insignificant (Scully, 1995; Sanderson & Siegfried, 1997; Fort & Quirk, 1999), while some others reveal that it is actually significant (Forrest & Simmons 2002; Wiseman & Chatterjee, 2003; Szymanski, 2003). Fort (2003) reviewed the correlations between the total wages paid to the athletes by the teams in Major League Baseball (MLB) and winning percentage in the seasons between 1900 and 1999 in a study and found a significant correlation. Likewise, Wiseman and Chatterjee (2003) found that there is a strong positive correlation between a team's performance on the field and the average wages paid to the athletes. It is stated that there is a positive correlation between wages and performance in English and Italian leagues (Szymanski & Kuypers, 1999; Forrest & Simmons, 2002). Baruch, Wheeler, and Zhao (2004) found out in a study that the premiums paid to the athletes in China to increase their performance also increases their motivation. Fair Wage-Effort Hypothesis which addresses the wage-performance correlation from a different perspective is also a much-debated issue in literature

(Akerlof & Yellen, 1990). The dramatic wage inequality in a team may impair the harmony and performance of the team. Levine (1991) advocates the Pay Equity Hypothesis and states that pay inequality will lead to jealousy and distrust among the players of a team, and consequently, general team performance will decrease.

In a study conducted by Wang, Cheng, and Jane (2014) on the correlation of the distribution of wage payment and team performance in Korean Professional Baseball League, it is revealed that the performance increases the wage, but the wage does not increase the performance. No study in this respect is found in Turkey about the relationship between player's salary and team performance, yet. On the other hand, Ergül (2017) have searched the relationship between financial success of the sport companies with sportive victories of sport clubs in football are being tested. They found that, it has been occurred that the success of the Turkish sports clubs on the football have a positive effect on the financial statements of the related sports companies.

5 Salary cap in sports

The salary cap model, which was first introduced in the NBA in 1946, is about the limitations of payments to be made to players by a team. According to this system, wages of players cannot exceed the limit determined by the committee. The purposes of Salary Cap are preserving and maintaining the competitive environment and the balance of power among teams (preventing powerful teams to have star players and disturb the balance with other teams), maximize the competition and preventing the financially powerful teams from disturbing the competitive environment. As the teams made by rich clubs by collecting star players will decrease the pleasure of watching, this system entered into force in NBA in 1984 and NFL (National Football League) in 1994 for continuity of competition. It should be noted that the salary cap does not limit the wage of players, but limits the total wages to be paid to all players (Doğru, 2010).

The fact that the administrative and economic functioning of European leagues are different from those in USA alienates them from the salary cap system. The structure in Europe controls the distribution of talents, and the mobility between the leagues are high and this ensures the continuity of competition. However, with the thought that this balance has been disturbed, FIFA started the financial fair play application in 2010 and put it into practice in 2015 and brought the financial structure under control in the football leagues in Europe (Ülker, 2019). Due to the legal, administrative, and economic structure of the clubs in professional Turkish Football Leagues, it is difficult to determine the base pay. Because Turkish clubs are not financially transparent, and required and proper accounting transactions and financial statement analyses are not performed (Ataçocuğu, 2012).

6 Unionization in professional sports

The organizations established to protect and improve common economic and social rights and interests in labor relationships between employees and employers are called trade unions (Demircioğlu & Centel, 2003). Professional sports is a fact which really rises in the changing world and popularity of which is increasing every passing day. The most important contribution to its popularity is made by the athletes who create this value. As the athletes are the employees of their clubs, they are in a conflict of interest with their employers. The economic and social interests of athletes can be protected by themselves, as well as by professional organizations they can affiliate with. Professional sports sector is not composed of star athletes only and lower leagues include numerous athletes besides stars who may have economic problems (Aydın, 2009). In consequence of economic attraction of sports and its commercialization due to the impact of globalization, the number of persons who prefer this profession gradually increases and as a result, not only economic and legal problems but also social problems encountered in this profession are increasing in number. The athletes who have a large media coverage are in the limelight not only with their sportive successes or failures but also with their private lives. Sometimes various events occur because of both reasons. In this sense, the unions do not protect only the economic interest but also protect social rights and interests of the athletes who are socially in the limelight.

When the development of sports trade unions in the world is reviewed, it is seen that the oldest sports trade union was established in 1885 in the USA by the Brotherhood of Professional Baseball Players. Unionization efforts of American baseball players continued between the years of 1900 and 1946 and the "Major League Baseball Players Association (MLBPA)" was founded in 1946 and it is still active at the present time (Aydın, 2007, 2009). The Major League Baseball Players Association in the USA established the "Major League Baseball Players Pension Plan" in the end of the 1940s. This was the first formation that bestows the pension right to athletes. In the following years, the National Football League Players Association, National Hockey League Players Association, and National Basketball Players Association were founded in 1956, 1957, and 1964, respectively (Öner, 2011).

Unionization in professional sports has a long history also in Australia and it is quite widespread. The attempt to establish the first sports union in Australia was made by footballers in 1913. Later on, there have been attempts to establish unions in other sports branches. Australian Football League Players Association (estd. 1973), Rugby League Players Association (estd. 1979), National Basketball League Players Association (estd. 1989), Professional Footballers Australia (estd. 1993), Rugby Union Players' Association (estd. 1995), and Union and Australian Netball Players Association (estd. 2002) are active in Australia today (Aydın, 2007).

Unionization was seen in Europe, and particularly in England and France. Professional Footballers Association (PFA) was founded in England in 1907 and it is an exemplary union still continuing its operations. National Union of Professional Footballers (Union Nationale des Footballeurs Professionnels-UNFP) is an important union. Apart from the unions founded in these two European countries, German Football Association in Germany and Italian Footballers' Association in Italy are important and powerful unions. When we take a look at Africa in respect of unionization, South African footballers Union (SAFPU) (estd. 1997) has an important place in the sports industry in the country. Apart from all these unionization at a national level, the International Federation of Professional Footballers' Associations (Federation Internationale des Footballeurs Professionnels-FIFPro) was established in 1965 by national football unions of five countries and today it has more than 40 members (Aydın, 2007, 2009).

Sports unionization in Turkey is only related to football. Existence of professional football had an important effect on this. The first example of unionization in professional sports in Turkey was "Turkish Professional Footballers Union" founded in 1965. The union changed its name into "Turkish Professional Footballers, Coaches, Managers and Monitors Union" in 1969. The name of the union was changed into "Futbol-İş (Turkish footballers, Coaches and Masseurs Union)" in 1975 and the union decided to affiliate with the Confederation of Turkish Trade Unions (Türk-İş). But the union was terminated in 1984 on the ground of nonfeasance (Baştürk, 2007; Aydın et al., 2017; Aydın, 2009).

It is seen that Futbol-İş Union was not sufficiently active because the clubs were not companies, and consequently, not employers at the time and they were regarded as associations and thus, industrial relationships were not organized in football. Another reason is stated as the lack of interest in unionization in sports and negative attitude towards the athletes who were active in this respect. The first step taken for athletes' union since 1984 was the establishment of the Sports Workers' Union (Spor-Sen). Then in 2010, "Turkish Progressive Sports Workers' Union (Spor Emek-San)" was established in the hospitality and entertainment sector (Aydın, 2007).

7 Naturalized athletes' policy

Nowadays, the countries focus on the potential international prestige brought by representation of successful athletes and naturalized athletes have become quite popular in international sports organizations (Bruce & Wheaton, 2011). Consequently, the concept of "olympic citizenship" received broad acceptance. More and more countries prefer "naturalized athletes" every passing day to use sports as a political tool and be successful in sports organizations. For example, France has naturalized 41 athletes, United States of America 25 athletes, Spain 21 athletes, Canada 11 athletes, Qatar 7 athletes, and Bahrain 4 athletes between 1998–2011 (Bulmuş, 2018).

Naturalized athletes policy has become an integral part of national sports policy and sports administration in Turkey to be successful in sports quickly. When we look at the athletes who participated in international sports organizations in the period after 2010, it is seen that Turkey has been gradually represented by more "foreign athletes" along with the countries in continental Europe. Turkey joined the 2016 Rio Olympics with 103 athletes and 29 (28%) of them were naturalized athletes (Bulmuş, 2018; Altunsöz & Koçak, 2017; İmamoğlu, 2016). Nine naturalized athletes won medals for Turkey in 2016 European Athletics Championship and it was criticized in international media. It was emphasized in the news that naturalized athletes were used for pragmatic purposes such as gaining international prestige and visibility and this implementation went beyond its purpose. As Turkey awards high prizes to athletes who come out in Olympic Games and Paralympics and World and European Championships, it has become a country preferred by the athletes (Bulmuş, 2018; Şahin & Dal, 2019).

8 Sport migration

As of 1970, athlete migration underwent a structural alteration due to the increase of supply and demand in sports, establishment of athletes' unions, national and international competition in sports, increase in the economic return of the Olympics, increase in sports investments, Bosman ruling, involvement of the managers, who play an important role in signature of contracts between athletes and clubs in sports, and the fact that professional sports has become a larger-scale industry. Even if the most important factor affecting the motivation to migrate is economic earnings, it is not the only factor that affects the decision of the athletes. Cultural and historic traditions as well as institutional and structural factors play an essential role in forming the migration typologies (Bulmuş, 2018; Çalışkan & Çelik, 2018; Durdubaş & Koruç, 2017).

Magee and Sugden (2002) classifies migrating athletes into five categories: mercenaries, settlers, ambitionists, nomadic cosmopolitan, and exiled athletes forced to migrate from the country for a number of political reasons. The *athletes in mercenary's category* mostly consider sports as an economic gain and migrate to earn money. The *athletes in settler's category* continue their professional careers for long years in the country they migrated to, settle in those countries and their perception of home changes. The *athletes in ambitionists category* migrate to countries where competition and quality are higher in order to improve their talents and careers. The *athletes in nomadic cosmopolitan category* migrate to experience the life in cosmopolitan cities and different cultures in relatively later periods of their careers. Exiled athletes leave their countries for a number of political reasons and may be forced to continue their careers in other countries. For example, Slaven Bilic and Sasa Ilic left Yugoslavia by giving the war in their country as a reason and continued their careers in other countries (Magee & Sugden, 2002).

Turkey has been a country containing the fact of migration within itself for many years. In the context of the external migration movement started in 1960s and continued in 1970s, a significant migration wave occurred from Turkey to countries in Western Europe, Germany being in the first place. Irregular and transit immigrants and refugees who came to our country from Asian countries to go to European Union were mainly from Afghanistan, Bangladesh, Iraq, Iran, and Pakistan. The largest number of immigrants who came to Turkey in recent years was from Syria due to the civil war in their country (Kirişçi, 2003; Arslan, & Yıldız, 2019).

In addition to current developments in migration movements, Turkey's success in sports and the investments made led to emigration of athlete laborers and Turkey has become an attractive country for many foreign athletes to continue their career with better standards. Unlike the naturalized athletes, the athletes who prefer to live in Turkey migrate to Turkey for various reasons without acquiring Turkish citizenship. These reasons are as follows (Bulmuş, 2018):

1 They select Turkey as a destination country or a country of transit where the sportive competition is increased and where they want to improve their talents and careers.
2 Turkey is considered as a "tax heaven" especially in football industry (income tax in football is 15%).
3 Political-economic crises in the countries of athletes.
4 Religion and cultural traditions.

Some athletes (footballers) who prefer Turkey as a destination country or country of transit compete on behalf of one or more than one teams till the end of their career, but some athletes give outstanding performance and attract attention of big European teams and transfer to those teams with higher transfer fees and yearly wages. Another reason for emigration to Turkey is the lower income tax ratio. Income tax rate is 20% in Turkey for footballers and this is the second lowest rate in Europe. According to Income Tax Law in effect, income tax is applied to athletes playing in the upper leagues as 20%. The highest income tax rate (56.9%) applied to the athletes in Europe is in Sweden. Sweden is followed by Portugal (56.5%), Spain (52%), France (50.3%), Austria (50%), Italy (47.9%), Germany (47.5%), and England (45%) (Bulmuş, 2018; Mahir, 2013).

9 Effect of exercise and physical activity on labor market

Humans are the most important production factor in businesses that produce economic goods and services and the most valuable asset of all businesses. Basic objectives of businesses are producing goods and services of higher quality than other businesses in the market, being the industry leader in terms of technology, constantly increasing sales volume and profitability, prevent waste by reducing expenses, increasing motivation of employees and strengthening reputation of the business. Achievement of these objectives is possible by making the labor force productive. Organizational objectives can be achieved with efforts of humans and the degree of productivity and efficiency of an organization depend on the productivity of employees (Yumuşak, 2008). Increasing the productivity of labor force is very important as it also increases the productivity in the economy and welfare. Individuals who are engaged in sports and exercise become healthier, and furthermore, they work in a disciplined manner, successfully manage the stress and more prone to team work. These factors increase the productivity of employees and also affects individual success in labor market. For this reason, it will be to the point for companies to develop policies that would direct the employees towards active life style (Lechner, 2015).

Positive effect of physically active life and regular exercise on health is revealed in the literature in detail (Bouchard, Blair, & Haskell, 2007; Gilmour, 2007; Özer, 2001). These studies illustrated that the regular physical activity takes under control the blood pressure and blood sugar, reduces the colon cancer and coronary heart disease risks, provides weight control, prevents vein and muscle-skeleton system diseases. Besides these physiological effects, the regularly performed physical activity also affects the mental and emotional heath positively (Cindaş, 2001; Özer, 2001). Research indicated that the regular physical activity positively effects the mental health, reduces stress and anxiety symptoms, helps controlling the emotions like rage and aggression, increases the quality of sleep (Kennedy & Newton, 1997). It is said that the physical activity increases self-understanding and self-respect (Gleser & Mendelberg, 1990) as it balances the health, physical structure, elasticity, and weight of the individual and the increasing endorphin leads to a positive emotional status (Daley, 2002).

There are numerous studies revealing that exercise increases cognitive performance as well as the physical, social, and psychological benefits it provides (Cotman & Engesser-Cesar, 2002; Swain et al., 2003). Many studies reveal that regular exercise increases oxygen consumption, blood build up in brain, and the number of brain cells. It also improves the attention, perception, learning, and problem-solving skills and positively affects creativity with various neurotransmitter substances (Kramer et al., 1999, Voss, Vivar, Kramer, & Van Praag, 2013; Cotman, Berchtold, & Christie, 2007; Cabral, Rice, Morris, Rundek, Pascual-Leone, & Gomes-Osman, 2019). As these positive effects of exercise on cognitive development also affect performance in work environment positively, it is an issue that should be addressed with importance in labor market (Baumann & Boutellier, 2012; Pronk & Kottke, 2009).

Exercise is prescribed as a medicine by healthcare authorities at the present time (Lobelo, Stoutenberg, & Hutber, 2014). In the latest physical activity guideline published by Physical Activity Guidelines for Americans the "moving more and sitting less" principle is emphasized (Piercy et al., 2018). There are studies in the literature stating that sitting for a long time is more or equally as harmful as smoking (Baddeley, Sornalingam, & Cooper, 2016; Mensing & Mekel, 2015).

Even though the positive effect of physical activity on health is addressed many times, studies on the productivity of physically active people in work environment is rather scarce. Physical activity and exercise may take additional time in the day but it develops various skills. Active individuals look physically healthier and attractive and their soft skills (team work, stress management, psychological durability, self-discipline) are developed more and they have higher creativity (Lechner & Sari, 2015; Lechner, 2015). Positive effect of physical activity on all these properties increase the earnings of companies and individuals. A study conducted by using the German Socio-Economic Panel (GSOEP) revealed that the females whose physical activity level is high and who have at least three years of work experience have a higher rate of finding a job. The studies also reveal that physically active females can better cope with the psychological barriers when looking for a job (Cabane, 2014). In a study conducted with males between the ages of 26 and 45, a negative correlation is found between unemployment and level of participating in sports and a positive correlation is found between employment and participation in sports. No difference is found in this study in unemployment or employment rates by types of sport (Lechner & Downward, 2013).

The studies in physical activity and labor market literature have addressed another subject related to physical activity and earnings and examined the participation of adults in sports and exercise on their current earnings. The results of the data obtained from GSOEP show that the males exercising at least once a week generate 5% more income than sedentary males (Cornelissen & Pfeifer, 2008). Another study revealed that the females who work out from 15 years of age generate approximately 6% more income than the females who don't work out (Lechner, 2009). The study revealed that the males who work out more between the ages of 26 and 45 earn 4.300£ to 6.500£ more and the females who work out more in the same age group earn 3.400£ to 5.300£. The said study revealed that the annual income changes with respect to the type of sport. An increase is observed in annual earnings of males working out outdoors and in fitness centers, of females between the ages of 26 and 45 who do racket sports and those between the ages of 46 and 64 who work out outdoors (Lechner & Downward, 2013). In a study conducted in Canada on the effect of the severity of physical activity on annual income, it is revealed that there is no significant increase in the income of those who were inactive but switch to being moderately active but annual income of those who switch to be highly active from being moderately active showed an increase by 10–20% within 8–12 years (Lechner & Sari, 2015).

Conclusion

Sports industry has reached a very different dimension within the globalizing world. It appeals to the service sector in terms of its health protection and improvement aspects while it appeals to the production sector in terms of its entertainment and show business aspects. It is also closely related to politics in terms of the recognition and reputation of the countries. This sectoral diversity that exists in the nature of sports has led to the diversification of workforce in sports. Athletes, coaches, referees, administrators, and such staff that serve in the sports services sector with an amateur spirit have started to take part in the business life with a professional approach in big sports organizations, which have become products. Particularly, perception of sports activities as a profession has brought about the need for identification of the positions of those working in the field of sports in terms of business and social security law, which has led to the trade union movement. While the share of sports, particularly football, which is an industry that continuously grows within itself, is growing every day, there is a requirement for programming, regulation, inspection, and of course organization in this sector. Sports is observed to have been organized within the order of trade unions in foreign countries; however, this awareness does not yet exist in Turkey. Such factors as athlete migration and athletes switching nationalities are among the factors that affect employment in sports. Athletes could leave their countries and emigrate to another country for their athletic careers or financial profit. They can continue their careers in the country they immigrated to and could get the opportunity to represent these countries as athletes switching nationalities in their national teams based on their performances in time. The level of sports migration is important as it would affect such factors as the playing period of the athletes trained in the infrastructure teams in the leagues of the country as well as their athletic improvement. In this respect, keeping the sports migration under control by countries would positively affect the athletic development and labor market of that country. Another topic handled within the context of labor market is the salary system. Similar to the business world, such factors as performance, position and league are the factors determining the price in sports. The studies conducted in general have shown that there is a positive relationship between the salary and performance. Salary balance within the sports clubs is a factor that should be kept under control as it affects the unity and solidarity within the team and the attractiveness of the league. Therefore, those who manage various sports leagues that operate at the professional level have been developing strategies to keep the salary balance under control.

One of the factors affecting the labor market in sports is the effects of exercise and physical activity on employees. Experimental studies investigating the relationship between the labor market and sports and exercise reveal strong positive relationships. Findings obtained from the studies show that sports and exercise have positive effects on cognitive and non-cognitive skills, physical appearance, and health. In addition, findings indicating that the physically active individuals had better employment opportunities, they earned better salaries and they had higher productivity levels at work constitute another finding related to the positive effect of physical activity and exercise on labor. Therefore, taking measures to support active lives of their employees would be beneficial for the institutions and organizations.

References

Akerlof, G. A., & Yellen, J. L. (1990). The Fair Wage-Effort Hypothesis and Unemployment. *The Quarterly Journal of Economics*, 105(2), 255–283.

Akşar, T. (2005). *Endüstriyel Futbol* (1. Baskı). Literatür Yayınları.

Altunsöz, I. H., & Koçak, S. (2017). Transfer of Allegiance in the Olympic Games. *Spor Bilimleri Dergisi*, 28(3), 115–127.

Andreff, W. (2008). Globalization of the Sports Economy. *Rivista di diritto ed economia dello sport*, 4(3), 13–32.

Arslan, N., & Yıldız, K. (2019). International Migration and Socio-Economic Aid in Turkey: Beliefs and Realities. *Uluslararası Yönetim İktisat ve İşletme Dergisi*, 15(1), 241–258.

Ataçocuğu, M. Ş. (2012). Analysing Football Sector in Terms of Labour Economics, Marmara University, Health Science Institute, Department of Sport Management, Master Thesis, Supervisor: Assist. Prof. Serap Mungan Ay, İstanbul, Turkey.

Ataçocuğu, M. Ş., & Zelyurt, M. K. (2016). Labour-Capital Relations in Professional Football: A Qualitative Research on the Phenomenon of Wage, Social Security and Labour Union in Lower Leagues. *Sportif Bakış: Spor ve Eğitim Bilimleri Dergisi*, 3(2), 99–115.

Aydın, S. (2009). Turkey's Economic Security in the Globalization Process. *Journal of Academic Studies*, 11(42).

Aydın, U. (2007). *Unionization in Professional Sports*, TÜRK-İŞ Yayını, Ankara.

Aydın, U., Canbey Özgüler, V., Kocabaş, F., Yalız Solmaz, D., Katırcı, H., Demirkaya, S., . . . Etci, H. (2017). Working Conditions and Organisational Tendencies of Professional Sportsmen in Turkey: The Case of Footballers and Football Teams. *Çalışma ve Toplum*, 55(4).

Baddeley, B., Sornalingam, S., & Cooper, M. (2016). Sitting Is the New Smoking: Where Do We Stand? *British Journal of General Practice*, 66(646), 258–258.

Bairner, A., & Molnar, G. (2010). *The Politics of the Olympics: A Survey*. Abingdon, UK: Routledge.

Baruch, Y., Wheeler, K., & Zhao, X. (2004). Performance-related Pay in Chinese Professional Sports. *The International Journal of Human Resource Management*, 15(1), 245–259.

Baştürk, F. (2007). *İş Hukukunda Profesyonel Futbolcu*. Beta Basım Yayım, İstanbul.

Battre, M., Deutscher, C., & Frick, B. (2008). Salary Determination in the German "Bundesliga": A Panel Study. No:811 IASE Conference Papers. *International Association of Sports Economists*, Monterrey, México.

Baumann, C. E., & Boutellier, R. (2012). Physical Activity: The Basis of Learning and Creativity. *The Future of Education, Conference Paper* (pp. 1–6), Florence, Italy.

Boniface, P. (2007). *Futbol ve Küreselleşme*, Çev., İsmail Yerguz, NTV Yayınları, 1. Baskı, İstanbul.

Bouchard, C., Blair, S. N., & Haskell, W. L. (2007). *Physical Activity and Health*. Champaign, IL: Human Kinetics.

Bruce, T., & Wheaton, B. (2011). *Diaspora and Global Sports Migration: A Case Study in the English and New Zealand Contexts: Sport and Migration: Borders, Boundaries and Crossings* (pp. 189–199). London and New York: Routledge.

Bryson, A., Rossi, G., & Simmons, R. (2014). The Migrant Wage Premium in Professional Football: A Superstar Effect? *Kyklos*, 67(1), 12–28.

Bulmuş, M. S. (2018). *Global Sport Economy and International Athletic Labor Migration: Case of Naturalized Athletes in Turkey*, Hacettepe University, Social Sciences Institute, Department of Political Science and Public Administration, Master's thesis, Supervisor: Prof. Dr. Berrin Koyuncu Lorasdağı, Ankara, Turkey.

Cabane, C. (2014). Unemployment Duration and Sport Participation. *International Journal of Sport Finance*, 9(3), 261–280.

Cabral, D. F., Rice, J., Morris, T. P., Rundek, T., Pascual-Leone, A., & Gomes-Osman, J. (2019). Exercise for Brain Health: An Investigation Into the Underlying Mechanisms Guided by Dose. *Neurotherapeutics*, 1–20.

Çakmak, M. N., İşlek, M. S., & Keskin, U. (2017). An Evaluation of Turkish Football Culture in Terms of Globalization Concepts and Processes. *KMÜ Sosyal ve Ekonomik Araştırmalar Dergisi*, 19(33), 125–133.

Çalışkan, K., & Çelik, V. O. (2018). An Evaluation of Sports Labour Migration as an Outsourcing Activity, *International Congress of Recreation and Sport Management*, 10–13 Mayıs, Bodrum, Turkey.

Çınarlı, S., & Ersöz, G. (2007). The Rights and Liabilities of Professional Football Clubs and Football Players, *Performans Dergisi*, 13.

Cindaş A. (2001). General Principles of Exercise Practice in the Elderly. *Geriatri*, 4(2), 77–84.

Çırka, S. (2017). A General Evaluation of Sport in Globalization Process. *Anadolu Bil Meslek Yüksekokulu Dergisi*, (45), 127–146.

Cornelissen, T., & Pfeifer, C. (2008). Sport und Arbeitseinkommen – Individuelle Ertragsraten von Sportaktivitäten in Deutschland. *Jahrb. Wirtschaftswissenschaften* (Rev. Econ.), 59(3), 244–255.

Cotman, C. W., Berchtold, N. C., & Christie, L. A. (2007). Exercise Builds Brain Health: Key Roles of Growth Factor Cascades and Inflammation. *Trends in Neurosciences*, 30(9), 464–472.

Cotman, C. W., & Engesser-Cesar, C. (2002). Exercise Enhances and Protects Brain Function. *Exercise and Sport Sciences Reviews*, 30(2), 75–79.
Daley, A. J. (2002). Exercise Therapy and Mental Health In Clinical Populations: Is Exercise Therapy a Worthwhile Intervention? *Advances In Psychiatric Treatment*, 8, 262–270.
Demircioğlu, A. M., & Centel, T. (2003). *İş Hukuku*. 9.baskı, Beta Basım Yayım, İstanbul.
Desbordes, M., & Richelieu, A. (Eds.). (2012). *Global Sport Marketing*. Abingdon, UK: Routledge.
Devecioğlu, S. (2005/2). Development of Sport Sector' s Strategies in Turkey. *Verimlilik Dergisi*, 2, 117–134.
Doğru, C. (2010). A Mathematical Approach for Establishing of Competitive Balance at the Footbal Industry: Salary Cap Model. *Uluslararası İktisadi ve İdari İncelemeler Dergisi*, (4).
Durdubaş, D., & Koruç, Z. (2017). Postkolonyalizm Bağlamında Türkiye'deki Sporcu Göçü. *Spor Bilimleri Dergisi*, 28(3), 155–166.
Ergül, N. (2017). The Investigation of the Relationship Between Financial Success of Sport Companies and Football Victories of Sport Clubs. *Hacettepe University Journal of Economics & Administrative Sciences*, 35(3), 43–71.
Forrest, D., & Simmons, R. (2002). Team Salaries and Playing Success in Sports: A Comparative Perspective. *Zeitschrift fu¨r Betriebswirtschaft*, 62, 221–237.
Fort, R. (2003). Thinking (Some More) About Competitive Balance. *Journal of Sports Economics*, 4(4), 280–283.
Fort, R., & Quirk, J. (1999). The College Football Industry. *Sports Economics: Current Research*, 11–25.
Frick, B. (2007). The Football Players' Labor Market: Empirical Evidence from the Major European Leagues. *Scottish Journal of Political Economy*, 54(3), 422–446.
Gilmour, H. (2007). Physically Active Canadians. *Health Reports*, 18, 45–66.
Gleser, J., & Mendelberg, H. (1990). Exercise and Sport in Mental Health: A Review of the Literature. *Israel Journal of Psychiatry and Related Sciences*, 27, 99–112.
Gündoğdu, C., & Devecioğlu, S. (2008). View of Sports Services within the Framework of General Economy. *Fırat Üniversitesi Doğu Araştırmaları Dergisi*, 6(2), 117–124.
Horasan, E., & Keleş, E. (2017). Is the Only Football That Makes Money? Relationship between Football Players' Publicity and Their Market Values: Cross-Sectional Analysis of Turkish Football Super League. *Marmara Üniversitesi İktisadi ve İdari Bilimler Dergisi*, 39(1), 157–169.
Imamoğlu, O. (2016). Evaluation of Turkey's Degree in Rio Olympic Games. *International Journal of Sport Culture and Science*, 4(3), 774–788.
İnal, R. (2008). *Küreselleşme ve Spor*. Istanbul, Turkiye: Evrensel Basim.
Iyem, C. (2013). Bullying in Football Experiences of Turkish Professional Footballers. *Mediterranean Journal of Social Sciences*, 4(4), 479.
İyibozkurt, E. (1999). *Küreselleşme ve Türkiye*. Ezgi Kitabevi Yayınları, Bursa.
Kennedy, M. M., & Newton, M. (1997). Effect of Exercise Intensity on Mood in Step Aerobics. *The Journal of Sports Medicine and Physical Fitness*, 37(3), 200–204.
Kirişçi, K. (2003). Turkey: A Transformation from Emigration to Immigration. *Migration Information Source*, 1.
Kramer, A. F., Hahn, S., Cohen, N. J., Banich, M. T., McAuley, E., Harrison, C. R., . . . Colcombe, A. (1999). Ageing, Fitness and Neurocognitive Function. *Nature*, 400(6743), 418–419.
Lechner, M. (2009). Sequential Causal Models for the Evaluation of Labor Market Programs. *Journal of Business & Economic Statistics*, 27, 71–83.

Lechner, M. (2015). Sports, Exercise, and Labor Market Outcomes. *IZA World of Labor*, 126, doi:10.15185/izawol.126.

Lechner, M., & Downward, P. (2013). *Heterogeneous Sports Participation and Labour Market Outcomes in England*. Discussion Paper No. 2013–25. Department of Economics, University of St. Gallen, Gallen, Switzerland.

Lechner, M., & Sari, N. (2015). Labor Market Effects of Sports and Exercise: Evidence from Canadian Panel Data. *Labour Economics*, 35, 1–15.

Leeds, M. A., Von Allmen, P., & Matheson, V. A. (2018). *The Economics of Sports*. Abingdon, UK: Routledge.

Levine, D. (1991). Cohesiveness, Productivity and Wage Dispersion. *Journal of Economic Behavior & Organization*, 15, 237–255.

Lobelo, F., Stoutenberg, M., & Hutber, A. (2014). The Exercise Is Medicine Global Health Initiative: A 2014 Update. *British Journal and Sports Medicine*, 48(22), 1627–1633.

Magee, J., & Sugden, J. (2002). "The World at Their Feet" Professional Football and International Labor Migration. *Journal of Sport and Social Issues*, 26(4), 421–437.

Mahir, Ş. A. U. L. (2013). Work Migration from Sub-Saharan Africa to Turkey. *Ankara Üniversitesi SBF Dergisi*, 68(1), 83–121.

Mensing, M., & Mekel, O. C. L. (2015). Sitting Is the New Smoking-Modelling Physical Activity Interventions in North Rhine-Westphalia: Monika Mensing. *The European Journal of Public Health*, 25, 143–171.

Murathan, F. (2019). Investigation of the Physical Education and Sport Teacher Candidates' Attitudes Towards Teaching Practice Course. *Asian Journal of Education and Training*, 5(1), 106–111.

Oflaz, İ. E. (2013). *The Football Industry and the Financial Analysis of the Publicly-Traded Football Clubs in Istanbul Stock Exchange*, Çağ University, Socıal Scıences Instıtute, Department of Busıness Management, Master Thesis, Supervisor: Assist. Prof. Ahmet Gökhan SÖKMEN, Mersin, Turkey.

Öner, S. (2011). *Social Security in Sports*, Seçuk University, Health Scıences Instıtute, Department of Business Management, Master Thesis, Supervisor: Assoc. Prof. Turgut Kaplan, Konya, Turkey.

Özer, K. (2001). *Fiziksel Uygunluk*, Nobel Yayın Dagıtım, Ankara.

Piercy, K. L., Troiano, R. P., & Ballard, R. M., et al. (2018). The Physical Activity Guidelines for Americans. *JAMA*, 320(19), 2020–2028. doi:10.1001/jama.2018.14854.

Pronk, N. P., & Kottke, T. E. (2009). Physical Activity Promotion as a Strategic Corporate Priority to Improve Worker Health and Business Performance. *Preventive Medicine*, 49(4), 316–321.

Sage, G. H. (2015). *Globalizing Sport: How Organizations, Corporations, Media, and Politics Are Changing Sport*. Abingdon, UK: Routledge.

Şahin, M. Y., & Tunçkol, H. M. (2010). Effects of Workers' Movement on Historical Development Process of Football. *Türkiye Sosyal Araştırmalar Dergisi*, 1, 219–236.

Şahin, S., & Dal, S. (2019). Investigation of Transfer of Naturalization of Athletes in the Olympic Games According to Sport Sciences Students. *European Journal of Physical Education and Sport Science*, 5(12), 201–214.

Sanderson, A. R., & Siegfried, J. J. (1997). The Implications of Athlete Freedom to Contract: Lessons from North America. *Economic Affairs*, 17(3), 7–12.

Scully, G. (1995). *The Market Structure of Sports*. Chicago: University of Chicago Press.

Sivrikaya, K., & Demir, A. (2019). An Evaluation of the Policies of Sports Economy Applied in Turkey During 2001–2018. *Süleyman Demirel Üniversitesi Vizyoner Dergisi*, 10(23), 126–136.

Swain, R. A., Harris, A. B., Wiener, E. C., Dutka, M. V., Morris, H. D., Theien, B. E., . . . Greenough, W. T. (2003). Prolonged Exercise Induces Angiogenesis and Increases Cerebral Blood Volume in Primary Motor Cortex of the Rat. *Neuroscience*, 117(4), 1037–1046.

Szymanski, S. (2003). The Economic Design of Sporting Contests. *Journal of Economic Literature*, 41(4), 1137–1187.

Szymanski, S., & Kuypers, T. (1999). *Winners and Losers: The Business Strategy of Football*. London: Viking.

Taks, M., & Schubert, M. (2016). The Sports Labor Market. *Global Sport Management: Contemporary Issues and Inquiries*, 1, 270.

Talimciler, A. (2002). *Futbolun "Meta"laşması*, Toplumbilim, Futbol Özel Sayısı, Ekim, Bağlam Yayınları, Sayı:16, İstanbul.

Talimciler, A. (2008). It Is Not Football, It Is Business: Industrial Football. *İletişim Kuram ve Araştırma Dergisi*, 26, 89–114.

Ülker, E. S. (2019). Football Clubs Financial Statement Analysis under Financial Fair Play: Bist Case: Social Sciences. *Management and Economics Journal*, 1(2), 51–63.

Voss, M. W., Vivar, C., Kramer, A. F., & van Praag, H. (2013). Bridging Animal and Human Models of Exercise-Induced Brain Plasticity. *Trends in Cognitive Sciences*, 17(10), 525–544.

Wang, J. S., Cheng, C. F., & Jane, W. J. (2014). Buying Success or Redistributing Payment: Bidirectional Causality in Korean Professional Baseball League. *Eurasian Business Review*, 4(2), 247–260.

Wiseman, F., & Chatterjee, S. (2003). Team Payroll and Team Performance in Major League Baseball: 1985–2002. *Economics Bulletin*, 1(2), 1–10.

Yumuşak, I. (2008). The Economic Importance of Human Capital and Turkey's Human Capital Potential. *Sosyal Siyaset Konferansları Dergisi*, (55).

13 How patriarchal power structures undermine women's empowerment and gender equality

The case of Nigeria

Özgür Tüfekçi and Mohammed Hashiru

1 Introduction

Though it is common knowledge, Nigeria is highly characterised by patriarchy from time immemorial (Aina, 1998). Despite deliberate attempts by governments and NGOs, patriarchy appears to dominate all spheres of the Nigerian economy and politics, thereby only entrenching patriarchy in the state. Generally, the highest populated African state continues to define the roles and responsibilities of men and women as manual and domestic, respectively.

The nature of patriarchy in traditional Nigerian society not only paves the way for men to dominate women but also impedes the activities of women in formal and informal decision making, which further weakens women's empowerment in the country. Evidently, women in the largest economy of Africa are not key players in political nor economic circles. It is a worrying phenomenon, especially now that women in leading economies have exhibited a significant level of ability in shaping political and economic discourses. A country which is a hub of African commerce continues to struggle to bring a significant number of women in the same round table with their male counterparts for decision making despite the constitutional provision of equal rights and privileges among male and female citizens. Patriarchy prevails amidst gross violations of women's rights through domestic violence, female genital mutilation, among others. Politically, women have been relegated to political offices at the lower level, with an insignificant number of them occupying those spots.

Unlike previously written papers and articles on the subject matter, analytical examination in this chapter will be in the context of feminist theory of discrimination and constructivist theory of identity. Employing an interdisciplinary approach of secondary data analysis and literature review, this chapter is divided into three subsections with objectives of examining gender equality in Nigeria, assessing women's empowerment attempts, progress and hindrances while juxtaposing them with the role of patriarchy in undermining them.

2 Theoretical framework

A theoretical appreciation of feminist theories with regards to discrimination against women will help to throw more light on the topic discussion. These theories take both economic and political shapes. In the realm of economics, feminists consider gender more than the study of women's status, which is at the heart of analysis. Radical and institutional analyses explain that discrimination theory of feminists accepts that labour markets structure and other social and economic institutions inspire individual economic actors. Postmodern and socialist feminists have pushed for the recognition of power culture and ideology gender composition in addition to the systematic elements and material oppression of women which is frequently integrated into patriarchy theories. Gender theory emphasises the process by which social and economic institutions are shaped by gender (Figart, 2005: 513). According to Bergmann (1987: 145), feminist economists have a self-imposed task to produce the design for a future which is more equitable. Figart (2005: 513) defines discrimination as not a dummy variable. He mentions that labour market discrimination is a multidimensional economic, political, social and cultural forces interaction in both the family and workplace which results in differential outcomes involving status, employment and pay. In general terms, gender discrimination refers to a situation of unfavourable attitude, behaviour and treatment apportioned to either males or females as motivated by tradition and culture of a group of people. It explains the pattern of behaviour which is apparent in the belief and opinion of people regarding what the political, social, cultural, economic and religious mode of relations between women and men (Onwutuebe, 2019: 2).

Among the universal theories of discrimination among women in public spheres is the one developed by Sanday. She explains that women's contribution to earning a living remains a major factor which determines their status. In performing its three functions – earning a leaving, protecting itself and reproducing – men exhausted their energy into earning a living and defending in the human community. This allowed them to have greater control over strategic resources. The overdependence of women on men to a larger extent resulted in male domination (Sanday, 1974: 190). In a nutshell, division of female and male activity is a major determinant of discrimination against women. This leads to the occupation of a lower position by women in both social life and in the labour market. Related to this universal theory is Sacks' developed feminist socialist theory, which proves that handicapping women did not emanate from a private property because it is not all men that have such. Instead, employment given to men allowed them to work more often than women for privileged classes. A vast difference between public life and household life limited the duties of women to the household, and as women got excluded from social production, automatically their status waned as compared to men (Sacks, 1974: 208). Another theory is the patriarchy-capitalism theory which tries to bring together capital system analysis of Marks and Engels and patriarchy feminist analysis. With the aim of presenting class and gender divisions as a goal owing to the charges of destroying the unity of working-class movement and diverting attention from the conflict of the main class, patriarchy-capitalism theory explains the handicap of women in the capitalist system via the inconveniencing of women with housekeeping and gender professional segregation. Women's production is therefore reduced by housework as lower salaries due to professional segregation increases the dependence of women on their husbands. This creates a vicious circle that makes it impossible for women to earn a higher salary and ultimately justifies such a division of household duties (Acker, 1988: 62).

A constructive framework, on the other hand, paves the way for a theoretical conceptualisation of the struggle of activism. The struggle of feminists situates power in social structures and pursues to fight this power. Against other universal theories of discrimination, this one emphasises that women are not necessarily powerless and can be made powerful through struggle. Prugl (1996: 16) maintains that constructivism views go with global governance. While realism emphasises on the international system structure and liberalism on actor agencies, constructivism involves both structure and agency. Under the impact of globalisation, sovereignty transformation has paved the way for women in the political space to turn into visible participants in the subjects of law and international relations (Sassen, 1998: 81). Sassen further argues that the critique of feminists' sovereignty must be developed because globalisation creates loopholes for nonstate actors and subjects to participate. Women and other nonstate actors can access more representation in international law and as well contribute to its making in the circumstance where the sovereign state is no longer seen as the special representative of its population in the international arena. For instance, the Optional Protocol to CEDAW which allows complaints to be made with the UN against countries that refuse to protect the human rights of women. The Protocol makes it possible for a group or individual women to submit their violation complaints on CEDAW to the committee (Kardam, 2004: 103).

3 Gender equality in Nigeria

Despite several strides made in the fight against gender inequality, in many regions in the world today men and women do not always enjoy equal opportunities and conditions in education, economic, legal, institutional fields, social and human development (Bulut and Yildirim, 2020). One of these regions in the world is sub-Saharan Africa. Although many states have made significant progress in economics and politics, disparities of income continue within and between states as poverty becomes generally more prevalent in sub-Saharan Africa than in other African regions. 2015 Global Monitoring Report according to the Education For All (EFA), not less than 41% of the sub-Saharan population is languishing in abject poverty on less than 1 USD per day. Besides poverty, inequalities can be seen more obviously in comparison to other developing regions (UNESCO). Nigeria, the largest economy in Africa with the largest population, is situated in this region.

In Nigeria, according to the World Poverty Clock, about 96 million of the total population, which is 48%, are living in extreme poverty, among which about 47 million are women (www.worldpoverty.io). Aisha Jummal Alhassan (former Minister for Women Affairs and Social Development of Nigeria) writes that Nigerian women specifically and African women at large have long been appealing for equality. Several efforts by the public have not been enough to alleviate the predominant difficulties they have faced throughout the years. They continue to be inadequately acknowledged for their inputs towards the country's national, social and economic development. The destitute status of rural women and the dominance of gender stereotypes limit access of women to power and decision-making, resources, opportunities and rights fulfilment. Though the Ministry of Women Affairs and Social Development is the government body responsible for bringing together strategies for addressing gender inequalities in Nigeria, in order to achieve gender transformation that will hasten sustainable development, it is crucial to address the fundamental dynamics that obstruct the progress towards equality (FAO and ECOWAS, 2018: VII). Suffyan Koroma, the FAO representative in Nigeria, adds that the Federal Republic of Nigeria has been trying towards further branching out of its economy amidst the prominence of oil in the country's economic wealth. Agriculture continues to contribute meaningfully to the economy of Nigeria, and its growth is important for general economic progress. The agricultural division still delivers employment to over 70% of the population. This contributes to not less than 30% of the state's GDP. With a population of almost 200 million, agricultural development and food security are crucial for both sustainable development and national development. There is no doubt about the key role women play in agriculture and food and nutrition security, from the farm to the kitchen where many of them end up. They make up an essential part of the agricultural labour force and their impact is critical to the success of the Economic Recovery and Growth Plan (ERGP) in Nigeria. Significant gender inequalities still exist in the sector of agri-food despite affirmative action. The split between the limited availability of sex-disaggregated data and policy and implementation to supervise progress towards gender equality have challenged the efforts towards the empowerment of women in the sector (FAO and ECOWAS, 2018: IX). This is a clear indication that the economic situation could improve when the gap between men and women is closed through women's empowerment especially in this period when one of the economic agendas of the nation is to concentrate on strengthening its non-oil economic sector.

A March 2019 article available on the Council for Foreign Relation's (CFR) website cites the new digital report of Women and Foreign Programs under the theme *Economies Through Gender Parity* that if women had significant participation in the economy equal to that of men, Nigeria's GDP could grow by $229 billion or 23% by the year 2025. In the same vain the article adds that the IMF equally projects that strengthening gender equality in Nigeria could change the economic narratives of the country and could result in higher productivity and more significant economic stability (Bro and McCaslin, 2019).

Politically, women and men in Nigeria have equal rights to participate in all political procedures and portfolios. Despite Nigerian women's active participation in the membership of political parties, women are mostly supporters for men to attain political spots. Party hierarchies are controlled by men and hence give them the advantage in influencing the internal politics of parties. Makama (2013: 116) writes that though women represent about half of the population of Nigeria, they barely occupy 10% of political positions. Meanwhile, chapter II of the 1999 Constitution addresses the Directive Principles and Fundamental Objectives of State Policy. Section 17(1) has it that the social order of the state is established on the principles of freedom, justice and equality. Section 17(2) also records that in the continuance of the social order: (a) before the law, every citizen shall have equal rights, obligations and opportunities; and (b) the sanctity of the human being shall be acknowledged, and human dignity shall be upheld and improved (Constitution of the Federal Republic of Nigeria, 1999). Section 17 implies that there should be no inequality of any kind. This means all citizens, regardless of their gender, must be treated equally. Clearly it connotes that male citizens should not dominate their female counterparts in any sector of the country.

The Gender Inequality Index (GEI) ratio of women's participation has a mean score of 17.8, with women in parliament having a mean score of 3.0, compared with men, giving the country a ranking of 30th in Africa. At just 5.9%, Nigerian women have one of the worst levels of representation in national legislatures, which comprises 469 members (Figure 13.1). Women at the ministerial level have a mean score of 34.9, while women judges have a mean score of 15.4 in GEI ratings. Women's household rights have a mean score of 58.8; women's legal rights have a mean score of 40.6 (GEI), out of 52 African country ratings (FAO and ECOWAS, 2018: 10)

Figure 13.2 captures the proportion of seats held by women from 2000 to 2019. In both figures, 2007 and 2009 were the peak of female parliamentary representation while the latest, i.e. 2019, is not something good to write home about for female political representation. This defeats the collective efforts being made to ensure a significant increase of female representation in Nigeria and calls for rather drastic measures that will expedite the processes of bringing more women to the

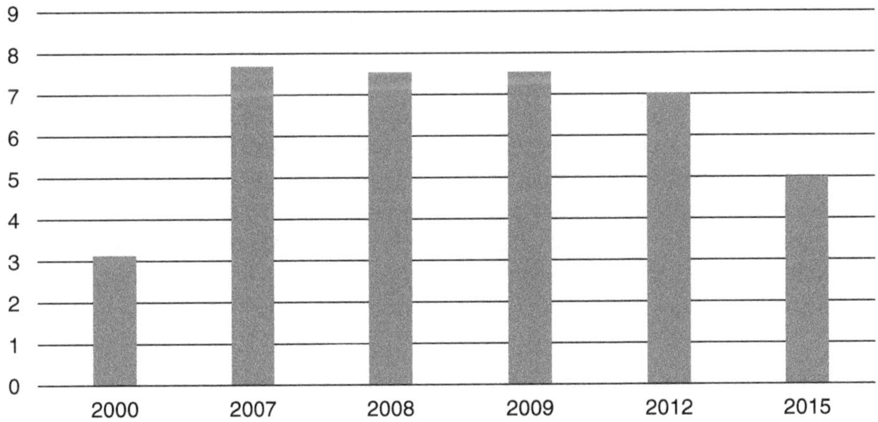

Figure 13.1 Trends in Seats by Women in Nigeria's National Parliament (%)
Source: FAO and ECOWAS (2018: 11)

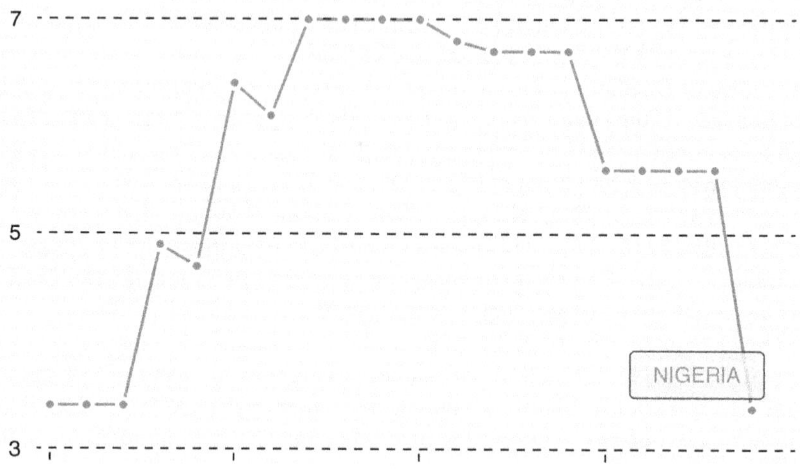

Figure 13.2 Proportion of Seats Held by Women in National Parliaments (%) – Nigeria
Source: World Bank, https://data.worldbank.org/indicator/SG.GEN.PARL.ZS?locations=NG

political arena. Nigeria is not isolated in this. Other sub-Saharan African states that have the same setback narrative are Ghana and Kenya, for instance. Ghana has a similar political and historical background of Nigeria. During the pre-colonial and colonial periods, Ghanaian women have contributed massively to the progress of the country (Adjepong, 2015: 26). However, there are a few women in parliament despite the fact that the Ghanaian Constitution just like that of Nigeria, recognises equal political rights.

Additionally, the country is a signatory to several international instruments that uphold the political rights of women. Out of the 200 parliamentary seats in 1995 women only occupied 16 of them and in the 2004 national election, 25 out of 230 seats (Sossou, 2011: 1). Similarly, Kenya shares a political history and cultural background with Nigeria. Despite their involvement in mobilisation for independence, women in Kenya did not have equal political participation after independence. The movement of women, however, adopted an agenda for 30–35% female representation in parliament and political appointments (Nzomo, 1997: 233–245). This resulted in their improved participation in politics. Although gender parity has yet to be achieved, the increased number of women in politics has brought about a fundamental change in the promotion of women's rights in Kenya.

4 Efforts to ensure women's empowerment in Nigeria

The situation in other African countries like South Africa, Senegal, Namibia and Rwanda is different; there many women have been elected to parliament. While in South Africa, women make up around 42% of members of parliament, 62 women were elected into the Nigerian parliament in the recent elections, representing less than 5% of elected officials, which connotes a decline from the 2015–19 periods where about 6% of elected officials were women.

Statistically, the 2019 election witnessed 235 women, which formed 12.34% of total candidates, contesting for a seat in the Senate out of which seven (6.42%) were elected. The ruling All Progressives Congress (APC) and the main opposition, the People's Democratic Party (PDP) which are the two main political parties, contested with seven and ten candidates respectively. Five hundred and thirty-three women contested for the House of Representatives, with APC and PDP fielding a total of 31 candidates. Only 11, however, have been elected, representing 3.05%. This is a severe setback, because previously 22 female lawmakers made it to the house. This means almost half have lost their seats. At the national stage, no woman governor was elected. Women formed 3.07% of the total candidates. Four women in Enugu, Kaduna, Ogun and Rivers states were elected out of the 275 women, making 11.40% of candidates for the deputy governorship. Despite that, the number of female deputy governors recorded a drop from six in 2015–19 to four (CDD, 2019). One of the first steps adopted by the Nigerian state to ensure women's empowerment is to ensure their protection. The most robust protection is to have states law's protection. It is against this background that besides the constitution, other national legislation has provisions that protect the rights of women in Nigeria. The Criminal Code and Penal Code, the Marriage Act, the Violence against Women Prohibition Act and Trafficking in Persons (Prohibition) Law Enforcement and Administration Act, 2003, among others, also add to the laws that ensure women's protection (Eniola, 2018: 5).

To further entrench these laws, individual states, based on their resolve to empower women through protection, have made criminal female genital mutilation, and prescribed penalties for violators of the law; amongst them are Female Circumcision and Genital Mutilation Prohibition Law (Edo State in 1999); Girl Child Marriages and Female Circumcision (Prohibition Law) (Cross River State in 2000); Abolition of Female Circumcision Law (Rivers State in 2001); Female Circumcision and Genital Mutilation (Prohibition) Law (Ogun State in 2000); and Gender-Based Violence (Prohibition) Law (Ekiti State in 2001). Other laws, such as Protection of Widows and Widowers Fundamental Rights Law (Enugu State in 2001), Widow's Empowerment Law (Oyo State in 2002) and Malpractices against Widows and Widowers Prohibition Laws (Anambra State 2004) among others, have been adopted to ensure the protection of the fundamental rights of widows. To curb the negative impacts of cultural practices on the realisation of women's rights, some states also have laws like the Prohibition of Early Marriage Law in Kebbi State, Retention in School and against the withdrawal of Girls from School Law in Kano State; and Violence against Women Law in Lagos State among others. Checks on Imo, Anambra, Ekiti, Plateau and Kogi states reveal that they are ahead of the federal government in enacting Gender and Equal Opportunities Law. One of the objectives is to provide equal opportunities for all, irrespective of gender, and to prohibit gender-based discrimination (Eniola, 2018). It is essential to state that places where these laws have been passed become serene environments for ensuring equal rights in all spheres, including the political one among men and women.

Besides the provisions in the constitution that support and advocate for political participation of women, Nigeria is a signatory to a number of international instruments that cater to gender inequality. Article 7 of the Convention on the Elimination of all Forms of Discrimination Against Women (CEDAW) mentions that state parties shall take all appropriate actions to eradicate discrimination against women in the sphere of politics and public life of the state and shall particularly guarantee to women equal rights with men. One entity pushing the agenda of gender equality through women's empowerment is the UN Women in Nigeria. They work on policies and programs together with a variety of allies to concentrate on four key result areas that have the prospect of transforming the gender equality landscape of the country. These include expansion of the voice of women, leadership and involvement, economic empowerment of women, prevention of violence against women and girls and the expansion of access to service, increasing leadership in the peace of women, and the response of security and humanitarian. This body supports the amendment of laws of discrimination, policy regulation, systems and practices at national and local levels and the expansion and execution of a gender policy within Nigeria's security forces in order to boost the protection of women and girls against sexual and gender-related violence. It also takes part in a DGD-financed governance program designed to cement and increase participation of women in democratic governance through enhancing their political and public awareness as well as political responsibility on gender equality and human rights of women (africa.unwomen.org).

Additionally, besides the international and regional treaties that promote political representation of women, some international conventions support gender equality in political participation. The Beijing Declaration and Platform for Action (BDPA) addressed numerous aspects of women's lives related to the achievement of their human rights. The BDPA has it that states should take measures to safeguard equal access of women to and total involvement in power structures and making of the decision and must increase the capacity of women to make them participate in decision making and leadership. Nigeria also has some policy frameworks in place to ensure gender parity in political participation.

Nigerian women still suffer many kinds of discrimination in both the private and public spheres in spite of these robust legal frameworks. Some reasons are accounting for this continuous discrimination against women; one of them is the patriarchal power structure.

5 The patriarchal power structure in Nigeria

Generally, a social system in which the role of a male as the principal authority is central is called a patriarchy. In this system, men have power over women, children and other possessions. Patriarchy, as a male rule and privilege institution, depends on female subordination. Traditionally patriarchy reveals itself in political, legal, social and economic institutions of different cultures. In a nutshell, it explains male supremacy in which the power is in the hands of men at the vulnerability of women. Nipokoski (2020) relates "power" to privilege. Therefore, a system that empowers men more than women only ensures men wield some privileges women are not entitled to. As cited and argued in our previous work (Hashiru and Tufekci, 2019), when President Buhari publicly pronounced that his wife belongs to his kitchen and his living room and the other room (BBC, 2016) because she publicly criticised his government, a lot could be understood about the patriarchal structures and background that informed such pronouncement of a president who could have lauded his wife's actions not only to promote women's empowerment but to pave the way for the democratic consolidation of the state in the long run.

Nigeria personifies a typical patriarchal African society where a system of social stratification and gender discrepancy equips men to control and dominate women in all circles of life. The hegemony of patriarchy as Connell (2005: 830) referred to in his own words "hegemonic masculinity" has a massive influence on social hierarchy and the activities of women, especially in the south of the globe. Patriarchy Power Structure (PPS) in this study means structures which make patriarchy conducive or helps male counterparts wield more power in every aspect of human life in a given society. Our research done from a pool of available literature on the subject matter informed our categorisation of the PPS into three main parts. These include religion, tradition and culture and the political atmosphere. We do not seek to blame these institutions for being the sole agents of discrimination against women as the situation is not same everywhere, rather, we maintain that patriarchy continues to use them to perpetrate more discrimination against women. The PPS established by the patriarchy uses these same institutions as references for fighting actions, programs, modules and outreach works designed to empower women.

5.1 Religion

According to Johnson (2014: 17) people take part daily in institutions, such as education, politics, science, art and the economy, which are founded on the roots of patriarchy. This also involves faith-based establishments that are responsible for how women are perceived and valued. It further touches all scopes of human lives, such as communities, families and legal structures. It is applicable to the church as well. The nature of the church structures is filled mostly by men, who tolerated, gave support to and supervised the suppression of women (Wood, 2019). This caused the denial of their full potential in the spheres of the church, economy, politics and society. Although Johnson and Wood did not mention other religions, the same can be said about other religious structures in Africa. Essien and Ukpong (2012: 289), in their case study of the Akwa Ibom State of Nigeria, find that both Anglican and Lutheran churches in the country continue to clutch strictly to the patriarchal structure of denying privileges to women of the ministerial priesthood, thus boosting the patriarchal structure. They take a clue and follow the leads of the powerful clergies' interpretation of the biblical texts like that of John Paul II who stressed that Jesus' liberally picking and establishing the apostles as priests meant that Jesus' marginalised women from the Twelve demonstrated their unsuitability for the priesthood. In order words, men are the sole custodians of leadership positions in the Church. Although the aforementioned Orthodox Churches promote patriarchal structures, Organization of African Instituted Churches (OAIC) refrain from barricading women from administrative positions. In general, patriarchy is not tolerated in these denominations.

Similarly, the Evangelical Fellowship of West Africa (ECWA) provides equal opportunity for male and female congregants. They observed that the practices of Christian churches are not identical. However, the practice of patriarchy and gender inequality is similar to a demon in churches with historical solidity and advanced theology and ecclesiastical discipline. Meanwhile, they maintain that there is an impressive attempt to recognise in ecclesiastical life and ministry the fundamental and ontological equality of every human person in the communities and movements of recent history, but this has not transformed into a formation of a new culture of equality in Nigeria owing to entrenched religious prejudice against women.

Christian Aid (2015) quantitative research reveals that women lament that church activities were time-consuming, and do not leave them with adequate time to attend to domestic issues. Additionally, young Christian men in Enugu of Nigeria are not ready for preaching based on gender equality, a reason why religious leaders preach gender equality with caution using scripture and emphasising obedience of women even in gender equality discourses. For instance, a male pastor in Lagos mentioned that gender equality could not be preached in rural churches because it would connote trying to make men become weak and not in control. Views from the church compounds with the traditional views that gender equality would be a problem that could result in separation of couples. Apparently, many churchgoers who are against equity in the community had their patriarchal orientation from the society because they were unable to provide scriptural support for their claims.

In the realm of Islam, the arrival of Islam had a double influence on the status of women in Nigeria (Bawa, 2017: 153). Firstly, Islam fortified the already existing patriarchal nature of the society by cementing supremacy of men and emphasising submission of women. Secondly, Islam invigorated and paved more of a way for education and literacy for women. Many groups have used various sets of strategies to halt this patriarchal and misinterpretation of Islam to justify the subordination of women. The movement of Muslim women is an ordinary outcome of the situation they have been forced to deal with. Feminists have always pointed at this much-debated statement of the Quran, which is often translated as "Men are maintainers and protectors of women" (2: 228) as central in discussions about patriarchy and Islam. The mistake of patriarchy is its imposition of sexism, and whereas aggressive sexism may infer that women are incompetent of maintaining themselves and consequently need a male guardian for their protection, generous sexism frequently advocates that women are given a high position and therefore must be valued and attended to by men (Davary, 2013). It is in connection with these second explanations of the verse that women are thought of like the honour of the man. From the very beginnings of its spread to various parts of the world,

Islam gave in to cultural adaptations and concurrent development with a multiplicity of cultures. There are however states that use Islam to justify and institutionalise patriarchy, particularly when the ancient customs of the land approve of it. Despite that, they have not been able to mute the voices of women who contest patriarchal subjugation in both the family unit and state. Formulation of the Sharia in a context of patriarchy has given it a patriarchal colour; Islam is, however, a message of unity and justice that promotes neither gender duality nor justifies its hierarchy (Davary, 2013).

5.2 Tradition and culture

The Nigerian society, both recent and premodern has been stained significantly with odd cultural practices that are effectively hostile to women's emancipation of women (Nmadu, 2000: 166). These include early and forced marriages, inheriting of a deceased person's wife and precarious widowhood practices. Bhavani and colleagues (2003) opine that in order to rescue women from poverty and empower them such uneven social and gender relations need to be changed. Gender stereotyping is established within the family unit, as long as self-identify of daughters as females are with their mother and sisters, and sons as males are with their father and brothers (Haraway, 1991). The dominant religious narratives in both colonial and colonial aftermath Nigerian society certainly privileges men at the disadvantage of women, even in accessibility of education, as discussed earlier. Nigerian society remains entangled in the analogy of history (Mamdani, 1996). The socio-cultural dependency of women is one of the critical harmful factors to their political participation in the public political sphere. Women also find it difficult to participate in politics because of the limited time available to them owing to their dual roles in the productive and reproductive spheres. With their primary roles as mothers and wives and competing for domestic responsibilities and care work, they are left with little time to participate in politics. This means that cultural factors have a ripple effect on their political participation in the sense that domestic responsibilities become a barrier for women's political participation. Women in Nigeria are confronted with cultural constraints on their mobility. The instruments of sex discrimination and purdah are used to limit their mobility (Makama, 2013: 133). Politics necessitates the exposure of women to interact with male and female constituents and address a public meeting.

It is established that the traditional Akwa Ibom society like other societies in Nigeria is dominated by the thinking that women are subordinates of men. Even in matters of birth, male children are mostly preferred to female children, and it is deeply entrenched in the culture of many states. Men are not merely considered as the head of the family but also go ahead to assume headship in traditional structures in the villages and the clans. Out of about 2,000 villages in Akwa Ibom State, no village proudly appoints a woman as a head and even thinking of such looks like a taboo to the people. Because a woman is perceived as part of a man's property, a man is at liberty to marry as many women as he can afford; a woman meanwhile barely keeps a friend (mostly make friends) apart from her husband.

So, to be married, whether as a second or third or fourth or fifth wife is something acceptable (Udoidem, 2006: 95). Able men are expected to bear the cost of marriage alone as that allows men to flex their muscles. The average cost for getting a wife is approximately 1 million nairas (app. 2800 USD) for people who have low income. The cost of marriage almost appears irrelevant until one understands its PPS influence. These high costs of marriage further keep women in the constant suppression of men. This often breeds domestic violence as the men mistakenly consider the woman as their properties. To a large extent, verily gender has been a minor issue in traditional Nigerian societies (Essien and Ukpong, 2012: 287). The traditional social structures which are PPS inclined have been contributing little motivations for the amendment of the existing power distribution between men and women.

Men in Nigeria generally believe women are unwilling to take up leadership positions because of cultural or traditional beliefs. Some others believe that the place of a woman is in the kitchen and women must seek the permission of their husbands in order to aspire to leadership positions. It is also believed, particularly by male respondents, that women are weak and fragile, and would not be able to make good leaders. However female respondents believe men or the society would not give them the necessary support and boosters if they aspire to leadership positions despite the fact that they aim to be more involved in leadership (www.christianaid.ie).

5.3 Politics

The nature of Nigerian politics has been described as a ground meant for the hard and strong (Akinola, 2009), and candidates cannot sponsor their elections themselves without recourse to "godfather" alternatives (Soyinka, 2004). This godfather complex involves a patron to client or servant to master relationship which is hardly free of violence. This exclusively happens in the area of disagreements, where a candidate fails to comply with prior agreed negotiations and contracts. This godfather politics hardly favours women. No women can withstand the resultant consequence of not yielding to the demands of godfathers as was witnessed in Oyo and Anambra states some years ago. Of course, this godfather complex cannot favour women as it involves the adoption of big affluent men who could find reasons to use these women as sex objects or abuse them sexually instead of investing in them to build on the already existing but struggling women's empowerment outreach in the country. Obviously the godfather complex is mostly yet another PPS established and funded by the patriarchy to further create a haven for the continuous undermining of the women's empowerment struggle, making democratic consolidations efforts minimal.

Elections in Nigeria have been branded violent with several electoral irregularities and various criminal happenings. Nevertheless, the continuous campaign for women to be actively involved in the democratic process has produced little results compared to the increasing number of women in other domain-seeking essential positions. The broader democratic framework and level of democratisation also impact the political participation of women. In Europe and in some developing countries, secular democracies have created relatively more space for participation of women in politics as compared to states where religious orthodoxy shapes democracy and politics. Adherence to discriminatory gender ascriptions persisted after the end of colonial rule in Nigeria (Makama, 2013: 133). This means that religious orthodoxy is a threat to female empowerment through political participation. This claim is supported by the preceding discussion and findings captured in the culture and religion subheading. The replacement post-independence political leaders made a deliberate effort to weaken women's organisations previously involved in an active campaign for emancipation through enhancing the militarisation of the polity and growing the statist of the economy (Ake, 1996). Gender blindness has meant that the variance influence of colonialism on African men and women has not been given attention until lately (Mama, 1997).

Domination of males in politics, political parties and culture of formal political structures is another factor that hinders the political participation of women. Male-dominated political parties often have a male perspective on matters of national significance that let down women, as their viewpoints are often overlooked and not reflected in the politics of their parties. Women are also frequently not voted for at the position of power within structures of the party because of gender biases of male headship. Just like mentioned in the culture and tradition subheading the society does not condone women keeping late at night though most political conferences and meeting often happen in the mid-nights, particularly in times when one is keenly involved and wants to seek a political post. Women who are mothers with children and a husband at home do not usually find it easy. Makama (2013: 132) further finds it significant to comment that most successful women in politics are those with helpful husbands, those who have turned into husbands, those lacking husbands, those who are done with childbearing, and those who are associated with the military, for example, daughters of past leaders and politicians. Some exampes of these people are Akunyili (helpful husband) Iyabo Obasanjo (a divorced and daughter of the former president), Condoleezza Rice (single), Sara Jubril (widow), and Hillary Clinton (a former flagbearer and wife of a former president).

6 Conclusion

Going through the literature of PPS it is evident that this famous African adage – *until the story of hunting is written by the animals too, the hunter would continue to be glorified by hunting tales* – summarises the panacea. It means that until women who have not given in to a patriarchal psyche become exegete of religious verdicts, texts, societal norms and culture male exegetes shall continue to build on the PPS of the society in the name of God. This goes to reply the famous patriarchal argument that women do not need to lead in order to feel or be empowered when in essence the body of patriarchy, which shapes the power structure in the society, can do so owing to the leadership advantages their own structure continues to provide. Both Islam and Christianity, which are the leading religions in Nigeria, have been used by the PPS to further bring women under the control of men through the repetition of verses and their exegesis by the patriarchal exegetes who determine the meaning what God and His prophets' decree for the society. Though these religions were alien to the lands of Nigeria, the culture and tradition of the land before the advent of Christianity and Islam seem to be mostly encouraging and supporting PPS even though women were actively instrumental in those times. It is these collective shapes, influenced by the religion, culture and tradition, that translate into the patriarchal political nature of the state. As evident is the poor performance of women in the most recent general elections held in 2019. The government of President Buhari appointed very few women in his government in the wake of several women among the least who contested but lost elections. Not only are women poorly represented in the highest political portfolios, but the same is the case in the local and national party positions. The violent elections in some areas that barricade many females who want to vie for political positions are largely perpetrated by men and have resulted in some women perceiving politics to be "dirty" and meant for only the masculine gender. The largely occupied masculine in the game of politics has also discouraged women who are nurturing political ambitions, and even if they do, they go in for less competitive positions where they end up not inspiring the massive representation of women because they are least represented in the party decision-making body. One of the effective solutions to this problem is, first and foremost, to identify and accept the problem itself. When people (women) toil to ensure that they get equity in every sphere of life, they show lackadaisical attitudes towards established policies to salvage them since the PPS is so deeply rooted in the society. The kind of epistemological orientation of these women is the one influenced by the PPS. Breaking away from the PPS epistemology would require a form of rigorous education of women on the need to survive a world without the PPS.

References

Acker, J. R. (1988). "Class Gender and Relations of Distribution", *Signs*, 3(13): 473–497.

Adjepong, A. (2015). "The Role of African Women in the Political Development of Pre-Colonial Africa: A Historical Analysis", in *Women in Development Essays in Memory of Prof. D.O Akintunde*, edited by S. A. Ajayi and J. K. Ayantayo (Ibadan: John Archers Publishers Ltd.), 17–39.

Aina, I. O. (1998). "Women, Culture and Society", in *Nigerian Women in Society and Development*, edited by Amadu Sesay and Adetanwa Odebiyi (Ibadan: Dokun Publishing House).

Ake, C. (1996). *Democracy and Development in Africa* (Washington, DC: The Brookings Institution).

Akinola, A. (2009). "Godfatherism and the Future of Nigerian Democracy", *African Journal of Political Science and International Relations*, 3: 268–272.

Bawa, A. B. (2017). *Muslim Women and Sharia Implementation in Northern Nigeria: An Overview of Fomwan* (1st ed., Vol. 18) (Awka, Anambra State, Nigeria: Unizik Journal of Arts and Humanities). doi:10.4314/ujah.v18i1.8.

BBC (2016). "Nigeria's President Buhari: My Wife belongs in Kitchen", www.bbc.com/news/world-africa-37659863.

Bergmann, B. R. (1987). "The Task of a Feminist Economics: A More Equitable Future", in *The Impact of Feminist Research in the Academy*, edited by C. Farnham (Bloomington: Indiana University Press), 131–147.

Bhavani, K. K., Foran, J., and Kurian, P. (2003). *Feminist Futures: ReImaging Women, Culture and Development* (London: Zed Press).

Bro, A. and McCaslin, J. (2019). "Nigeria's Laws Hold Women Back, and the Economy Suffers", www.cfr.org/blog/nigerias-laws-hold-women-back-and-economy-suffers [Accessed on 10 January 2020].

Bulut, A. T. and Yildirim, T. M. (2020). "Gender Differences in Policy Priorities among Legislators", in *Political Stability, Democracy and Agenda Dynamics in Turkey*. Comparative Studies of Political Agendas (Cham: Palgrave Macmillan).

Christian Aid (2015). *Masculinity and Religion in Nigeria Findings from Qualitative Research*, Christian Aid Nigeria Country Programme, Abuja.

Connell, R. W. (2005). "Hegemonic Masculinity: Rethinking the Concept", *Gender and Society*, 19(6): 829–859.

Constitution of the Federal Republic of Nigeria [Nigeria], Act No. 24, 5 May 1999, www.refworld.org/docid/44e344fa4.html [Accessed on 30 January 2020].

Davary, B. (2013). "Islam and Patriarchy the Oxford Encyclopedia of Islam and Women", www.oxfordislamicstudies.com/article/opr/t355/e0066 [Accessed on 30 January 2020].

Eniola, B. O. (2018). "Gender Parity in Parliament: A Panacea for the Promotion and Protection of Women's Rights in Nigeria", *Front. Sociol.*, 3(34). doi:10.3389/fsoc.2018.00034.

Essien, A. M. and Ukpong, D. P. (2012). "Patriarchy and Gender Inequality: The Persistence of Religious and Cultural Prejudice in Contemporary Akwa IbomState, Nigeria", *International Journal of Social Science and Humanity*, 286–290. doi:10.7763/ijssh.2012.v2.111.

FAO and ECOWAS Commission. (2018). *National Gender Profile of Agriculture and Rural Livelihoods: Nigeria*. Country Gender Assessment Series, Abuja. 92 pp.

Figart, D. M. (2005). "Gender as More Than a Dummy Variable: Feminist Approaches to Discrimination", *Review of Social Economy*, 63(3): 509–536. doi:10.1080/00346760500255692.

Haraway, D. J. (1991). *Simians, Cyborgs, and Women: The Reinvention of Nature* (New York: Routledge).

Hashiru, M. and Tufekci, O. (2019). "Women Empowerment through Political Participation in Rising Powers: Comparison of Turkey and Nigeria Cases", in *A Comparative Perspective of Women's Economic Empowerment*, edited by M. I. Yenilmez and O. B. Çelik (Abingdon, Oxon: Routledge).

Johnson, A. G. (2014). *The Gender Knot: Unraveling Our Patriarchal Legacy*, Revised and updated edition (Philadelphia, PA: Temple University).

Kardam, N. (2004). "The Emerging Global Gender Equality Regime from Neoliberal and Constructivist Perspectives in International Relations", *International Feminist Journal of Politics*, 6(1): 85–109. doi:10.1080/1461674032000165941.

Makama, G. A. (2013). "Patriarchy and Gender Inequality in Nigeria: The Way Forward", *European Scientific Journal*, 9(17): 115–144. doi:10.19044/esj.2013.v9n17p%25p.

Mama, A. (1997). "Shedding the Masks and Tearing the Veils: Cultural Studies for a Post-Colonial Africa", in *Engendering African Social Sciences*, edited by A. Imam, A. Mama, and F. Sow (Dakar: CODESRIA), 61–77.

Mamdani, M. (1996). *Citizen and Subject: Contemporary Africa and the Legacy of Colonialism* (Princeton: Princeton University Press).

Nigeria. https://africa.unwomen.org/en/where-we-are/west-and-central-africa/nigeria [Accessed on 30 January 2020].

Nmadu, T. (2000). "On Our Feet: Women in Grassroot Development", *Journal of Women in Academics*, 1(1): 165–171.

Nzomo, M. (1997). *The Gender Dimension of Electoral Politics in Kenya: Capacity Building of Women Candidates for 1997 and Beyond* (Nairobi, Kenya: The Commission).

Onwutuebe, C. J. (2019). "Patriarchy and Women Vulnerability to Adverse Climate Change in Nigeria", *SAGE Open*, 9(1). doi:10.1177/2158244019825914.

Prugl, E. (1996). "Gender in International Organizations and Global Governance: A Critical Review of the Literature", *International Studies Notes*, 21(1): 15–24.

Sacks, K. (1974). "Engels Revisited: Women, the Organisation of Production and Private Property", in *Woman, Culture and Society*, edited by M. Rosaldo and L. Lamphere (Stanford, CA: Stanford University Press).

Sanday, P. (1974). "Female Status in the Public Domain", in *Woman, Culture and Society*, edited by M. Rosaldo and L. Lamphere (Stanford, CA: Stanford University Press).

Sassen, S. (1998). *Globalization and Its Discontents* (New York: The New Press).

Sossou, M. A. (2011). "We Do Not Enjoy Equal Rights: Ghanaian Women's Perceptions on Political Participation in Ghana", *Sage Open*, 1–9. doi:10.1177/2158244011410715.

Soyinka, W. (2004). "Obasanjo's Action Promoters Godfather", August 27, 2004, http://www.vanguardngr.com\articles [Accessed on 26 January 2020].

Udoidem, S. (2006). *Dreams and Visions of Akwa Ibom: From Promise to fulfilment* (Lagos: African Heritage Research Publications).

Wood, H. J. (2019). "Gender Inequality: The Problem of Harmful, Patriarchal, Traditional and Cultural Gender Practices in the Church", *HTS Teologiese Studies/Theological Studies*, 75(1): a5177. https://doi.org/10.4102/hts.v75i1.5177.

The World Bank (2020). "Proportion of Seats Held by Women in National Parliaments (%): Nigeria", https://data.worldbank.org/indicator/SG.GEN.PARL.ZS?locations=NG [Accessed on 10 January 2020].

Index

Note: Page numbers in *italics* indicate figures; page numbers in **bold** indicate tables.

Abadan-Unat, Nermin 193
advertising: gender stereotypes in 216; stereotypes and gender roles 208–209; women in campaigns 216–217; women's empowerment in 204–205, 209–210; women's representations in 208–209; *see also* femvertising
Africa, gender balance index *66*
agriculture: female percentage employment in 26, **27–28**; gender employment distribution by country *140*, 141
Alhassan, Aisha Jummal 241
All Progressives Congress (APC) 245
Always 205, 212, 213; Like a Girl campaign 213–214
Arab States: financial sector employment share by gender **60**; women employment in financial services *61*
Argentina: female employment in agriculture 26, **27**; female employment in industry **29**; female employment in services 28, **30**, **31**; female labor force participation rate 22, **22**; female percentage of own-account workers **31**, **32**; female percentage of wage and salaried workers **34**; gender parity index **33**
Asia Pacific, gender balance index *66*
Atatürk, Mustafa Kemal 204, 207
athlete migration, sports industry 230–231
Australia: female employment in agriculture **27**; female employment in industry **29**; female employment in services 28, **30**, **31**; female labor force participation rate 22, **22**; female percentage of own-account workers **31**, **32**; female percentage of wage and salaried workers **34**; gender budgeting initiative 47; gender-responsive budgeting 48
Australian Football League Players Association 228

Baltagi-Wu test 36, **37**
Bangladesh: female employment in agriculture 26, **27**; female employment in industry **29**; female employment in services **30**, **31**; female labor force participation rate 22, **22**; female percentage of own-account workers **31**, **32**; female percentage of wage and salaried workers 34, **34**
banking industry, double glass ceiling in *64*
Beijing Declaration and Platform for Action (BDPA) 153, 165, 246
Big Data 54
Bosman Ruling 225
Brazil: employment indicators of 77, **78**; female employment in agriculture **27**; female employment in industry **29**; female employment in services **30**, **31**; female labor force participation rate 22, **22**; female percentage of own-account workers **31**, **32**; female percentage of wage and salaried workers **34**; gender inequality and 7; gender inequality in 12–13; gender parity index **33**; government women programs 13–14
BRICS (Brazil, Russia, India, China and South Africa): contributing family workers 85, *85*; econometric model for 102; employment indicators in 76–85;

labor force participation rate *83*, *84*; unemployment rates 85, *86*; wage and salaried workers 83, *84*; *see also* VAR (Vector Auto Regression) analysis model
British Football Association 225
Brotherhood of Professional Baseball Players 228
budget *see* gender-responsive budget

Canada: female employment in agriculture **27**; female employment in industry **29**; female employment in services 28, **30**, **31**; female labor force participation rate 22, **22**; female percentage of own-account workers **31**, **32**; female percentage of wage and salaried workers **34**; gender parity index **33**; Master File of Survey 115
Central and Western Asia: financial sector employment share by gender **60**; women employment in financial services *61*
Chartered Financial Analyst 62, 70n7
China: employment indicators of 77, **80–81**; female employment in agriculture 26, **27**; female employment in industry 28, **29**; female employment in services **30**, **31**; female labor force participation rate 22–23, **23**; female percentage of own-account workers **31**, **32**; female percentage of wage and salaried workers **34**; gender parity index **33**
Christian Aid 248, 250
Christianity, in Nigeria 248, 251–252
Classical economics: employment 73; wages in 108
Clinton, Hillary 251
coefficient of variation 131, 149n3; for unemployment *133*
Collins, Patricia Hill 173
Confederation of Turkish Trade Unions 229
consumer price index (CPI), response of GDP to 146, *147*
consumption, term 101
Convention on the Elimination of All Forms of Discrimination against Women (CEDAW) 44–45, 50, 153, 165, 241, 246
Council for Foreign Relations (CFR) 242
Crenshaw, Kimberlé 172, 173
Cuban women migrants 193
Current Population Survey (2004 and 2006) 116

De los Reyes, Paulina 174
democracy: gender equality and 12; as independent variable 9
discrimination, labor market for Roma women 179–181, 183
Dove, Real Beauty campaign 204, 212–213
Dream Crazier, Nike 215
Dream with Us campaign, Nike 214–215
Durbin-Watson test 36, **37**

East Asia and Pacific (EAP), gender equality in education 152, 155–160
Eastern Asia: financial sector employment share by gender **60**; women employment in financial services *61*
Eastern Europe: financial sector employment share by gender **60**; women employment in financial services *61*
economic development, as independent variable 8–9
Economic Recovery and Growth Plan (ERGP), Nigeria 242
economic theory, minimum wage issue in 108–110
education: adult literacy rates *155*; enrollment rates 156–158; female academic staff in tertiary *159*, 160; female teachers in primary *159*; female teachers in secondary *159*, 160; formal, in Turkey 160–164, *161*; gender equality in 152–160; gender equality index in 39; gender equality in Turkish 164–168; as independent variable 10; influencing female labor participation 5–6; literacy rates 154–155; preprimary enrollment rates 156, *156*; primary enrollment rates 156, *157*; recommendations for gender equality 13–14; secondary enrollment rates 156, *157*; teachers' and/or professors' situation 158; tertiary enrollment rates 156, *158*; youth literacy rates *155*
Egypt: female employment in agriculture 26, **27**; female employment in industry **29**; female employment in services **30**, **31**; female labor force participation rate 23, **23**; female percentage of own-account workers **31**, **32**; female percentage of wage and salaried workers **34**; gender parity index **33**
emerging markets, labor markets and female employment 74–76

employment: description in mainstream economics 73; diversity by gender 74; female, in emerging markets 74–76; gender gap, rate by country *139*; gender gap and 138–139; minimum wage and *109*; rate 74; sectoral, and gender gap 140–141
employment indicators: of Brazil **78**; BRICS and Turkey 76–85; of China **80–81**; contributing family workers 85, *85*; empirical study 86–95, 97; of India **79–80**; labor force participation rate *83*, *84*; labor markets and female employment in emerging markets 74–76; of Russia **79**; of South Africa **81–82**; of Turkey **82–83**; unemployment rates 85, *86*; wage and salaried workers *84*; *see also* VAR (Vector Auto Regression) analysis model
employment study: analysis of 11–12; equation for gender equality 10; gender equality as dependent variable 8; independent variables 8–10; method 8–10; model for 10–11; policy recommendations 12–14
empowerment: definition of 21; ensuring women's, in Nigeria 244–246; gender equality and women's 215–216
equal opportunities in education, concept of 164
Equileap 57, 70n3
ethnic niche, Roma women in Turkey 177
Europe: financial sector employment share by gender **60**; gender balance index *66*; gender gap in earnings in 206; unadjusted gender pay gap in *67*; women employment in financial services *61*
European Commission: European Economic and Social Committee (EESC) 191; gender pay gap 206–207
European Court of Justice 225
European Employment Strategy 53
European Institute for Gender Equality 65
European Labour Force Survey 193
European Union (EU): footballers 225; gender equality in education 152, 155–160
Eurostat, website 169n3
Eurostat Database 128, 129
Evangelical Fellowship of West Africa (ECWA) 248
exercise: labor market and 231–233; *see also* sports industry

Fair Wage-Effort Hypothesis 226
family beliefs, influencing female labor participation 5
feminism, women's rights and 207–208
feminist economic theory 2–3
feminization of poverty 20–21
FEMIPOL (Integration of Female Immigrants in Labor Market and Society, Policy Assessment and Policy Recommendations) 191
femocrats 48
femvertising 204–205; concept of 210–212; famous implementations of campaigns 212–215; Like a Girl campaign 213–214; Nike's Dream with Us campaign 214–215; Real Beauty campaign 204, 212–213; term 204; *see also* advertising
finance sector: employment share in total employment by gender and region **60**; gender balance index *66*; gender diversity and women representation in 58–59; gender diversity in 69–70; gender employment gap in 59, 61–62, 64–65; gender wage gap 66–67, *67*; reasons for gender gap in 67–69; share of employees in senior positions in *68*; women in management 57–58; women share on band boards by country *63*
FLFP (female labor force participation): description **36**; equation 35
football, labor market in 225
France: female employment in agriculture **27**; female employment in industry **29**; female employment in services 28, **30**, **31**; female labor force participation rate 23, **23**; female percentage of own-account workers **31**, **32**; female percentage of wage and salaried workers **34**; gender parity index **33**
Frees test 37, **37**
Friedman test 37, **37**

GDI (Gender Development Index) 8
gender, employment diversity 74
Gender Balance Index (GBI) *65*, 71n9; central banks 65, *66*; scores by year *65*
gender blindness 45
Gender Budgeting Practices Survey 46

gender empowerment (GEM), as independent variable 9
gender equality: concepts of 152–154; democracy and 9, 12; in education 12, 152, 154–160; equation for 10; index value **33**, 33–34; in Nigeria 241–244; ordinary least squares estimates of determinates of **11**; urbanization rates 12; women in advertising 215–217; women's empowerment and 215–216; World Bank on 3; *see also* education; VAR (Vector Auto Regression) analysis model
Gender Equality Index: description 35, **36**; primary and secondary education 39; World Bank 10
gender equity 154
gender gap: employment and 138–139; estimation results 145–146, **146**; impulse-response functions *147*; labor force participation 137–138; in labor market 127–128, 147–149; model specification 144–145; New York City 67; sectoral employment 140–141; sensitivity to unemployment level 141–143; in Turkish labor market 3; unemployment GDP and inflation 143–146; unemployment and 131–137; unemployment definition 136; unemployment rates for young and adults by gender **134–135**
gender inequality: societal feature 75–76; term 75
Gender Inequality Index (GEI) ratio, Nigeria 243
gender parity 169n2
gender parity index **33**, 33–34
gender-responsive budget: Big Data and 54; challenges of 51–52; commitment of government stakeholders 48–49; concept of 44; defining 44–45; future endeavors in 52–53; initiatives for 47–48; lessons learned from 48–51; level of government in 49–50; need for 45–46; participation of stakeholders in 53–54; political environment 50; potential for 54–55; technical expertise and data availability 50–51; term 45
gender theory 240
general government health expenditure (GHEP) 35, **36**
German Football Association 228
German Socio-Economic Panel (GSOEP) 232–233
Germany: female employment in agriculture **27**; female employment in industry **29**; female employment in services **30**, **31**; female labor force participation rate 23, **23**; female percentage of own-account workers **31**, **32**; female percentage of wage and salaried workers **34**; gender parity index **33**
Global Financial Crisis (2008) 62, 70
Global Gender Gap Index 129, 130, **130**
global score, gender balance index *66*
government final consumption expenditures (GCEP) 35, **36**
government programs, recommendations for gender equality 13–14
gross domestic product (GDP) 8–9, 10; Nigeria 242; response of consumer price index (CPI) to 146, *147*
groupthink, term 70, 71n14

Hansen's J test 150n17–18
Hausman test 35, **36**
HDI (Human Development Index) 8

income, functional distribution of 17
income effect 4
Income Tax law 231
India: employment indicators of 77, **79–80**; female employment in agriculture 26, **27**; female employment in industry 28, **29**; female employment in services **30**, **31**; female labor force participation rate 23, **23**; female percentage of own-account workers 28, **31**, **32**, 33; female percentage of wage and salaried workers 34, **34**; gender parity index **33**
Indonesia: female employment in agriculture **27**; female employment in industry **29**; female employment in services **30**, **31**; female labor force participation rate 23, **24**; female percentage of own-account workers 28, **31**, **32**, 33; female percentage of wage and salaried workers **34**; gender inequality in 12–13; gender parity index **33**; government women programs 13–14
industry sector, female percentage employment in 26, **29–30**
infrastructure, as independent variable 9
International Federation of Professional Footballers Associations 229
International Labour Organization (ILO) 10, 70n2, 190, 194, 198–199

International Organization for Migration (IOM) 188
international sports organizations 223
International Standard Classification of Education (ISCED) 156
intersectionality 173–175; concept of 194; Crenshaw's conception of 173; in labor market 174–175
Islam, in Nigeria 248–249, 251–252
Italian Footballers' Association 228
Italy: female employment in agriculture 26, **27**, **28**; female employment in industry **29**, **30**; female employment in services **30**, **31**; female labor force participation rate 23, **24**; female percentage of own-account workers **31**, **32**; female percentage of wage and salaried workers **34**; gender parity index **33**; women migrants in labor market 194–197

Janis, Irvin L. 71n14
Japan: female employment in agriculture 26, **27**, **28**; female employment in industry **29**, **30**; female employment in services **30**, **31**; female labor force participation rate 23, **24**; female percentage of own-account workers **32**; female percentage of wage and salaried workers **34**
Jubril, Sara 251

Kaitz index 115
Keynesian economics 73; employment 73; wages in 108
Kóczé, Angéla 179
Korean Professional Baseball League 227
Koroma, Suffyan 242
Kotex 204, 213

labor force: component of market 73–74; gender segregation 1, 172; participation of women in 17
labor force participation: Baltagi-Wu tests 36, **37**; dependent variables 35, **36**; Durbin-Watson test 36, **37**; evaluation of 39–41; factors affecting women's 26, 37, **38**, 39; female rate in emerging markets 75; Frees test 37, **37**; Friedman test 37, **37**; gender equality index 40–41; gender gap and 137–138; independent variables 35, **36**; labor market and wage 18–20; method and model 35–37; model estimations **38**; Pesaran test 37, **37**; rates for female (2000–2018) **22–25**; role of women in society 41; self-employment and women 40; variables and data descriptions **36**
labor market: demand curve 19, *109*; descriptive analysis of 129–141; in emerging markets 74–76; exercise and physical activity on 231–233; in football 225; gender disparity 1; gender gap in 127–128; integration of women migrants into 190–194; intersectionality in 174–175; minimum wage law and 106–107; participation of Roma women in Turkish 175–178, 183; in professional sports 224; supply curve 18, *109*; wage and 18–20; women migrants in Italian 194–197; women migrants in Turkish 197–199; women's situations in 205–207
Labor Force Survey (LFS) 116
land and property rights reforms 14
Latin America & the Caribbean: financial sector employment share by gender **60**; gender balance index *66*; gender equality in education 152, 155–160; women employment in financial services *61*
Law on Foreigners and International Protection (No. 6458) 197
leadership, women's involvement in 2
Lehman Brothers 70
Like a Girl campaign, Always 213–214

macroeconomic indicators, employment term 73
macroeconomic stabilization, as independent variable 10
MAIC (modified value of Akaike information criteria) 145, **145**, 150n16
mainstreaming 47
Major League Baseball (MLB) 226
Malthus, Thomas 108
manufacturing sector, gender employment distribution by country *140*, 141
Martelli Law 195
MBIC (modified value of Bayesian information criteria) 145, **145**, 150n16
Mexico: female employment in agriculture 26, **27**, **28**; female employment in industry 28, **29**, **30**; female employment in services **30**, **31**; female labor force participation rate 23, **24–25**; female percentage of own-account workers **32**; female percentage of wage and salaried workers **34**; gender parity index **33**

microfinance institutions 64, 70–71n8
Middle East, gender balance index *66*
Middle East and North Africa (MENA): gender equality in education 152, 155–160; region 194
migration: young male 187; *see also* women migrants
minimum wage: average wages and of full-time workers *114*; descriptive statistics of variables **118**; estimation equation for effect on employment 117–118; estimation results 120–123; histogram of minimum-to-mean wage ratios *120*; impact on female youth employment 123, **123**; impact on male youth employment **122**, 122–123; issue in economic theory 108–110; labor market and 106–107; youth employment and 124–125
Ministry of National Education (MoNE) 160, 162, 165
Ministry of Women Affairs and Social Development, Nigeria 242
MQIC (modified value of Hannan-Quinn information criteria) 145, **145**, 150n16
multidimensionality 173

Nakano Glenn, Evelyn 175
National Basketball League Players Association 228
National Basketball Players Association 228
National Education Basic Law No. 1739 160
National Football League (NFL) 227
National Football League Players Association 228
National Hockey League Players Association 228
National Union of Professional Footballers 228
net replacement rates 125n4
networking 2
New York State Department of Labor 67
Nigeria: Economic Recovery and Growth Plan (ERGP) in 242; elections in 250–251; ensuring women's empowerment in 244–246; female genital mutilation in 245; gender equality in 241–244; Gender Inequality Index (GEI) 243; patriarchal power structure in 246–251; patriarchy in 239; Patriarchy Power Structure (PPS) 247, 250, 251–252; politics in 250–251; President Buhari 247, 252; religion in 247–249; seats by women in National Parliament *243*, *244*; tradition and culture in 249–250
Nike 204, 205, 212–215; Dream with Us campaign 214–215
North America: financial sector employment share by gender **60**; gender balance index *66*; senior positions in financial firms 68, *68*; women employment in financial services *61*; women representation in financial services *61*; women representation in subsectors of finance firms *62*
Northern Africa: financial sector employment share by gender **60**; women employment in financial services *61*

Obasanjo, Iyabo 251
OECD (Organization for Economic Cooperation and Development) 190, 216; Action Plan for Youth 111, 113; Social, Employment and Migration Working Papers 190
OECD countries: data and model specification 117–118, 120; dependent variables by country *119*; descriptive statistics of variables **118**; equation for estimating minimum wage effect 117–118; estimation results 120–123; gender gap and employment 128; histogram of minimum-to-mean wage ratios *120*; Im-Pesaran-Shin (IPS) test statistic 120; literature review of wage policy in 114–117; minimum and average wages of full-time workers *114*; minimum wage in 107; panel estimation for female youth employment **123**; panel estimation for male youth employment **122**; panel estimation for total youth employment **121**; population projections of youth cohort in *111*; youth employment and wages in 110–114; youth employment rate in *112*
OECD Statistics Database 117
Okun's law 87, 143, 144, 149n12
olympic citizenship, concept of 229
Olympic Games 224, 229, 230
Organization of African Instituted Churches (OAIC) 248
Orkid 215; Like a Girl campaign 214
own-account workers: female percentage 28, **31–32**, 33; variable description **36**

Pakistan: female employment in agriculture 26, **27**, **28**; female employment in industry **29**, **30**; female employment in services **30**, **31**; female labor force participation rate 23, **24–25**; female percentage of own-account workers **32**; female percentage of wage and salaried workers 34, **34**; gender parity index **33**
Pantene 204, 212, 213
patriarchy-capitalism theory 240–241
Patriarchy Power Structure (PPS), Nigeria 247, 250, 251–252
Pay Equity Hypothesis 227
People's Democratic Party (PDP) 245
Pesaran test 37, **37**
Philippines: female employment in agriculture **27**, **28**; female employment in industry **29**, **30**; female employment in services **30**, **31**; female labor force participation rate 23, **24–25**; female percentage of own-account workers **32**; female percentage of wage and salaried workers **34**; gender parity index **33**; gender-responsive budgeting 48–49
Phillips Curve 143, 144
physical activity, labor market and 231–233
Polity IV Project Online 10
post-traumatic stress disorder (PTSD) 194
poverty: concept of women's 20; definition 20; feminization of 20–21; gender-based, in Roma community 183
Procter and Gamble 213, 214
production, term 101
Professional Footballers Association (PFA) 228
professional sports: labor market in 224; *see also* sports industry

qualified labor factor, term 73

Real Beauty campaign, Dove 204, 212–213
Recommendation on Gender Equality in Public Life 46
Refugee Convention (1951) 197
Ricardo, David 108
Rice, Condoleezza 251
Roma women in Turkey: challenges in access to labor market 178–183; dependence on social transfers 182–183; discrimination in labor market 179–181; ethnic niche 177; intersectional policies 183; in labor market 172–173; lack of education, skills or opportunities 181–182; literacy and 177, 181; methods and data 175; participation in labor market 175–178, 183
Roosevelt, Eleanor 1
Russia: employment indicators of 77, **79**; female labor force participation rate **24–25**
Russian Federation: female employment in agriculture **27**, **28**; female employment in industry 28, **29**, **30**; female employment in services **30**, **31**; female percentage of own-account workers **32**; female percentage of wage and salaried workers **34**; gender parity index **33**
Rwanda, gender-responsive budgeting 49

self-employment: female percentage 28, **31–32**, 33; impact on labor force participation 39; OWFP (own-account female percentage) 35, **36**
service sector: female percentage employment in 28, **30–31**; gender employment distribution by country *140*, 141; sports as economic activity in 223
sex sells, concept 212
She Media (formerly SheKnows Media) 204, 210, 211
Skey, Samantha 211
social exclusion, concept of 21
SODAM (Social Solidarity Center) 182
South Africa: employment indicators of 78, **81–82**; female employment in agriculture **27**, **28**; female employment in industry **29**, **30**; female employment in services **30**, **31**; female labor force participation rate 25, **25**; female percentage of own-account workers **32**; female percentage of wage and salaried workers **34**; gender inequality in 12–13; gender parity index **33**; government women programs 13–14
South African Footballers Union (SAFPU) 229
Southeastern Asia and the Pacific: financial sector employment share by gender **60**; women employment in financial services *61*
Southern Asia: financial sector employment share by gender **60**; gender equality in education 152, 155–160;

women employment in financial services *61*
South Korea: female employment in agriculture **27**, **28**; female employment in industry **29**, **30**; female employment in services **30**, **31**; female labor force participation rate 23, **24**; female percentage of own-account workers **32**; female percentage of wage and salaried workers **34**; gender parity index **33**
sports industry 223–224; athlete migration 230–231, 233–234; exercise and physical activity in labor market 231–233; globalization of 223; international sports activities 224; labor market in 234; labor market in football 225; labor market in professional sports 224; naturalized athletes' policy 229–230; performance-wage correlation in 226–227; salary cap in 227; unionization in professional 227–229; wages in sector 225–226
Sports Workers' Union 229
sticky floors 8
Sub-Saharan Africa: financial sector employment share by gender **60**; gender equality in education 152, 155–160; women employment in financial services *61*
Survey of Gender Budgeting Practices 48
Syrians in Turkey, women migrants in labor market 197–199

Taiwan, Kaitz index 115
Temporary Protection Regulation 197, 198
This Is Us, Nike 215
Turkey: athlete migration 230–231; barriers to women's employment opportunities 4–8; contributing family workers 85, *85*; econometric model for 102; employment indicators of 77, **82–83**; enrollment rates in tertiary education *167*, 167–168; expectations of women workers in 2; female employment in agriculture 26, **27**, **28**; female employment in industry **29**, **30**; female employment in services **30**, **31**; female labor force participation rate 25, **25**; female percentage of own-account workers **32**; female percentage of wage and salaried workers **34**; female teachers in *166*; formal education in 160–164; gender equality in education system 164–168; gender gap 3; gender inequality in 12–13; gender inequality in employment 1; gender parity index **33**; gender stereotypes in advertising 217; government women programs 13–14; labor force participation rate *83*, *84*; labor force participation rates 83, *83*, *84*; labor market for footballers 226; literacy rates in *166*; nonformal education in 164; perception of family unit 3; preschool education in 161–162; primary education 162; Roman women in labor market 172–173; school enrollment rates in *166*; secondary education 162–163; sports unionization in 229; structure of formal education system *161*; unemployment rates 85, *86*; voting rights for women 204; wage and salaried workers 83, *84*; women migrants in labor market 197–199; women's economic situation in labor market 205–207; *see also* Roma women in Turkey; VAR (Vector Auto Regression) analysis model
Turkish Professional Footballers Union 229
Turkish Statistical Institute (Turkstat) 205

UK Labour Force Survey (LFS) 116
UK Women's Budget Group 54
Under Armour 204, 212, 213
unemployment 35; component of market 73–74; gap *vs* real GDP per capita *136*; gap *vs* relative cohort size *137*; gender gap, GDP and inflation 143–146; gender gap in labor market 131–137; gender gap sensitivity 141–143; rates for young and adults by gender **134–135**; response of, gap to GDP 146, *147*; variable description **36**; variations across countries *133*; youth and adult rates by country *132–133*
unionization, professional sports 227–229
United Nation Population Fund 154
United Nations (UN): 2030 Agenda for Sustainable Development Goals 190; Millennium Development Goals (MDGs) 3, 57, 70n1, 153; Refugee Agency 191; Sustainable Development Goals (SDGs) 153, 190
United Nations Department of Economic and Social Affairs (UN DESA) 189
United Nations Educational, Scientific and Cultural Organization (UNESCO) 154, 168, 169n4, 170n9

United Nations Population Division 117
United Nations Women 198, 209
United States: female employment in agriculture 26, **27**, **28**; female employment in industry **29**, **30**; female employment in services 28, **30**, **31**; female labor force participation rate 25, **25**; female percentage of own-account workers **32**; female percentage of wage and salaried workers **34**; gender parity index **33**; gender-responsive budgeting 50
Universal Declaration of Human Rights 153, 168
Unstereotype Alliance 209

VAR (Vector Auto Regression) analysis model 87–88; CADF (cross sectionally ADF) test 87–88, **88–89**; CIPS (cross sectionally IPS) test 88, **89**; cross-section dependency test **88**; gendered unemployment inflation and GDP 144–145; gender gap and macroeconomic variables 128–129, 148; Granger causality analysis 90, **91**, 95, **96–97**; lag order selection from 87, **90**, 95, **96**; Monte Carlo simulations 146; tests determining degree of 87; variance decomposition 87–88; variance decomposition model (female) **92–95**; variance decomposition model (male) **98–101**
Vietnam: female employment in agriculture 26, **27**, **28**; female employment in industry 28, **29**, **30**; female employment in services **30**, **31**; female labor force participation rate 25, **25**; female percentage of own-account workers 28, **32**, 33; female percentage of wage and salaried workers 34, **34**

wage(s): definition 18; female labor participation 6, 8; labor market and 18–20; in OECD countries 110–114; in sports sector 225–226
wage and salaried workers 35; female percentage 34, **34**; variable description **36**
Wald chi2 test 36, **36**
Wald test 87
Williams, Serena 215
women: role in society 41; social belief of role of 2
women migrants 187–188; challenges and risks 199–200; integration and 188–190; integration into employment market 190–194; in Italian labor market 194–197; limitations and challenges for 193; in Turkish labor market 197–199
Women's Budget Initiative 47
women's employment, barriers to opportunities 4–8
Women's Rights Day, Turkey 207
World Bank 3, 70n2, 70n4, 129, 179; database 35; Online database 10; World Development Indicators (WDI) 10, 156, 170n4, 170n9
World Conference on Education for All (EFA) 153, 158, 241
World Economic Forum 6, 206, 207
World Population Prospects (2019) 117
World Poverty Clock 241
World War II 74, 101

youth employment in OECD countries 110–114

Lightning Source UK Ltd.
Milton Keynes UK
UKHW020202070922
408454UK00005B/144

9 780367 694012